VICTIM-CENTRED PEACEMAKING
Colombia's Santos–FARC-EP Peace Process

Roddy Brett

BRISTOL
UNIVERSITY
PRESS

First published in Great Britain in 2026 by

Bristol University Press
University of Bristol
1–9 Old Park Hill
Bristol
BS2 8BB
UK
t: +44 (0)117 374 6645
e: bup-info@bristol.ac.uk

Details of international sales and distribution partners are available at bristoluniversitypress.co.uk

© Bristol University Press 2026

British Library Cataloguing in Publication Data
A catalogue record for this book is available from the British Library

ISBN 978-1-5292-3880-8 hardcover
ISBN 978-1-5292-3881-5 paperback
ISBN 978-1-5292-3882-2 ePub
ISBN 978-1-5292-3883-9 ePdf

The right of Roddy Brett to be identified as author of this work has been asserted by him in accordance with the Copyright, Designs and Patents Act 1988.

All rights reserved: no part of this publication may be reproduced, stored in a retrieval system, or transmitted in any form or by any means, electronic, mechanical, photocopying, recording, or otherwise without the prior permission of Bristol University Press.

Every reasonable effort has been made to obtain permission to reproduce copyrighted material. If, however, anyone knows of an oversight, please contact the publisher.

The statements and opinions contained within this publication are solely those of the author and not of the University of Bristol or Bristol University Press. The University of Bristol and Bristol University Press disclaim responsibility for any injury to persons or property resulting from any material published in this publication.

Bristol University Press works to counter discrimination on grounds of gender, race, disability, age and sexuality.

Cover design: Liam Roberts Design
Front cover image: Photographs by Jonathan Moller, www.jonathanmoller.org

Bristol University Press' authorised representative in the European Union is:
Easy Access System Europe, Mustamäe tee 50, 10621 Tallinn, Estonia,
Email: gpsr.requests@easproject.com

For my son and teacher, FB, for your irreverence, comedy and humanity. You have remade the world and it is a far better place.

Contents

About the Author		vi
Acknowledgements		vii
Introduction		1
1	A Concise History of Violence	36
2	Colombia's Aberrational Cold War	69
3	Getting to Havana: From International Pariah to Innovative Peacemaking	86
4	The Havana Talks: A Victim-Centred Peace?	106
5	A Participatory Process? Victim Inclusion and Representation in Havana	135
6	Victims as *Peacebuilders*: The Relational Impact of the Victims' Delegations	170
7	The Impact of the Victims' Delegations: Victims as *Peacemakers*	207
Conclusions		250
Annex 1: Interview Format		280
Annex 2: Participation in the Victims' Delegations		287
References		291
Index		306

About the Author

Roddy Brett is Professor of Peace and Conflict Studies in the School of Sociology, Politics and International Studies at the University of Bristol, where he directs the Global Insecurities Centre.

Acknowledgements

This book is the outcome of the extraordinary kindness, humanity and insight shared with me across countries, continents and over various decades by friends and colleagues. The book would not have materialized without them, and I am indebted to them all.

The idea for the book emerged from the work I carried out for the United Nations System in Colombia, assessing the impact of the victims' delegations on the Havana talks in 2015. This research was supported by the UN's ethics board and published by the UNDP in 2017, as *La Voz de las Víctimas en la Negociación: Sistematización de una Experiencia*. Many of the quotes included in this monograph were published in this report, as were aspects of the analysis. As such, some of this research has already been made public. I am profoundly grateful to the participants in the delegations, the United Nations, the Episcopal Conference of the Catholic Church, the Universidad Nacional de Colombia, and other state and nonstate entities I interviewed under the auspices of this investigation. Above all, I am deeply grateful to the participants in the delegations for their unremitting generosity, understanding and kindness, and for sharing their lives and stories with me. Their clarity and determination drove forward my own comprehension. I would not have been able to carry out this research without their extraordinary support, trust and humanity. This volume fails to do justice to their courage. However, it is hoped that the research presented here might spotlight their contribution to Colombia's history and to bringing to a close one of the country's most brutal periods of violence.

I would also like to thank many other interviewees, who offered me their time during the research stages for this book. In particular, I would like to extend my gratitude to President Juan Manuel Santos for his generosity during his time at the University of Notre Dame, where we were able to converse at length.

I am also deeply grateful to the United Nations System in Colombia, in particular Alessandro Preti, who gave me their support and trust, commented on the original ideas and authorized this monograph. Of course, the content of the book is uniquely my own, as are the errors and my own critiques.

Much of the book was written during my tenure as a Visiting Fellow at the Kroc Institute for International Peace Studies, University of Notre

Dame, during 2022 and 2023. In this respect, I have a series of significant debts to acknowledge. Enormous gratitude goes to Asher Kaufman and Erin Corcoran for their tremendous individual support and the generous institutional backing offered at Kroc, where the intellectual community has been fundamental in developing this research. The unrelenting support of my dear friend and colleague Josefina Echavarría Alvarez has been deeply influential in the crafting of the arguments and ideas developed here, as have been the camaraderie and insight shared by other friends at Notre Dame: Norbert Koppensteiner, Ernesto Verdeja, Colin Barr, Maria Paula Prada, Madhav Joshi and Jason Quinn, among others.

I would also like to acknowledge the unrelenting kindness, intellectual support and friendship of Richard English, who has, as ever, been central to the formulation of this book and the clarification of my arguments. Insightful observations and comments on drafts and chapters and wider support have been given by other scholars and friends, to whom I would like to show my gratitude. Colleagues at the School of Sociology, Politics and International Studies, University of Bristol, including specifically in the Global Insecurities Centre, have offered imperative advice, assisting in my improving the quality of the research, as well as institutional support. My colleagues at Bristol, in particular Ana Juncos Garcia, Eric Herring, Tim Edmunds, Terrell Carver, Ryerson Christie, Clara Voyvodic Casabó and Therese O'Toole, provided enthusiastic support for the research, as well as important ideas on how to develop and refine my arguments. I would also like to thank a number of other friends and colleagues for their intellectual insight during numerous discussions and their comments on early drafts, including Roger Mac Ginty, Andrei Gomez Suarez, Valerie Rosoux, Elise Féron, Leigh Payne, Mo Hume, Ezequiel Gonzalez Ocantos, Alex Prichard, Lara Montesinos Coleman, Per Engstrom, Cath Collins, Thia Sagherian-Dickey, Olga Burkhardt-Vetter, Rosy Cave, Jonathan Leader Maynard, David Simon, Catherine Panter-Brick, Pablo Rueda and Tim Wilson. I would also like to acknowledge the support of Sean Loughna, Brandon Hamber, Francesca Lessa, Catalina Ortiz, Paul Seils, Ben Jolliffe and Sean Corbett during this prolonged process of crafting this book.

The material in Chapters 1 and 2 of this volume draws on my contribution to *The Cambridge History of Terrorism*, Chapter 16, 'Political Violence and Terrorism in Colombia', edited by Richard English and published in 2021. It is reprinted here with the permission of Cambridge University Press.

I would like to extend my thanks to Jonas (Jonathan) Moller who, yet again, provided stellar and apposite photographs for the book cover.

Last, although by no means least, I would like to express my profound gratitude to Lina Malagón and my son Federico Brett, whose love, support and laughter made the loneliness of writing on such harrowing topics far less difficult to shoulder.

Bristol, May 2024

Introduction

Violence unhinged

Since the 19th century, Colombia has experienced diverse, complex and mutually reinforcing forms of political and criminal violence, embedding throughout the country a series of entrenched and, at times, overlapping conflicts driven by inequalities and political and economic exclusion, and sustained by increasingly acute societal cleavages. Recurrent patterns of political violence have been manifest through elaborate and habitually strategic acts of unhinged brutality and acts of terror perpetrated by diverse armed groups (Brett 2021). According to one female survivor of violence perpetrated by multiple armed actors interviewed as part of this study in 2015:

> In July 1988, my brother was killed (by paramilitaries) in a massacre in Carmen de Bolívar. Then, in August 2000, the FARC-EP guerrilla exploded a bomb at precisely the moment my niece was on her way home from school on a motorbike with three other school friends. As they were passing the hardware store, the bomb went off, and they were burnt alive … the bomb was enormous, and the flames went up higher than the town church. A man managed to get my niece out, he was also burnt, but they couldn't do anything for her. What she suffered was very hard. I can still remember the sound of the ambulance, and when I hear ambulances today it's terrible, and smell burning; you would think that these things don't leave scars, but they do.[1]

During protracted episodes of violent conflict in Colombia, patterns of violence have evolved, phenomena neither static nor isolated from broader domestic and transnational political and economic processes. Such violence has followed a macabre logic of contingent communicative performance. According to a survivor of multiple violations:

---

[1] Interview, Bogotá, Colombia, May 2015.

On 26 August, it was our turn; seven killed, three our own, and four others in our village. It was there they killed my husband. They left their letters painted on the walls, Autodefensas Unidas de Colombia [AUC, paramilitaries], and they wrote 'death to rats, guerrillas and informers', in large letters. On the wall on the other side of the building they wrote 'AUC is present here'. From that moment, everyone felt scared. Many massacres followed, week after week. That's when I was displaced.[2]

Acts of terror and ritualized violence perpetrated in Colombia by state and nonstate actors alike have undergone manifold and episodic reiterations, ultimately characterized by a 'tragic circularity' (Hylton 2006). For more than a century, massacre, execution, torture, sexual and gender-based violence, disappearance and displacement have become commonplace occurrences, deployed as enduring strategies by multiple armed actors to obtain, contest and preserve political and economic power and military advantage. Such horror has left devastation and trauma in its wake (Bushnell 1993). The actions of armed actors, state and nonstate alike, have, moreover, destroyed individual lives and eviscerated community dynamics, as evidenced by one survivor of a landmine left by the guerrilla army the Revolutionary Armed Forces of Colombia (FARC-EP) in rural Colombia:

In 2007, I went with a friend and my family to a farm, a day before the Easter holidays ended. We went down to the river ... We were playing football, which was one of my hobbies. And when we were on our way back, we were unfortunate enough to come across a minefield. First, my friend fell, he lost his left foot. Four of us managed to pick him up. We made a stretcher out of our shirts and carried him. Some two hundred metres further along, I myself stood on a mine and I flew. I lost my left leg. I lost my life's project, my life was completely destroyed.[3]

Such egregious violations, perpetrated by multiple and competing armed groups, have been characterized as a 'complete and harrowing geography of violence' (Sánchez and Bakewell 1985: 790), the ubiquity of which has led scholars to attest to their 'banal', ordinary quality (Pécaut 2008: 142). For the victims and survivors, of course, such violence is far from banal. Under such conditions, aberrational violence and the systematic violation of national and international norms by state and nonstate armed actors have become customary in Colombia. According to one survivor:

---

[2] Interview, Bogotá, Colombia, March 2015.
[3] Interview, Bogotá, Colombia, April 2015.

In October, a man appeared at our house ... he threatened my brother, he said to him 'people who think like you do end up dead like a dog in the street'. And then on the 14 November they took him. He had one day left before he completed his secondary school. My brother went out to buy some paper for his homework and never came back. We knew about forced disappearances, and we searched for him for days. On the fourth day, we went to the sixth station of the F2, the intelligence police, and one of the police commanders suggested we go and search the morgues. The next day, we did that, and they showed us two cadavers. At first, we didn't recognize him, because he had been tortured, and had been shot in the head, but then we realized it was my brother. Even during his burial, they came to intimidate my other brothers and tried to take his body away.[4]

For Sánchez and Bakewell (1985: 790–796), Colombia has been a country of 'permanent' and endemic 'warfare', typified by three stages of war and violence: first, a long and violent 19th century, shaped by civil wars between elites throughout the country; second, *La Violencia* during the mid-20th century, a period of mass violence moulded by a combination of anarchy, peasant insurgency and official terror, the most evident motor of which was the viscerally hostile fracture between the Conservative and Liberal Parties, resulting in approximately 300,000 killings; and, finally, a third cycle of violence imposed during Colombia's complex and protracted Cold War internal armed conflict, which represents the primary focus of this book. Boasting a homicide rate akin to *La Violencia*,[5] the internal armed conflict commenced in the 1960s and remains ongoing at the time of writing, despite the formal closure of the armed conflict between the state and the FARC-EP guerrilla in 2016. The conflict has been waged between multiple armed groups, including the Colombian state, guerrilla insurgencies and paramilitary organizations. From the 1980s onwards, the conflict become yet more complex, as drug cartels came to play an increasingly decisive role in the violence. The configuration of and relationship between violent actors, the nature of their atrocious acts, the localized expression of political violence and the resulting massive scale of victimization has, in many senses, made the Colombian conflict unique. Individuals and collective groups, in such a context, have often been victim of multiple armed groups or to successive violations:

---

[4] Interview, Bogotá, Colombia, April 2015.
[5] The National Centre for Historical Memory identifies 95 terrorist attacks with 1,566 victims between 1988 and 2012.

> In 1988, my brother was killed by the FARC-EP, because he refused to be recruited into their ranks. That's when we left [and went to a neighbouring town], where they killed another three of my brothers. So we were displaced again. Two brothers killed by the FARC-EP, and two killed by the AUC. After that, our lives were extremely difficult ... After the second displacement, I went to live in Quindío. The first months were too harsh, because we had to go without food and sleep on the floor.[6]

> I have been a victim of two crimes: forced displacement and torture by the paramilitary block, in Chocó in the year 2000, when I was in the council in charge of the municipal budget. These events have been very difficult for me, both the displacement and when the paramilitaries came to my house to kill me.[7]

Atrocious violence has then shaped Colombian society for more than a century, imposing profound damage upon individuals and communities (Steele 2017), forging relations of power through blood and torment, and, in many cases, shaping the moral codes and core beliefs undergirding collective group identity. In such a context, for the many who have benefited from the violence or whose identities have been deeply shaped by it, bringing an end to the country's protracted violent conflict and forging a truce that might neutralize Colombia's acute societal divisions gradually became increasingly inadmissible.

Counterinsurgency, insurgency and militia violence has led to systematic massacres, the murder of men, women and children, extrajudicial execution, torture, rape and other forms of sexual and gender-based violence, forced disappearance, kidnapping, the unencumbered use of landmines, forced displacement and the recruitment of child soldiers. Unimaginable carnage has been wrought in the name of partisan political struggle, of righteous rebellion, of the integrity and security of the state and, on all sides, of freedom, security and emancipation. Since independence, political parties and their militia and military, paramilitary and guerrilla actors and drug cartels have employed egregious violence in order to spread terror, to achieve their political, economic and territorial objectives and, in many cases, to wrest and assert control over the state, its institutions and its coffers. Accordingly, the waging of armed conflict and the concomitant infliction of suffering and humiliation have been consistently justified by all armed groups, and often by their social and political constituencies, as a legitimate defence of their group

---

[6] Interview, Bogotá, Colombia, April 2015.
[7] Interview, Bogotá, Colombia, May 2015.

values, norms and humanity in the face of unjust victimization by their adversaries, whether real or imagined.

Under such unremitting conditions, civilians have suffered disproportionately, as the testimony of one survivor highlights:

> In 1996, I was the victim of sexual abuse by the guerrilla, in a small hamlet within the banana-growing region ... We never talked about it because we were scared. Then in 2002, I was victim of sexual violence again this time committed by [paramilitaries] that was one of the groups operating in the region ... this really marked me, because I had only just survived one attack and then came the next ... the *finca* [plantation] owners were linked to the paramilitaries, and you could see how workers were killed ... how women were raped too in some of the *fincas* ... they used snakes to kill people to hide the fact that there were many murders ... or they used crocodiles to kill people and dispose of the bodies, or they cut them up with chainsaws.[8]

As in other Latin American countries, such as Guatemala and Argentina, civilians have borne the brunt of the cruelty inflicted by armed groups, representing more than 90 per cent of the victims of Colombia's political violence. Decades of atrocity have moulded a society deeply divided by embedded and often mutually reinforcing ideological, ethnic, racial and political cleavages. Protracted violent conflict has bestowed upon some armed actors in Colombian society a moral framework that, for many, validates their acts of obscene cruelty against those that are perceived as representing a threat to their group, whether this be a political party, armed faction, human rights organization, trade union or otherwise. In the words of one young man forcibly recruited into the paramilitaries:

> Our town was split in two; on the hill was the guerrilla, and on the plains were the paramilitaries, and between them they disputed the territory. I mended motorbikes, repairing them for both the guerrilla and the paramilitaries, as well as for townspeople. From one moment to the next, the guerrilla accused me of collaborating with the paramilitaries ... And they threatened to kill me unless I left town. They went to the workshop twice to look for me. I was only 13, almost 14. My boss fired me because he was scared his own life was in danger. The paramilitaries took advantage of my situation and proposed that I join them. I joined the group when I was 14. In my region, it was complicated, because there were hostilities every day.[9]

---

[8] Interview, Santa Marta, Colombia, April 2015.
[9] Interview, Bogotá, Colombia, April 2015.

Building peace amid atrocity

The impact and legacy of Colombia's violence has represented a grave challenge to those seeking to bring an end to such unfettered brutality and to build peace for future generations. In fact, under such conditions, the present has been habitually lived through the societal cleavages forged and fought over in the past, which, in turn, often impedes the imagining of a shared, collective future. Nevertheless, Colombia's chronicles of grotesque violence have been equalled by the country's history of innovative peacemaking and peacebuilding initiatives struggled for and implemented at the local, subnational and national levels for decades (Karl 2017). In such a paradoxical context, this book addresses the fundamental question of how, in the face of unrelenting barbary and adversity, survivors of political violence and atrocity have sought to assert agency and contest power as they painstakingly forge a path through which to bring an end to political violence, craft the effective means through which to reckon with the past, and reconstitute their political and moral communities. This book is then, in part, about how war is fought, what its impact is, particularly on civilians, and the means that armed groups employ in order to achieve their ends. However, it is also more emphatically about how those who survive atrocious violence narrate and make sense of war and attempt to construct peace, and, in so doing, transform political subjectivity, shape formal peacemaking processes and accountability mechanisms, and reconfigure relations of power.

Amid this unremitting history of violence, then, Colombians have assiduously prosecuted pioneering peacebuilding initiatives, often at the local and subnational levels, such as the remarkable Zones of Peace and Peace Communities, including in San Jose Apartado (Burnyeat 2018), and through the country's many Afro-Colombian, human rights, indigenous and women's organizations, such as the Ruta del Pacífico (Hancock and Mitchell 2007; Kaplan 2017; Santamaría et al 2020; Allen et al 2022). Historically, despite a range of failed negotiations since the 1980s, the country has also undergone significant episodes of successful peacemaking between armed factions, such as the demobilization, disarmament and reincorporation of the M-19 in the 1990s, initiatives often themselves driven forward by the survivors and the victims of the bloodshed as much as by those who perpetrated it.

Most recently, at the end of November 2016, the Colombian Congress ratified a comprehensive and unprecedented package of peace agreements negotiated meticulously over four years between the two administrations of President Juan Manuel Santos (2010–2014, 2014–2018) and the FARC-EP. After having been initially rejected through a public referendum – *el plebiscito* – on 2 October 2016, and subsequently (and urgently) revised over the following weeks, the ratification of the political settlement ultimately brought formal closure to Colombia's brutal 52-year armed conflict with the FARC-EP. However, war with the country's other longstanding insurgency, the National Liberation Army (ELN), remains ongoing at the time of writing. Moreover, by February 2020, two dissident factions of the FARC-EP had returned to the armed struggle, while paramilitary groups – supposedly demobilized under the 2005 Justice and Peace Law (Law 975) – continue their carnage throughout the countryside, slaughtering social activists and former FARC-EP combatants. Simultaneously, drug-producing and trafficking organizations continue to assert horrific violence throughout the country, including the notorious Clan del Golfo. Peace, conflict and violence in Colombia have never been mutually exclusive, but rather have constituted a complex mosaic, itself characterized by continuity between the past and the present, as efforts to consolidate peace are moulded by the impact of ongoing violence and merge with the legacy of historical barbarie.

Beyond succeeding where previous peace processes had failed, what was unique about the Santos–FARC-EP negotiations was that survivors and victims of the political violence perpetrated by all armed actors during the conflict were afforded a formal role in the peace talks (Mendes 2019; Brett 2022). In June 2014, after two years of talks and with three agreements already reached, the negotiating parties undertook the unprecedented step of issuing a joint press communiqué inviting five delegations of 12 victims each to present their individual testimonies and proposals for the Victims' Agreement, the fifth point of the negotiating agenda (Point Five), at the peace talks that, since 2012, had been taking place in Havana. The negotiating parties intended to give victims a say in shaping the content of Point Five – the agreement that would consecrate the transitional justice provisions for victims and perpetrators of all political violence. In fact, according to one of the organizers interviewed in 2015, the negotiating parties were keen to achieve their ambition of 'placing the victims at the centre of the peace process'.[10] The words of one of the members of the victims' delegations place this objective into meaningful perspective:

> I was a Congresswoman, and then Secretary of Education and then in the Senate. I was kidnapped in 2001 ... and held in the jungle for seven years by the FARC-EP as a prisoner. The years went by in sadness and anguish. Worry, fear, despair. I had to confront many things: besides the privation of liberty, there is the distance from one's family, being isolated in a prison in the depths of the jungle. In the jungle, I found out about the death of my husband a year after I had been taken. I was

---

[10] Interview, Bogotá, Colombia, April 2015.

profoundly concerned about my daughters and felt guilty for having got involved in politics ... I lived this war, and I know what it's like to have to run through the jungle from the bombs and try to escape death ... To live with a rifle in the ribs and pointed at my neck.[11]

The formal inclusion of the victims' delegations took place under the auspices of the discussions over the transitional justice provisions relative to the 8,944,137 victims of Colombia's protracted armed conflict and the country's diverse spectrum of armed actors. Accordingly, at the behest of the negotiating parties, during the second half of 2014, the UN, the Colombian National University (NUC) and the Episcopal Conference of the Catholic Church (ECCC) organized the five visits of the so-called *victims' delegations* to Havana, seating 60 of the almost nine million victims and survivors at the peace talks with the aim of sharing their testimonies and making proposals for Point Five. The Victims' Agreement was eventually signed in December 2015, a year after the last of the five delegations had returned from Cuba.

This book tells the story of this experience from the perspectives of those who took part in the process as part of the victims' delegations, and presents an analysis of what, in particular, said delegations signified for the individuals who participated in them and, more generally, for peacemaking and transitional justice in Colombia. It simultaneously seeks to understand what, if anything, the experience may mean for peacemaking and transitional justice practices and thinking elsewhere.

Themes of the book: the wider significance of the victims' delegations

The research presented here contends that the participation of the victims' delegations in the Santos–FARC-EP peace process was significant for a series of reasons that speak both to the specific context of Colombia and to broader debates pertaining to peacemaking, transitional justice, and the practices and theories of reconciliation.

Transitional justice and peacemaking

Since its emergence, transitional justice discourse has situated, at its core, the satisfaction of the rights of victims of political violence. This ubiquitous narrative was echoed by Francisco de Roux, the President of Colombia's Truth Commission, at the UN Security Council on 13 February 2020. In de Roux's words: 'The victims of armed conflicts are the raison d'etre of

---

[11] Interview, Bogotá, Colombia, May 2015.

transitional justice, leaving behind the pain of human tragedy in order to search for solutions of coexistence and reconciliation.'[12]

As has been well documented, from the 1980s, the transitional justice paradigm emerged as a set of practices, mechanisms and concerns based on human rights norms, frameworks and international standards, aimed at confronting and redressing the legacy of large-scale human rights violations perpetrated principally during the authoritarian episodes that had characterized the Cold War (Minow 2000; Teitel 2000; Bell 2009; Payne, Olsen and Reiter 2010; Shaw, Waldorf and Hazan 2010; Roht-Arriaza and Mariezcurrena 2012; Sikkink 2011). The primary focus of transitional justice was on the mechanisms, both judicial and nonjudicial, formulated by states and international actors oriented not only towards accountability for past crimes (trials, truth commissions and lustration), but also victim-oriented restorative justice mechanisms (reparations, monuments and public memory projects) and so-called mechanisms of security and peace (amnesties, pardons, constitutional amendments and institutional reform). In authoritarian countries undergoing liberalizing transition, the fundamental objectives of the paradigm were initially driven then by the push to guarantee the restitution of the individual and collective dimensions of victims' rights (the rights to truth, justice, reparation and nonrecurrence) and, arguably, by efforts to craft interpersonal reconciliation and sustainable peace in the aftermath of political violence, as had, for example, been the case of the *Núnca Más* report in Argentina in the 1980s (Minow 1998; Teitel 2000; Bell 2009; Gonzalez Ocantos 2020).

In the 1990s, the application of transitional justice interventions moved gradually away from its original focus on authoritarian regimes and post-authoritarian societies, shifting increasingly towards the provision of a notional *postconflict* justice. In particular, in the aftermath of the launch of the United Nations Agenda for Peace unveiled by the then Secretary-General Boutros Boutros Ghali in 1992 and its supplementary protocol, transitional justice mechanisms have been increasingly employed in conflict and postconflict scenarios, such as those of Guatemala and Colombia, arguably modifying considerably the original parameters of the paradigm (Lundy and McGovern 2008; Lambourne 2009; McEvoy and McConnachie 2012a, 2012b; García-Godos 2016). Accordingly, transitional justice has since become an integral component of the so-called liberal peace repertoire, intrinsic in that regard to postconflict state and nation building and increasingly embedded within the dominant global peacemaking and peacebuilding architecture (Brett and Malagón 2013; Sharp 2013; García-Godos 2016). The framework of rights

---

[12] See https://comisiondelaverdad.co/actualidad/noticias/discurso-francisco-de-roux-en-naciones-unidas-febrero2020 (accessed 14 February 2020).

that first undergirded transitional justice interventions since the 1980s – victims' rights to truth, justice, reparation and nonrecurrence – has thus itself become gradually pivotal to mainstream peacemaking and peacebuilding initiatives, and has become critical to the global dissemination of those norms linked to liberalism and neoliberalism (Robins 2017). The more limited configuration of rights upon which the liberal peace paradigm was initially forged (fundamental human rights, and individual civil and political rights) has, in turn, been extended over time, as victims' rights frameworks have come to shape spheres of peacemaking and peacebuilding directly. It is this transformation that has been of core significance to attempts to make peace over the last two decades in Colombia, as we shall see, and, in particular, to the country's experience of victim-centred peacemaking and transitional justice.

As it has been incorporated into the liberal peacemaking framework, so the transitional justice paradigm has been consolidated as a staple of peace negotiations and postconflict reconstruction, becoming central both to disarmament, demobilization and reintegration (DDR) and to broader provisions relative to democratization, statebuilding, reconciliation and human rights protection. With the growing inclusion of transitional justice practices within peacemaking and peacebuilding interventions, policy makers and scholars have further contemplated the degree to which transitional justice mechanisms and their objectives represent central tenets of sustainable peace (Mendeloff 2004), arguing that truth telling (Minow 1998), reparations (Brett and Malagón 2013; Firchow 2017) and justice guarantees (Payne et al 2010) represent pillars of successful peacebuilding and reconciliation. Scholars have argued that transitional justice processes are integral to peacebuilding and reconciliation, leading, at best, to the recovery of truth, the healing of individual victims and of their respective nation/society, while also potentially providing victims with justice and accountability, reforming state institutions, strengthening the rule of law and guaranteeing the nonrecurrence of human rights violations. Nonetheless, such ambitious claims are questionable and have rarely been rooted in empirically tested practice (Mendeloff 2004: 355–357).

Nevertheless, a clear articulation between transitional justice and the liberal peace paradigm has been indisputably forged over time, as the case of Colombia presented in this book will show. The key concerns of the transitional justice paradigm – amnesty, truth, justice, reparations and nonrecurrence – came to represent a core component of the Santos–FARC-EP peace negotiations, decisively shaping controversial discussions over how to deal with perpetrators and how to redress victims and satisfy their rights. At the same time, transitional justice concerns were integral to those broader provisions central to the task of bringing closure to Colombia's armed conflict, in particular to DDR provisions and political reform relating to democratization and inclusion. In this respect, conversations concerning the configuration of DDR provisions and the eligibility of those individuals to which these provisions would apply were closely determined by the thinking in relation to the conditions that those state and nonstate actors accused of or sentenced for human rights violations would enjoy. Similarly, the core concerns of justice and amnesty for past crimes were integral to the discussions, considerations and final decisions taken regarding whether and, if so, under which conditions those accused of or sentenced for specific crimes would be able to run for political office.

Such debates may, in part, appear abstract. However, the words of one of the female members of the Organizing Committee of the victims' delegations are illustrative in this respect:

> From the perspective of human rights, one of the gravest issues of the conflict has been negation, the denial by all armed actors of their violent acts. The fact that 60 individuals in flesh and blood went to Havana and gave testimony to the atrocities carried out represented a means of overcoming this denial ... The participation of the victims' delegations in Havana made visible the country's history of pain and suffering and began to demolish the wall of silence and denial, to dismantle the stigmatization of victims.[13]

The Colombia experience evidences explicitly how the concerns of transitional justice have become embedded within broader political discussions and pronouncements inherent in the deal making at the centre of peace negotiations. In this context, this book then examines the degree to which the victims' delegations shaped the dynamics of the negotiations and the final content of the peace agreements, ultimately exploring how, if at all, survivors and victims may contribute to formal peacemaking initiatives between armed actors. It also raises the question of whether the victims' delegations had any longer-term impact on the sustainability of the peace process.

Victim-centred transitional justice

Beyond demonstrating the increasingly complex articulation between the transitional justice paradigm and the liberal peacemaking/peacebuilding architecture, Colombia's victims' delegations were of significance for a second key reason, which is of central interest to this book. In recent years, transitional justice as a field has been increasingly critiqued and 'challenged'

---

[13] Interview, Bogotá, Colombia, April 2015.

by 'survivors of mass violence' as exclusionary and unrepresentative (Shaw and Waldorf 2010: 3). Survivors, victims, activists and scholars have, in this regard, made mounting and justifiable claims that victims' interests, experiences and perspectives are persistently excluded from the design and orientation of transitional justice mechanisms and that, as such, these mechanisms have failed to take into account victims' demands, needs and priorities. Going further, as one female member of the delegations stated in an interview:

> In a peace process, it's impossible to talk about nonrecurrence, if those affected by the violence don't participate, because otherwise those negotiating are those who wielded the power of the weapons ... to include the perspectives of those who have had to bear the greatest suffering legitimizes the process and, at the same time, affords it with a route forward. It is crucial to validate the testimonies of those that suffered the violence and to be able to say that they are the reflection of millions of Colombians.[14]

Survivors of atrocity and political violence have coherently claimed that the satisfaction of their needs and the guarantee of their rights have been consistently subordinated to wider interests and initiatives, including to those of the state, illegal armed groups and heavyweight international actors determining transitional justice, peacemaking and peacebuilding interventions (Shaw and Waldorf 2010; Robins 2011, 2012, 2015, 2017). For example, victims' demands have often been outranked by the prerogatives and interests of high-level political and armed actors during political transition and peace processes, subordinated as they have been to the task of maintaining the stability and impetus of fragile political transitions and negotiations, ultimately leaving other issues to be prioritized in their place (Hayner 1994; Berat and Sahain 1995).

Moreover, recent scholarship has shown how victims have often tended to focus their demands less upon conventional transitional justice issues, such as truth and justice for past crimes, instead prioritizing housing, employment and the satisfaction of basic needs (McEvoy and McConnachie 2012b). The words of a male peasant farmer who visited Havana as part of the delegations are telling in this regard: 'My proposal was that we ourselves represent the pillars through which the country builds peace. That proposal included everything at the root of our peasant economy.'[15]

In this respect, the Colombia experience speaks to empirical data collected from victims and affected communities that has demonstrated how the range

---

[14] Interview, Bogotá, Colombia, May 2015.
[15] Interview, Santa Marta, Colombia, April 2015.

of often complex and context-specific victims' demands[16] – such as the fulfilment of basic needs, the restitution of economic and social rights, and redress of the structural causes of conflict – has been habitually excluded from the mandates of transitional justice mechanisms (Jacoby 2015; Robins 2017). Interventions have instead tended to prioritize a legalistic rights discourse that spotlights civil and political rights, while sidelining meaningful engagement with the violations of economic and social rights and the causes of structural violence (Arbour 2006; Miller 2008; LaPlante 2015). As Miller has argued, 'poverty and inequality tend to be depicted merely as the landscape against which murder, disappearance, torture and other gross human rights violations are committed' (2008: 276).

In response to these critiques, policy makers, practitioners and scholars have gradually begun to advocate what Brinton Lykes and Murphy have described as 'soft reforms' (2023: 363),[17] seeking closer alignment between the demands of survivors of political violence, the priorities of transitional justice norms and entrepreneurs, and the configuration and mandates of transitional justice mechanisms (Garcia-Godos and Knut Andreas 2010; Garcia-Godos 2016; Méndez 2016; de Waardt and Weber 2019; Brinton Lykes and Murphy 2023). There has, in this context, been a growing consensus within policy and academic spheres that victim participation should be central to the design, adoption and implementation of transitional justice mechanisms and institutions. Accordingly, terms such as 'victim-centred approach' and 'victim-oriented perspective' have become increasingly common parlance within the transitional justice paradigm (McEvoy and McConnachie 2012a), and the language of 'victim-centrism has come to permeate all approaches to transitional justice' (Robins 2017: 42). The United Nations System and the European Union (EU), for example, have adopted a 'victim-centred' approach across much of their policies oriented towards dealing with the legacy of past atrocities, seeking to ensure that victims are guaranteed a role in both designing and implementing transitional justice initiatives.

Broadly speaking, the arguments in favour of victim and civil society inclusion in both peace negotiations and in the design and implementation of transitional justice mechanisms are framed from two perspectives. The first argument, from a moral standpoint, contends that those individuals and stakeholders most affected by violent conflict should not be excluded

---

[16] From the perspective of Jacoby (2015), victims seek a host of goals: justice, a voice, truth, peace, monetary compensation, martyrdom, independence or political representation, depending on what they consider valuable and worthy of achievement in terms of their own norms and political goals.

[17] Other scholars have called for more 'radical' reform to transitional justice thinking and practice, with respect specifically to the decolonization of the paradigm (de Andreotti et al 2015; Essay 2022; Lykes and Murphy 2023).

from discussions concerning their future. The second argument is framed from the point of view of efficacy – in short, that inclusion brings to the negotiating table and to discussions concerning accountability mechanisms alternative perspectives based on the self-defined needs and demands of conflict-affected populations. By bringing more diverse themes to the negotiating table, discussions are, so the argument goes, pushed beyond those themes habitually prioritized by the negotiating parties, such as DDR, security sector reform and amnesty. At the same time, victim inclusion may identify unseen patterns of victimization and affectation, which allows for more representative provisions. In turn, the inclusion of victims' self-defined local and subnational agendas generates wider legitimacy, and the acknowledgement and recognition of victim/survivor histories. Such a transimission chain, it is argued, may lead to broader societal appropriation of the peace talks and of accountability mechanisms. In the end, the gambit is that participation will strengthen post-accord settlements, making them more resilient to recidivism and delivering better-quality peace.

As policy makers have sought to craft more effective responses to victims' and survivors' demands that mechanisms and institutions represent their specific needs and claims (Shaw and Waldorf 2010; García-Godos 2016), so the latter have come to participate increasingly in so-called 'victim-centred' practices through consultation processes, dialogue with perpetrators and, more recently, direct engagement in the design, planning and implementation of transitional justice mechanisms (Nussio, Rettberg and Ugarrizzo 2015). Colombia's victims' delegations simultaneously manifest the tendency towards victim inclusion in discussions over transitional justice and in wider peacemaking/peacebuilding initiatives – the so-called victims' turn in transitional justice and local turn in peacebuilding respectively. The delegations also demonstrate the consolidated tendency of incorporating transitional justice into the broader endeavour of peacemaking. In this regard, they represent a core example of the evolution of both the peacebuilding and transitional justice paradigms, towards respectively a more inclusive and victim-centred approach. The delegations were thus a *hybrid* mechanism, at once explicitly incorporated into a formal peacemaking process, while, in turn, bound to a victim-centred transitional justice practice.

The so-called 'victims' turn' in transitional justice has been characterized by 'more widespread' interaction and dialogue between victims and perpetrators within transitional justice interventions, in an effort to strengthen the capacity of accountability mechanisms to represent victims' demands and voices directly (Quinn and Freeman 2003; David and Choi 2005; Robins 2015; Méndez 2016; Sajjad 2016). The 'victims' turn' emerged in the mid-2000s, as increasing attention was paid by policy makers and scholars to the broader spectrum of victims' rights (Garcia-Godos 2016). The establishment of the victims' fund within the International Criminal Court and an increasing receptivity towards the theme within the UN and other intergovernmental and nongovernmental organizations were also key factors in consolidating the so-called 'victims' turn' (Engstrom 2013). In this context, Méndez has gone so far as to argue that 'victim participation has become a well-established norm' in transitional justice practices, as victims have become 'prominent protagonists' through their participation 'in the design and execution of all programmes of truth telling and reparations, *and not simply as witnesses or recipients of benefits*' (Méndez 2016: 1–2, emphasis added). Other scholars have posited that growing attention to the promotion and protection of victims' rights within international and national policy/academic arenas over the last decade has, in fact, positioned victims as priority targets in national and international policy (Nussio, Rettberg and Ugarrizo 2015).

Characterizing Colombia's 'victims' delegations' as a key manifestation of so-called local turn in peacebuilding and of the victim-centred transitional justice approach, themselves embedded within the broader peacemaking initiative of the Santos–FARC-EP peace process, this book analyses the degree to which the delegations effectuated the meaningful participation of survivors of atrocity and placed victims and their demands at the centre of the process, as the negotiating parties professed. The research at the same time explores the degree to which the ambitions of victim-centred transitional justice practices were, in fact, achieved in the case of Colombia.

Whether such practices permit the effective exercise of victim agency, the incorporation of victims' demands and the representation of their self-defined needs, priorities and interests, while generating appropriation of the provisions of the peace accords and making them more resilient, is far from resolved, as the case of Colombia will show. Despite assertions of 'victim-centredness' made by policy makers and scholars, in practice there remains 'something of a mismatch between the claims of transitional justice institutions and the views of those victims who are the supposed beneficiaries of such initiatives' (McEvoy and McConnachie 2012a: 528). McEvoy and McConnachie have cogently argued that the 'victim-centeredness' of transitional justice practice is, above all, closely related to the quest by governments and policy makers to demonstrate their own 'bona fides', given the 'enormous financial, political, legal and psychological effort' of establishing and maintaining transitional justice processes. From their perspective, victim inclusion and 'centeredness' in transitional justice is thus determined in, large part, by a quest for self-legitimation and is often linked to the 'pursuit of larger political or social goals' by states and other elite actors (McEvoy and McConnachie 2012b: 490). By promoting transitional justice as a discourse and practice that defers to victim experience and knowledge, endorses victim participation and acknowledgement, and, on paper, places victims at the centre of transitional justice design, victim-centred practices may be framed as morally legitimate and politically inclusive. Legitimacy may then, in turn, be conferred upon those state and internationally led processes being pursued – be they peace negotiations or transitional justice practices themselves – a quality, argue McEvoy and McConnachie (2012a, 2012b), that such top-down processes often lack. The inclusion of survivors of political violence in the Colombian peace process may, to a certain extent, be seen through this lens; however, as will be argued later on, this critique does not tell the whole story, given that many who went to Havana saw the process as emancipatory. In the words of one of the delegates:

> The experience changed me and made my heart rest when I gave my testimony. Having the perpetrators before you, you can rest ... looking them in the face and in the eyes, they were crouched down, you know, like the reaction you have when you're really saying things, expressing the pain that you've felt and you've caused.[18]

Other scholars, such as Sajjad (2016), Grewal (2016) and Robins (2015, 2017), have similarly argued that 'victim-centred' transitional justice is driven by the needs of the state, over and above the needs of victims, and, accordingly, does little to incorporate or respond effectively to subaltern voices. For Robins (2017), while victim participation should be considered an ethical imperative, victims often lack meaningful agency and may ultimately be instrumentalized by state and international actors within nominally 'victim-centred' transitional justice practices. McEvoy and McConnachie offer a pertinent critique in this regard, positing that 'instrumentalization' represents '*the defining characteristic* of the relationship between victims and the mechanisms of transitional justice'. From their perspective, victims lose out 'in the pursuit of larger political and social goals such as reinforcing the rule of law, deterring future offenders, getting to the "truth" of past violence and ... the pragmatic deal-making that is inherent in making peace' (2012b: 499–502). From this perspective, transitional justice processes aimed at consolidating the rule of law, strengthening democratic institutions and uncovering the 'truth' related to past episodes of violence, as well as those transitional justice practices linked to peace negotiations, limit the exercise of victims' agency. Victims thus 'participate as instruments of those mechanisms, rather than on their own terms' (Robins 2017: 42–44), signifying that victim-centred transitional justice practices habitually objectify victims, while 'creating new narratives for states to build their legitimacy upon' (Robins 2017: 48).

The question of agency then represents a core aspect of the critique of victim-centred transitional justice. Scholars have problematized the role of

---

[18] Interview, Bogotá, Colombia, April 2015.

those (national and international) actors seeking to represent the perspectives and interests of victims within victim-centred transitional justice practices, with specific reference to the former's episodic lack of will to acknowledge and engage with and transform power relations, such as those relating to caste, gender, economy and ethnicity. McEvoy and McConnachie (2012b: 495–500) accordingly assert that the 'dominant mechanisms of trials and truth commissions accommodate victims only as nominal or instrumental actors', and advocate an approach that, on the contrary, would seek to maximize victim agency. Grewal (2016) calls for a radical shift in transitional justice practices in order to move beyond legalistic discourse and practice, and reconceive the political core of the paradigm as a means of giving voice to marginalized actors. Referring to the case of Nepal, Sajjad (2016: 44) similarly argues that victims were defined and constrained by their role as 'subjects' rather than having been active 'participants' in what had, on paper, been billed as a victim-centred transitional justice process. For Sajjad, the parameters of participation ignored realities on the ground, such as education and illiteracy rates. Moreover, local actors were obliged to learn and articulate the 'appropriate language' of (internationally led) transitional justice. Participation and inclusion were thus ultimately restricted and tended to reinforce existing power structures. In a similar vein, Robins has cogently argued that victims have become a 'fetish' in transitional justice. For Robins (2017: 53), despite the increasing assertion that the transitional justice paradigm is oriented towards victim participation and agency, victims 'remain almost entirely their object with no capacity to exert significant impact on a prescribed process that unfolds according to a global model, largely unchanged by rituals of consultation'.

Empirical evidence then has suggested that, even in spite of its apparent focus on victims, the claims made by 'victim-oriented' transitional justice practice have not been borne out in practice. Despite key innovations, transitional justice processes continue to 'fall short of achieving the "victim-centered" threshold' (Sajjad 2016: 26). Victims have rarely participated directly in the design and implementation of transitional justice mechanisms and, as has been well documented, participation in such cases has brought minimal sustained impact. Not only has participation been restricted, but the demands, needs and interests of victims within 'victim-centered' transitional justice also continue habitually to be left unaddressed. Victim-centred transitional justice from this perspective has thus rarely led to the guarantee of broader victims' rights or to the inclusion of their demands (Lundy and McGovern 2008). Moreover, the contention that victim-centred transitional justice practices may engender broader buy-in of both the peace settlement and accountability mechanisms, and, crucially, make peace settlements more resilient, similarly remains hard to prove, a further point that will be explored in the case of Colombia.

In light of the preceding discussions, scholars have correctly signalled the importance of crafting measured expectations with respect to the agency that victims might assert within victim-centred mechanisms, in particular as regards their capacity to make their voices heard and the degree to which such processes are likely to lead to the guarantee of victims' rights. Jones et al (2023) coherently propose that evaluation of whether victim participation is 'meaningful' or 'beneficial' – including in terms of both procedure and outcome – should be measured according to how participants themselves evaluate their experience. Situated within the earlier debates, this book examines the degree to which the victims' delegations replicated other experiences of victim-centred transitional justice or whether, on the contrary, Colombia's experience departs from these tendencies and has brought about a more meaningful process of empowerment for survivors of atrocity.

Conciliation/reconciliation, peacemaking and transitional justice

Finally, the victims' delegations were significant for a third reason, which will be of central importance to the development of this book. The Colombia case provides original insight concerning the relationship between peacemaking, victim-centred transitional justice practice, and the broader concept and practices of conciliation/reconciliation. The book is then at once about how survivors of political violence contribute to peacemaking, how they might shape transitional justice and accountability frameworks in the context of peace negotiations, and what the spaces for contact and encounter between victims and their perpetrators established during victim-centred initiatives may ultimately mean for intragroup and intergroup relations. It is also about what, if anything, it might mean to talk about conciliation and reconciliation in a context such as Colombia, where over a century of grotesque killing and maiming has made such a proposition problematic.

In the wake of violent conflict, victims, perpetrators, former enemies and their constituencies often live as uneasy neighbours, their relationships shaped by mutual distrust and discrimination and by memories of violence, whether recent or more long term (Brett 2022). Such antagonisms are likely to be particularly severe in the wake of egregious and historically protracted intergroup violence that has cut across and exacerbated societal cleavages, and has affected broad geographical areas. In contexts where there has been a high incidence of mutual dehumanization and the suspension of moral codes (Theidon 2010), such has been the case in Colombia, intergroup reconciliation will understandably be difficult, suggesting that our expectations should be well managed.

Overcoming violent intergroup antagonism faces further acute obstacles when powerful actors remain armed and where elites contest or oppose peace talks, including specifically narratives of inclusion and mechanisms for accountability consecrated within peace agreements (Brett 2021a). Despite the formal end to peace negotiations and, often, the incorporation therein of a wide array of provisions oriented towards overcoming intergroup antagonism, as has been the case since the Santos–FARC-EP peace talks, post-accord coexistence habitually remains begrudging, as communities and individuals experience the present and imagine the future through the societal cleavages and violent memories and hostilities of the past. Colombia is no exception in this respect, an unsurprising state of affairs given that the wider armed conflict remains ongoing and only eight years have elapsed since the peace agreement signed with the FARC-EP. Beyond the achievement of formal negotiations and political accommodation between former protagonists, transformation on this scale takes generations, particularly where the conflict identities and collective beliefs that framed and shaped violent conflict persist. Furthermore, the superation of intergroup antagonism faces acute impediments, particularly where a conflict has been indivisible in character. Zero-sum conflicts, 'waged over territory, secession, or cultural politics', are likely to be especially hard to overcome, often leading to the 'hardening' of divisions based on ethnicity, ideology (Cheng et al 2018: 3),[19] race or identity. Such cases culminate in 'deeply divided societies' (Guelke 2012), where all social issues are ultimately framed through the lens of the predominant societal cleavages, as has been the case in Colombia.

Compounding the struggle over territorial, economic, political and material benefits, the onset, continuation and termination of violent conflict are shaped by the development and persistence of perceptions, beliefs and motivations that determine the relationship between social groups (Staub 2011; Aiken 2013; Bar-Tal 2013, 2014; Leader Maynard 2019; Castano, Muñoz-Rojas and Čehajić-Clancy 2020; Brett 2021a). From the discipline of social psychology, Bar-Tal (2013) has argued that a so-called 'conflictive ethos' plays a key role in both the outbreak and perpetuation of political violence.[20] Particularly in cases of intractable conflict, scholars have argued that individual and groupthink are shaped by a psychological infrastructure, itself undergirded by so-called societal beliefs that enable individuals and communities to cope with its protracted and violent nature. For Bar-Tal (2013), the conflictive ethos represents a worldview that constructs an image and rationale of the conflict, shapes individual and group perceptions of one's own group (ingroup) and of the adversary's group (outgroup) and moulds

---

[19] Cheng et al (2018: 3) argue that 'divisible' conflicts are 'fought over access to the state, resources, political rights and rent-sharing arrangements' and 'offer greater scope for negotiation and compromise'.

[20] Bar-Tal's concept of societal beliefs coincides closely with what Leader Maynard (2019) has referred to as 'atrocity-justifying ideologies' – in short, 'justificatory mechanisms' that explain how ideology may shape/feed into perpetrators' willingness to kill.

group identity. The ingroup often perceives itself and its goals as glorious, and justified, while believing itself to be the only victim in an unjust violent onslaught against it by the outgroup. In such a context, violence wielded by the ingroup is, from its perspective, justified and legitimate: it perceives its own acts as committed in self-defence against an unjust opponent. As has been well documented, the ingroup often dehumanizes its adversary; such negative trait characterization, it is argued, justifies and may incentivize the violence wielded against the outgroup. Violence may then not only be justified (as self-defence), but it may also be framed as necessary (to prevent the extermination of the ingroup by the outgroup). Historically, such dynamics have played a driving role in shaping the nature of the violence in Colombia, and in constructing the impediments to longer-term peace in the aftermath of the 2016 peace talks, as the research presented here will contend.

Significantly, as violent conflict escalates, societal groups habitually develop core beliefs that facilitate their understanding and justification of and coexistence with intractable conflict and the violence that is perpetrated within its confines (Brett 2021a). Such beliefs may justify and incentivize (violent) acts against the enemy, prepare group members for violence both from and against the enemy, motivate solidarity, mobilization and action, and create a sense of differentiation and superiority between societal groups (Leader Maynard 2019). Moreover, collective beliefs may also play a decisive role in impeding the closure of peace negotiations and the achievement of intergroup reconciliation, given that those individuals who reach out to the outgroup are perceived as traitors, as betraying their own group.

Such assertions may appear abstract, yet they are of central concern and relevance to the journey of the victims' delegations and the wider story of the Santos–FARC-EP peace talks, facilitating insight into the nature of the political violence and conflict waged, and the factors that shaped the negotiations. Referring to the perspectives of the negotiating parties, one of the members of the Episcopal Conference that organized and accompanied the victims' delegations stated that:

> I saw them evolve [the negotiating parties], a process that commenced especially when the victims began to give their testimonies. At first, the parties thought they had committed political errors. After this, they began to believe that they had made military mistakes. And finally, the negotiating parties recognized that they had made human mistakes, and, by acknowledging that they had made human mistakes, they themselves came to be affected.[21]

---

[21] Interview, Bogotá, Colombia, April 2015.

Far from essentializing a conflict and the identities of those armed actors and their constituent groups that wage and sustain it, an approach that seeks to understand the collective beliefs of and relationships between warring parties and their social constituencies gives important insights into how we might understand the contingent factors that drive protracted political violence. Such an approach may, in turn, shed light on the potential approaches and processes that may be developed in order to engage effectively with the factors that sustain conflict and impede conciliation. In fact, important peacebuilding scholars such as John Paul Lederach (1997) have, for many years, argued that the transformation of antagonistic relationships between social groups and the beliefs, ideologies and motivations that undergird them – and which were often key to the onset and perpetuation of the violence in the first place – is central to peacemaking, peacebuilding and reconciliation. In short, unfreezing and transforming collective beliefs and intergroup relations, and rebuilding damaged relationships after episodes of political violence are essential for laying the foundations for the cognitive changes necessary to facilitate the prospects for sustainable peace and take serious steps towards crafting conditions for coexistence and reconciliation (Murphy 2010). However, this is not, on its own, sufficient: structural inequalities, economic and political exclusion, and structural drivers of conflict must also be addressed. From this perspective: 'Reconciliation goes beyond the agenda of formal conflict resolution to changing the motivations, goals, beliefs, attitudes and emotions of the great majority of society members regarding the conflict, the nature of the relationship between the parties and the parties themselves' (Bar-Tal and Bennink 2011: 12). Such a shift lies at the heart of conflict transformation and is highly pertinent to our analysis of the role of the victims' delegations.

Reconciliation is then a long-term, complex process occurring on a multilevel, multidimensional basis through which a society moves away from a divided past towards a shared future (Bloomfield, Barnes and Huyse 2003). It requires changes in group attitudes, aspirations, emotions and beliefs, changes which often understandably represent a painful challenge (Hamber 2009; Brett 2021a). Significantly, in this regard, Hamber has cogently argued that reconciliation processes are 'non-linear, messy and deeply ambivalent', in particular at the community and individual levels, the latter due to the obstacles to closure (2009: 193).

Reconciliation is not then a 'one-track' process, but rather a social, psychological, political, educational and cultural one. Such a process must include diverse levels and dimensions across institutions and infrastructures (Bar-Tal 2013). Similarly, Adler and Bartlett (1998: 43) posit that, at the core of the reconciliation process, is: 'An active process of redefinition or reinterpretation of reality – what people consider real, possible, and desirable – on the basis of new causal and normative knowledge.'

A fundamental component of this process is what Lederach (2010) terms the construction of the *Moral Imagination* – in short, the capacity of individuals, societal groups and communities to create a shared imaginary and to imagine/perceive themselves as being part of a wider web of relationships, while also imagining what has previously been unimaginable with respect to mutual recognition between groups.

Departing from the position that Colombia's history of violence has sculpted deep, complex divisions, and, in turn, shaped (and been shaped by) multiple, often overlapping collective group identities, this book will analyse the degree to which the Santos–FARC-EP peace process and specific experience of victim-oriented transitional justice therein shaped and transformed the country's engrained conflict identities. The chapters will accordingly explore what it means to talk about conciliation and reconciliation in the context of the victims' delegations. In order to develop this analysis, the research argues that the victims' delegations represented both a means through which a limited number of survivors could articulate their demands to the negotiating parties (peacemaking) and an unintentional ad hoc space of encounter and contact between them. As such, the book explores the degree to which the delegations were able to play a role as peacemakers and peacebuilders, in the latter case through transforming the relationships between victims and perpetrators in Havana and beyond. The testimonies given by the delegations were confidential – the audience was restricted to the negotiating parties and national/international actors accompanying the process. Within this space, important dialogue was sustained, albeit temporarily, between the members of the delegations and the negotiating parties, dialogue that had not initially been a core objective of the delegations. These spaces for dialogue ultimately brought significant relational transformation, specifically of the perceptions held by many that participated in the Havana process. According to one of the members of the victims' delegations:

> I changed a lot. I saw the FARC-EP from another perspective. I was trained to fight them, to eliminate them. But the fact of sharing with them, looking over different cases, I began to think that those of us who are here, we are all children of peasant farmers, we are the same.[22]

Scholars of contact theory contend that sustained interaction (contact) between adversarial groups 'directly reduces prejudice, challenges stereotypes and misperceptions, and can break down rigid perceptions of the Other as a monolithic and inherently hostile group' (Aiken 2013: 34). Contact theorists

---

[22] Interview, Bogotá, Colombia, April 2015.

argue that encounters between adversarial groups, both during hostilities and in their aftermath – as was the case with the victims' delegations – may serve as a crucial first step in the processes towards (re)humanization and acknowledgement. Such contact, it is argued, may lead enemies to begin to perceive one another as individuals situated within the same moral sphere and thus entitled to the same rights and protections, particularly when it is sustained and regulated (Allport 1954; Staub 1998; Aiken 2013; Hughes 2017).

Contact theory may thus provide some insight into the question of how to overcome the embedded narratives and perspectives driving violent intergroup conflict, such as dehumanization, mutual distrust, delegitimation of the outgroup and so on. The purpose of approaches undergirded by positive contact is to permit actors to craft empathy develop and reasonable expectations each other's future behaviour (Staub 1998), with the aim of challenging the reversal of morality that legitimized the past use of violence. The success of contact processes, it is argued, is contingent upon reductions in negative stereotyping taking place across all members of the group, relegitimation and repersonalization; these changes must be generalizable, particularly given the likelihood that only a small number of individuals will form part of any formal process. Staub's words concisely summarize the potential effect of intergroup contact: 'As the members of each group describe the pain and suffering of their group at the hands of the other, they can begin to open up to the pain of the other. They can grieve for themselves, for the other, and assume responsibility for their share in the historical antagonism and violence' (Staub 1998: 255).

Thus, the Colombia case is of central relevance to the debates pertaining to the feasibility of the positive outcome of contact between survivors and victims of political violence and its perpetrators within formal victim-centred mechanisms, and the degree to which this may lead to conciliation and reconciliation. The discussions presented here are framed within the scholarship on intergroup conciliation and reconciliation, and reflect insights from broader scholarship that highlight the complex path taken by intergroup interaction across specific cases (Nee and Uvin 2010; Druliolle and Brett 2018).

The argument

Advocating a context-specific understanding of the role of survivors and victims as political actors (Baines 2015: 320; 2017), the research presented in this book will explore the complex factors determining the nature, role and impact of 'victim-centred' peacemaking directed towards defining transitional justice practices in Colombia. The research will ask whether victim inclusion in the Santos–FARC-EP peace talks mattered, from two complementary perspectives. First, to what degree did the victims' delegations shape the formal peace process in terms of the dynamics and content therein? Second, did the space of encounter that the delegations represented bring about a transformation in the relationships between the negotiating parties and the participating victims themselves and the mutual beliefs and perceptions they held of each other?

Of central importance to this task is to explore whether and, if so, to what degree Colombia's victim-centred transitional justice process represented and benefited victims directly, or whether the delegations remained 'an arm of global liberal, and often neoliberal, governance', and, as such '… driven by the needs of the state' and international actors, 'rather than of the victims of political violence' (Robins 2017: 51). In other words, did the delegations represent a transformative and empowering space for their participants or, rather, did they institutionalize practices of instrumentalization and depoliticize and disempower survivors of atrocity? Finally, the research will also aim to answer whether the victims' delegations were able to foster wider buy-in for the peace talks and a more resilient post-accord settlement, both key justifications for inclusive peacemaking.

The argument that victims are instrumentalized within broader social and political processes led by the state or by international actors, and that, therein, their agency is constrained, their demands sidelined and voices silenced, is, at least in part, convincing. The experiences rigorously analysed by scholars such as Robins, McEvoy, McConnachie and Sajjad for cases such as Nepal and Northern Ireland demonstrate this argument persuasively. Should we then expect to identify similar patterns of instrumentalization and exclusion of victims, and their demands in the Colombia case analysed in this book?

The answer to this question is a complicated one. In fact, the narrative developed here is, in part, at odds with research addressing contexts elsewhere. What this book proposes instead is that such a contention – of instrumentalization – only partially explains the dynamics inherent to the experience of the victims' delegations in Colombia. In short, revictimization, retraumatization, instrumentalization and the marginalization of survivors' demands and interests did take place in Colombia in the context of the victims' delegations. However, to prioritize this experience over and above a narrative of empowerment and restoration is to disclose only one aspect of an otherwise complex and, in part, transformative process for those that took part. Moreover, to concede that instrumentalization and exclusion were the predominant characteristics for the case of the victims' delegations negates the fact that the delegations ultimately represented a space for disputation, disruption and agency, a space that was itself acutely contested, as this book will argue.

In the case of Colombia, an armed conflict that has persisted for over half a century and has left approximately nine million victims in its wake, complex patterns of mass victimization have occurred, themselves building on and reinforcing protracted, historical episodes of egregious violence and socioeconomic marginalization and structural violence, as will be discussed in Chapter 2. Such brutality has shaped collective identity in diverse and nuanced ways. In this context, and in a country with one of the highest indices of inequality on the planet, political and economic elites unsurprisingly continue to call the shots, or at least try to. Nevertheless, for over three decades, Colombian human rights, women's and victims' organizations have persistently punched above their weight, increasingly having a significant influence within both the political and juridical spheres and, more recently, on the dynamics of making and building peace and reckoning with the past. The argument presented in this book accordingly identifies those survivors of political violence who participated in the peace negotiations in particular and victims' organizations in general, as political actors who, through asserting their agency, have gradually reconfigured diverse spheres of political power, a point Rettberg (2015) has made eloquently. The book is then, at once, a story about the affirmation of political subjectivity and expression of subaltern agency by those survivors/victims who participated in the Havana talks as much as it is about top-down, formally driven peacemaking.

In this context of ubiquitous violence, mass victimization and continued elite prerogative, how, if at all, might subaltern actors assert their agency and reconfigure relations of power? Indeed, what might an effective victim-centred transitional justice process look like and what might realistically be expected from it? How and to what effect might survivors of political violence meaningfully participate in such a process on their own terms? And what impact on embedded identities and the wider sustainability of the peace settlement might victim-centred peacemaking and transitional justice practices affect? These are the questions with which this book is concerned and to which the core argument will speak.

Building on over 70 interviews carried out over five years in Colombia, the research presented in this book seeks to disclose a complex story, contending that the proposition of a sweeping narrative that articulates the reductive logic that victim-oriented peacemaking and transitional justice are paralysing and merely instrumentalize victims' narratives and experiences, and, in turn, collapse spaces for agency, contestation and resistance, is insufficient as an explanatory framework. Moreover, in this case, such an argument disparages and sidelines the extraordinary courage and the agency of those survivors of political violence who participated in the talks, and fails to divulge an adequate account of how they engaged with and, in part, transformed peacemaking and transitional justice practices in Colombia, or how they themselves were transformed as a consequence.

A more nuanced reading is thus required, one that reflects the changing perspectives over time of those who took part in the victims' delegations and acknowledges the micro- (interpersonal) and macro- (political) level consequences of the delegations, while at the same time, and significantly, acknowledging the evident and powerful limitations and challenges that the delegations did, in fact, face. By drawing upon the direct experiences of participants themselves, this book aims to craft a context-specific understanding of what delegates experienced during their participation in the victims' delegations, and what whether they perceived participation as meaningful, beneficial and dignifying. The analysis develops from this point of departure, from a reading of delegates' own assessments of their participation in the victims' delegations.

The hope here is that a more nuanced history will be crafted and an accurate analysis reached, one that has been shaped by the harrowing experiences of the members of the victims' delegations in the precarious and uncertain terrain that a face-to-face encounter with state and nonstate perpetrators in Havana represented. Characterizing the victims' delegations as practices that were uniquely instrumentalizing and, in fact, silenced subaltern voices is then imprecise; moreover, it fails to do justice to those individuals who courageously confronted the armed actors in Havana and the consequences that such an encounter precipitated.

A perhaps more refined analysis of the experience of the victims' delegations presented in this book will reveal how a composite set of factors did indeed impose significant limitations on the capacity of survivors of atrocity to shape those technocratic, political and legal mechanisms and interventions oriented towards protecting and guaranteeing the rights of victims and enshrining the obligations of duty bearers to redress past horror. Such constraints derive from the limitations of the transitional justice paradigm and, specifically, the restricted and disproportionate nature of victim participation in Havana, as we shall see; they are also directly linked to what transpired in the aftermath of the visits of the victims' delegations to Havana, in particular to the way in which political power exerted by both those driving and those opposing the peace talks was asserted and its effects played out. Under such conditions, the capacity of victim participation to secure the incorporation of provisions within the Final Agreement aimed at guaranteeing the right to nonrepetition and to wider structural transformation was severely constrained. Similarly, the mechanism was also unable to foster wider societal buy-in of the peace process and accountability mechanisms agreed upon in Havana or, ultimately, to strengthen the resilience of the peace settlement. It is here, then, that the concept of instrumentalization assumes its core relevance. However, the argument crafted in this book is that when analysing the factors that led to the instrumentalization of survivors of political violence in Colombia's victim-centred transitional mechanism, it may be useful to disaggregate the influence of the provisions for and nature of participation itself (including both procedures and outcomes) from post facto factors, such as the capacity of spoiling actors and congressional sovereignty.

As such, the primary data upon which this book is based suggest the need for further, more meticulous examination of Colombia's victims' delegations away from a reductionist conclusion of mere depoliticization and disempowerment of those victims who participated in the Havana talks. In this regard, the research is careful not to propagate a view that survivors are unable to shape victim-centred transitional justice mechanisms in post-atrocity and postconflict societies, or that they themselves are uniquely silenced through or remain unchanged by their participation within formal processes and mechanisms. Rather, the contention here is that the victims' delegations were not solely quarry to or subordinated by the impositions of elite national and international actors. Participation, in fact, brought with it significant dividends at a range of levels: at the *national level*, in terms of shaping the content of the peace agreement; at an *individual level* for many of those that took part in the delegations and for those negotiating peace; and at a *collective level* for some victims' organizations and the core agenda of these collectives in relation to their demands for and platforms supporting peacebuilding and transitional justice during and in the wake of the peace talks. In this respect, the process of transformation was a circular one, as the participants' testimonies effectuated individual transformation of those negotiating peace, which, in turn, engendered changes in their perspectives on responsibility, accountability and de-escalation, as well as their relationships with victims and their negotiating adversary. Such a process itself led to the empowerment of many participants of the victims' delegations.

Victim participation and its significant impact were contingent upon two fundamental factors particular to the Colombia case: first, the weight of historical dynamics – in particular, of patterns of victim mobilization; and, secondly (and relatedly), the juridical transformations and political influence that these mobilizations, in part, shaped, in the run-up to the Havana talks. In this regard, the study will evidence how the victims' delegations emerged out of a process of long-term historical struggle, driven by survivors of political violence themselves. Over time, victims' struggles have shaped key legislative frameworks, while also gradually reframing the narrative around peacemaking and transitional justice in Colombia. The upshot of this was that by 2014, victims' and human rights organizations imposed a clear prerogative for victim participation that ultimately led to the invitation by the negotiating parties for participation in the peace talks. Once at the peace talks, delegates articulated a series of diverse demands and, by so doing, played a role in shaping the truth and accountability provisions consecrated within the Victims' Agreement. Many delegates advocated a shift away from an emphatically legalistic/punitive framework of justice towards what they perceived as a more integral approach that balanced the rights to truth, justice, reparation and nonrecurrence. Delegates were thus able, in part, to impose their own narrative on the peace negotiations, appropriating a space for agency and contestation, which 'produced a qualitative shift in the peace talks and transformed them profoundly', according to one of the organizers of the delegations.[23] This book will argue that this so-called integral approach to transitional justice indeed reflected the demands of many members of the victims' delegations, ultimately signifying that the Final Agreement closely resembled many of their own specific proposals. Consequently, the delegations facilitated the assertion of victims' agency, sculpting the design of the transitional justice mechanisms around their own experiences and demands.

However, as previously discussed, the book is also careful to present a nuanced analysis of the question of whether and, if so, how survivors' demands were incorporated into the Final Agreement. In this regard, the so-called integral approach to justice – favoured by many of the delegates themselves – was rejected by many who did not go to Havana and who demanded widespread prison time for perpetrators. Significant divisions thus emerged within the wider victims' movement. Simultaneously, the integral approach to transitional justice closely reflected and responded to the demands and interests of both the government/state security forces and the FARC-EP levying the peace talks. The negotiating parties unsurprisingly favoured amnesty (including partial amnesty), alternative sanctions, truth telling, and reparations mechanisms over and above retributive justice. The parties, from the outset, sought explicitly to limit strict penal justice provisions for past crimes and to prioritize other forms of sanctions, accountability and redress, ultimately restricting the potential prison time to be served by armed actors found guilty of human rights violations and abuses. The convergence of the demands for alternative justice mechanisms articulated by the negotiating parties with those made by many members of the victims' delegations in this respect shielded the process from a potential crisis, which would likely have occurred had the members of the victims' delegations instead prioritized demands for strict retributive justice for past crimes. Significantly, it is also here that the Colombia process is opened up to one of the core critiques articulated by scholars for processes elsewhere, namely that survivors of political violence are instrumentalized and subordinated to the demands and interests of elite actors.

Beyond the content of Point Five, at the individual level, interviews illustrated how the presence of the victims' delegations facilitated a meaningful, although unintended space for dialogue between survivors and perpetrators of political violence in Havana. In this respect, the victims' delegations fostered a key moment of contact between the survivors and the negotiating parties. These dialogues did not take place under the formal

---

[23] Interview, Bogotá, Colombia, May 2015.

auspices of the victims' testimonies – when the negotiating parties were not authorized to respond directly – but rather, during informal breaks, lunches and conversations. These encounters, in many cases, transformed the relationship between members of the victims' delegations and the negotiating parties, as well as their perceptions of one another. In many respects, this contact began to break down the wall of denial held by the negotiating parties, and the embedded perspectives and beliefs that had shaped mutual perceptions between participating victims and the negotiating parties. In this regard, the interviews emphatically illustrated important episodes of dialogue between members of the victims' delegations and the negotiating parties themselves that took place during the visits, which transformed the dynamics and relationships between the negotiating parties and those who had survived the violence perpetrated by them. This dialogue also arguably precipitated a shift in the perspectives of the negotiating parties towards acknowledging 'victims' and accepting responsibility for their violent acts.

The contention of this research, then, is that the hybrid mechanism of the delegations shaped the peacemaking process and transitional justice design, while at the same time crafting incipient steps towards coexistence and potential conciliation between those who met in Havana. In this respect, the delegations partially sculpted what early transitional justice practitioners and scholars had posited as one of the paradigm's original objectives: that of interpersonal dialogue and conciliation in the aftermath of political violence (Minow 1998). Moreover, the delegations illustrated the potential of approaches towards peacemaking and peacebuilding based on contact theory. What, in part, emerged out of the victims' delegations was what Theidon (2010: 71; 203) has described as 'postconflict social repair', which, at least temporarily, led in this case to the reconstruction of 'the human (in a context of dehumanizing violence)', and the fracturing of individual and collective identities based on the ethos of conflict.

However, and significantly, the dialogue between survivors and perpetrators that had commenced in Havana was not given formal continuity in the wake of the visits, nor was it extended towards other societal groups or spaces, obliterating its sustainability and capacity to scale up and out. The influence on the trajectory of the peace process of those powerful political actors opposed to it ultimately threatened the fragile steps towards co-existence that had taken place in Havana. Such a factor was compounded by the fact that the limited dissemination by the government and the UN of the progress made in Havana also restricted the degree to which the delegations were able to wield broader societal impact; in short, what happened in Havana ostensibly stayed in Havana. Once again, then, in this regard, what transpired post facto – after the visits of the delegations – was fundamental in limiting the degree to which the experience was able to assert any further or wider meaningful or sustainable influence on peacemaking and peacebuilding in

Colombia. In this case, the transformative implications of contact between perpetrators and victims remained temporary, as it has done for other cases elsewhere, such as in Northern Ireland.

In this respect, the Colombia case evidences how approaches to intergroup reconciliation dependent on contact alone are unlikely to overturn macro-level perspectives, policies and prerogatives, as Prieto (2012) correctly argues. Scholarship has in fact documented cases where, even in spite of sustained everyday contact, such as in the cases of returnees in Bosnia and Herzegovina and Rwanda, intergroup antagonism, prejudice and stereotypes remain ongoing, 'along with new hatreds and resentments' (2012: 543). Referring similarly to the context of Northern Ireland, Hughes (2017) vehemently critiques contact theory. The author correctly questions the degree to which norms, values and behaviour can be modified progressively through positive contact between individuals from antagonistic groups, even when conditions are sustained, nonhierarchical and unthreatening, and the process is mediated by adequately trained outsiders. For Hughes, macro- and structural factors, such as poverty, exclusion and ongoing segregation in housing and education, play a decisive role in impeding the potential impact of contact. Drawing on Allport, Hughes identifies the fundamental difficulties that the process of overcoming prejudice is likely to face and thus the challenges that practitioners and policy makers may confront in their attempts to 'build' a shared identity, particularly at the national level. Mendeloff (2004: 370–373) shares this insight, signalling the difficulties and dangers in 'manipulating' existing identities in the wake of violence and atrocity:

> forging new identities almost always fails when groups share a history of substantial intercommunal violence ... Manipulation of identities may generate enormous popular resentment and further harden and radicalise communal identities. Most important, manipulating identities can threaten [ethnic] elites who are much more willing to fight than to give up power.

In this case, it will be argued that the victims' delegations asserted an important role, transforming, in part, aspects of the relationships between the negotiating parties and the victims themselves; these changes led to unprecedented (albeit transitory) episodes of conciliation in Havana. Nevertheless, the peace process has followed a difficult path. The agreement was rejected in 2016 through a national plebiscite and there remains continued opposition to the process in many spheres of Colombian society. Paramilitary organizations have perpetrated horrific carnage since the peace process, murdering social activists and former FARC-EP combatants throughout the country. In 2019, dissident factors of the FARC-EP re-emerged. All of this has been accompanied by the ongoing capacity of elite actors opposing the negotiations – particularly those linked to the government of former Presidents Ivan Duque and Alvaro Uribe – to wield significant influence on its trajectory. As a result, the research in this book argues that the consequences of the contact that took place in Havana were restricted and temporary. Whether a peacemaking process – and specifically a victim inclusion mechanism – can be designed effectively to anticipate these problems is an important question that will be addressed in this book.

In the end, the research presented here will argue that the participation of survivors of political violence had not insignificant consequences for the content of the peace agreement, as well as for the dynamics between the negotiating parties and the victims themselves, ultimately leading to the dismantling of the wall of perpetrator denial, to public acts of apology, to the enactment of episodes of temporary conciliation in Havana and, albeit in part, to the shaping of the provisions for transitional justice. Consequently, the contention here is that by assuming an unprecedented role in formal peacemaking channels, survivors strengthened their status as legitimate political actors and asserted subaltern agency, in the end facilitating important transformations. However, the delegations also brought the revictimization and instrumentalization of survivors of political violence across some spheres of action, and, significantly, in the wake of the delegations, fundamental weaknesses in the process became evident, as broader factors driven by the exercise of political power and agency constrained the influence that the delegations were able to wield.

However, the research presented here is cautious not to define the victims' delegations as a uniquely 'depoliticizing project', the term adopted by Rajca (2018) in his important work on memorialization sites in Argentina, Brazil, and Uruguay. Rather, the victims' delegations sculpted a partial path for empowerment and politicization, at the very least for those who took part in the process, a path that was perhaps, in the end, a single-track one. The delegations nevertheless represented a site through which to contest the depoliticization of survivors of atrocity in Colombia, reflecting the insights of Rojas-Perez (2017) on the potential for victims to become political subjects in Peru. However, aspects of depoliticization also occurred, arguably precipitating both silencing, retraumatization and instrumentalization, as will be discussed later on. As such, the book proposes that an appropriate manner through which to understand the capacity of victims to affect transformation during and as a consequence of victim inclusion initiatives is an *instrumentalization–empowerment spectrum*. In sum, in such scenarios, both empowerment and instrumentalization may occur across diverse fields and levels, at times simultaneously; in other words, the phenomena are not necessarily mutually exclusive. The research presented in this book will explore how the instrumentalization–empowerment spectrum may be shaped by the extent to which victims and survivors are able to navigate and negotiate relations of power linked to elite political, economic and military/armed actors.

From the standpoint that victim agency is complex and nuanced, this approach (and the Colombia case in particular) poses a partial corrective to the scholarship that, at best, refutes and, at worst, negates the capacity of victims as political actors in peacemaking and victim-centred transitional justice practices, framing victims instead as uniquely instrumentalized and lacking meaningful agency. The argument followed in this book is that our conceptualization of power should be refined if we are to understand accurately how survivors of atrocity shaped the peacemaking process in Colombia. In short, the argument contended here is that in the context of the Havana negotiations, subaltern actors were, in fact, able to actively 'negotiate and renegotiate their own place in the social, political ... spheres' (Mac Ginty 2011: 391–402) and consequently write themselves into history, shaping the transitional justice mechanisms consecrated within the Victims' (and Final) Agreement and precipitating key transformations in the relationships between the negotiating parties and survivors of the violence that they had perpetrated. Nevertheless, in seeking to challenge and redefine how power is configured and represented in formal peacemaking interventions, the victims' delegations were ultimately subject to important limitations. The argument may be unsatisfactory for those who believe there to be a categorical answer to whether and how survivors of political violence may shape peacemaking and transitional justice practices. However, it is one that remains faithful to the complexities of survivor experience and participation as illustrated in the testimonies and interviews that represent the core research data and inspiration for this book.

Methodology

The research is based on 70 semi-structured interviews carried out under the auspices of a UN investigation led by the author in 2015 to determine the impact of the victims' delegations on the peace talks. Within the framework of the UN investigation, the author was mandated to conduct in-person interviews, and all in-person interviews were carried out by the author in Spanish. Interviews were carried out in Bogotá, Santa Marta and Cali, Colombia. The empirical data from the interviews were collated and a report subsequently published by the UN in 2017 (Brett 2017a). Interviews were carried out with 52 participants across all five victims' delegations. The composition of each delegation in terms of specific participants, including the gender and other characteristics of each delegate, is set out in Annex 1. Fieldwork consisted of interviews with a further 16 individuals from state institutions, three academic experts, one accompanier and one guarantor country, and with members of the UN system, the NUC and the ECCC.

Follow-up in-person interviews with select members of the victims' delegations were conducted in 2016 and 2018, as part of an individual research project. All interviews were transcribed and data were put into a database, before the interpretation of data and analysis were developed using grounded theory (Charmaz and Thornberg 2017). In 2017, prior to the publication of the UN report, the findings of the investigation were disseminated virtually to the participants of the victims' delegations and the organizers. All interviews are anonymous, given the sensitive nature of the investigation. Fieldwork was approved by the UN in Bogotá in 2015.

Given that the original research for this monograph was carried out under the auspices of a UN investigation, a note on positionality is important here. The interview questions (see Annex 1) and original report were approved by the UN in Colombia, prior to publication in the case of the report. However, the content, including its weaknesses, remain very much my own. For the case of this volume, my access to all materials was approved in 2017 by the United Nations Development Programme (UNDP), and the content of this book is my own; no external institutions have approved or had access to it in that respect. During the investigation and for the specific published report, I was permitted to critique the process of the victims' delegations, as I have done in this book. However, these perspectives are my own.

It is apposite to signal that, due to research constraints, a key weakness of this book is that interviews were not carried out with the negotiating parties, although Sergio Jaramillo Caro and President Juan Manuel Santos were interviewed (in 2016 and 2022 respectively). While the perspectives of the negotiating parties on the themes developed in the book were addressed specifically during interviews with all other interviewees, they remain a missing piece of the puzzle, and an important avenue for future research.

The book

Chapter 1 offers a longitudinal historical perspective of the evolution of patterns of political violence and victimization in Colombia, with the aim of contextualizing the historical processes that shaped the testimonies and proposals presented by the victims' delegations that visited Havana in 2014. An understanding of the experiences of survivors framed within the wider historical trajectory of the armed conflict is fundamental in order to understand how the conflict has perdured and why victims made the demands they did in Havana.

Chapter 2 addresses Colombia's aberrational and grotesque internal armed conflict under President Alvaro Uribe. It explores how Uribe's war on Colombia weakened the FARC-EP guerrilla, pushing it back to peripheral zones of the country, and how this strategy precipitated an unprecedented humanitarian disaster. As such, the chapter details the massive patterns of victimization and state-sponsored human rights violations that occurred under Uribe, as a means of contextualizing the demands made by many participants in the victims' delegations to Havana.

Chapter 3 builds on the argument that beyond the military dynamics of a hurting stalemate presented in Chapter 2, two further factors are critical in explaining the path towards making peace in Havana and the inclusion of the victims' delegations within this process: first, the role and leadership specifically of President Santos and his journey of from hawk to dove during the peace process; and, second (and significantly), building on wider global processes and shifts in peacemaking/peacebuilding norms and practices, the evolving role of Colombian civil society and victims as domestic political actors.

Chapter 4 develops the analysis of the role that Colombia's victims' delegations played in the Havana talks, detailing the antecedents to direct victim participation, before turning to the rationale for victim inclusion. Drawing specifically on the perspectives of those who participated in and organized the victims' delegations, the chapter contends that the Havana talks and the nature of victim inclusion therein demonstrate the evolving trajectory of both the liberal peacebuilding and transitional justice paradigms. The argument presented is that a complex, nuanced and context-specific understanding of participation should be adopted when evaluating victim inclusion.

Chapter 5 examines the process through which participants were selected for the victims' delegations, with a particular focus on the issues of representation and gender. The research discusses whether the delegations were politically effective and able to provide a meaningful, representative reflection of historical patterns of political violence and victimization. Drawing on interviews with members of the victims' delegations and other relevant actors in the peace talks, the chapter explores the efficacy of the principles of inclusion developed by the organizers.

Chapter 6 explores the role of the victims' delegations as *peacebuilders*, looking specifically at the degree to which the delegations were able to effect relational change across three levels: (i) the individual level; (ii) the intragroup level; and (iii) the intergroup level (victims-perpetrators and perpetrator-perpetrator). It argues that the delegations were, in part, an emancipatory project, while also signalling how the delegations precipitated episodes of depoliticization, retraumatization and revictimization. The chapter develops further the argument that victim *empowerment* and *instrumentalization* may occur across a *spectrum*.

Chapter 7 explores the extent to which the participants in the victims' delegations played a role as *peacemakers* during the Havana talks, addressing whether the delegations explicitly shaped the content of Point Five and the Final Agreement. It argues that the delegations were able to influence the content of the agreements across diverse spheres. However, this capacity was more closely subordinate to wider structural factors and relations of power than was their capacity to wield relational transformation: victims' petitions were incorporated only when they converged with and reflected the interests of the negotiating parties.

The final chapter brings together the conclusions from the empirical and wider research pertaining to transitional justice and peacebuilding, arguing for a nuanced and victim/survivor-led analysis of the process and outcome of participation framed through an *instrumentalization–empowerment spectrum*. The chapter also offers a series of policy recommendations pertaining to inclusion mechanisms.

1

A Concise History of Violence

Introduction

This chapter will offer a longitudinal historical perspective of the evolution of patterns of political violence and victimization in Colombia, with the aim of contextualizing the historical processes that shaped the testimonies and proposals presented by the victims' delegations that visited Havana in 2014. An understanding of the experiences of survivors framed within the wider historical trajectory of the armed conflict is of fundamental significance if we are to understand how the conflict has persisted and why victims made the demands they did in Havana. The chapter begins by discussing the patterns of violence that shaped Colombia's post-independence period and turbulent mid-20th century. The analysis will then turn to the country's internal armed conflict, outlining the causes of the conflict, the principal state and nonstate actors who have participated therein and the nature of the violence that they have perpetrated.

A violent post-independence

States and societies do not tend to follow a linear or sequential logic in the aftermath of civil war, violent conflict and mass atrocity (Cheng et al 2018). Poor-quality peace, post-accord violence and conflict relapse regularly occur in the aftermath of initially successful peace negotiations (Brett 2021a). In certain cases, as we shall see for Colombia, conflict, violence and peace coexist, are 'mutually constitutive' or 'entwined', their logics driven by 'complex conflict systems' (Miller 2020: 262) and ongoing direct and indirect violence, predominantly affecting the most vulnerable groups (de Coning 2016). It would thus be misleading to identify a dichotomy between war and peace, and particularly so in the case of Colombia (Karl 2017). Rather, countries remain peaceless, habitually experiencing what can be characterized as a *conflict-peace continuity nexus* (Brett 2021a), in particular with respect to the enduring scars that the causes and consequences of political violence sculpt upon the social and political landscapes of societies emerging from genocide, internal armed conflict, authoritarianism and civil war. These scars frequently impose a legacy that obfuscates the past, present and future, while reinforcing the historical status quo. Under such circumstances, the past is lived in and shapes the present, moulding intergroup relations and often forging profound justifications for the continuation of atrocious violence (Bar-Tal 2013; Brett 2021a).

Throughout much of the 19th century and well into the 20th century, Colombia experienced ongoing war and political violence, punctuated by episodes of both bipartisan peace and incipient institution building (Brett 2022). From the 1830s, internal wars were waged across every decade, as the Conservative and Liberal Parties and their political, social and economic constituencies fought to establish hegemonic rule, control over the state and the ownership and management of national, subnational and local resources, such as land. From 1886, on the eve of the 20th century, until 1930, the Conservative Party asserted political and military hegemony, with the Thousand Days' War (1898–1902) leading to the third consecutive military defeat for the Liberals and the albeit temporary end to their 'military adventurousness' (Posada-Carbó 1997: 246). The commencement of the period of Conservative hegemony was inaugurated by the 1886 Constitution, which consecrated provisions to restrict the political activity of the Liberal Party. According to Posada Carbo, the 1886 Constitution represented 'a definitive historical moment' which 'shaped modern terrorism', given that subsequent struggles to achieve liberal reforms have been 'at the centre of Colombia's violent history' (Posada-Carbó 1997: 246).

Following the political defeat of the Conservative Party in 1930, for 16 years, a series of Liberal Party-run administrations, the so-called *Liberal Republic*, sought to consolidate Liberal hegemony and craft a more liberal government and society. With variegated levels of success, the administrations aimed to overturn Conservative domination, introducing, for example, land reform policies that limited ancestral privileges. During the Liberal Republic, partisan violence began to spiral, as Liberals carried out acts of vengeance against Conservatives throughout the country. Liberal policies 'unleashed furious political opposition from the Conservatives' (Molano 2007: 3). By the end of the *Liberal Republic* in 1946, a century of confrontation between the Conservative and Liberal elites seeking to impose their own 'model of modernisation' through embedded 'local partisanship' throughout the country had exacerbated existing and acute societal cleavages framed across political party lines (Safford and Palacios 2002). Such conditions represented the tinderbox that would ignite extreme and prolonged violence and terror, 'La Violencia', that would come in the wake of the assumption to the presidency on 7 August 1946 of Conservative leader Mariano Ospina Pérez.

'La Violencia'

By the middle of the 20th century, ruling class divisions manifest through bipartisan conflict, the limited reach of central government and pronounced regionalism shaped by patterns of land ownership had become embedded in social, political and economic relations (Hylton 2006: 9). Against this backdrop, the end of the Liberal Republic was precipitated by the early resignation of President Lopez Pumarejo in 1944, which put the country on 'the brink of a catastrophic confrontation ... and augured a revolutionary explosion of unforeseen consequences' (Sanchez and Merteens 2001: 11). The abrupt end to the Liberal Republic in 1946 and the collapse of the Liberal Party itself (Safford and Palacios 2002), ushered in Colombia's modern period of political violence and partisan terror, 'a germinal period ... which sowed ... myths, representations, and modes of behaviour that would be harvested in later phases' (Safford and Palacios 2002: 349).

Conservative Mariano Ospina Pérez assumed the presidency in 1946, incorporating Liberals within what was to be a nominal transitional government. Despite a degree of goodwill on both sides, many Liberals throughout the country were unwilling to accept political defeat, while a wave of violent score settling against Liberals accompanied the return of the Conservative Party to government. Violence precipitously increased after 1946, as Liberals formed armed groups to protect themselves from armed Conservatives and to 'harass government agents', such as those in the Eastern Llanos. In parallel, pro-government militias, the so-called 'pajaros' (armed assassins) and 'chulavitas' (Conservative police), grew in strength and numbers, and violence 'eventually engulfed most of the country'. In this context, Liberals gradually coalesced around political leader Jorge Elécier Gaitán, who eventually withdrew Liberal support for the ruling coalition with the Conservative Party (Bushnell 1993: 201–207).

Bar-Tal (2013, 2014) has argued that intractable conflicts (those of a protracted, irreconcilable, violent, zero-sum and totalizing nature) 'are dependent on the appearance of particular perceptions, beliefs, attitudes and motivations, all of which must change for conflict resolution to occur', manifest through what he has termed a *conflictive ethos* (CE) (Bar-Tal 2000: 352). The CE represents a worldview which furnishes individuals and collective groups with images of the ingroup and of its adversary, the outgroup. As violent conflict escalates, so the CE and the societal beliefs which undergird it gradually shape key aspects of collective group identity, enabling/obligating societal groups to develop core beliefs that facilitate their understanding and justification of, antagonism towards and coexistence with each other and with the violence perpetrated within the confines of the conflict. The CE and its corresponding societal beliefs may first break down social capital between groups, and then erode the ability of the ingroup and outgroup to empathize with each other. A collective sense of *woundedness*, or 'chosen trauma', such as the (real, invented or imagined) memory of an historical wrong perpetrated against the ingroup by the outgroup often persisting over generations, habitually develops, as victimization becomes part of the fabric of constructed collective memory (Volkan 2001). The mobilization of such memories may perpetuate antagonism as they are deployed to ignite and maintain violence, as the violence in the Balkans in the 1990s made abundantly and tragically clear.

By the mid-20th century, bipartisan intergroup violence and polarization in Colombia had become further edified through ideological and identitarian frameworks linked intimately to the Liberal and Conservative Parties and their beliefs and platforms, frameworks that in part evidenced some of the characteristics of a conflictive ethos. Under such conditions, a dramatic evolution and transformation in the nature, scale and dynamics of bipartisan violence took place, following the emergence of Gaitán.

Gaitán was a polarizing figure, who allegedly split the Liberal vote at the 1946 election, arguably leading to the Conservative victory. While formally a Liberal, his populist policies diverged to some degree from the official party line (Sánchez and Bakewell 1985: 797; Mazzei 2009: 75). In fact, Gaitán's calls for land reform and for Colombians to unite against both Liberal and Conservative elites were perceived as representing a significant threat to elite (partisan) hegemony (Sanchez and Merteens 2001: 11–17). In this context, government repression of popular protest increased, leading the country to breaking point. On 9 April 1948, Gaitán was assassinated in Bogotá, which led to subsequent accusations of his murder against elites from both national parties. An outbreak of spontaneous terror throughout the country followed, which would ultimately last for a decade and set the historical antecedents for the internal armed conflict across diverse generations of Colombians.

In the immediate aftermath of Gaitán's execution, Liberal-led popular insurrections and rioting combined with generalized and ritualistic violence broke out initially in the Colombian capital. The so-called Bogotazo, a vehement expression of 'popular rage' (Hylton 2006: 40), affected the entire country, as Revolutionary Boards (juntas), popular governments and peasant militias formed in response to the assassination. Reaction to the Bogotazo and to the generalized revolutionary uprising was itself no less than a 'barbarous reprisal' (Sanchez and Merteens 2001: 11), as state forces were sent by the government to quell the uprising. Accompanying acts of state terror sought simultaneously to punish and communicate a clear message to the rebels. State forces cut off perpetrators' testicles, slashed open the bellies of pregnant women and executed babies, allegedly with the objective of preventing 'the seed of future rebellion'. This immediate partisan terror represented the first phase in what would become 'a war of incredible cruelty' (Pearce 1990: 49–51). By the end of 'La Violencia' in 1964, approximately

300,000 people had been killed – 80 per cent of whom were men – and two million people displaced (Hylton 2006: 40). The cruelty imposed during 'La Violencia' would be reiterated and replicated in the decades of internal armed conflict that followed it.

During previous decades, both Liberals and Conservatives had systematically instrumentalized 'atrocity-justifying ideologies' (Leader Maynard 2019) against their respective adversary, dehumanizing and constructing their opponents as an immediate threat, with the aim of motivating, legitimizing and rationalizing their own killing campaigns. Such ideologies meant that all members of the adversary group were consistently identified as legitimate targets and were held to be collectively responsible for the suffering of the ingroup, signalling the effective use of depersonalization processes/narratives (Bar-Tal 2000). As *La Violencia* escalated, historical partisan cleavages were further exacerbated, as political leaders constructed the opposition as a definitive threat, often through the employment of historical and mythical knowledge.

In such a context, partisan violence was 'used or threatened with a political aim', as Liberals and Conservatives employed violent force to generate 'terror or fear among a directly threatened group and … wider … audience in the hope of maximizing political communication and … redressing … power relations' (English 2010: 3–5). As such, from as far back as the 19th century, partisan violence evidenced characteristics of terrorism, as its perpetrators sought to generate widespread fear across the country's social and political landscape, in turn sculpting and reinforcing political identities and cleavages. Significantly, over time, armed actors in Colombia have not limited their armed actions to a unique category of violence: political parties and their militia, armed groups, including leftist insurgencies and paramilitary organizations, drug cartels, and government and state actors have regularly employed terrorist methods and carried out acts of terrorism (Holmes 2019; Palma 2019), while also resorting to irregular warfare, conventional warfare, widespread attacks on infrastructure, political activity and so on (Palma 2019: 266), patterns of victimization to which the victims' delegations attested.

Party militias employed atrocious political violence to communicate explicit messages. For example: 'Conservatives cut out the tongues and the eyes of … Liberals, and disembowelled others.' Similarly, in rural zones, 'killing obeyed a sinister calculus of pain and cruelty'. Reflecting genocidal intent: 'Pregnant women were disembowelled and foetuses destroyed, so new members of the opposition party would not be born' (Hylton 2006: 43; see also Pearce 1990: 65). Partisan actors made continued use of ritualized violence to terrorize and communicate to party affiliates and their allies; bodies were mutilated and enemies were murdered using different 'cuts' – for example, the *necktie*, the *florists' cut* and the *monkey's cut* – as a means of signalling to party members that they should either flee or remain silent (Palacios 2007: 49–51).

The narratives undergirding Colombia's partisan political violence – and arguably each act of violence itself – gradually eroded the moral codes and frameworks governing the behaviour deemed acceptable by each group. In other words, as the narratives incentivizing outgroup killing and maiming and the acts themselves became increasingly widespread and systematic, so customary beliefs in tolerance, decency and mutual obligation towards each group's political adversary were, in large part, obliterated. Staub has argued that the dehumanization and delegitimation of one's adversary and the transformation of the ingroup's moral order represent requisite conditions for the escalation of intergroup violence, repression and other gross human rights violations committed on a massive scale (Staub 2006: 872–873). Such shifts were key to the processes through which the harm done by Conservatives to Liberals and vice versa became justified and, habitually, encouraged. In fact, locked in to this dynamic during the first half of the 20th century, gross human rights violations were perpetrated on a massive scale by each group and their armed militia in supposed self-defence. In turn, hostile relationships between the Conservatives and Liberals became ossified, impeding mutual empathy and reinforcing mutual distrust and fear, prejudice, stereotyping and so on.

In 1946 alone, 43,000 political killings took place, ushering in growing hostility between the two formal political parties and local bloodletting by party members and sympathizers (Palacios 2007). Much of the violence was 'state-sanctioned terror', of 'which the peasantry was the core victim' (Hylton 2006: 46). In the years that followed, state terrorism became a 'salient characteristic' of patterns of violence (Sánchez and Merteens 2001: 15). While in urban areas political violence was employed to 'silence' the working class, state-sponsored '[t]errorism then spread to the countryside as an anti-Liberal and anti-Communist crusade to crush the peasantry's democratic aspirations and reverse the social gains peasants had won from the landowners' (Sánchez and Merteens 2001: 15). Violent entrepreneurs engaged in creative ideological mobilization to justify and incite violence against increasingly cohesive targets through the appeal to values, normative codes, standards, ideal self-images and norms (Leader Maynard 2019) embedded in partisan identities. The act of framing the outgroup as deserving of rage, abhorrence or disgust is contingent on its construction as, at once, inherently threatening and inferior and its being situated outside the moral sphere of the ingroup (Bar-Tal 2014). Such ideological narratives habitually aim to justify violence against the adversary, while motivating solidarity, mobilization and action within the ingroup, in turn reinforcing perceived partisan differentiation and superiority, and framing the perpetration of violent acts against the adversary as permissible, desirable and necessary. Acts of terrorism in this context were employed not only to prevent liberal reforms, but also in the struggle to achieve them. For example, in the wake of Gaitán's murder, Liberals in Quindio and Tolima mobilized 'peasant clients into guerrilla militias' to carry out grotesque violence, fearing they would be targeted by Conservatives in vengeance attacks. Similarly, in Puerto Tejada in southern Colombia, for example, Liberals killed leading Conservative politicians and are rumoured to have 'decapitated them and played football with their heads in the main plaza' (Bushnell 1993: 202). As political violence escalated during the 20th century, then, entrenched collective group identities – at this point Liberal and Conservative – assumed a progressively monolithic quality, embedding societal and partisan cleavages across all facets of political, social and economic life (Guelke 2012).

In the months following the Bogotazo, the government armed Conservative peasant groups, while Liberal peasants were armed with the support of the Communist Party and, at least initially, support from the Liberal Party. In the years after 1948, the driving causes of 'La Violencia' evolved, shifting away from their predominantly bipartisan roots to include more diverse motives and causes, such as interpersonal conflict and violence motivated by wider structural factors, such as the prolonged and permanent struggle for land ownership, particularly in rural areas. Violence was thus increasingly shaped by both micro- and macro-antagonisms: 'political events had triggered the process and political rivalries kept it going' (Bushnell 1993: 201–202).[1]

While bipartisan animosity was a crucial initial factor driving conflict onset and subsequently remained a core justification for the terror, patterns of rural social and economic development increasingly played a key role in its perpetuation (Bushnell 1993: 202). As those groups carrying out the violence and their primary motives became more diverse and complex, so the shift away from bipartisan vengeance killings edged the country towards 'more of a generalized civil war', as ongoing political incentives simultaneously masked 'crass economic motives' (Safford and Palacios 2002: 349). While Conservative and Liberal peasants habitually carried out the killings, over time, perpetrators came to include 'bandits', criminals and political groups (Sánchez and Marteens 2001). Nevertheless, and significantly, the policy of the Conservative government in rural areas continued to be one of 'overt terrorism organized by local political bosses and landowners, in its crusade against communism and Liberalism' (Pearce 1990: 51). In other words, Conservatives wielded terror 'to suppress radical-popular politics and confine rising racial/ethnic and class conflict within bipartisan channels' (Pearce 1990: 50–51). Within the 'official terror, partisan sectarianism, and

---

[1] Kalyvas (2006) has identified similar dynamics as representing a core factor shaping the logic of violence in civil war, as he would define it.

scorched earth policy' that characterized *La Violencia*, government-led forces spawned 'new modes of terror' in a war increasingly bereft of rules or limits (Hylton 2006: 39–48).

1948–1953: the seeds of the internal armed conflict

The initial 1948 uprising in Bogotá was crushed by the Conservative-controlled military within a relatively short period of time. Nevertheless, the *Bogotazo* and accompanying rural violence came to mark the commencement of a period of political violence and terror at the national, subnational and local levels between 1946 and 1964 that would reach its 'most destructive force' between 1948 and 1953 (Safford and Palacios 2002: 345). The dynamics and patterns of violence evolving by the mid-20th century, and the collective damage, harm and trauma that they spawned, arguably edified competing narratives of competitive victimhood, a point to which we will return, given its centrality to the theme of this book. The spark that had led to the immediate popular rage of 1948 would subsequently ignite a series of longer and more complex processes of violence, terror and victimization, a 'galaxy of social conflicts' that shared a 'national political history', yet acquired 'full significance in a history of local and provincial contexts' (Safford and Palacios 2002: 346). These often sequential episodes of violence have built upon and shaped each other's trajectories and characteristics, and, in part, moulded evolving beliefs and norms, particularly as regards intergroup relations, perceptions and experiences of victimhood, and victim–perpetrator relations.

Scholars have usefully developed the notion of competitive victimhood, a concept that is pertinent to our discussion of the historic intergroup violence between Liberals and Conservatives and the legacy that such violence sculpted. Bar-Tal, Chernyak-Hai, Schori and Gundar (2009) argue that competitive victimhood closely articulates with the CE and plays the explicit role of generating the collective perception (within the ingroup) that it is the sole victim of unjust atrocious violence perpetrated against it by its adversary. What emerges, they argue, is the internalized collective perception that each group's victimization is unique. Competitive victimhood, of course, habitually develops as a consequence of lived violence and 'traumatic experiences', such as genocide, war, past colonial occupation, extensive physical harm or 'prolonged exploitation and discrimination' (Bar-Tal et al 2009: 229–231). Arguably, the longer a war goes on and the more entrenched antagonistic intergroup relations become, the more embedded competitive victimhood is likely to be. Violence perpetrated by the ingroup against the outgroup under such conditions will be deemed collectively as justifiable self-defence, wrought in the face of the ingroup's unjust victimization and, at worst, its potential annihilation by its adversary. Consequently, violence against the outgroup is constructed as permissible and, arguably, as necessary. It is under such conditions that collective groups often 'make efforts to nurture the beliefs and feelings embedded in the sense of collective victimization and try to assimilate them into the society's collective memory and ethos of conflict and collective emotional orientation' (Bar-Tal et al 2009: 237). As such, competitive victimhood may come to represent the sole lens through which the conflict in general and intergroup relations in particular are perceived and experienced.

Between 1949 and 1953, and emphatically during the presidency of Laureano Gómez Castro (1950–1954), partisan violence consolidated profound political and societal cleavages in Colombia. 'Indescribable acts of violence', such as massacres, '[d]ecapitations, mutilations and sexual crimes' were meted out in similar measure by both Conservative and Liberal armed militias, as 'criminality and senseless violence intermixed with political and social violence', further forging political identities around intergroup bloodletting (Pearce 1990: 52–55). Initially, Liberal peasant guerrilla armies were organized by landowners in the coffee-producing regions of Valle and the minifundia regions of Boyacá, the Santanders and the Eastern Llanos to confront the state's Conservative forces. However, peasant farmers themselves carried out and bore the brunt of the killing (Hylton 2006). In 1950 alone, approximately 50,000 people were executed principally in the name of partisan hostility and by peasant clients in bloody vendettas against neighbouring villages (Safford and Palacios 2002: 350; Hylton 2006: 46).

In parallel, between 1950 and 1953, the 'foundations of the Cold War national security state were established' in Colombia, which, in turn, transformed and diversified historical societal cleavages and their legacies in a significant manner (Hylton 2006: 47). The mid-20th century brought with it a gradual shift away from the Liberal–Conservative rift as the exclusive and predominant public marker determining intergroup violence, towards more complex patterns of allegiance and identification and, in turn, more complex societal cleavages. From the 1950s, 'Cold War objectives meshed with those of partisan sectarianism', leading to the perpetration of acts of terrorism as a central government policy linked to the wider ideological and political context (Hylton 2006: 47). The Cold War security state would become a fundamental arena for the political violence and terrorism that would later envelop the country after 1964, as we will see.

From 1950, the Colombian state – and the sitting Conservative government – began to collaborate directly with paramilitary forces to levy terror against both armed Liberal factions and organized workers and peasants in its anti-communist/anti-Liberal crusade (Sánchez and Merteens 2001: 17–20). Nevertheless, the commission of atrocious violence as a political strategy was not unique to Conservatives. In rural areas, in a 'popular peasant convulsion', both Conservatives and Liberals executed acts of terrorism against their adversary, leading to a 'permanent state of siege'. Within this context: 'Massacres of entire families were frequent, accompanied by rape, the burning of homes, theft of cattle and coffee, and the destruction of harvests' (Palacios 2007: 135). Such violence and plunder precipitated mass migration to those areas controlled by the party with which the victim identified, arguably leading to 'politically homogeneous' neighbourhoods. Rural terror thus 'rearranged social classes and power/leadership' and shaped patterns of habitation, consequences that would become further consolidated as the Colombian armed conflict got under way (Sánchez and Merteens 2001: 18–21). These patterns were subsequently repeated cyclically throughout the following six decades, as victimization became increasingly widespread and systematic and, eventually, cleft across ever more complex societal divisions.

Within the political vacuum of the early 1950s and out of the structures of sectarian violence of the 1940s, armed Liberal groups, often referred to as Liberal 'guerrilla movements', emerged across the country, often with the support of Communist party activists (Sánchez and Merteens 2001: 15). Many who joined these groups had themselves survived the first years of brutal partisan violence, subsequently coming to form the first nuclei of the rural armed resistance. It is from this perspective that Paredes Zapata has coherently argued that the '[s]eeds for modern terrorism in Colombia were sown in rural regions of the country in the 1940s' (2003: 81). In the departments of Tolima, Huila, the Eastern Llanos, Boyacá, the Santanders, Antioquia and Caldas, these 'small guerrilla groups' were constituted by approximately 10,000 males. Nevertheless, Liberal elites themselves gradually distanced themselves from the peasant guerrillas, refusing to accept requests for concrete alliances with or support to them. The lack of direct support from Liberal elites to Liberal guerrilla groups ultimately permitted the Conservative Party to triumph in the 1950 presidential election and subsequently to intensify its counterinsurgency campaign against the guerrillas (Mazzei 2009: 75–80). By 1951, Liberal guerrillas began formally to break ranks with the Liberal landowning elite, given that the latter had rejected (and 'resented') the former's 'demands for money and supplies'. Within this context, social issues began gradually to influence the struggles of Liberal guerrillas, a transformation in their platforms and demands that would ultimately get off the ground in the 1960s (Pearce 1990: 57). Significantly, however, it was the armed groups influenced by communism within the coffee-growing areas in Tolima that became increasingly radicalized, establishing the basis for the country's long-term guerrilla insurgencies that would form in the 1960s, and would play a crucial role in the dynamics of armed conflict and subsequently shape patterns of victimization and, in part, the demands of the victim movements and victims' delegations.

With the assumption of Laureano Gómez to the presidency in 1950, bipartisan violence evolved into a full-blown armed confrontation (NCHM

2012: 113). In the wider context of the Cold War, the Conservative Party imbued the conflict with its Liberal enemy with a moral, religious and anti-communist justification, thus escalating what had previously been severe differences along partisan lines into an ideological clash of worldviews articulated through a globally emergent constructed threat narrative (Pécaut 2003). Simultaneously, party-led terrorism against the respective political adversary became increasingly organized, as the Conservative *chulavitas* and *pájaros*, on the one hand, and Liberal guerrillas and communist self-defence groups on the other, rampaged against each other, employing violence not only to communicate with but also to punish their rival (NCHM 2012: 115).

In 1953, Laureano Gomez was toppled in a coup d'état by General Gustavo Rojas Pinilla (1953–1957), and a brief military dictatorship was installed. General Rojas Pinilla, an anti-communist military strongman, was backed by elements in both traditional parties and, significantly, by the US government in Washington DC. Assuming a mandate to pacify the country and bring an end to 'La Violencia', Rojas Pinillas offered amnesty to the Liberal guerrillas and peasant self-defence groups. The former accepted the terms of his amnesty, while many self-defence groups, with the exception of peasants linked to the Communist Party in Sumapaz and eastern Tolima, rejected it. With only limited success in its pacification programme, the regime became 'increasingly heavy-handed' against both the civilian opposition and armed groups (Paredes Zapata 2003 53–57, 216). For example, in 1955, the dictatorship launched a brutal military operation in those rural zones representing the regional strongholds of the Liberal guerrillas and where communist defence groups had crafted their political home. With the backing of Washington and framed within the National Security Doctrine (NSD), a doctrine that continues to shape the security forces to this day, Rojas Pinilla bombed guerrilla and opposition peasant positions (Bushnell 1993). These operations arguably radicalized peasant defence groups yet further, precipitating, in some cases, their subsequent transformation into revolutionary guerrillas.

During the mid-1950s, rural zones, such as Tolima and the Eastern Llanos, suffered severely, in terms of both the quantity and systematic nature of the killing and the displacement caused by the violence (Palacios 2007: 160–168). A considerable number of refugees from military campaigns fled to the city of Ibague, Tolima, while others were displaced and hid in local forests. Ongoing military operations against communist and peasant defence groups and communities further radicalized armed peasants, many of whom reached a consensus not to disarm (NCHM 2012: 115); such groups came to form the 'early bastions of the communist FARC-EP guerrillas of the 1960s' (Palacios 2007: 160–168). Patterns of violence further evolved after 1954, as violence became increasingly localized and intensified, driven by 'small-town tensions and complicities, mostly revolving around property and wealth' (Palacios 2007: 160–168).

Prolonged experience of partisan terror had brought with it high numbers of victims of homicide, sexual violence, massacre, torture and displacement. Such violence imposed deeply felt grievances and narratives of collective/competitive victimhood, as well as enduring psychological effects. Palacios, for example, cites the case of urban Liberals 'who stopped wearing red neckties in order to avoid being beaten by the police' (Palacios 2007: 160–168). Marginalized peasants radicalized by their experiences of state-sponsored terror in the first half of the 1950s were thus obliged 'to choose between persisting or perishing' (Palacios 2007: 160–168). Such historical experiences of violence meant that gradually 'participants had become socialized to murder as a social instrument' (Safford and Palacios 2002: 351), arguably lowering the threshold of animosity towards the tolerance and employment of atrocious violence and consolidating yet further a society shaped by competing narratives of collective victimhood. Under such conditions, the impetus towards all-out civil war escalated.

The National Front and the pillars of the armed conflict

In 1958, after the failure of Rojas Pinilla to put an end to 'La Violencia', Conservative and Liberal elites reached a bipartisan power-sharing agreement, the so-called National Front (NF). The accord, which would endure formally for four presidential terms until 1974 and would overlap with the armed conflict, obliged the Conservative and Liberal parties to alternate presidential power and governmental/public office every four years.[2] Partisan violence was reduced during the NF. However, the agreement consolidated elite political control within the Conservative and Liberal Parties (Pearce 1990: 64; Molano 2007), marginalizing other political parties – notably the Colombian Communist Party (CCP) – from participating in the political system. Consequently, the NF played a key role in precipitating the emergence of subsequent guerrilla insurgencies and the perpetration of widespread and systematic violence by diverse state and nonstate actors, cementing as it did oligarchic rule while excluding the CCP and alternative political groups. In fact, the latter remained subject to violent repression during the terms of the NF. In a sense, then, the NF did what it was proposed to do, bridging the gap between Liberal and Conservative elites. However,

---

[2] Bushnell (1993: 225) posits that in fact, coalition rule lasted until 1986, when Virgilio Barco (Liberal) took power. See also Karl (2017).

it simultaneously sculpted profound divisions across the rest of society and exacerbated prerevolutionary conditions.

The initial NF governments offered conditional amnesty to those guerrillas agreeing to disarm. With the aim of winning over the peasant population, the NF ushered in a series of economic reforms and implemented a range of civic projects in rural areas, employing the national military to build roads, schools and health clinics. However, simultaneously, the first NF governments pursued a policy of accelerated economic development, which led to further mass displacement and increasing landlessness, phenomena that exaggerated the already acute grievances felt by the rural population and consolidating further fertile ground for rural rebellion (Brittain 2010: 4–16; Montesinos Coleman 2024).

In a context of accelerated rural discontent, growing poverty and displacement and formalized political exclusion, the CCP began to create militia units in those communist enclaves that had been consolidated during the previous decade, while at the same time seeking to strengthen its links with active Liberal guerrillas (Mazzei 2009: 75; NCHM 2012: 115). The development of armed self-defence units within the so-called communist enclaves, such as in southern Tolima, Huila and Cauca, posed a significant threat to the NF, to the Colombian state and to the rural elites (Brittain 2010: 9–12; LeGrand 2003). Moreover, the failure of the Liberal Party itself to support effective reform programmes and incorporate more radical actors, such as the CCP, stoked the prerevolutionary conditions. In fact, the Liberal Party gradually came to align itself against CCP members, many of whom had sought refuge in communism during *La Violencia*, often 'carrying out aggressive actions and even cooperation with the Colombian military' (Brittain 2010: 4–8).

The NF did not put an end to violence, as party elites had proposed. Rather, despite decreasing homicide levels, peasant support for violent groups in rural areas continued, as the motives for violence shifted away from a uniquely political rationale to incorporate ideological targeting and 'criminal economic enterprise'. In fact, Meertens and Sanchez posit that from 1958 until 1965, the phenomenon of 'political banditry' became the predominant armed expression. An 'an anarchical desperate peasant response', political banditry was precipitated by 'the changing relations between armed rebels and the state, the political parties, and the local and regional powerbrokers': violence was thus no longer linked solely to political affiliation, but was also increasingly shaped by the struggle for economic power (Sánchez and Merteens 2001: 21–22).

What, in part, consolidates narratives of competitive victimhood and acts as the glue that keeps collective victim (and perpetrator) groups together are the common societal beliefs, norms, attitudes and emotions constitutive of a shared sense of identity and cohesion, which gradually become integral to social identity. Logically, such collective beliefs are often constructed in opposition to those beliefs, attitudes and emotions held by the adversarial group. During the 1950s, then, Colombia became divided along more diverse and complex cleavages (beyond political partisan identity). As the wielding of political violence and terror became increasingly ubiquitous and permissive, while being perpetrated by more variegated groups, so patterns of victimization evolved, as wider groups engaged in and suffered violent acts. Shifts in allegiance that had resulted initially from the emergence of peasant guerrillas and the accompanying closing of ranks by Conservative and Liberal elites against them, recalibrated the historical practice of political violence and, in part, transformed collective narratives of victimhood away from being uniquely embedded in partisan identity. The 1950s then represents a key decade in the consolidation of a complex politics of victimhood in Colombia, which would become a core factor shaping patterns of competitive victimhood once the armed conflict began to take its toll.

Furthermore, after the prolonged violent experiences of the late 1940s and 1950s, individual and collective barriers inhibiting the use of violence were progressively lowered. The terror of *La Violencia* had persisted for more than two decades, resulting in the passing on of violent strategies across two generations (Schnabel, Halabi and Noor 2013; Druliolle and Brett 2018). The use of terror by both state and nonstate actors became increasingly embedded as a permissible social and political strategy, particularly given that the formal political system remained in the hands of Conservative and Liberal elites. In this context, the instrumentalization of terror by elite actors and peasants appeared logical. The former continued to benefit considerably from acts of terror against those seeking to challenge their rule; for the latter, 'terror became not only an integral part but also, in most cases, the overarching element of their actions', incentivized by frustration, desperation and vengeance (Sánchez and Merteens 2001: 25). For those peasants who had survived the carnage and humiliation of *La Violencia* and who were subsequently unable to organize collectively, 'disproportionate cruelty and massacres appeared as primitive but extreme expressions of power – as the only expressions available to them' through which they would be able '*to instil both awe and fear*' (Sánchez and Merteens 2001: 25, emphasis added).

In this context, then, horrific violence perpetrated during the first two governments of the NF represented less the last remnants of *La Violencia* than the embers that would kindle the full-blown guerrilla insurgency and paramilitary brutality that began in the first half of the 1960s. Such violence, itself shaped by a history of state and nonstate/partisan confrontations, would be manifest through large-scale and widespread guerrilla resistance across diverse political expressions, paramilitary terror, and the legal and illegal state reactions to leftist insurgencies. Objective structural conditions, accompanied by a century of unbridled opposition terror, and progressively more complex political and societal cleavages, brought the country, once more, to a turning point at the beginning of the 1960s. The violence of the internal armed conflict was to follow, violence witnessed and suffered directly by the participants in the victims' delegations to Havana.

The internal armed conflict (1964 to present)

Political terror and violence in Colombia have been cogently characterized as possessing an 'historical sense of tragic circularity and repetition' (Hylton 2006: 113). From Hylton's perspective, '[p]atterns of counterinsurgent terror' employed against civilians during *La Violencia* were 'reinforced during the cold war, and repackaged under the anti-terrorist rubric after 11 September 2001' (2006: 129). In this respect, political violence and acts of terrorism therein have been reinterpreted and often replicated episodically over a period of 150 years: torture, homicide, massacre and dispossession have been consistently used against noncombatants by state and nonstate actors alike, culminating in a 'limitless terror' (Hylton 2006: 129). The use of such violence accelerated during the second half of the 20th century and the first decade of the 21st century during the armed conflict, as will now be discussed. Such historical patterns, of course, marked the context towards which the transitional justice mechanisms crafted during the Santos–FARC-EP peace talks were to be oriented, given that those participating in the victims' delegations had suffered from this violence: torture, kidnapping, landmines, disappearance, sexual and gender-based violence, massacres and extrajudicial execution.

When 'La Violencia' came to an end, the pillars of Colombia's internal armed conflict had been constructed. By the early 1960s, guerrilla groups linked to the CCP and, in some cases, to existing Liberal guerrillas gradually began to develop into sophisticated armed organizations (Gutierrez Sanin et al 2007; Arias and Goldstein 2010). The grievances faced by the rural population had accelerated under the NF (Molano 2007), as economic development policies precipitated an increased reserve army of workers in urban areas and the consolidated monopolization of rural land by urban-based elites. Historical dispossession of land from rural peasants thus accelerated during the NF, as elites orchestrated mass illegal land expropriations. In the 1960s, land owned and controlled by large commercial farms accordingly increased by 21 per cent, as the number of landless peasants grew in parallel (Brittain 2010: 7–8). As will be discussed in later chapters, historical patterns of landlessness and unjust land ownership so acutely accelerated during the internal armed conflict became central demands for redress articulated by many participants in the victims' delegations. These demands would remain unaddressed (see Chapter 7).

In this context, Colombia's historical experience of armed conflict was shaped by a series of cross-cutting societal cleavages: ideological (left–right; social class) and demographic (urban/rural and, to a lesser extent, ethnic group identity), some of which evidenced continuity with past causes of violence. These cleavages were reinforced by a series of systemic conflict drivers: *structural drivers* – rural exclusion/poverty/inequality (unequal land distribution/tenure) and the closure of the formal political system to effective political alternatives; and *proximate drivers* – drug trafficking and production and access to land for (il)legal resource extraction. Embedded within the ideological, military, political and economic logic of Latin America's Cold War, Colombia's revolutionary movements were a response to these historically embedded structural drivers of conflict. In the aftermath of *La Violencia*, as the economic impact of the NF collided with the repercussions of the formal exclusion of the CCP from the political sphere, so armed groups gradually consolidated their organizational structures and military strategies with the aim of confronting repression, political fraud, corruption, inequality and exclusion (Pearce 1990: 65).

The onset of the armed conflict was precipitated with the creation of the ELN in 1962 and the FARC-EP in 1964, auguring in waves of left-wing guerrilla violence that have persisted until the time of writing (Safford and Palacios 2002: 354). Shaped by a combination of Marxist-Leninism and, although albeit less so, liberation theology, the ELN emerged in the middle Magdalena Valley of Santander. Formed by guerrillas trained in Cuba, the ELN initially became embedded in Santander and Norte de Santander (Deas 1995). The group lacked roots in a 'genuine peasants' movement', conforming instead to a more conventional model of Latin American insurgency by drawing upon the disaffected middle class (Bushnell 1993: 244). The political platform of the ELN focused on land distribution, poverty, corruption, access to resources and political participation. After military engagements with the Colombian armed forces in the early 1970s, the movement was in part weakened. Subsequently, the ELN became a less major military force, obtaining finance from kidnapping, extortion of petroleum companies, war taxes and, ultimately, from the illicit drug trade.

The FARC-EP grew out of grassroots peasant self-defence organizations formed across Tolima in communist rural enclaves of the upper Magdalena Valley. At least initially, the FARC-EP was less an offensive guerrilla than a defensive organization, 'not given to sabotage or terrorism, nor to ambushes of the police or army'. The organization's focus was on protecting peasant communities from other communities themselves 'protected by clientilistic armed forces' (Bushnell 1993). However, in response to state military operations in the wake of the Yarborough survey, such as Plan Lazo in 1962, which employed counterinsurgency doctrines applied by the US in Vietnam,[3] and specifically to the bombing of the communist enclave of Marquetalia in 1964, the organization adopted more offensive guerrilla strategies. As Colombia's insurgencies became consolidated, so the 'unfinished business of La Violencia' merged with the country's incipient Cold War (Hylton 2006: 58).

Operation Marquetalia represented a turning point in Colombia's armed conflict – a chosen trauma. In the aftermath of the operation, Manuel Muralanda Velez, alias Tirofijo, a communist leader who had survived the bombing, garnered increasing support for his claim that armed struggle was the only feasible path towards transformation. The FARC-EP subsequently became a sophisticated military organization under Muralanda's leadership (Brittain 2010: 12–16), over time becoming the largest and most capable armed group in Colombia (Leech 2011: 25–37). During the 1960s and 1970s, the activities of the guerrillas were concentrated in rural areas. Their territorial domination progressively expanded (Villamizar 2017), due, in part, to limited institutional presence across much of Colombia's vast territory. Consequently, the ELN and the FARC-EP – and other illegal armed groups – were gradually able to wield partial territorial control in diverse rural areas. As left-wing insurgencies grew, so the state's response to them escalated. Military operations aimed at defeating the guerrilla groups spiralled in the 1960s, while death squads were legalized through Decree 3398 (1965) and subsequently Law 48 (1968).

The approval of Decree 3398 signalled a key moment in the evolution of the armed conflict and would set a precedent for the employment of future acts of terrorism, precipitating widespread patterns of victimization. By authorizing the creation and provision of arms to defence patrols, the Ministry of Defence effectively legalized paramilitary groups, actors that would subsequently play a significant role in the armed conflict. Units were composed principally of reservists and retired soldiers, police and armed peasant farmers. The groups served both to fight alongside the military against insurgent groups and as a core component of the government's intelligence network (Hristov 2009: 61). However, at the same time, wealthy landowners also provided resources to the paramilitaries with the aim of preventing guerrilla hostilities, such as killings and kidnappings (Mazzei 2009: 80).

Other guerrilla organizations emerged during the Cold War, as the FARC-EP's consolidation from the 1970s onwards was accompanied by the increasing capacity of diverse insurgencies to mobilize and craft effective

---

[3] Between 1961 and 1967 the US provided Colombia with $100 million for military equipment and $60 million for economic development and military assistance (Hristov 2016: 80; see also Hylton 2006: 56).

social bases.[4] In the aftermath of allegedly fraudulent elections in April 1970, for example, the M-19 (19 April Movement) was formed. The M-19 espoused an ideology of nationalism, revolutionary socialism, equality/inclusion and populism, reflecting, in part, the experiences of insurgencies in the Southern Cone (Villamizar 2017). The M-19 had a 'gift for the spectacular', carrying out notorious high-publicity operations, such as the theft of the sword of Simon Bolivar, the robbery of a mass weapons cache from a military base in Bogotá in 1978 and the occupation of the Embassy of the Dominican Republic in 1980. For Bushnell (1993: 246), the M-19 were instrumental in 'rural terrorism', as he accuses their ranks of having assassinated key figures, such as trade union leader Jose Raquel Mercado.

The evolution of political violence and patterns of victimization

The preceding century in Colombia had seen acts of terrorism employed against civilians in the context of the bipartisan violence that followed the post-independence period. This dynamic evolved during 'La Violencia', when grotesque, ritualistic violence was used systematically against civilians and armed opponents by political parties, state forces and nonstate groups seeking to consolidate political and economic power. Subsequently, as Colombia's internal armed conflict evolved over the 1970s and 1980s, so atrocious violence would be progressively meted out by state and nonstate groups alike. In fact, by the 1980s, homicide became the leading cause of death in Colombia, the homicide rate tripling as conflict-related killings were accompanied by increasing urban violence, itself progressively linked both to the armed conflict and to the growing drug-trafficking/production activities.

The armed conflict escalated during the 1970s, and, by the 1980s, the ranks of diverse insurgent groups had grown, while their geographical reach, military prowess and strategic capacity continued a process of consolidation. The response of the state was no less decisive, as military and paramilitary actors increased in number, preparing the ground for spiralling political violence between adversaries and what would be the enduring strategic employment of acts of terrorism (Hristov 2009; Brittain 2010; Leech 2011). With the assumption of Julio César Turbay Ayala (1978–1982) to the presidency, the so-called Security Statute was passed, a law that restricted fundamental freedoms and imposed an almost permanent state of emergency, while simultaneously framing counterinsurgency policy within the NSD. According to one of the members of the victims' delegations, the Turbay

---

[4] For example, the People's Liberation Army (EPL) in 1966 and the Indigenous movement Quintin Lamé in 1972.

administration was characterized by widespread 'repression, persecution and torture', in particular against civilians who mobilized against the regime.[5] This female participant, whose family had been 'eliminated' during 'La Violencia', was victimized directly during the Turbay regime and in its aftermath. Of five brothers, one was taken arbitrarily by the police and murdered while in custody. Another brother was disappeared by the military in 1988, and a further brother, who studied in Colombia's National University, had been persecuted by the state security forces and was finally killed in a hit-and-run accident in 1994. For the members of the victims' delegations, then, Colombia's Cold War violence has been a defining aspect of their lives.

As state-sponsored, insurgent and drug-related violence increased under Turbay (Iturralde 2003), so the NSD was extended. Counterinsurgency operations spread away from solely targeting revolutionary groups to target those legal groups perceived by the government to represent the guerrillas' political wing, such as trade unions, human rights organizations and other sectors of the legal political opposition, as well as civilians (Gutiérrez and Barón 2006). Officials in the Turbay government 'at least tacitly accepted' the use of illegal methods against armed guerrilla groups (Bushnell 1993: 257) and their perceived social base, resulting in ferocious levels of military and paramilitary violence against trade unions and human rights organizations, among others. Framing the counterinsurgency campaign through the NSD, the government identified civilians – particularly those with links to the CCP – as the *internal enemy*, conflating civilians with insurgent groups. Civilians – whether left-wing activists or not – were thus signalled as a 'legitimate' counterinsurgency target for the regime, leading to systematic levels of violence against trade unions and human rights organizations by state and paramilitary forces (Bushnell 1993: 256). Many of those who took part in the victims' delegations to Havana had suffered acts of victimization precisely within this rubric, such as a trade unionist leader, and individuals whose family members had been executed or disappeared by the state security forces.

By the end of the Turbay administration, despite the acceleration in counterinsurgency strategy, the FARC-EP had increased its size from a movement of approximately 500 combatants to a small army of 3,000, and, after having consolidated its forces in the Upper Magdalena Valley and the Eastern Llanos, established new guerrilla fronts. By the following year, it would become an 'authentically offensive guerrilla movement' (Safford and Palacios 2002: 356; Waisberg 2008), boasting a centralized hierarchical structure, a general staff and military code, a training school and a political programme (Monning 2002). The ELN replicated this tendency, growing

---

[5] Interview, Bogotá, Colombia, April 2015.

from 800 members to eventually reach 3,000 combatants (Safford and Palacios 2002: 360–362). Simultaneously, the M-19 also grew steadily during the 1970s and, by the 1980s, numbered over 2,000 combatants. Insurgent activity also expanded geographically, spreading from marginal rural areas to strategically more important zones and, eventually, to urban areas (Molano 2007).

The 1980s saw a considerable increase in guerrilla and death squad activity and combat hostilities between guerrilla groups, military forces and paramilitary organizations. The 1980s similarly represented a key moment in which drug-trafficking groups imposed their presence. According to Palma, in fact, the term 'terrorism' was first employed by the Colombian government in public discourse during the presidency of Virgilio Barco (1986–1990), who referred to 'drug-dealing terrorism' even before the term was used to refer to leftist insurgencies (Palma 2019: 251). While in some cases, initial alliances existed between guerrillas and drug traffickers, an upsurge in violent hostilities between the revolutionary armed left and the latter took place during the 1980s, due, in part, to the fact that the latter were amassing land and the guerrilla itself was targeting wealthy landowners and cattle ranchers. As the insurgent threat grew, so alliances between ranchers, small farmers, police and narco-traffickers were forged with the aim of combating the guerrilla. Self-defence militia were formalized by wealthy landowners, cattle ranchers and drug lords throughout rural areas (Safford and Palacios 2002: 265), a direct antecedent to the paramilitaries of the 1990s, which would have their origins in the death squads of the Magdalena Medio Valley (Hylton 2006: 68). As we will see, many of the delegates to the Havana talks were victims of those paramilitary and guerrilla groups consolidated during this period of time, as well as of the military.

In this context, between 1981 and 1982, the organization Death to Kidnappers (MAS) was formed in Medellin by members of the Medellin Cartel, active and retired police and military, small industrialists, wealthy cattle ranchers and representatives of the US-based corporation Texas Petroleum. The group was founded in 1981, when Pablo Escobar, Gonzalo Rodríguez Gacha and Carlos Lehder met with drug traffickers from the Ochoa family in the immediate aftermath of the kidnapping of their sister, Martha Nieves Ochoa, by the M-19. The MAS was established as a response to the wave of kidnappings of and intimidation and extortion against wealthy landowners and their families by left-wing guerrilla groups, including the M-19 and the FARC-EP, and simultaneously to defend the former's economic interests. The organization confronted the guerrilla groups head-on, while subsequently perpetrating acts of terrorism against human rights defenders, members of left-wing political parties, journalists and lawyers. For example, in January 1982, the MAS assassinated trade unionist Luis Javier Cifuentes in Medellin, followed in March by the planting of a bomb in the house of journalist María Jimena Duzán. As it stepped up its violent methods, two male cadavers were found the same month on the outskirts of Bogotá, strangled, impaled and hung from a tree, with MAS signs written on them. MAS violence sought to communicate an unequivocal message, reminiscent of the bipartisan terror employed during *La Violencia*.

As paramilitary groups grew in number, a broad 'functional alliance' between the private sector, landowners, drug barons, sectors of the security forces and paramilitaries was built; together they waged a *Dirty War* against the guerrilla and the political left (Bushnell 1993: 195; Hylton 2006: 68). By the mid-1980s, diverse rural and urban theatres of insurrectional and mafia war had thus appeared throughout the country, evidencing the emergence of 'drug-traffickers, guerrillas, and paramilitaries … intermixed, in alliance or in conflict, with clientilistic politicians, cattle-owners, the military and police' (Bushnell 1993: 195; see also Hylton 2006: 68). At the same time, a sharp rise in 'urban terrorism' took place, linked to growing narco-activity and the unchecked power of the drug lords, which was exacerbated by the escalating grievances of the urban poor and the incapacity of successive governments to address such discontent (Bushnell 1993: 250–254).

In their bid to consolidate economic and political power, the drug cartels perpetrated egregious violence, taking on both the guerrilla (through the MAS, for example) and the government, as they did. Significantly, any attempts by the national government to move against the cartels were met with brutal and decisive force. In 1984, for example, during the government of President Belisario Betancur, Justice Minister Rodrigo Lara Bonilla was assassinated by Pablo Escobar's Medellin cartel due to the latter's attempts to persecute the cartels. The execution of Lara Bonilla pushed President Betancur to approve a law securing extradition to the US for cartel members, which the cartels took as a declaration of war. Over the following years, the cartels employed acts of terrorism, supported by their 'virtually parallel security system', ravaging urban and rural Colombia (Bushnell 1993: 194). Magistrates connected with extradition cases were assassinated. Guillermo Cano, the editor of the Colombian newspaper *El Espectador*, was killed in 1986 after publishing an editorial on the mafia. In 1989, an airliner allegedly carrying police informants exploded in mid-air, killing all 107 people on board. The same year, a car bomb attack on the country's intelligence agency in Bogotá killed over 50 people and wounded over 1,000 others. In both cases, the Medellin cartel, and Pablo Escobar and Gonzalo Rodriguez Gacha in particular, were purportedly responsible (Bushnell 1993: 194).

In this context, an emblematic episode took place on 6 November 1985, when the M-19 carried out a typical high-profile operation, occupying the Palace of Justice in downtown Bogotá (Pearce 1990: 181). The guerrilla's objective was allegedly to hold a symbolic trial of President Betancur, who, unsurprisingly, rejected the group's demands he go to the Palace to be tried by them. Once the M-19 had secured their position within the building, allegedly killing two security guards as they did so, they took over 300 people hostage, including all Supreme Court Magistrates and over 20 other judges. The military operation to retake the Palace of Justice began the following day, coordinated by Colonel Alfonso Plazas. The armed forces stormed the building, utilizing armoured cars and tanks to do so. During the military's blitzkrieg operation, over 100 people were killed, including 12 magistrates (Uran Bidegain 2020), civilians and five M-19 leaders, as both the guerrilla and the military unleashed their furies. In the aftermath of the operation, 11 individuals were forcibly disappeared by the military, a crime for which both Colonel Plazas and his commanding officer, General Armando Arias, were convicted in 2010 and 2014 respectively. Moreover, the Inter-American Court of Human Rights (IACHR) stated in 2012 that the Colombian authorities had carried out both torture and forced disappearances during the Palace siege.[6] By the mid-1980s, then, acts of terrorism by state and nonstate terrorist actors had become uncontainable. Members of the victims' delegations were victims of and witnesses to this violence, as we will see later on.

Violence against the political opposition

In the same year as the sacking of the Palace of Justice, as part of the peace agreement between the FARC-EP and the Betancur government, former FARC-EP combatants, dissidents from the CCP and social activists came together to establish the political party the Patriotic Union (UP) (Pearce 1990; Gomez-Suarez 2017). In the context of the peace talks, and with a broad section of the country pushing for peace with the guerrilla, the UP rapidly became a political force. In the 1986 general elections, the party gained important inroads, winning 4.4 per cent of the presidential vote, five seats in the Senate and nine in the Chamber of Representatives, alongside key wins at local level, including 14 deputies, 351 councillors and 23 municipal mayors.

The UP's achievements precipitated a severely violent reaction from Colombia's political elites and right-wing illegal armed groups, culminating in emblematic crimes that constituted the wider 'genocide of the UP' (Hylton 2006; Gomez-Suarez 2017). Acts of terrorism against the UP carried out by a 'perpetrator bloc' decimated the party, leaving more than 3,000 of

---

[6] The rationale for the M-19 operation has sparked deep controversy. During the operation, records for approximately 6,000 legal cases were destroyed, including files for the criminal case against Pablo Escobar, precipitating unproven accusations that the M-19 were working with the backing of the drug lord.

its politicians, including presidential candidates and parliamentarians, and UP supporters dead within less than a decade and a further 1,000 dead by 2002 (Gomez-Suarez 2007: 648). Others were tortured, forced into exile or displaced. According to one of the members of the victims' delegations, an acknowledged UP leader who narrowly escaped an assassination attempt in the early 1990s:

> My neighbours would say to me, 'they're waiting for you' ... we had very little protection from the state, just two cars, and the day of the attempted assassination, there was only one car with two bodyguards behind us. Our lives were saved miraculously. The rocket was fired at me from a truck, everything happened so quickly – when my driver saw the rocket, he was able to move the car, and the rocket passed overhead and exploded five cars behind us.[7]

The 'bloc' itself was constituted by the armed forces, paramilitaries and self-defence groups, drug traffickers, political entrepreneurs and government officials, often in association or collaboration. The killing campaigns themselves were habitually formalized, taking place within the framework of three key military plans: the Baile Rojo (Red Dance Campaign) in 1986, the Plan Golpe de Gracia (Coup de Grace Plan) in 1992 and the Plan Retorno (Return Plan) in 1993 (Gomez-Suarez 2007: 468). In a strategy reminiscent of Valentino's (2004: 201) concept of 'collective punishment', or Goodwin's (2006) concept of 'categorical violence', the killing campaigns identified the entire political party, including the leadership and the social base, as a collective enemy to be physically eliminated. Massacres of UP members occurred throughout the country, including in regions such as Segovia in the Magdalena Medio Valley, where the triumph of the UP precipitated alliances between traditional political parties and paramilitary groups. In the department of the Norte de Santander, perpetrators used crematoria, chainsaws and alligators to dispose of the bodies of assassinated UP officials. The extermination was ongoing throughout the 1990s, carried out through 'selective assassination of UP public figures, raids on UP offices and illegal detentions, assassinations and threats to relatives, families and local activists' (Gomez-Suarez 2007: 167).

The extermination of the UP was a key factor in radicalizing those fighters who had previously demobilized, and once more pushing them back to the armed struggle, at the same time as the memory of the 'genocide' in turn prevented many combatants from disarming. The message that the perpetrator bloc communicated was unequivocal. The formal political

---

[7] Interview, Bogotá, Colombia, April 2015.

sphere was closed to actors that chose to mobilize within the UP and radical transformation was not permissible; those who ignored the message would be punished. Such a message was not, of course, without precedent – it had been employed frequently during *La Violencia* and in the Security Statute/NSD pursued by President Turbay. Moreover, acts of terrorism against civilians (the 'internal enemy') would continue under President Virgilio Barco and, some years later, would reach their zenith during the government of President Alvaro Uribe, as we will see. Significantly, many of those participating in the victims' delegations had survived such atrocious emblematic crimes and some would ultimately be afforded the opportunity to confront their perpetrators in Havana, as we will see.

Barco and the Statute for the Defence of Democracy

In 1986, Virgilio Barco was elected to the presidency, as the elimination of the UP was underway (Nagle 2005: 17). Midway through his term, Barco approved anti-terrorist legislation, the so-called Statute for the Defence of Democracy, which sought to control and bring to justice both the drug cartels and armed insurgencies. The Statute created 90 Specialized Judges of Public Order and Public Order Courts, at the same time as it authorized military forces to arrest individuals suspected of terrorist activities and, if required, detain them for up to ten days. The Statute restricted civilian freedoms, permitting the government to utilize the law to lay siege to leftist activists, trade unionists and human rights activists, at the same time as the military carried out a 'policy of terror' against civilians, including bombings, intimidation, torture, killings and disappearances (Pearce 1990: 234; Iturralde 2003). Rather than representing a legitimate instrument against terrorism, then, the Statute institutionalized state terror. Moreover, violence continued unabated: between 1988 and 1990, over 14,000 Colombians died in terrorist attacks, such as the killings of UP members and the 'terrible massacres' carried out by paramilitaries in Uraba and Cordoba (Safford and Palacios 2002: 366–367).

By the late 1980s, the paramilitaries had 'erased the broad Left from the electoral map, reinforced clientelist political controls, and began to acquire vast landholdings, chiefly through massacre and expropriation' (Hylton 2006: 75–78). Paramilitary 'social cleansing' of UP affiliates in banana, logging and cattle-ranching regions – through massacres beginning in the 1980s – became a common feature of paramilitary modus operandi. For example, paramilitary leader Fabio Castaño (Rambo) launched a violent crusade against the guerrilla after his father was kidnapped and disappeared, subsequently massacring a considerable number of peasant farmers after torturing them to obtain information concerning the guerrilla. At the same time, 'urban terrorism' by the paramilitaries and the cartels began to have a significant effect: judges, activists and politicians were executed and city districts were cleansed of 'petty thieves, prostitutes, homosexuals and other undesirables' (Hylton 2006: 75–78). In the urban area of Barrancabermeja, for example, paramilitaries linked to the cartels and the private sector were responsible for continual killings and kidnappings, such as the murder in 1988 of trade union leader Manuel Gustavo Chacón (Pearce 1990: 240). One participant in the victims' delegations had been a witness of paramilitary violence in Barrancabermeja, his son disappeared and murdered. During 1988, in fact, at least 200 leaders and activists were executed, including CCP officials and sympathizers in Puerto Boyaca, and mine workers and UP party activists and politicians in Medellin.

In this context, the state itself became 'part of an anachronistic political order', in which past and present violence propagated by political and economic elites became interconnected. Colombia's ruling class 'led its people into one of the bloodiest civil wars of the twentieth century, and three decades later, it unleashed a wave of right-wing terror against people that demanded their rights' (Pearce 1990: 256). The enduring 'tragic circularity and repetition' of political violence and terrorism in Colombia would in fact characterize the following two decades of violence in the country. Moreover, it would be the motivating force for the emergence of the victims' and human rights movements in Colombia, and, latterly, the participation of the victims' delegations in Havana.

The 1990s: terrorism in the aftermath of the Cold War

Echoing processes across Latin America, the post-Cold War context brought a series of successful peace initiatives to Colombia, including the DDR process of the M-19 and Quintin Lame, among others. Despite the political will of these insurgent groups, by the end of the 1980s, the FARC-EP's escalating military and political strategy had already begun to represent a significant threat to the economic status quo, as the guerrilla began increasingly to assert control in rural areas. However, in the aftermath of the Cold War, the FARC-EP's military and organizational consolidation (Safford and Palacios 2002: 86–88) came at a cost: the progressive loss of its political legitimacy, as it further turned to drug production and trafficking to finance its armed struggle, 'increasing its involvement in the cocaine producing trade chain' (Palma 2019: 254). Moreover, as the FARC-EP sought to secure control and guarantee the sovereignty of its local territories, the group perpetrated significantly higher levels of selective assassination and kidnappings, as the profile and membership of the victims' delegations demonstrated. The FARC-EP simultaneously perpetrated diverse and systematic forms of violence against civilians during this time, such as the use of sexual violence, as the testament of one of the participants in the victims' delegations made evident. At the same time, the FARC-EP adopted the indiscriminate use of anti-personnel mines throughout rural areas as part of its wider armed strategy. One delegate to the Havana talks had lost his leg when he stepped on a landmine during a football game close to his rural home. The consequence of the FARC-EP's escalating war was increasingly egregious, as it employed horrendous violence that culminated in paradigmatic episodes of violence, such as sexual and gender-based violence, kidnapping, improvised explosive devices (IEDs), landmines and executions.

By the mid-1990s, violence across the country had once again spiked, as the paramilitary response to growing insurgent capacity escalated and terrorist actions – such as car bombings – by the cartels (in particular the Medellin cartel) became routinized. Paramilitary violence similarly escalated, drawing civilian populations increasingly into the conflict. Many participants in the victims' delegations told harrowing stories of the egregious paramilitary violence to which they had been subject.

It was in this context that the original structural causes of the conflict, which had, in turn, precipitated and decisively shaped the political violence of the second half of the 20th century, mutated and evolved. Following the termination of financial support to the FARC-EP from the former Soviet Union, the organization began to develop strategies aimed at securing finance, including both through kidnapping and involvement in illicit activities (Pécaut 2008). According to Sánchez, this development, along with the egregious paramilitary and cartel violence, precipitated the 'degradation' of Colombia's armed conflict. Involvement in narco-activity represented one of the factors that permitted both the FARC-EP and the paramilitaries to consolidate as effective military machines in the late 1980s and 1990s. Importantly, as Moyano (1995) has argued in the case of the Argentine guerrillas, during the 1990s, the FARC-EP began to transform the norms and ideological foundations that had previously regulated the guerrilla's relationship with its traditional social base, which had in turn controlled the nature of the violence the group was prepared to exercise against it.[8] In this context, the FARC-EP began to execute increasingly arbitrary, diverse and widespread forms of violence, including against its own social base, subsequently alienating it from elements within its existing social constituency and broader Colombian society. Two of the members of the victims' delegations had survived, having been kidnapped by the FARC-EP. One member of the police who participated in the delegations was kidnapped during the military occupation of Mitú, the capital of Vaupés, in 1998, and was held in captivity for 11 years. One female delegate, a politician from

---

[8] See Weinstein (2011) for an eloquent discussion on the factors shaping the relationship between insurgencies and their social constituencies.

southern Colombia, was kidnapped in 2001 and was held as a political prisoner for seven years. Describing the pain of the kidnapping, the latter narrated how: 'You can only imagine the anxiety, the pain, the frustration, and the sadness, everything that a human being might feel being deprived of their liberty and without understanding the motives of such an act.'[9]

The commission of extrajudicial executions, sexual and-gender based violence and threats, and, significantly, the employment of individual and collective kidnappings by the FARC-EP became a cornerstone of their military strategy, representing not only grave violations of international humanitarian law, but also ultimately becoming key factors that whittled away potential political or social support to the group from within wider civil society.

In part as a consequence of its increasing military strength fuelled by drug money, the FARC-EP gradually expanded further into rural and semi-urban zones, an expansion that ultimately signified that, by the end of the 1990s and the beginning of the 2000s, the guerrilla represented a significant threat to the Colombian state in diverse areas across the national territory. Significantly after 1990, the FARC-EP grew from under 8,000 to approximately 18,000 members in 2000. Between 1996 and 2003, the group averaged 1,000 offensive military actions, in contrast to 500 annually during the 1980s (Nasi 2009: 44–7). By 1997, both the FARC-EP and the ELN would be placed on the US Department of State list of Foreign Terrorist Organizations, and in 2002 on the European Union Terrorist Organization list.

The response to the FARC-EP's increasing military capacity was an expanded and progressively coordinated wave of paramilitary terror sponsored by the state and the political and economic elites against the organization and its perceived social and political support base. Paramilitary expansion drew upon the historically enduring presence of private armed and militia groups, culminating in 1996 with the establishment of the United Self-Defence Forces of Colombia (AUC), an umbrella group that brought together diverse paramilitary fronts linked to the political and economic elites. During the late 1990s, as alliances were cemented with the military and between the paramilitary blocs themselves, increasing acts of terrorism, including massacre campaigns, were executed against noncombatants throughout rural and semi-urban areas. Significantly, as was the case with the FARC-EP and the ELN, both paramilitary and state security forces became intimately involved in drug production and trafficking during the 1990s, acutely transforming the nature of the armed conflict.

Grotesque paramilitary terror resulted in severe consequences throughout the country, leaving widespread and egregious patterns of victimization.

---

[9] Interviews, Bogotá, Colombia, April–May 2015.

Many participants of the victims' delegations had survived paramilitary terror or had family members who had not. One member of the victims' delegations recounted the impact of her son's kidnapping and disappearance by the paramilitaries in Magdalena Medio in 1998: 'it's so difficult, to pass through life, because every day we get up and say to ourselves that today our children will come home, and the day goes by and they don't arrive. When the night comes, we think just maybe there'll be a knock at the door. But we've still not lost hope, to find them alive or dead'.[10]

By the 1990s, the paramilitaries had crafted a degree of autonomy, collaborating variously with the state and military, landowners, cattle ranchers and cartels. No longer self-defence groups, they came to pursue an offensive strategy, eliminating areas of subversive activity and annihilating their supposed supporters through massacre and forced displacement, the latter often permitting cartels to move in or international companies to plant African palm. Paramilitaries often 'linked to drug cartels ... worked closely with Colombian military officers to eliminate suspected guerrilla sympathizers, while at the same time they attacked Colombian authorities investigating drug trafficking and paramilitary activity' (Tate 2001: 166). With respect to their collaboration with state institutions, paramilitaries were frequently employed as 'de facto shock troops', sent into rural areas suspected of supporting guerrilla activity prior to a formal military assault operation (Nagle 2005: 19). By the 1990s, once they had achieved relative autonomy, paramilitary groups were consolidated throughout the country, bolstered by income from illicit activities and, in some cases, legal decrees that formalized their mandates. For example, in 1994, Decree 356, promulgated by the subsequent Colombian President Alvaro Uribe, created the so-called *Convivir*. Convivir security cooperatives were private organizations mandated with tasks of surveillance, information gathering and rural security that articulated cooperation in security matters between the rural landowning elite and Colombia's armed forces. The group was established to combat the FARC-EP, and subsequently perpetrated egregious crimes against civilians, often in collaboration with military and police units.[11]

As paramilitary acts of terror spiralled between 1997 and 1999, organizations' ranks doubled; massacres represented a particular modus operandi of the groups, increasing from 286 in 1997 to 403 in 1999 (Safford and Palacios 2002: 95–101). In 1996, across four municipalities of the so-called *Banana Axis*, the homicide rate was 500 per 100,000. In this context, the military frequently allegedly removed troops tasked with the protection

---

[10] Interview, Bogotá, Colombia, April 2014.
[11] The decree establishing the Convivir was struck down by the Constitutional Court in 1997; many of its ranks passed to the AUC.

of civilians from the paramilitaries. For example, the massacre in the town of Mapiripan, perpetrated over five days in July 1997, included five days of torture and murder, assisted by the military itself. Paramilitary terror had a significant effect on the capacity of the FARC-EP to control its territories. In 1996, for example, in the wake of a 'campaign of indiscriminate terror and cruelty', the Cordoba and Uraba self-defence forces were able to displace the FARC-EP to neighbouring Choco (Safford and Palacios 2002: 95–101).

However, perhaps the key development with respect to paramilitary capacity to employ egregious violence and strategic acts of terrorism was the establishment in 1996 of the AUC by Carlos Castaño. Castaño sought to strengthen the anti-subversive campaign through a 'definitive and conclusive war against the guerrillas' (Mazzei 2009: 93). Despite protestations that it would remain isolated from the narco-sphere, the AUC took advantage of the illicit business both to finance its own struggle and to drive capital accumulation of its members, eventually appropriating 40 per cent of the drug economy.

The AUC emerged with approximately 3,000 members, expanding rapidly; by 2005, they numbered between 8,000 and 11,000 armed combatants, with a logistical support base of approximately 18,000 members (Mazzei 2009: 93–94).[12] By 2003, it wielded a presence in over 25 of Colombia's departments and in a third of the country's municipalities. Castaño has claimed that the AUC ranks included 800 ex-guerrillas, 135 former military officers and over 1,000 former soldiers (Hristov 2009: 71). The organization enjoyed broad operational, financial and technical support from the military high command, at the same time as it coordinated closely with landowning elites – often paid directly by them – and with local and national state and government officials.

The AUC often employed a three-component strategy. A first stage of 'incursion' was characterized by the distribution of distributed pamphlets warning of their arrival. Immediate incursion was followed by a 'social cleansing' campaign against the guerrilla, its perceived social base (trade unionists, human rights lawyers and activists, and academics) and thieves, drug addicts, the homeless, homosexuals and prostitutes. The AUC also destroyed houses, community buildings and infrastructure. After 'incursion', the AUC focused on 'consolidation', when the population was informed it could cooperate, flee or be killed. Civilians were terrorized into submission, while businesses were taxed and potential state and private collaborators were consolidated. Finally, the AUC sought to 'legitimize', including through social projects and community work (Hristov 2016: 313–314).

---

[12] There are estimates that the group numbered over 30,000 by the time of its DDR process in 2007.

Acts of AUC terror and paramilitary activity were commissioned throughout the country. Like other key zones of contention, the city of Barrancabermeja, at the heart of one of Colombia's oil exploration regions, was devastated by paramilitary violence as the group struggled to weaken the historical foothold of organized trade union and leftist politics and, latterly, armed organizing. Of the considerable number of delegates affected by paramilitary violence that visited Havana, several were from Barrancabermeja. In 1998, one delegate's son was kidnapped and subsequently disappeared by the AUC, due to his involvement in student politics. Similarly, the brother of another female delegate was murdered by the AUC in Quindio. However, in the latter case, her two other brothers had previously been killed by the FARC-EP, making her a survivor of diverse perpetrator violence. Victimization by multiple perpetrators was, tragically, a frequent pattern in Colombia, as evidenced by the participants in the delegations. The impact of the violence was also severe for one social organizer from the region of Montes de Maria. In 1998, the female delegate's brother was killed by paramilitaries in Mercado Nuevo. Shortly afterwards, her niece was killed in an explosion in Carmen de Bolívar perpetrated by the guerrilla.[13]

The AUC has been identified as a significant terrorist actor in Colombia, linked, according to Nagle (2005), to international terrorist organizations. Collusion between the Colombian Armed Forces and the AUC was systematic from its creation up until the DDR process with the group which began in 2005. By 2000, the rapid spread of the AUC and its strategic use of acts of terrorism against noncombatants had polarized Colombian society yet further, transforming the social and political landscape. By the mid-2000s, paramilitary terror played a key role in pushing both the FARC-EP and the ELN to withdraw from many areas in which they had historically asserted control and into peripheral zones of the country. The violence perpetrated by the AUC was both decisive and widespread in scale and grotesque in nature. In 2000, massacres increased by 22 per cent, while approximately 319,000 people were forcibly displaced (Human Rights Watch 2001: 5). Acts of terrorism – including the perpetration of massacres – were often facilitated or accompanied by state agents, either through its direct collaboration in commissioning violence, or through acts of omission or nonintervention, such as when state security forces would not respond to notifications of an imminent or probable paramilitary attack. For example, the police and military ignored warnings of a likely paramilitary operation by local officials in Chengue, Sucre, during late 2000 and January 2001; 50 paramilitaries subsequently murdered more than 24 people in the village, in a massacre aimed at 'eliminating all the men and women of the community',[14] according

---

[13] Interview, Bogotá, Colombia, April 2015.
[14] Interview, Bogotá, Colombia, April 2015.

to one of the survivors of the Chengue massacre, who went to Havana as a member of the victims' delegations. Rather than responding to the local population's pleas, the military had in fact facilitated the attack, holding a mock battle, which sealed off the roads to the village.

The paramilitaries' reach also extended into the political sphere. Between 2002 and 2006, 77 per cent of national Congressional representatives were linked to the paramilitaries; these links were replicated at the local level (Hristov 2016: 103–104). Significantly, the group also closely coordinated with transnational corporations, such as Chiquita Banana, on whose behalf it allegedly carried out terrorist actions against over 100 noncombatants, including organized Chiquita workers (Coleman Montesinos 2024). For example, in 1998, the AUC forced Chiquita employees to watch as two co-workers were executed. In 1999, two AUC members beheaded a Chiquita employee with a machete on a Chiquita plantation, followed two years later by an action in which AUC members rounded up male civilians and smashed their skulls with stones and sledgehammers. However, in spite of such activity, the AUC would only be placed on the US Department of State list of Foreign Terrorist Organizations in September 2001, five years after its establishment.

The interminable conflict?

This chapter has offered a longer-term historical perspective on political violence and state and nonstate terrorism in Colombia, providing a rigorous historically oriented and contextually driven analysis of violence perpetrated since the 19th century by diverse actors. The chapter has depicted how complex interrelated political, economic, legal and social processes, themselves shaped by historical context, have determined how, when and by whom political violence has been employed in Colombia.

Since Colombia began its process to break free from Spanish rule in 1810, the country has 'suffered constant violent political confrontations ... devastated by nineteen separate internal armed conflicts, each attributable to a myriad of forces' (Nagle 2005: 10). Independence ushered in a long period of violent instability throughout the 19th century, during which time civil war and poverty were significant factors determining the country's social and political dynamics. Broadly speaking, violent confrontation during the 19th and the first half of the 20th centuries was shaped by and further consolidated the cleavage between the Conservative and Liberal Parties, and was manifest in complex patterns of conflict at the national, subnational and local levels. Systematic, grotesque violence became the norm in Colombia's bipartisan conflict, as party elites and members and the armed militia groups through which their wrath was made manifest executed acts of terrorism against civilians. 'La Violencia' represented the unfinished business of the post-independence period. However, the pillars of Colombia's internal armed conflict were, in turn, crafted during 'La Violencia' and the NF power-sharing agreement that sought to bring it to an end. Subsequently, with almost no meaningful or protracted hiatus, and in spite of important peacebuilding initiatives, the country embarked on what has been over five decades of egregious political violence, in which acts of terrorism against civilians have been employed systematically by multiple armed actors: the participants in the victims' delegations were testament to this horror.

Drawing on interviews with the members of the victims' delegations, the chapter has evidenced how, since the 1980s, violence in Colombia has become characterized by its sheer unfettered scale and its complexity, in particular in the aftermath of the Cold War, as the original structural causes of conflict mutated and evolved.[15] According to Sánchez, this development represented a moment of 'degradation' of the internal armed conflict. Guerrilla, paramilitary and state security forces became intimately involved in drug production and trafficking during the 1980s and, emphatically, the 1990s, acutely transforming the nature of the armed conflict and, in fact, exacerbating rural grievances as paramilitaries expropriated vast tracts of land. Since the early 1990s, drug trafficking organizations, criminal organizations and illegal armed groups – and not infrequently military and police forces – have generated complex alliances as they seek to maintain control of economic resources, including drug production and other illegal enterprises. In this regard, a mosaic of often connected sub-nationally and locally-driven conflicts have emerged, converging around a set of objective conditions, common actors and patterns of violence, oftentimes melding political violence and criminal activity (Paredes Zapata 2003: 87). The shifting motivations behind and targets of armed violence, including acts of terrorism, and the blurred line between political and criminal violence have since imbued the conflict with an unprecedented level of intricacy, in turn problematizing the 'classification of violent acts' (Holmes 2019). Armed actors have consistently resorted to acts of terrorism, often as a

---

[15] The violence exerted by the guerrillas included massacres, torture, homicide and disappearances, and the insurgents were responsible for the highest levels of kidnapping of civilians and members of the security forces aimed at levying political pressure against the government or economic resources for the war (Leech 2011: 109–110). On the other hand, according to the NCHM, the paramilitary groups were the main perpetrators of massacres and selective assassinations, often in collaboration with the armed forces. They also systematically practised sexual violence (2012: 84) and other types of violence such as selective assassination, forced disappearance, torture, threat, massive forced displacement and economic blockades against civilians (2012: 44). Consistently, the goal behind such activities was to increase civilian collaboration and force civilian support. Drug cartels have been responsible for massacres, homicides, torture, bombings and intimidation.

default strategy, while simultaneously waging regular and irregular warfare against conventional and unconventional forces, as well as engaging in the formal political sphere.

The continuity of political violence within broader and more complex armed confrontations has been coherently shown in this chapter. Moreover, the chapter has demonstrated how the employment of atrocious violence has not been the sole preserve of leftist insurgencies; party militia, right-wing paramilitaries, mafias, drug cartels and the state have, in turn, methodically commissioned widespread acts of terrorism, often collaborating together and, at other times, acting with the direct or indirect collusion of the private sector and transnational corporations, with egregious impacts on the civilian population. In the following chapter, I turn to an analysis of how, in a context of such grotesque violence, the Santos–FARC-EP peace talks emerged, and how the survivors and victims of Colombia's darkest episodes of violence crafted a key role in shaping the country's peace process.

2

Colombia's Aberrational Cold War

This chapter addresses how, despite the post-Cold War context of international rapprochement, Colombia's grotesque and, in global terms, aberrational war continued under President Alvaro Uribe, channelled explicitly through his policy of Democratic Security. It explores how Uribe's war on Colombia weakened the FARC-EP guerrilla, gradually pushing it back to peripheral zones of the country, while precipitating an unprecedented humanitarian disaster, characterized by massive patterns of victimization and state-sponsored human rights violations, patterns that would later closely influence the parameters of inclusion for the victims' delegations to Havana. However, despite Uribe's progress towards debilitating the FARC-EP, the insurgency's military resilience and its capacity to regenerate strategically – including by financing the armed struggle through illegal drug trafficking activities and kidnapping – also meant that, as an armed force, the FARC-EP was able to persist. The guerrilla's capacity to maintain its armed struggle, even in spite of the superior capacity of the Colombian Armed Forces, ultimately signified that, by the end of the first decade of the 2000s, the armed conflict had reached a hurting stalemate. It was out of these darkest episodes of political violence perpetrated during the two Uribe administrations that the Santos–FARC-EP peace talks eventually emerged, bolstered by both the partial military hurting stalemate and the significant impact brought by civil society and victims' organizations as they consolidated themselves as political actors.

Introduction: The Cold War and its aftermath

Across the globe, the end of the Cold War in the 1990s precipitated significant change. In Latin America, the Southern Cone's transitions from authoritarian rule were gradually consolidated and, by the middle of the decade, Central America's brutal internal armed conflicts were formally brought to an end through internationally monitored peace processes (O'Donnell, Schmitter and Whitehead 1986). Moreover, by the mid-1990s, security doctrine, political institutions and narratives across Latin America had begun to move on from the bipolar frameworks that had been so ubiquitous and influential during the preceding decades. In tandem, in the aftermath of the launch of the UN Agenda for Peace in 1992, international peace support initiatives began to shift away from their historical emphasis on peacekeeping, as policy makers sought to meet the challenges brought by changing patterns of conflict and violence and address more effectively their causes and consequences (Lipson 2007). Such transformation – manifest in developing normative standards, evolving institutional mechanisms and an increasingly robust and interventionist global peacemaking and peacebuilding architecture – played a key role, for example, in the Guatemalan and El Salvadoran peace processes. However, Colombia was, in part, an exception to this wider global phenomenon and the new peacebuilding architecture would only much later come to have a meaningful bearing upon how Colombia's Santos–FARC-EP peace process would develop.

Decades before the negotiations between the Santos government and the FARC-EP, during what Goulding (1993) has characterized as the *Golden Age* of peacekeeping (1956–1974), international peacekeeping operations (PKOs) had focused principally on the monitoring of ceasefires and frontier lines and the interposition between belligerents. The 13 PKOs carried out during the Cold War were, in this context, of significant importance, leading to the establishment of a customary body of principles determining peacekeeping, including their *Unitednationsness*, the requirements of the respective parties' consent to intervention and the mandatory impartiality of the parameters shaping the operation in question.

During the Cold War, UN PKOs had been limited and, in fact, were absent in Latin America, due to the intrastate conflicts that had characterized the region and the UN's focus, in part, on interstate wars. Moreover, the UN was deadlocked and the Security Council was effectively paralysed by the strategic employment of member vetoes in the interests of the superpowers and their allies, and by the rigid interpretation of state sovereignty. Such conditions ultimately ruled out the prospect for greater consensual intervention. However, with the end of the Cold War, fundamental changes in the international system brought about new opportunities for international engagement and cooperation in mediating international and internal armed conflicts. The thawing, followed by the eventual termination of the Cold War, precipitated a rapprochement in superpower relations and accompanying shifts in foreign policy paradigms, which led to the increased acceptance of international engagement in peacemaking and peacebuilding by heavyweight states and international governmental organizations (Mayall 1996). At the same time, ideational changes within the Gorbachev regime and key perestroika reforms, augmented by the decline of Reagan-era hostility towards both the former USSR and the UN, ushered in increasing cooperation between the permanent members of the Security Council (Durch 1994).

In the ten years after 1989, demand for multilateral peace operations grew. No fewer than 33 UN peace operations were carried out, as a degree of comparative success in the UN's early multifunctional missions during the closing years of the Cold War forged an atmosphere of optimism and enthusiasm for UN peacekeeping. The evolution in peace support practice and thinking at the global level brought about a change from classic PKO approaches towards complex multidimensional operations, as shown, for example, in the UN Transition Assistance Group (UNTAG) in Namibia and the UN observer missions in El Salvador (ONUSAL) and Guatemala (MINUGUA) (Durch 1994). Such fundamental shifts in UN practice resulted in a qualitative move away from the quiet diplomacy of the UN Secretary-General, and gradually towards more visible UN operations that stretched of the principles of impartiality, consent and persuasion, leading to the adoption of increasingly coercive techniques and a questioning, in part, of the principle of sovereignty (Paris 2000; Richmond 2004; Lipson 2007).

A new era of cooperation, it appeared, had begun. However, such profound shifts in peacemaking and peacebuilding norms and practices had a far more limited impact in Colombia than they had done in Central America at the start of the decade. The 1990s, in fact, represented a decade of contradictions in Colombia. On the one hand, the decade saw an acute escalation in the scale and dimension of Colombia's armed conflict and in the brutality of the violence that accompanied it. Sánchez has argued that in this regard, the 1990s precipitated the 'degradation' of Colombia's conflict, as armed actors targeted civilians through egregious military strategies and turned to drug trafficking and kidnapping to fund their armed struggle, in the case of the FARC-EP, due, in part, to the drying up of Soviet-era funding. The FARC-EP simultaneously distanced itself from international norms and customary conventions governing the treatment of noncombatants, as had arguably been the case for the Argentine guerrilla in the 1970s (Moyano 1995), employing increasingly horrific actions against noncombatants and ultimately alienating it from broader Colombian society. These patterns were heightened by the exacerbation of the complex factors shaping the dynamics of Colombia's armed conflict, such as the diversification of those armed actors involved in hostilities, the growing fragility of state reach and increasing territorial expansion of the guerrilla across the country's vast fragmented territory, and, significantly, the spiralling of drug-trafficking income to fund armed protagonists (Brett 2021b).

However, on the other hand, and significantly, the decade's ascendant global peacemaking and peacebuilding character were also reflected within Colombia. A series of unprecedented domestic peace initiatives, including the demobilization, disarmament and reintegration processes of the M-19 and other guerrilla groups, such as the Quitin Lame, were levied successfully between 1990 and 1991. The 1990s similarly witnessed important and unprecedented widespread mobilizations by civil society, and specifically by victims' and human rights movements, in favour of peace, movements that were supported by international actors. The 1990s also saw – albeit more briefly – considerable effort by the armed actors themselves towards bringing an end to the war with the FARC-EP. In this context, by the end of the 1990s, brief and unsuccessful peace negotiations between President Andrés Pastrana (1998–2002) and the FARC-EP took place, as will be discussed later on; such talks would present a series of lessons learned for the Santos–FARC-EP talks later in the century.

The Caguán talks

In January 1999, as hostilities continued, within the wider context of the shifting, post-Cold War global environment, ongoing pressure from domestic and international lobbies for peace gradually opened up a path to talks between the government of President Andres Pastrana and the FARC-EP in Colombia. The Caguán peace process (1999–2002), as it came to be known, was carried out in the traditional guerrilla stronghold of Caguán, under conditions of a bilateral ceasefire, while the FARC-EP was afforded an extensive demilitarized zone, where it would not be subject to military interventions.

Operatively, the Caguán negotiation agenda was broad, incorporating issues of human rights, land reform, structural transformation and discussions concerning the recalibration of Colombia's economic model. Supporting this agenda, during the talks, civil society groups were mandated with a strategic role, specifically to carry out hearings with the negotiating parties along thematic lines (Haspeslagh 2021). In this respect, the Caguán talks reflected, at least in part, the new peace support thinking and practice contemplated in the 1992 UN Agenda for Peace and later its 1995 Supplementary Protocol oriented towards more inclusive peacemaking and peacebuilding processes. Specifically, the process was characterized by the unprecedented inclusion of civil society organizations, an attribute shared by the Guatemalan peace process some years earlier (Brett 2008).

The Agenda for Peace had been crucial in consolidating a renovated global paradigm for peacemaking and peacebuilding, moving the UN away from its prior focus on peacekeeping, historically one of UN's 'most significant innovations ... [the] most conspicuous single manifestation of the UN's role in the world' (Roberts and Kingsbury 1996: 3). The new peacebuilding paradigm was manifest through the diversification of international and national responsibilities linked to both peacemaking (peace negotiations) and peacebuilding (post-accord reconstruction). Within this framework, from the beginning of the 1990s, increasingly complex peace support initiatives were deployed both as part of the negotiation of political solutions to armed conflict – an approach reflected in the Caguán agenda – and, in their aftermath, as part of intricate post-accord reconstruction interventions.

Within this remit, the role of the UN and other international actors was at the same time broadened, away from the explicit task of peacekeeping and towards the deployment of both military and civilian advisors and observers mandated to carry out tasks such as disarmament, demobilization and reintegration, the resettlement of refugees, the training of police, judges and other state officials, and election monitoring. After 1992, therefore, civilian participation in peacemaking and peacebuilding initiatives became increasingly common, including, for example, civilian involvement in electoral monitoring and the training of political parties, humanitarian relief, economic restructuring, human rights monitoring and training, development initiatives, institution building, security sector reform (SSR), civil society strengthening and so on. UN operations in Latin America carried out within this framework included the operations in El Salvador – through the UN Mission to El Salvador (ONUSAL, 1991–1995) – and Guatemala – through the United Nations Verification Mission to Guatemala (MINUGUA, 1994–2004) – which closely reflected changes in international peace support thinking, although ONUSAL itself had begun before the formal launch of the Agenda for Peace in 1992 (Malone and Wermester 2000).[1]

The Agenda for Peace called for the adoption of more inclusive processes – in short, the wider participation of nonstate actors in peacemaking and peacebuilding. Along these lines, civil society actors increasingly assumed a more visible, although habitually secondary, consultative role in formal peace processes. Within these parameters, for example, the first formal inclusion mechanisms, the so-called Civil Society Assembly (ASC), was established in 1994 in Guatemala, mandated by the negotiating parties to send formal, nonbinding proposals for the peace accords to the government and guerrilla delegations (Brett 2008, 2017b). Civil society participation, particularly

---

[1] Moving beyond peacekeeping and preventive diplomacy, the Agenda for Peace qualified a multi-stage approach to peace support, identifying *peacemaking* as those practices directed at 'bringing hostile parties to agreement' by 'reconciling political and strategical attitudes through mediation, negotiation, arbitration and conciliation', principally to be carried out at elite level through peace negotiations. At the same time, the Agenda consolidated the notion of subsequent post-conflict *peacebuilding* support as representing those practices aimed at 'the practical implementation of peaceful social change through socio-economic reconstruction and development'. Said practices were aimed at preventing a recurrence of the violence through the generation of conditions of security, development and confidence, aimed ultimately at consolidating the foundations for a self-enforcing peace. See https://www.un.org/ruleoflaw/files/A_47_277.pdf (accessed 3 February 2020).

at a secondary level, has since come to represent an increasing modality employed during peace negotiations, a discussion that will be returned to later on (Paffenholz 2015; Vogel 2016).

Such significant shifts at the end of the Cold War were both audacious and unprecedented. However, given the fact that Colombia's Cold War has persisted beyond the 1990s, interventions framed within the new peace support paradigm were slower to take effect to the same extent in the country. Furthermore, as will be seen in the case of the Santos–FARC-EP talks, Colombia's political, economic and military elite has historically tended to oppose UN interventions that aspire to a similar ambition and scale as those initiatives successfully levied in Central America. As such, UN peace support operations had a hard time consolidating a meaningful presence in the country, at least until 2016, when the UN Verification Mission in Colombia was mandated in the wake of the Havana talks. Colombian elites have openly resisted the 'fundamentally altered conceptions of state sovereignty' that post-Cold War UN interventions have compelled, undoubtedly due to resistance to their 'often … strikingly intrusive nature' (Malone and Wermester 2000: 38). Consequently, during the Caguán talks and, arguably, since, the UN system has remained up against the ropes in Colombia, pinned there by a recalcitrant economic, political and military elite, whose anachronistic Cold War has served to justify their exceptionalism.

From their inception, the Caguán talks languished ineffectively. Despite such a bleak panorama, the UN aspired to play an instrumental role, with James LeMoyne being appointed by then UN Secretary-General Kofi Annan in November 2001 as his Acting Special Adviser on Colombia. LeMoyne elevated the UN's role and presence, even meeting with the FARC-EP during the latter stages of the Caguán talks. However, his presence in Colombia was relatively short-lived, as he, and the UN more generally, became increasingly constrained and, ultimately, blackballed by the government, particularly after LeMoyne's controversial declaration to the newspaper *El Tiempo* in May 2003, where he stated: 'I have two questions for the upper class of this country to respond to … First: Are your sons, nephews or grandsons in the army? … Who makes the sacrifices in this country when there is combat?' LeMoyne finally suspended activities in January 2005, after the Uribe government had consistently refused to cooperate and, controversially, had accused the UN of supporting and justifying terrorism under LeMoyne. The Head of the Office of the UN High Commissioner for Human Rights in Colombia, Swedish diplomat Anders Kompass, suffered a similar fate. After arriving in April 1999 during the Caguán process, Kompass encountered an executive unwilling to accept UN advice or countenance official UN findings on human rights violations committed by state and paramilitary forces. By May 2003, Kompass had been obligated to use a bulletproof vehicle after a prominent Colombian general had accused him of being an enemy of the state and of the Armed Forces. Kompass left the country the following month.

Although the Caguán talks were hailed as innovative due to the mass participation of civil society actors, they ultimately became more significant for their consequences for war than their consequences for peace. Neither the FARC-EP, nor the Colombian government and state, particularly the military, was deeply committed to the negotiations. The guerrilla came to the talks from a militarily and politically robust position, bolstered by the impact of its politico-military strategy and its illegal assets that had allowed territorial expansion and, increasingly, by its key victories against the military. The executive, while demonstrating a degree of political will, failed to enjoy widespread political support, particularly from within the ranks of the military. Both negotiating parties were hesitant on major commitments as a consequence, being reluctant to compromise their political and ideological positions and, ultimately, reticent to relinquish their perceived military superiority. The talks subsequently collapsed in July 2002, after the FARC-EP carried out an armed offensive, to which the government immediately responded by bombing guerrilla enclaves with the support of the US (Chernick 1999; Villamizar 2017: 654).

The Caguán talks came to represent a key episode in Colombian political and military history, a *never again*, or 'chosen trauma' in Volkan's words, in the country's collective memory. Despite the lack of commitment by both parties, public opinion became increasingly consolidated around the narrative that the FARC-EP had duped the government during the talks, leaving an 'empty seat' (*silla vacía*) at the negotiating table, which humiliated President Pastrana, while making use of the demilitarized zone and ceasefire to reorganize militarily. The government, of course, was itself equally insincere, meaning that the talks were most likely stillborn. In both cases, the approaches and attitudes towards the talks echoed what Richmond (1998) has defined as the 'devious objectives' of negotiating parties. In reality, the collapse of the talks responded to a complex series of factors, including, on both sides, hubris, fear and an assumed belief in military superiority. Significantly, however, the collapse of the Caguán process paved the way for the election of President Alvaro Uribe (2002–2006 and 2006–2010), whose electoral platform had rejected negotiating with the FARC-EP.

Si vis pacem, para bellum: Uribe's war on Colombia

Against the immediate backdrop of the failed Caguán talks, President Uribe was elected to office in August 2002, in a context of escalating acts of atrocity against civilians, a severe economic crisis and increased drug trafficking violence. During the Cold War and in its wake, patterns of violent conflict at the global level had shifted towards a higher incidence of intrastate conflict, bringing changing forms and manifestations of political violence and victimization. While, as English (2013) has coherently argued, the absence of customary constraints on political violence and concomitant attacks against civilians have historically represented core components of warfare,[2] the 20th century ushered in extraordinary levels of horrific violence against civilians by state and nonstate actors alike. At the commencement of the 20th century, approximately 90 per cent of victims of war and political violence across the planet had been combatants; by the 1990s, an estimated 90 per cent of those killed in armed conflicts were civilians (English 2013). Colombia, of course, has been no exception in this regard: approximately 90 per cent of victims of the country's abhorrent, unfettered political violence have been civilians, victims of systematic rape and sexual violence, massacre, extrajudicial execution, disappearance, torture and displacement, which were employed by both state and illegal armed actors as deliberate strategies of war (NCHM 2012). During the Uribe administrations, systematic killing of civilians became a key feature, as an all-out war was waged with decisive support from Washington DC against the FARC-EP, and a dirty war was executed against the guerrilla's social base and those individuals and organizations that either opposed Uribe's war or demanded the armed actors adhere to international humanitarian and human rights standards.

The atrocious violence holding the entire country hostage from the end of the 1990s, and the collapse of the peace talks in the Caguán, had been decisive factors precipitating Uribe's rise to power. The election of Uribe to the presidency brought with it a dramatic escalation in the killing and, within this grotesque context of tit-for-tat political violence, noncombatants bore the brunt of the horror. The eight years of Uribe's two administrations saw rural terror by state and nonstate groups alike extend into urban areas, as 'attacks became urban and increasingly complex' and sophisticated (Paredes Zapata 2003: 82). Even before his assumption to office, during 2002, more than 19 'terrorist attacks' were executed, attributable to leftist and right-wing armed groups, all but one of which were bombings (car bombs, horse and bicycle bombs, and collar bombs) against political, military and commercial assets (Paredes Zapata 2003: 82). In May 2002, months before Uribe's inauguration, in fact, the FARC-EP perpetrated one of its most emblematic acts of terrorism. During hostilities between the guerrilla and the paramilitaries in the town of Bojayá, the FARC-EP fired a cylinder bomb at paramilitary positions located around the church and civilian residences. The gas cylinder fell on the church where civilians were seeking refuge, killing 119 people. The Bojaya massacre came to represent one of

---

[2] English (2013) contests the argument that the 1990s ushered in so-called new wars, contending that the targeting of civilians has been a historically consistent modality of war.

Colombia's most paradigmatic episodes of horrific violence and the victims and community were, significantly, represented in Havana by a community leader who survived the massacre, whose words are highly moving: 'Only by listening to the testimony of the victims could the damage be understood.'[3]

The following year, a further emblematic act of violence was perpetrated in February, when the El Nogál club in Bogotá was bombed, killing 36 people and injuring over 200 civilians. No group initially claimed responsibility, although the FARC-EP has since accepted responsibility for carrying out the attack. In response to the bombing, the UN Security Council issued an unprecedented proclamation, Resolution 1465 (2003), in which it took the step of terming the attack an act of terrorism and a 'threat to international security'. Significantly, as with the case of the massacre of Bojayá, this atrocity was also represented at the Havana peace talks by a mother who had lost her youngest son in the bomb and whose other son had barely survived the bombing. In her words: 'As he is entering the club, the bomb explodes, and my younger son dies immediately. My other son, who was in the sports cafeteria, fell from the 5th floor due to the impact of the bomb. A beam fell on top of him, causing him to be left with a diffuse adzonal cranioencephalic injury.'[4]

In the first year of Uribe's presidency, then, political violence escalated dramatically, as state and nonstate forces grappled to gain the upper hand in a war increasingly bereft of rules and limits. In the immediate aftermath of Uribe's first election victory, joint forces carried out a series of critical operations, including Operation Orion in Medellín's Comuna 13 in October 2002, in which FARC-EP and ELN rebels and alleged sympathizers were removed from the neighbourhood. The operation left the Comuna in the hands of paramilitary organizations that arguably still wield control over the zone today. The Armed Forces also implemented Operations Freedom I and II, successfully frustrating the potential encircling of Bogotá and restoring state control across urban areas and transport infrastructure in Cundinamarca and other central areas of the country. Finally, through Plan Patriot (2003–2006), the military carried out its largest ever offensive, involving 18,000 troops across the departments of Caquetá, Meta, Putumayo and Guaviare, key FARC-EP strongholds. The operation had a significant impact on the eastern and southern blocs of the FARC-EP, its most powerful structures (Crisis Group 2012). The military operations precipitated widespread human rights violations and mass displacement, crimes and patterns of victimization that would be represented by the victims' delegations to Havana 13 years later.

---

[3] Interview, Bogotá, Colombia, April 2015.
[4] Interview, Bogotá, Colombia, April 2015.

President Uribe's assumption to power took place in the wider context of the global war on terror. He immediately adopted a dramatically different approach to the war than that of his predecessor, President Pastrana, in particular with respect to the FARC-EP, which had executed his father some years before (Monning 2002: 164; Nagle 2005: 22). Finding echo in and seeking legitimation and justification through President Bush's war on terror, Uribe appropriated the discourse of a global war on terror, declaring, in his inaugural address, that 'any violence against a [democratic state]' would now be defined as terrorist activity (Nagle 2005: 22). The US war on terror, which had begun only a matter of months prior to the assumption of Uribe to the presidency, was thus a critical factor in the permissibility with which Uribe's discourse and actions were received, both internationally and by some sectors within Colombia. In the aftermath of 9/11, in a discursive conflation between the war on terror, war on drugs and war on insurgents, and the conceptualization of the FARC-EP as 'narco-terrorists' was given robust support from Washington, a discourse that was ultimately operationalized through the so-called Plan Colombia. Significantly, 'the vast majority of abuses' in Uribe's 'war of terror' were perpetrated 'against Colombia's civilian population'. In fact, the war precipitated the most dramatic humanitarian disaster in the Western hemisphere: over five million people were displaced, thousands murdered and entire zones destroyed (Stokes 2003: 578).

Plan Colombia

Presidents Uribe and Bush quickly became staunch allies in their respective wars on terrorism. Colombia joined the 'coalition of the willing', and Bush channelled millions of dollars to Colombia's war on drugs (and later war on terror) through Plan Colombia, originally established in 1998 (Nagle 2005: 58; Haspeslagh 2021). Plan Colombia, a multibillion-dollar funding plan, had originally commenced under President Pastrana, conceived as a Marshall Plan for Colombia, which had initially engaged multiple donor governments and had been focused on development (Monning 2002: 164). Under President Clinton, the US government had agreed to $1.3 billion support, oriented towards military assistance and illicit crop eradication. During the Bush administration, funding was expanded and the original restrictions on wider support for counterinsurgency operations were vetoed. Plan Colombia was formulated as a national/international collaboration through which to restore the rule of law, combat drug trafficking and address the insurgent threat. However, the Plan morphed into a primarily military intervention programme, and, during President Uribe's first term, its original objectives came to converge with and bolster Uribe's own counterinsurgency and counterterror policies, shaping US counterterrorist policies. The programme had an immediate impact on hemispheric relations, as neighbouring countries increased security along their frontiers in anticipation of increasing flows of refugees and combatants from Colombia resulting from the plan's implementation (Hristov 2009; Nagle 2005: 60).

Between 1996 and 2010, Colombia, the US's closest ally in the region and third-highest recipient of US aid at the global level, received $6.14 billion in military and economic aid, $5.56 billion of which was channelled through Plan Colombia after 2000. The appropriation of the discourse of the global war on terror by Uribe was key in terms of securing both an effective militarized state response to the FARC-EP and, significantly, garnering US support for his war (Palma 2019: 259). The framing of internal violence within broader global narratives was not new to Colombia, where, as was discussed in the previous chapter, the NSD had been appropriated during the previous three decades to justify horrific state-sponsored violence. Framed within the broader language of the war on terror, the discourse of narco-terrorism was consolidated under Uribe, permitting him to frame 'the decades-old problem of violence in Colombia merely as a terrorist threat' and thus to intensify counterinsurgent strategy (Palma 2019: 259–264).

Defining the FARC-EP as 'narco-terrorists', Uribe rejected the narrative that Colombia was experiencing an armed conflict, framing the state's military strategy as one of counter-terrorism. In August 2002, Uribe declared a state of emergency, while building up a network of 'citizen spies' and 'peasant soldiers' (Hylton 2006: 100–107). Shifting the narrative from both a counterinsurgency campaign and war on drugs to his war on terror, Uribe assumed a hardline approach against the insurgencies through military campaigns and state reform bankrolled by a receptive White House. In an effort to reassert state control across Colombia's vast territory, Uribe legislated a war tax to increase military revenue, while drawing upon Plan Colombia to improve and intensify military training and hardware.

The policy of democratic defence and security

Less than a year into office, in 2003, President Uribe formulated his government's security policy, the *Policy of Democratic Defence and Security* (Democratic Security, DSP). Prioritizing the elimination of the 'narco-terrorist' FARC-EP, the counterinsurgency/counter-terror strategy was undergirded by a series of interrelated goals, including strategic military pacification and stabilization. Heavily financed by the White House, the Uribe government waged an all-out war against the FARC-EP and its social base, and those state institutions and human rights and civil society organizations that opposed Uribe's DSP and its humanitarian and human rights impact.

The DSP sought to regain and consolidate state control and presence throughout the national territory with the aim of denying sanctuary for illegal armed actors and perpetrators of violence ('terrorists'); to guarantee the protection of civilians through increasing state presence/control and reducing violence; to combat the illegal drug trade and eliminate resultant revenues financing illegal armed groups ('terrorism'); and to guarantee and efficiently manage resources with the aim of reforming and improving the performance of the government. Moreover, undergirded by increased defence spending, the DSP was to be implemented and achieved through the inclusion of the civilian population (informants); general support to the military; the augmentation of intelligence capability; the restoration of control over transport infrastructure; the demobilization of illegal groups; and the integration of the armed forces. Consequently, the DSP became a critical aspect of the search for a military solution to Colombia's armed conflict, the restoration of state territorial control and the strengthening state institutions (Brett 2021b).

Within the framework of Plan Colombia and the DSP, the armed forces and intelligence services were systematically reformed and military hardware was upgraded, logistical procedures were streamlined and military personnel were trained. Military personnel also underwent strategic training in counterinsurgency operations. The increase in military spending allowed the Colombian armed forces to mushroom, acquiring significant military hardware, including approximately 80 Black Hawks, 30 Huey IIs and 11 UH-1Ns, subsequently guaranteeing air superiority over the FARC-EP (Crisis Group 2012). The military was reformed and its ranks considerably augmented. Under President Uribe's predecessor, the Armed Forces had grown by 60 per cent to 132,000. By 2010, the military had increased to 283,000 and the national police force to 159,000, including an increase in professional soldiers from 22,000 to 55,000 and regular soldiers from 46,000 to 73,000. At the same time, elite counterinsurgent combat units were created, including Task Force Omega (in 2003), and, with US support, the Joint Commands were established to facilitate coordination between the Army, Air Force and Navy. Smaller rapidly deployable units and specialized jungle and mountain units were also established (Palma 2019: 259), improving mobility and logistics, enhancing reaction time to insurgent threats and operations, and improving capacity for night operations, all of which effectively brought the fight to the guerrilla. US financial assistance and training simultaneously permitted the reform of intelligence structures and networks, ultimately precipitating more streamlined and effective intelligence-gathering procedures (Crisis Group 2012).

While waging war on the guerrilla, the state and the political and economic establishment also outsourced the war to illegal paramilitary organizations, which were financed directly by the economic elite, and trained and armed by the Colombian military (Hristov 2009; Hylton 2006; Hristov 2016). Of significant importance to this process were Uribe's personal ties and those of his government and political allies with Colombia's paramilitaries, with whom he had established a close relationship since the creation of the Convivir in 1994 during his term as Mayor of Medellin, Antioquia. Uribe, although only in part, abdicated the dirty war against the guerrilla's social base to the paramilitaries, who themselves subsequently became embedded in and captured state institutions and national and subnational political institutions, including through their legal arm, Colombia Viva.

After its creation in 1996, the AUC had enjoyed broad operational, financial and technical support from the military high command and became a key instrument of Uribe's counterinsurgent dirty war. Across rural and urban areas, the military financed and trained paramilitary forces in a war of terror precipitating vast numbers of abuses against the civilian population (Stokes 2003). The command structure of the AUC worked closely with landowning elites – often paid directly by them – and local and national state and government officials (Hristov 2016). Over time, the AUC extended its network and mandate beyond combating the insurgency and became a key actor in the illicit drug trade.

However, combining state and paramilitary forces, Uribe's all-out war on the FARC-EP and its social base came at a significant cost. State institutions – such as the Constitutional Court – politicians and activists who opposed or questioned the Uribe administration and international organizations, such as the UN and diverse embassies, were all subject to illegal surveillance by the Administrative Department of Security (DAS). At the same time, acts of terrorism against civilians carried out by the paramilitaries – frequently in coordination with the military – were as effective as they were brutal, as human rights and civil society organizations that opposed the DSP were identified as legitimate targets. Enjoying broad operational, financial and technical support from the military high command, paramilitary forces waged a war of terror against civilians, precipitating vast numbers of killings, massacres, torture, sexual and gender-based violence, disappearance and displacement across rural and urban areas (Stokes 2003; NCHM 2012).

Notably, many participants in the victims' delegations that visited Havana were survivors of paramilitary violence and their testimonies of paramilitary-sponsored horror were harrowing, as we will see. The security forces, in fact, acted with equal measure of egregiousness and impunity, including the so-called DAS, which was mandated as a highly secretive security apparatus. One of the members of the victims' delegations recounted how, in 2004, her brother had been initially kidnapped by the DAS in broad daylight. Despite their denying the episode, after sustained lobbying of the DAS offices and local government in Barranquilla, her brother was released from custody. However, some months later, he was executed in broad daylight on his way to the Universidad Simon Bolívar. A paramilitary henchman and a DAS official were finally prosecuted for the murder.[5]

Members of the military during both Uribe administrations also kidnapped poor civilians, luring them to remote parts of the country affected by the armed conflict with offers of work. The individuals were subsequently dressed in guerrilla uniforms, summarily executed and presented to state authorities as insurgents killed in battle (Montesinos Coleman 2024). The initiative, called the *false positives* scandal, which culminated in over 3,300 extrajudicial executions, sought to boost guerrilla body counts and justify military aid within the context of Plan Colombia. Officials responsible for the illegal operations and contraventions of international humanitarian law were rewarded with promotions, salary raises and time off. As with the Bojayá massacre, the Nogal bombing and the DAS killings, the families involved in the *false positive* scandal participated in the Havana peace talks, represented by a mother whose son had been kidnapped in 2008, sold to the 15th Mobile Brigade of the Army, and subsequently presented as a FARC-EP combatant in Villavicencio.[6] In her reflection on the experience of being in Havana, she expressed her deep-felt suffering: 'There was much pain. The pain of each one of us was a single pain. The pain of our country was a single pain, but it was lived in different ways.'

The hurting stalemate

Beyond precipitating a massive humanitarian disaster, the overall impact of the DSP on the guerrilla was to weaken its command structure and strategic operational capacity emphatically, while partially fracturing communications capability, arguably pushing the insurgents ever closer to the negotiating table (Brett 2021b). The capacity of the government to inflict such an impact on the FARC-EP was facilitated through the constitutional reform approved in 2005 permitting then President Uribe to stand for a second four-year term. Uribe subsequently won the presidential elections in 2006, affording stability and continuity to the DSP (Crisis Group 2012; Brett 2021b).

By the end of Uribe's second presidential term, in many rural zones, counterinsurgency operations had successfully forced the guerrilla to cede territory and shift strategy from breadth of presence to strategic and selective attacks. The FARC-EP was pushed back from the country's central Andean departments, at the same time as it was forced to cede its presence and operational capacity in diverse urban areas. The military's onslaught – combined with illegal paramilitary operations – pushed the FARC-EP

---

[5] Interview, Barranquilla, Colombia, May 2015.
[6] Interview, Bogotá, Colombia, April 2015.

towards increasingly peripheral areas of Colombia and, in turn, weakened the group's control over strategic corridors (Crisis Group 2012). Yet, with the exception of specific zones of historical support for the guerrilla such as Caquetá and Catatumbo, the FARC-EP was displaced from a range of its traditional strongholds, including in the coastal region of Montes de Maria. Such zones were subsequently designated for 'consolidation'. The strategy held a high military component that, while bringing decreasing levels of direct violence and reinforcing the withdrawal of the FARC-EP, systematically restricted the civil and political rights of the most vulnerable inhabitants.

Zones where Uribe's military strategy, combined with paramilitary operations, were able to neutralize the guerrilla threat, were subsequently designated for the implementation of a consolidation strategy. In this regard, in 2007, DSP was supplemented with the Democratic Security Consolidation Policy (DSCP), stabilization activities focusing on the consolidation of territorial gains by increasing state presence in conflict zones. In 2009, a strategic shift was made to the National Territorial Plan of Consolidation (PNCT). Both the DSCP and the PNCT emerged out of an evolving DSP, although did not break with the latter's primary military focus (Crisis Group 2012). The consolidation strategy brought about a series of stabilization initiatives with the aim of imposing initial military presence to be followed with the restoration of civilian authority structures, public services and development. The programme has been consistently criticized for not following through quickly enough with the construction of effective civilian authorities, leaving consolidation zones militarized and underdeveloped.

Within the framework of the DSP, and with the technological, military and financial support of the US within the parameters of military assistance and Plan Colombia, the military had also executed a plan of targeted assassinations of high-value targets, including members of the Joint General Staff (EMC) and the Secretariat, the FARC-EP-EP's most important decision-making entities. The programme, which sought to decapitate the guerrilla by eliminating its leadership, led to the killings of Negro Acacio (head of the 16th Front and a key member of the illicit drug business) in 2007; Martín Caballero (37th Front), in 2007; Raúl Reyes (member of the Secretariat) in 2008, in an illegal bombing operation into Ecuador; Mono Jojoy (the FARC-EP's then military leader) in 2010; and later, under the subsequent President, Juan Manuel Santos, of Alfonso Cano (the guerrilla's supreme leader) in 2011. While the FARC-EP was able to recover from these assassinations, they arguably had an effect on both the morale of middle and low-ranking combatants, as well as causing a minor destabilization of the group's military structure and its network of contacts and communications capabilities, ultimately making negotiations a more likely option (Brett 2021b).

In specific numeric terms, the impact of Uribe's war was devastating. Between 2003 and 2009, the security forces killed over 12,000 FARC-EP combatants and captured a further 12,000, dramatically reducing the insurgency's numbers. In 2002, the FARC-EP had wielded operational presence in 377 municipalities; by the end of Uribe's second term, approximately 17,000 combatants had demobilized, leaving only 9,000 FARC-EP fighters remaining active with operational presence in only 142 municipalities (Crisis Group 2012). The DSP similarly achieved its objective of extending state presence and, by 2006, the security forces had achieved operational presence in all the country's 1,100 municipalities (Crisis Group 2012). Many of the participants in the victims' delegations had suffered from the patterns of egregious violence perpetrated by the military and paramilitary organizations during this period, testifying to its horrific impact on them, their families and their communities.

As a result of its military success of bringing the strategic withdrawal of the guerrilla and its temporary disengagement from key zones of the country, direct paramilitary activity ended by 2007. The demobilization of the AUC and other paramilitary groups took place between 2003 and 2006 within the framework of the so-called Justice and Peace Law (Law 975) passed in 2005 and its predecessor laws (Law 782 of 2002 and Decree 128 of 2003) (Hristov 2016). The AUC took the decision to demobilize as a result of secret negotiations with President Uribe in El Ralito, in which Uribe agreed to guarantee that former paramilitary combatants would enjoy immunity from prosecution and have the option of assuming a role as formal political actors. However, the law that Uribe promoted (the Law of Penal Alternatives) was deemed partially unconstitutional by the Constitutional Court, forcing Uribe and his supporters in Congress, allegedly linked to paramilitary organizations, to formulate a law that was constitutionally acceptable and adhered to international standards – Law 975. The subsequent DDR process pertaining to the paramilitaries was a resounding failure, a point that will be revisted later on. While approximately 32,000 paramilitaries formally demobilized, only 3,700 individuals applied as beneficiaries of Law 975 and thousands of individuals have since integrated into post-AUC, so-called *neo-paramilitary* organizations (OHCHR 2015),[7] groups which continue to represent the principal challenge to peace and security in Colombia and which have played a key role in weakening the possibilities for sustainable peace in the wake of the Santos–FARC-EP peace process.

---

[7] See Annual Report, Office of the United Nations High Commissioner for Human Rights in Colombia, 23 January 2015, A/HRC/28/3/Add.3.

Concluding remarks

By 2010, despite such devastating effects on the FARC-EP and its support base from Uribe's military strategy and the illegal dirty war waged by the paramilitaries, the guerrilla had not been defeated; rather, it retained a degree of military integrity, arguably remaining a threat as Uribe's second term came to an end. Under these conditions, the presidential elections of 2010 were held, with Uribe designating his former Defence Secretary, Juan Manuel Santos, as his heir. Santos won the election comfortably, leaving Uribe and the economic, military and political elites secure that the country would remain on a war footing once Santos assumed office. However, the assumption to the presidency of Juan Manuel Santos would open a dramatic new chapter in Colombian history, ultimately leading to a political settlement with the FARC-EP and the consolidation of victims as political actors, peacemakers and peacebuilders. It is to this discussion that the following chapter will turn.

3

Getting to Havana: From International Pariah to Innovative Peacemaking

The argument developed in the previous chapter was that a key factor driving the government and the FARC-EP to the negotiating table in Havana had been the execution under former President Uribe of a determinant, brutal and, in part, illegal military onslaught that weakened, although failed to defeat a resilient FARC-EP insurgency, which was able to adapt strategically by returning, relatively quickly, to the use of conventional guerrilla tactics. While the military dynamics of a hurting stalemate tell part of the story, two further factors are critical in explaining the path towards making peace in Havana and, specifically, the inclusion of the victims' delegations within this process: first, the journey of President Santos from hawk to dove and his leadership during the peace process; and, second, building on wider global processes and shifts in peacemaking/peacebuilding norms and practices, the evolving role of Colombian civil society and victims as domestic political actors. This chapter addresses these issues in turn.

Introduction

The détente that settled with the end of the Cold War was accompanied by an ascendant global liberalism and increasing turn towards multilateralism, facilitating, in turn, a less encumbered UN. Building on the provisions of the UN Agenda for Peace,[1] what followed was unprecedented international

---

[1] Beyond the importance of the Agenda for Peace as a founding text of the paradigm, other national, regional and international documents played a role in enshrining the values of the liberal peace and its associated norms, such as the Inter-American Democratic Charter, launched in 2001.

cooperation in renovated peacemaking and peacebuilding operations at the global level, which came to represent the core of the so-called Liberal Peace paradigm. The paradigm, previously referred as 'getting to Denmark' (Fukuyama 2015), was, from its inception, undergirded by the supposition that simultaneous liberalization within the political and economic spheres represented the most effective means through which to transform the conditions driving and the consequences of armed conflict and civil war. Such direct intervention was aimed at re-engineering and rebuilding conflict-affected states and societies. This *Wilsonian Triad* (of peace, democracy and free trade), it was supposed, would prevent the reoccurrence of conflict (Mac Ginty 2012) and lead to self-enforcing peace through the establishment of open political systems (democratic governance, the rule of law and human rights) and neoliberal economics (fiscal discipline, deregulation and macro-economic stability). In practice, the paradigm was premised on four key principles: the insertion of political and economic liberalism into peace settlements; the provision of expert advice during implementation; conditionality attached to economic assistance; and proxy governance (Paris 2000, 2012). As will be discussed later on, the Havana talks were, in part, approached through the framework of the liberal peace paradigm, explaining, to a degree, their successes and failures.

In the 1990s, liberal peacebuilding was employed successfully to bring closure to some of the 20th century's most protracted conflicts, including in Latin America (Guatemala and El Salvador). The paradigm was subsequently consolidated further in the first decade of the 21st century within a series of key UN policy documents. In 2000, the Brahimi Report proposed that peacebuilding reach beyond the mere absence of war to include objectives such as strengthening the rule of law, improved respect for human rights, democratic development, conflict transformation and reconciliation. In 2009, a report from the UN Secretary-General's Office specifically identified five recurring priority areas for international assistance that consolidated the UN's approach to liberal peacebuilding: support to basic safety and security; support to political processes; the provision of basic services; the restoration of core government functions; and economic revitalization. As such, post-accord peacebuilding came to revolve around three intertwined narratives relating directly to the core functions of the state: the provision of *security*, *welfare* and *representation*.

Accordingly, over the following decades, humanitarian intervention, post-accord peacebuilding and conflict mediation became increasingly common components within political and diplomatic initiatives in conflict-affected states (Bell 2006, 2011; Jamison 2011), in turn later coming to influence the Havana peace talks. International actors, including intergovernmental organizations (IGOs) and International non-governmental organization (INGOs), and individual states themselves, have, under such conditions, gradually formulated increasingly complex multilevel and multidimensional strategies, which seek to craft sustainable peace and improve its quality through ambitious stabilization, peacebuilding and statebuilding programmes (Cheng, Goodhand and Meehan 2018), a trend bolstered by the establishment of the UN Peacebuilding Commission and a series of integrated UN missions (Rambsbotham 2000; Lipson 2007). International norms and standards relative to human rights, victims' rights and transitional justice have since been linked ever more closely to peacemaking and peacebuilding norms, standards and objectives (Brett 2022), changes that are fundamental to the decision to establish the victims' delegations, as will be discussed later on.

However, the liberal peace paradigm has faced justifiable critiques. It has been charged as being driven by top-down, internationally led and Western-biased state-centric interventions that impose extraneous, standardized, culturally inappropriate norms, agendas, initiatives and mechanisms on conflicts that are acutely distinct in nature. Critics have accordingly contended that liberal peacebuilding imposes an ideological framework that compels societies emerging from armed conflict to assume liberal and neoliberal norms, values and governance structures, ultimately disciplining them into conformity with the international system (Sriram Lehka 2007; Baker and Obradovic-Wochnik 2016). Reflecting the critiques of the transitional justice paradigm, liberal peacebuilding has similarly been criticized for prioritizing universal, individual, civil and political rights, and excluding economic, social, cultural and collective rights, limiting the capacity of liberal interventions to transform the embedded structural causes of conflict (Sharp 2013), an issue that will be revisited for the case of the Santos–FARC-EP peace talks. Peace settlements levied through the Liberal Peace paradigm have, in fact, frequently failed to deliver on their commitments: over half of peace settlements reached through negotiations collapse within five to ten years, and, when they do hold, habitually lead to poor-quality peace (Joshi and Wallensteen 2018).

Liberal peacebuilding's internationally led, state-centric agenda has also tended to marginalize conflict-affected populations and exclude their experiences, perceptions and interests from the design of peacebuilding mechanisms, critiques similarly levied at the transitional justice paradigm (Brett and Malagon 2013). Since the 1990s, despite incipient progress towards including victims and conflict-affected parties within the design of peacemaking and peacebuilding interventions, the paradigm, it is argued, has failed to guarantee meaningful thresholds for the participation of non-elite actors (Andrieu 2010; Brett 2017b). Furthermore, liberal peace initiatives regularly fall short in guaranteeing the meaningful representation, participation and inclusion of women (Bell and McNicholl 2019). Peace agreements have frequently failed to establish specific institutions to address women and gender, while women are less likely to be incorporated into implementation frameworks (Bell and McNicholl 2019), even despite of the greater likelihood of the incorporation of a gender perspective in peace agreements signed after 2015 (O'Reilly 2016). By incorporating the victims' delegations and a very significant differential focus on gender, Colombia's agreement did, in fact, include an innovative series of mechanisms and approaches. However, at the same time, in failing to include victims' proposals oriented towards addressing the root causes of Colombia's historical armed conflict, the Havana peace process replicated the failings of the Liberal Peace and transitional justice paradigms, which will be discussed subsequently.

Emergent political actors within the new paradigm

A key related development shaping the incorporation of the victims' delegations in the Havana talks pertains to the gradual inclusion of civil society actors in formal peacemaking and peacebuilding since the 1990s, a process closely linked to the critiques of liberal peacebuilding set out earlier. Up until 1994, peace negotiations were ostensibly carried out between armed actors, despite the demands of civil society organizations and victims of violence for participation therein. However, the shifts in norms, practices and thinking precipitated by the end of the Cold War were, in turn, accompanied by broader transformations within the international system, supporting the increasing inclusion of nonstate actors within wider spheres of power and, eventually, within the formal peacemaking and peacebuilding architecture (Vogel 2016).

Directives and reports by both the UN Secretary General – for example, the *Secretary General's Report on Civil Society Participation in Political Processes and Peacebuilding* – and UN mechanisms relative to human rights, victims' rights, peacebuilding and transitional justice have, over time, challenged the historical invisibility of civil society actors. Consequently, there has, in part, been a gradual evolution in jurisprudence, international norms and customary practices towards greater civil society inclusion. The turn towards inclusion, framed as it was within the context of the broader 'local turn' in peacebuilding, was further strengthened and legitimized by the gradual consolidation of track two and track three engagement diplomacy, in particular after 1994 (Paffenholz 2015; Brett 2017b).

In the wake of the launch of the UN Agenda for Peace, then, civil society (including victims') organizations have come to play an increasing role in formal peacemaking and peacebuilding, especially after the Guatemalan peace process, which brought about a paradigmatic shift and set a precedent in this regard. In 1994, 82 civil society organizations, including, specifically, victims' organizations, were mandated with a formal role in the peace negotiations through the so-called Civil Society Assembly (ASC), after having demanded formal participation in the talks and more robust international and national protection measures and mechanisms since the end of the 1980s (Brett 2008). In the same decade, civil society organizations in Colombia were similarly mandated with a formal role in peacemaking during the Caguán peace talks (1999–2002), as detailed in the previous chapter (Haspeslagh 2021), further demonstrating the increasingly visible, albeit secondary role of civil society actors in peacemaking.

Inclusive peacemaking has since gradually emerged as a common practice in contemporary peace support, although, as yet, remains an incomplete and imperfect one. Significantly, for the research presented in this book, incipient civil society inclusion in peacemaking has been reinforced and complemented by the gradual acknowledgement of the prerogative of victim participation within the design and implementation of transitional justice mechanisms, which will be discussed in the next chapter.

This framework is crucial to our understanding of the dynamics shaping the Santos–FARC-EP talks, including with respect to the mandate conferred upon civil society actors and, specifically, the victims' delegations. The argument put forward in this book is that Colombia's victims' delegations represented a *hybrid* mechanism, through which victims were at once incorporated explicitly within formal *peacemaking*, while, in turn, being bound to a victim-centred transitional justice practice. As such, Colombia's victims' delegations emerged out of and came to embody the culmination of both the so-called local turn in peacebuilding and the victims' turn in transitional justice.

The first Santos administration (2010–2014): from hawk to dove?

President Juan Manuel Santos, Uribe's former Minister of Defence, was elected to office in 2010. Santos had been officially delegated by Uribe as his political heir and mandated to give continuity to Uribe's war against the FARC-EP and his policy of Democratic Security. Widely commended by supporters of Uribe and by the political and economic elite as the Minister of Defence under whom Uribe's war of shock and awe had been successfully waged, Santos was elected to office with a resounding majority. During his campaign, Santos had taken advantage of his image as a hawk,[2] crusading publicly on a platform that foregrounded his previous role as Minister of Defence, during which time he had been, in his own words, able to 'tilt the balance of military power in favour of the state' and 'get to [the FARC-EP

---

[2] Public talk, University of Notre Dame, US, September 2022.

commanders] ... for the first time they felt vulnerable and started to think maybe it's better to negotiate peace than to continue war'.[3]

The assumption of President Santos to office took place amid deteriorating security conditions and ongoing military confrontation, exacerbating the generalized hostility to the idea of negotiations with the FARC-EP, particularly given the societal polarization that had escalated under Uribe. Militarily, the Santos government gave continuity to the DSP, executing strategic operations aimed at further pacifying the guerrilla. Blows were rapidly dealt to the FARC-EP – three EMC members, 13 front commanders and five leaders of FARC-EP mobile columns were killed in the first two years of the Santos administration – and the insurgency's overall capacity to carry out large-scale actions was limited. Despite the military's strategy of bringing the war to the FARC-EP's rural strongholds and decapitating its leadership (Crisis Group 2012: 8), however, the FARC-EP continued to prove resilient in adapting; as such, IED incidents, anti-personnel mines and small-scale attacks continued unabated. Furthermore, the guerrilla continued to control important strategic zones of the country (such as Catatumbo, Meta and Cauca), while simultaneously maintaining its capability to carry out small and medium-scale attacks at a local level. Nevertheless, while the FARC-EP continued to avoid battlefield defeat and organizational fragmentation, it was unable to challenge the integrity of the state and redress the armed forces' increasing military superiority. According to Crisis Group (2012: 11), three fundamental factors account for the FARC- EP's resilience: ongoing access to finance; the capacity to replenish its ranks; and a robust 'institutional structure and organizational culture'.

In this context, at the start of the first Santos administration, the term 'armed conflict' continued to remain absent from official discourse, purged as it had been in unashamed Orwellian style during Uribe's two administrations in favour of the discourse of a war on 'narco-terrorists' (Santos Calderón 2016: 18; Haspeslagh 2021). Under such circumstances, and with hostilities ongoing, opposition to prospective peace talks was acute, aggravated by and particularly manifest in the opposition of Uribe and his political party (the Democratic Centre [DC]) to the possibility of peace talks (Santos Calderón 2016: 17). Opposition to talks was further shored up by the (albeit erroneous) consensus in public opinion that the FARC-EP had been cornered and was on the verge of defeat.

In retrospect, at the beginning of the first Santos administration, and as the war was becoming progressively 'degraded',[4] imminent outright victory

---

[3] Interview, President Juan Manuel Santos, University of Notre Dame, Kroc Institute for International Peace Studies, September 2022.

[4] Interview, President Juan Manuel Santos, University of Notre Dame, Kroc Institute for International Peace Studies, September 2022.

appeared an unlikely outcome for either side, making a political settlement increasingly attractive to the parties, at least in private. According to Enrique Santos Calderón, the brother of President Santos appointed by the President as his personal emissary to the guerrilla in 2010 and to kick-start secret talks in 2012, it was the gradual 'understanding by both sides that a total victory was neither possible, nor perhaps desirable' that 'opened the door to the ... cycle of dialogue with the guerrilla' (2016: 19, author's translation). In order for a political settlement to be reached, according to President Santos, it became increasingly urgent to guarantee the 'recognition of the existence of an armed conflict', which was 'a necessary condition for a peace process'. In his words, 'if you don't have an armed conflict officially recognized, you cannot apply transitional justice, you cannot invoke the Rome Statute and you cannot give the victims the importance that we gave them at the negotiating table'.[5] It is also likely that other factors shaped the government's decision to negotiate, in particular the broader sense at the international level that both the government and the guerrilla were increasingly bereft of legitimacy as a result of their military strategies. In this respect, the surveillance scandal in which the DAS – the country's secret service – was embroiled, the country's inability to sign a free trade agreement with the US government due to Colombia's worsening human rights record and the false positives scandal likely played a role in pushing the government towards the negotiating table.[6]

Under such conditions, in his inauguration speech in August 2010, President Santos stated that he held the 'keys to peace' in his pocket and that his government would not be opposed to peace talks under the correct preconditions. The gesture immediately distanced him from his former President and from Uribe's political cadres. Santos' preconditions represented the basic tenets of international humanitarian law: cessation to guerrilla hostilities, cessation of attacks on military, civilian or economic targets, cessation to kidnappings and extortion, and the immediate cessation to the use of landmines or recruitment of minors. From the perspective of the FARC-EP, of course, these conditions were tantamount to surrender or military defeat. Nevertheless, as the subsequent talks gained momentum, the guerrilla would gradually accede to them, as will be discussed later on. According to President Santos, talks, were they to take place, would not be accompanied by a bilateral ceasefire – a condition that ultimately played out after 2012. Negotiations amid the conflict logically brought a series of complex challenges, not least the pressure on the negotiating parties to

---

[5] Interview, President Juan Manuel Santos, University of Notre Dame, Kroc Institute for International Peace Studies, September 2022.

[6] Sophie Haspeslagh, public talk, University of Bristol, UK, October 2023.

remain at the table, and to effectively justify their presence to their own social and political constituencies in the face of battle deaths. Santos' decision was undoubtedly influenced by the experience of the Caguán talks, where, as previously discussed, the ceasefire had allegedly been used by the guerrilla to reorganize militarily.

Within the broader context of President Santos's political gambit – where he practised war but talked peace – game-changing legislation and public policy relative to victims was rapidly approved. In May 2011, after years of struggle by victims, human rights organizations and by some politicians, the Colombian Congress approved the bill promoted by the Santos government, which became the Law for Victims and Land Restitution (Law 1448). The introduction of the law represented a decisive step towards the recognition of Colombia's almost nine million victims and to formalizing the acknowledgement of Colombia's internal armed conflict, a red line drawn during the two Uribe administrations.

The legislation, which formally recognized the existence of the armed conflict, gave legal weight and legitimacy to victims' demands and at once created an innovative institutional framework establishing a set of procedures and mechanisms through which to guarantee victims' rights and to give comprehensive provision for reparations (Garcia-Godos and Knut Andreas 2010). As such, Law 1448 represented a crucial legal opportunity enabling victims of political violence after 1985 to access administrative, symbolic and financial reparations, including land restitution, in compensation for the violence they had suffered. The Victims' Law, as it is commonly known, consolidated legal instruments and opened up new administrative pathways for victims to access, while bringing public legal and political acknowledgement of victims, as well as recognition of the patterns of mass victimization precipitated by the conflict (Rettberg 2015). Arguably, the law opened an incipient path through which victims and their political/legal advocates could confront the historical culture of denial, negation and stigmatization to which victims had been subjected by the armed actors (Brett 2022). Law 1448 and the legal and political processes that it ushered in represented key precedents for the subsequent inclusion of the victims delegations at the Havana talks. Combined with Santos' recognition of the armed conflict, the Law's political and juridical acknowledgement of victims and the push for land restitution for which it gave partial provision, also sent a key message to the FARC-EP that the Santos government was serious about negotiating peace, at least under its prerequisite conditions.

The Victims' Law established key parameters that would subsequently be of significance in Havana. Specifically, it recognized and consolidated the rights of a broad spectrum of victims, including victims of forced displacement (Law 387 of 1997 had only referred to victims of displacement), recruited minors and victims of sexual violence perpetrated within the confines of the armed conflict. The Law also created the first single registry of victims of the conflict, while, in turn, imposing weighty obligations on the government with respect to the provision of humanitarian attention towards victims and their inclusion, effective participation, reparation (both individual and collective), socioeconomic stabilization and empowerment (Rettberg 2015). Moreover, by acknowledging and legitimizing victims, the Law reinforced their role and visibility as political actors in the run-up to the peace process.

However, the political role of Colombia's victims was not tied uniquely to the Victims' Law, but rather had evolved over previous decades. Victims had played a direct role in shaping the transitional justice model adopted during negotiations with the AUC (the Justice and Peace Law, No. 975) (Garcia-Godos and Lid 2010; Rettberg 2015). This capacity to mobilize human rights and victims' rights discourse and appropriate these frameworks to their specific context and struggles represented a key factor in bringing victims to the negotiating table in Havana, as will be discussed in due course.

While waging war against the FARC-EP, President Santos played a decisive role both in public – through his support for Law 1448 – and behind closed doors in pushing forward the search for peace by political means, a gambit that was a potentially risky one. Santos has been an opportunistic and ambitious politician who, over the course of his political career, had not been timid in making clear his aspiration to go down in history as the President who brought peace to Colombia. Despite having played a determinant role as Minister of Defence during Uribe's military onslaught, on assuming office, President Santos quickly consolidated his commitment to a political settlement. In this regard, he began to construct an image of himself as a peacemaker, as a 'dove' rather than a 'hawk', as he has characterized it, stating in 2012 that he would be happy to leave behind a legacy as the politician who 'betrayed his own class' to bring peace (Santos Calderón 2021). The individual dimension – embodied in a charismatic president with a clear commitment to and political will for peace under his own terms – compounded the wider political opportunity brought by the conditions of a degrading war and hurting stalemate.

While waging his continued war on the guerrilla, President Santos simultaneously began to explore options for a political settlement. In 2010, during secret meetings, the government and the FARC-EP reached agreement over which countries would be the guarantors of a potential peace process (Cuba and Norway), as well as a series of logistical issues, including the support of the International Committee of the Red Cross (ICRC). Between August and September 2010, the parties secretly expressed their disposition to negotiate without addressing the contentious issue of who had been victorious and who had been vanquished (Santos Calderón 2016: 22). At the beginning of 2011, the first secret meetings took place between the Colombian government and the FARC-EP on the Venezuelan border, with the direct collaboration and support of the late President Hugo Chavez, who was considered an ally by the guerrilla. It is likely, although not confirmed, that President Chavez assumed a role in creating and employing back channels with the FARC-EP, facilitating discussion of the logistics of the secret meetings. Eventually, the parties agreed to hold their first formal meeting in Havana, Cuba – which would subsequently become the permanent location for the peace talks. Favoured by the government, and supported by the guerrilla given the country's ideological and historical trajectory, the decision to hold talks in Cuba represented a crucial step towards securing the possibility of a political settlement. The island afforded security, confidentiality, isolation and a host that was serious, politically agile and partially sympathetic to and trusted by the FARC-EP (Santos Calderón 2016: 22).

A final piece of the puzzle was to get Colombia's neighbours on board. In this regard, President Santos' regional foreign policy was central to the onset and eventual success of the peace talks, illustrating his argument that peace could only be made 'when one's neighbours are onside'.[7] On assuming office, he quickly moved to re-establish relations with the political administrations of Venezuela and Ecuador. Relations with both countries had been in tatters since the Uribe administrations. Uribe and Venezuela's President Hugo Chavez had broken off diplomatic relations with each other on different occasions, antagonism driven by their ideological, political and personal disputes. Moreover, in 2008, under Uribe, the Colombian Air Force had illegally bombed a guerrilla encampment in Ecuador and killed, among others, Raul Reyes, the guerrilla's second in command and a member of the FARC-EP's secretariat. The attack destroyed diplomatic relations with Ecuador. Consequently, the game-changing shift in relations between both countries resulting from President Santos' holding out an olive branch to Hugo Chavez and Ecuadorian President Rafael Correa quickly brought mutually respectful and supportive diplomatic relations, shifts that were decisive in convincing the guerrilla of Santos' political will. Both Chavez and Correa subsequently became key supporters of the talks, with Venezuela appointed as an accompanier country to the Havana talks, while Ecuador would later become central to the subsequent peace talks with the ELN.

The first formal meeting between the delegations took place in February 2012. Six months of confidential meetings and confidence-building exercises followed, until President Santos made public the negotiations at the end of August. The objective of the talks from the government's perspective, and the foundational premise of the negotiations, was to end the conflict

---

[7] Interview, President Juan Manuel Santos, University of Notre Dame, Kroc Institute for International Peace Studies, September 2022.

rather than engage in debates regarding its causes and consequences, as had been the case in the Caguán (Haspeslagh 2021). Beyond the absence of a bilateral ceasefire, three further caveats were introduced by President Santos with the aim of anticipating opposition to the talks from powerful domestic actors: first, not to negotiate the predominant economic and political model of the Colombian state, a premise reflecting core liberal peacebuilding principles; second, not to negotiate the status of the Armed Forces (these first two caveats have ultimately weakened the capacity of the peace accords to usher in a stable post-accord settlement, as will be discussed later on); and, third, that *nothing was agreed upon until everything was agreed upon*.

Winning support for the peace process from a divided private sector, particularly given the vested interests of the economic elite in the war and, in many cases, their links to paramilitary organizations, represented an acute challenge for President Santos and his government. In its efforts to incentivize private sector support for the peace process, the government capitalized on Santos' own status as a member of the oligarchy, making explicit that the prevailing economic model was not open to negotiation. Hailing from one of the country's oldest and most established families, Santos was a strategic thinker with a distinguished career as a politician, diplomat and journalist, in whom much of the modernizing economic elite had come to trust. His role as Minister of Defence under Uribe had, of course, assured this status from the perspective of the economic and political elite. Under such conditions, Santos made clear that his search for peace was also aimed at pacifying the country in order to gain access to and guarantee national and international exploitation of the natural resources that were at the centre of his so-called 'locomotive of the economy'.

Fundamentally, many of Colombia's natural resource reserves have been located in remote zones, historically neglected by the state and in many cases under guerrilla control for decades. As such, a political solution to the armed conflict, at least from the perspective of those sectors of the economic elite that would come to support the talks, was ultimately driven by a vision of neoliberal economic modernization and, without doubt, of profit/profiteering. Reports from leading think tanks in Colombia, such as the Foundation Ideas for Peace, corroborated by international organizations, including the World Bank, stressed how Colombia's economy would likely increase as much as 3 per cent in GDP if the conflict were to be drawn to a close.[8] Accordingly, the Santos government made a strategic

---

[8] President Santos and his High Commissioner for Peace, Sergio Jaramillo, have indicated how peace could increase the country's growth rate and GDP by 3 per cent. Francisco Rodríguez, an economist from the Bank of America, has supported these assertions, although he has proposed that peace could boost growth only by as little as 0.3 per cent.

calculation that successfully concluded negotiations would likely offer the quickest path to generate access to these areas and thus to fuel an effective 'Democratic Prosperity', the slogan of his incumbent government. Sectors of the economic elite thus gradually got behind the peace talks, coming to the realization that peace might ultimately be more lucrative than conflict.

At the same time, in a tactically astute move, President Santos appointed Ambassador Luis Carlos Villegas as one of the negotiators in the government's initial team. Villegas had held positions including High Commissioner for the Economy, Ambassador to France, Deputy Secretary for International Affairs and, significantly, President of National Business Association of Colombia (ANDI). Villegas' appointment gave the business sector a seat at the negotiating table and direct representation in Havana. Such direct representation gave further credence to Santos' statement that the process would not negatively affect elite economic interests and that the economic model was not up for negotiation. In this respect, the peace process early on came to be framed within the conventional liberal peace paradigm, as discussed at the beginning of this chapter, given that talks would not address the fundamental economic causes of the conflict or threaten Colombia's macro-economic neoliberal model.

As a consequence of the government's lobbying, heavyweight industrial and commercial sectors gradually supported the peace process, recognizing the potential economic benefit that peace was likely to bring. In fact, the ANDI was regularly represented at and levied input into the peace talks in Havana, while closely advising the government, including around issues of reintegration and the economic benefits for former FARC-EP combatants.

However, the agricultural sector – in particular the cattle-ranching elite – was and remains a key actor opposing the peace process, given the enormous resources it continues to possess through land ownership and illegal expropriation and its links to the paramilitary project. Land distribution in Colombia remains violently unequal; in fact, it is among the most unequal in the world: 52 per cent of farms are owned by 1.15 per cent of landowners. Furthermore, only 22 per cent of potential arable land is cultivated and approximately 6.5 million hectares of land was illegally expropriated, abandoned or forcibly changed hands between 1985 and 2008 in the context of the conflict, in particular by paramilitary actions (Brett 2022).

The Colombian Federation of Cattle Ranchers (Fedegán), led by José Félix Lafaurie during the Santos administrations, vehemently opposed any political deal with the guerrilla, stating that the government was 'handing over the countryside to the guerrilla'.[9] However, Fedegán's arguments

---

[9] See http://www.semana.com/nacion/articulo/la-pelea-entre-fedegan-el-gobierno/456761-3

were unfounded – despite provisions supporting agrarian development, the peace accords made no radical provision for land reform, an issue that was at extreme odds with the demands made by many participants in the victims' delegations, as will be discussed later on. The group, driven by both political/ideological and economic interests, closely allied itself to Uribe and his political followers. As discussed in Chapter 2, historically cattle ranchers have been intimately linked to the AUC, given that the former paid large sums of money to the paramilitaries to 'protect' their lands. The sector continued to oppose the peace deal after its eventual signing in 2016, and blocked the implementation of the agreement provisions. Moreover, demobilized and remobilized paramilitaries have adopted a role as violent spoilers in the aftermath of the peace process and continue to be linked to elite political and economic actors.

Santos was unable to bring former President Uribe and his political cadres onside, and nor was he able to prevent their ascendance as a powerful oppositional force to the Havana talks. In fact, Santos became quickly positioned as a traitor to Uribe, nicknamed a *Castrochavista*, given his growing relationship with President Chavez in Venezuela. With the aim of anticipating further potential spoiling actions from other sectors, particularly the military, the government employed two strategies. First, Santos made clear that the position, role and doctrine of the security forces would not be discussed during the talks. Santos remained true to his word: no provisions pertaining to security sector reform were incorporated into the Final Agreement and, in fact, Colombia's security forces retain a doctrine that closely resembles the NSD. Colombia's armed forces continue to follow a counterinsurgent doctrine – as was evident in the response by the security forces to widespread social and political mobilizations in 2019 and 2021 during the COVID-19 pandemic. This decision went against the demands tabled by numerous participants in the victims' delegations to revise military doctrine and limited victims' rights to nonrecurrence, as will be discussed in detail in Chapter 7.

Second, beyond experienced negotiators such as Humberto de la Calle, the government's negotiating team included high-level negotiators from the security forces, whose long-term presence in Havana played a role in generating the trust of the security forces in and their aperture towards the peace talks. For example, General Oscar Naranjo, the former director of the National Police, who had seen combat and participated in operations against drug trafficking organizations, and General Jorge Enrique Mora, a former head of the Armed Forces and a heavyweight figure in the Colombian military who was well respected across ranks, were crucial to the government's negotiating team. Both figures were key in supporting the talks – at least while they remained ongoing – and in placating potential military opposition to them. They also embodied the commitment of the security forces to the talks, particularly at sensitive moments, such as the albeit brief kidnapping of General Ruben Dario Alzate by the FARC-EP in November 2014.

The path to Havana: the consolidation of victims and civil society

In the context of hurting stalemate and of an increasingly degraded war, the assumption of President Santos to office represented a critical enabling factor facilitating the commencement of the Havana talks. Building on the political and juridical opportunities precipitated by the Santos presidency, a second factor forged what became the irreversible path towards the inclusion of the victims' delegations in the Havana talks. Since the 1960s, the evolving visibility of a wide spectrum of Colombian civil society organizations and, during the 1990s, the consolidation of civil society actors and, specifically, of victims as political actors and peacebuilders made wider participation in Havana inevitable (Rettberg 2015; Malagón Diaz 2019).

Initially, human rights and victims' organizations formed across Colombia at the local, subnational and national levels during the mid-1960s in response to historical exclusion and the diverse patterns of political violence that were beginning to characterize the incipient armed conflict. During the first two decades of the Cold War, trade unionists', workers', peasants', women's, indigenous and Afro-Colombian organizations emerged, articulating human rights platforms that prioritized engagement with and redress of ongoing and past atrocities (Riano Alcala and Uribe 2016; Malagón Diaz 2019), as well as broader platforms linked to workers' rights, women's rights, land, and cultural and political identity, as had been the case, for example, in Guatemala (Santana 1989; Archila Neira 2003; Brett and Santamaria 2010). In the midst of the conflict, as well as protesting against state repression, organizations carried out strikes, land occupations and seizures, student protests and civic strikes for the right to access public services, education, health and housing (Malagón Diaz 2019), patterns of civil resistance similar to those in Argentina and Chile.

Diverse organizations built a robust national presence, including the Popular Feminine Organization (OFP) (1972), the Committee for Solidarity with Political Prisoners (CSPP) (1973), the Permanent Committee for the Defense of Human Rights (CPDH) (1980), the 'José Alvear Restrepo' Collective Bar Association (CCAJAR) (1980), the National Trade Union School (ENS) (1982) and the Association of Relatives of the Detained-Disappeared of Colombia (ASFADDES) (1982). As Malagón-Diaz (2019: 37) has eloquently argued, after the 1970s, it was these movements themselves that became 'the first organized victims of the armed conflict'. In fact, numerous participants in the victims' delegations had themselves been involved in these organizations and explicitly attested to the violence that they had suffered as a consequence of their political mobilization.

Echoing processes elsewhere in Latin America (Brett 2008), since the 1980s, the emergence of human rights movements in response to escalating patterns of violence in Colombia catapulted these organizations and their members on to the national agenda and into the international arena, as their demands for adherence to international human rights standards and humanitarian law and for concomitant domestic reforms made them a strategic target of the violence perpetrated by state and illegal armed groups (Malagón Diaz 2019). Since the 1980s, further organizations have emerged, many of which gradually crafted platforms and collective identities as victims, developing increasingly influential platforms that prioritized redress of ongoing and past atrocities, as well as demands linked specifically to their condition of victimhood (Rettberg 2015; Malagon Diaz 2019).

A watershed moment came in the early 1990s, with the formalization of Colombia's 1991 Constitution. The Constitution paved the way for the establishment of a series of institutions central to human rights protection, democratization and the rule of law, which would become fundamental instruments for civil society and victims' organizations, such as the Constitutional Court, the Public Prosecutor's Office, the Superior Council of the Judiciary, the Procurator's Office and the Human Rights Ombudsman's Office. The Constitutional Court has, in part, remained an efficient bulwark against state arbitrariness. It has also, for the most part, effectively protected fundamental human rights and avoided radical levels of politicization, as has, albeit to a lesser degree, the Human Rights Ombudsman's Office. In fact, the Constitutional Court came to play a key role in the Santos–FARC-EP peace process as an important arbiter with respect to critical legal decisions, such as the Legislative Act, finally approving it in December 2016. However, the Procurator's Office, while initially a stable institution, became deeply politicized under President Uribe, as did many other state institutions. Uribe's Procurator General, Alejandro Ordonez, systematically suspended public officials from office he believed to hold ties with the armed left, publicly attacked LGBTI+ and women's rights, and restricted fundamental rights of other marginal groups, making a mockery of the institution (Brett 2017c).

Beyond establishing core institutions and instruments, the 1991 Constitution consolidated important legal weapons for the struggle for human rights, such as the injunction (*tutela*), a legal mechanism through which to guarantee fundamental and human rights protection by limiting the arbitrary reach of the state. Moreover, the Constitution established the conceptual parameters for the formulation of public policy and legislation oriented towards the incorporation of inclusiveness and equity for ethnic groups (Article 7), as guiding principles. Of significance here was the rapid adoption of a series of laws and public policies related directly to ethnic inclusion, such as the adoption in 1993 of Law 70 Relating to Afro-Colombian Populations and Land (Brett 2017c). With constitutional underpinning, and shored up by widespread social mobilizations, the law came to represent the normative framework through which Afro-Colombian populations were able to claim their collective rights, including to communal lands, community development and political participation. Despite significant limitations (Bries Silva 2024), Law 70 has since become a crucial mechanism and central point of reference for Afro-Colombian struggles, in particular in relation to the struggle for land and inclusion, and its provisions were a point of reference for several Afro-Colombian victims that participated in the Havana talks, as will be discussed later on.

Within the context of the National Constituent Assembly, the National Women's Network was formed in 1991, bringing together 63 women's organizations that had developed across the country (Krystalli 2021), including in rural areas, since the late 1980s and early 1990s (Brett 2017c). The Constitution had significantly represented the first instrument through which gender inclusiveness as a guiding principle was widely established, through a series of mutually reinforcing articles (Articles 13, 40, 42 and 53), formally recognizing many of the demands articulated by women's organizations. In the years following the Constitution, a portfolio of laws and public policies were similarly formulated with the objective of consecrating and guaranteeing women's rights, and of promoting gender inclusion, at least on paper. Legislation was approved, including Law 82 (1993) relating to women as heads of family, Law 248 (1995) establishing legal and administrative guarantees to repair damage in the case of violence and discrimination against women, Law 294 (1996) penalizing domestic violence, Law 581 which established a quota system for women in relation to political participation and participation in public office. With respect to government policy, in 1992, the Integral Policy for Women was launched and reinforced by Sectoral Policy for Rural Women (1993), the Policy for Equity and Women's Equity (1994) and the Plan for Equality of Opportunity for Women (1999). A decade later, under President Santos, the Public Policy for Gender Equity for Women and the Integral Plan to Guarantee Women a Life Free of Violence were also launched (Brett 2017c). In this context, feminist activists and women's organizations gradually began to further consolidate the space their mobilizations had won at the national political level, emerging as important political actors in the decades before the Santos–FARC-EP talks. Significantly, women's organizations would come to play an influential role in the peace talks, manifest through the so-called Sub-commission on Gender, as they shaped the content of the Victims' Agreement (Point Five) to include significant provision to victims of sexual and gender-based violence, as will be discussed subsequently.

The new Constitution also embedded indigenous and Afro-Colombian rights in the institutional mechanisms of the state through a broad series of unprecedented initiatives. The Special Circumscription for Indigenous Peoples, for example, guaranteed two seats in the Senate for indigenous leaders with the aim of ensuring indigenous political participation. In the wake of the 1991 Constitution, in 1996, the National Commission for Indigenous Territories was established through Decree 1396, followed by the Direction for Ethnic Affairs, which evolved into the Direction for Indigenous Affairs, Roma and Minorities and the Direction for Black Communities, Afro-Colombians, Raizales and Palenqueras. These institutions have consolidated the formal representation of indigenous and Afro-Colombian populations within the Colombian state and strengthened the administrative pathway open to national-level mobilizations since the 1990s.

In the early 1990s, political and societal processes in Latin America were shaped by the progressive visibility of indigenous, Afro and peasant movements precipitated by the 500 Years of Resistance Campaign (Brett 2008). It was in this context that, in 1991, the Colombian state ratified both its new Constitution and Convention 169 concerning Indigenous and Tribal Peoples in Independent Countries of the International Labour Organization. A binding framework to guarantee the protection of indigenous peoples' fundamental rights, its provisions were subsequently translated into national law through Law 21 in 1991. Shortly afterwards, in 1993, the state approved legislation relative to the fundamental rights of indigenous peoples, including Decree 1088 (1993), pertaining to the regulation of traditional indigenous authorities as entities of political participation, Law 160 (1994) relative to indigenous territorial organization (land reservations) and Law 115 (1994) and Decree 2249, governing indigenous and Afro-Colombian education respectively (Huneeus and Rueda-Saiz 2021). These mechanisms – in play now for three decades – legitimated the demands of indigenous and Afro-Colombian organizations for inclusion, situating them increasingly on the national stage as relevant political actors, a process that only served to heighten the requisite importance of their inclusion in the Havana talks. However, in spite of core importance of indigenous and Afro-Colombian rights, the ethnic chapter of the peace accords was filed very late on in the peace process and was not comprehensive.

The political and juridical opportunities ushered in during the 1990s represented a watershed moment in the consolidation of the visibility, role and political consequence of human rights, women's, peasants', indigenous and Afro-Colombian organizations. Moreover, the decade brought with it the increasing visibility of victims as political actors and their representation within collective movements at the national level, either through organizations providing legal support for victims of the armed conflict – such as the Corporation for the Defense and Promotion of Human Rights

(REINICIAR) (1992) – or directly through organizations established by victims of the armed conflict seeking to address their needs, demands and experiences (Malagón Diaz 2019).

During the 1980s and 1990s, a number of key organizations, such as the Colombian Commission of Jurists (1988), the CPDH and the CCAJAR had aimed to provide juridical support to victims of all armed actors, although, given the dimensions and patterns of the violence itself, this often played out with a certain emphasis on victims of state crime. In such a context, as Malagón Diaz has persuasively argued, victims of guerrilla violence gradually became more organized (Malagón Diaz 2019). In an increasingly polarized context, human rights and victims' organizations established during the 1990s and in the early 2000s began, in part, to reflect the wider macro-cleavages of the armed conflict. Victims of insurgent groups established the Free Country Foundation (1992), the Colombian Association of Relatives of Public Force Members Retained and Released by Guerrilla Groups (ASFAMIPAZ) (1999) – an organization of relatives of soldiers kidnapped by the FARC-EP – and subsequently the Visible Victims Foundation (2001). Later, the National Movement of Victims of State Crimes (MOVICE) was established in 2005 (Malagón Diaz 2019). Despite their differences, these organizations came to play a collective role in the selection of the 60 members of the victims' delegations in 2014, as will be discussed in the next chapter. At the same time, members of these organizations also participated at an individual level in the Havana talks, as will be discussed later on.

Civil society and victims' organizations thus gradually asserted themselves as robust political actors (Rettberg 2015). From the perspective of Rettberg (2015: 113–115), a key turning point was 2003, after which victims became central interlocutors within the political sphere in Colombia, particularly as regards their contributions to debates over transitional justice models. In a context in which shifting normative parameters at the international level relative to peacemaking and peacebuilding further enabled and legitimized victims' struggles and, in turn, transformed expectations of the role victims might assume in peacemaking and peacebuilding, Colombian victims' organizations effectively took advantage of the domestic political opportunities afforded to them. In such a context, of key significance were 'the convergence of global transitional justice trends, the universalizing of human rights discourses and the pressure on nation states from supranational institutions such as the Inter-American Court of Human Rights and the International Criminal Court' (Riano Alcala and Uribe 2016: 10).

In such a context, at the beginning of the 2000s, victims' organizations became increasingly professionalized and effectual in lobbying the state and international actors for political and legal recognition. Within a decade, in fact, 7 per cent of victims had become organized in more than 3,000 organizations (Rettberg 2015: 115). From 2003, the negotiation process with the AUC precipitated the further emergence of victims as political actors and, relatedly, their direct engagement in the development of a transitional justice model built on victims' demands for the right to justice, truth, reparation and nonrecurrence in relation to accountability for paramilitary perpetrators. In this way, victims became increasingly central interlocutors in the debates over state policy and legislation and transitional justice models, including through their advocacy for the Ley de Alternatividad Penal project of 2003, which became the Justice and Peace Law in 2005. Victims' organizations also played a crucial role shaping and sustaining the National Commission for Reparations and Reconciliation, the first state agency dedicated specifically to victims (Rettberg 2015: 113–116).

Gradually, and in particular in the wake of the 2011 Victims' Law, the professionalization of victims' organizations led to the articulation of increasingly sophisticated legal strategies, political platforms and strategic repertoires. Rettberg (2015: 112) argues that the representative nature of victims' organizations and the reach of debates on victimization have remained partially limited to a 'small group of experts'. Nevertheless, overall, victims' organizations built on and subsequently broadened fundamental human rights discourse and practice, taking advantage of processes at both the national and international levels to push for the development of a complex transitional justice framework. As such, by the end of the first decade of the 21st century, the stage was set for their inclusion in the Havana talks.

Concluding remarks

This chapter has traced Colombia's path from international pariah under President Uribe to the onset of the Santos–FARC-EP peace negotiations in Havana. It has been argued that while the military dynamics of a hurting stalemate explains part of the story, two further factors played a critical role in consolidating the path towards making peace in Havana. Moreover, these factors provide insights for our understanding of how and why the victims' delegations took part in the Havana talks. In this regard, the chapter first plotted the specific leadership role assumed by Juan Manuel Santos in the wake of his inauguration as President in 2010.

The chapter subsequently traced the emergence of and role played by civil society and, in particular, of victims' organizations, in Colombia over recent decades. Building on and connecting with broader global processes and shifts in peacemaking, peacebuilding and transitional justice norms and practices, victims gradually carved out a fundamental role as domestic political actors. Explicitly, in the wake of their role in shaping Law 975 in the mid-2000s, victims' organizations assumed a similar role in the development of the Law for Victims and Land Restitution (Law 1448) during the second Uribe and first Santos administrations. Their role in supporting the crafting of Law 1448 was perhaps the final piece of the puzzle that ensured the acknowledgement of victims as political actors with a fundamental capacity to shape the national agenda. By lobbying Congress, pressuring both the Uribe and Santos administrations and working with international organizations to amplify their advocacy platforms, victims' and human rights organizations maximized their political capital and visibility. By 2014, then, the significant historical experience and success that victims' organizations had wielded in mobilizing human rights discourse, appropriating these frameworks to their specific context and struggles, and shaping national policy and legislation gradually paved the way to their incorporation in the Havana talks. In a context marked by wider political and juridical opportunities, it was the assumption of victims' organizations as political actors that ultimately guaranteed them a place at the negotiating table in Havana. In the following chapter, the discussion will turn specifically to the role that Colombia's victims' delegations played in the Havana talks and, therein, the extent to which victims were placed at the centre of the process, as the negotiating parties themselves claimed.

4

The Havana Talks: A Victim-Centred Peace?

The previous chapter set out the historical context framing Colombia's five-decade-long armed conflict and the factors pushing the Santos government and the FARC-EP guerrilla towards Havana. This chapter now turns to the analysis of the core theme of this book, namely the role that Colombia's victims' delegations played in the Havana peace process. First, it details the antecedents to direct victim participation in the Santos–FARC-EP negotiations – specifically, the victims' forums carried out in 2014 – before discussing the rationale for victim inclusion in the Havana talks, in both cases by drawing on the perspectives of both those who participated in and those who organized Colombia's victim-centred initiatives. The empirical discussion is situated in a broader framework which contends that the Havana talks and the nature of victim inclusion therein demonstrate the evolving trajectory of both the liberal peacebuilding and transitional justice paradigms. How transitional justice was addressed during the Havana talks illustrates the manner in which the foundational tenets and objectives of the paradigm have shifted over time, becoming embedded gradually within liberal peacemaking and peacebuilding, and, subsequently, in recent years, towards the conferral upon victims and survivors of a central role as protagonists driving the paradigm towards victim-centredness.

The international context: transitional justice and peacemaking

Since the 1990s, the application of transitional justice interventions has progressively shifted away from its original terrain of authoritarian regimes and post-authoritarian societies (Gonzalez-Ocantos 2020) towards the provision of a notional *postconflict* justice during and in the wake of war to peace transitions (Bell 2009). Since the launch of the UN Agenda for Peace in 1992, transitional justice has become increasingly embedded in the dominant global peacemaking and peacebuilding architecture and now sits alongside DDR, security sector reform (SSR), the rule of law, human rights, democratization and economic liberalization as part of the 'checklist' of liberal peacemaking and peacebuilding interventions (Leebaw 2008; Andrieu 2010; Sharp 2013), which are intrinsic in that regard to post-accord state and nation-building (Sriram Lehka 2007; Lambourne 2009). Accordingly, the framework of rights that had undergirded transitional justice interventions since the 1980s – victims' rights to truth, justice, reparation and nonrecurrence – has itself become gradually pivotal to mainstream peacemaking and peacebuilding interventions (Robins 2017: 56). In turn, the rights framework upon which the liberal peace paradigm was itself initially forged – fundamental human rights and individual civil and political rights – has been extended, as victims' rights frameworks have begun explicitly to shape peacemaking and peacebuilding thinking and practice.

Over recent decades, then, the principle of guaranteeing accountability for human rights violations has become central to liberal peacemaking and peacebuilding (Bell 2009, 2017). Such thinking has been fuelled by the growing assumption that durable peace – in the shape of a robust human rights culture and the rule of law, effective state institutions, a functioning civil society and the overcoming of intergroup antagonism – rests, among other factors, upon addressing the past (Baker and Obradovic-Wochnik 2016; Andrieu 2010). In short, transitional justice initiatives and the human rights frameworks that undergird them are increasingly recognized as crucial to the achievement of self-sustaining peace, as states and societies seek simultaneously to 'account for the past and satisfy international legal standards' (Bell 2009: 16). Nevertheless, in spite of this trend, and of guidance published in 2006 by the UN Department of Peacekeeping Operations encouraging closer links between DDR and transitional justice (Sharp 2013), there has been limited coordination between the pillars of liberal peacebuilding and transitional justice (de Greiff and Duthie 2009). Engagement by negotiating parties with transitional justice has tended to be ad hoc and usually in response to logistical and political problems emerging out of the respective negotiation process itself (Bell 2009; Sharp 2013). However, the case of Colombia suggests certain nuances to this argument, as will be discussed later on (Jamar and Bell 2018).

The consolidation of the connections between transitional justice and liberal peacebuilding has been accompanied by a shift in expectations and, gradually, in legal norms relative to the role accountability for perpetrators plays in peacemaking and peacebuilding (Leebaw 2008; Aggestam and Björkdahl 2013). In the aftermath of episodes of atrocity during the final decade of the 20th century, consensus grew concerning the *requirement* of (rather than the *option for*) accountability as the legitimate (and gradually the mandated) international and domestic response to the commission of atrocious violence (Kerr 2007). Central to this development was the symbiotic relationship between norm promotion and institutional innovation, which drove the consensus that broad/blanket amnesties for egregious human rights violations and violations of humanitarian law were inadmissible, although a degree of enabling amnesty was acceptable (Bell 2011).

By the time of the adoption of the International Criminal Court in 1999, UN policy had prohibited the endorsement of amnesty for genocide, war crimes and crimes against humanity, a position, in turn, that hardened in 2004, when the UN added gross violations of human rights to those crimes that could not be amnestied (Mallinder 2019). Not only was blanket amnesty for such crimes no longer an eligible option, then, but also accountability (through criminal prosecutions) for perpetrators of serious crimes became increasingly mandatory (Mallinder 2019). As will be discussed later on, such principles were of core significance to the decision to include transitional justice matters in the Havana peace agenda, determining discussions over what to do with perpetrators and victims of human rights violations and, ultimately, the configuration of the accountability mechanisms eventually agreed upon.

Since the early 2000s, the transitional justice paradigm has become progressively consolidated as core to the frameworks of 'human rights', 'conflict resolution' and 'international intervention' (Bell 2009). In fact, during the first decade of the 2000s, it was determined by 'a new wave of normativization and institutionalization ... emanating from diverse standard-setting initiatives and processes' (Bell 2017: 368). In other words, the paradigm has been gradually mainstreamed and 'normalized' as a postconflict response to political violence (Teitel 2003), linked to broader political settlements (Bell 2018). Under such circumstances, and in particular after the establishment of the ICC in 1999 (Sharp 2013), the expectation that peace and justice were integral to one another – in short, were mutually reinforcing – became increasingly edified. However, significant debate has continued over how to balance: (i) the obligation of state actors to guarantee victims' rights; (ii) the expectation that perpetrators face criminal prosecution; and (iii) the need to bring about a sustainable peace settlement. As will be seen, the Colombia experience, to which the chapter now turns, speaks directly to these dilemmas.

The Havana process: antecedents to the victims' delegations

As discussed in the previous chapter, in the context of a hurting stalemate and an increasingly degraded war, the election of President Santos to office in 2010 represented a critical enabling factor in the commencement of the Havana talks that would formally begin two years later. During

President Santos' first mandate, relatively rapid progress was made in the peace negotiations in Cuba. By 2014, three out of five agreements had, in fact, been signed: (i) *Towards a New Colombian Countryside: Comprehensive Rural Reform* (26 May 2013); (ii) *Political Participation: Democratic Openness to Building Peace* (6 November 2013); and (iii) *A Solution to the Illicit Drug Problem* (16 May 2014). However, despite the unprecedented progress that these agreements demonstrated, the peace process was briefly disrupted by the 2014 electoral cycle. The albeit temporary destabilization of the Havana talks represented a development of particular concern, given that the parties still faced the challenge of negotiating the remaining controversial topics of transitional justice/victims and the termination of the conflict, with or without Juan Manuel Santos in the presidency.

In 2014, the election of a new president hostile to the talks was, in fact, a very real prospect. Debate over the legitimacy and continuity of the peace talks was at the centre of the first round of presidential elections that took place in May 2014, a contest fought principally between President Santos and Oscar Zuluaga, former President Uribe's designated candidate. Santos and Zuluaga waged close-run confrontational campaigns, their platforms at loggerheads over whether to negotiate with the guerrilla and, if so, under what conditions, particularly given Uribe's opposition to the peace talks and his demands that the guerrilla serve maximum prison time for the abuses they had perpetrated.

Amid the political uncertainty and escalating rhetoric between those in favour and those against the Havana talks, on 7 June 2014, a week before the second round of voting took place, the negotiating parties issued a joint press communiqué, the *Declaration of Principles for Discussion Agenda Item 5: Victims*. The decision represented a game-changing moment in the peace talks, a before and after for the process. Building on the acknowledgement of human rights protection and victims' rights initially consecrated in the 2012 General Agreement, and reflecting the global normative shift towards the requirement for accountability mechanisms to be incorporated within peace settlements, the communiqué established ten principles through which the discussion of victims and accountability would be framed. Specifically, the declaration placed the recognition and guarantee of the rights of victims as a central pillar of the peace talks. Based on international standards for victims' rights, the Declaration sought specifically to ensure:

1. recognition of victims;
2. perpetrators' recognition of responsibility;
3. the satisfaction of victims' rights;
4. victims' participation;
5. the principle of truth;
6. reparations for victims;

7. guarantees of protection and security;
8. guarantees of nonrecurrence;
9. the principle of reconciliation;
10. a human rights-based approach.

In the immediate wake of the publication of the Joint Declaration, wider political debate was shaped not only by the imminent second round of presidential elections, but also by increasing expectations regarding the possibility of victim participation in Havana. Voting took place on 15 June. As the two highest-polling candidates in the first round, Santos and Zuluaga had gone through to the final round, a fractious affair out of which President Santos was eventually re-elected to the presidency with 50.95 per cent of the vote. Assuming office for a final four-year term allowed President Santos to give continuity to the peace talks and, despite the narrow margin between the candidates, afforded him the legitimacy to push on with the negotiations. However, the negligible majority upon which Santos had been elected simultaneously evidenced the sheer cleavage in Colombia with respect to the ongoing peace talks. Such deep division would continue to shape the wider discussions framing the legitimacy of the peace talks and, eventually, play out decisively during the 2016 plebiscite over the peace accord.

By the middle of 2014, with the peace talks still on track, the gradual path towards the participation of the victims' delegations at the peace talks had become irreversible. Such irreversibility was due, among other factors, to the growing pressure exerted by Colombia's diverse victims' movements, now consolidated as national political actors. As was argued in the previous chapter, civil society actors in general and victims' movements in particular had, since the 1990s, taken increasing advantage of global shifts in peacemaking and transitional justice norms and practices, and of the international pressure that accompanied such developments. In so doing, they had incorporated relevant norms and platforms into their progressively effective advocacy strategies. The victims' delegations, as such, would represent the culmination of these developments and Colombia's victim-centred experience in peacemaking.

Beyond establishing the ten core principles framing the theme of victims within the Victims' Agreement (Point Five), the Joint Declaration designated a series of mechanisms that would structure the discussions concerning victims and transitional justice.

First, the joint statement established the Historical Commission of the Conflict and its Victims, constituted by 11 national experts and one international expert. The Commission was not envisioned as a formal truth commission – this would come later – but, rather, sought to instigate discussion concerning the historical causes and the impact of the conflict from diverse perspectives. In this sense, the commission aimed to generate debate concerning the 'meta-causes' of the conflict, as Fisas (2004) has termed it. Given the distinct positions – in terms of political ideology and historical analysis – that the 12 experts represented, the commission at once demonstrated both the diverse perspectives regarding the trajectory of the armed conflict and the lack of agreement on what the meta-causes and consequences of the violent conflict had been. Second, in the Joint Declaration, the parties requested that the United Nations System in Colombia and the National University of Colombia (NUC) organize public forums to discuss the broad set of themes addressed within the mandate of Point Five. The forums were to be held in 2014 in cities that would facilitate the participation of conflict-affected populations from across the country (Villavicencio, Barrancabermeja, Barranquilla and Cali). Third, the communiqué formally proposed the formal inclusion of victims of the armed conflict at the Havana talks. Specifically, it invited the UN, the NUC and the Episcopal Conference of the Catholic Church (ECCC) to organize five delegations of 12 victims who would visit the negotiating parties in Havana. The objective of the delegations was 'to present proposals and expectations about building peace in Colombia's territories and concerning the satisfaction of the rights of victims (to truth, justice, reparation), including guarantees of nonrecurrence' (Joint Communiqué No. 37).

Framing victim participation

The rationale behind the provisions incorporated into the June 2014 joint communiqué was driven by the wider evolution of the transitional justice paradigm over recent decades towards a purportedly more victim-centred practice. As was discussed earlier, beginning in the 2000s, the push towards victim-centred transitional justice had emerged out of the charges made by survivors and victims of mass violence that the transitional justice paradigm was exclusionary and unrepresentative.

Victims' claims that their interests, experiences, demands and perspectives have been sidelined from the design and orientation of transitional justice mechanisms and subordinated to the interests of the state, illegal armed groups and heavyweight international actors have shown the disparity in scale and power inherent in the paradigm (Shaw and Waldorf 2010). Since the 2000s, the response of policy makers and practitioners to such claims has been progressively interventionist and inclusionary, at least on paper. The development of thinking and practice in this respect has led to the increasing employment of terms such as 'victim-centred approach' as common parlance within the paradigm (McEvoy and McConnachie 2012b). At the same time, the so-called 'victims' turn' has been characterized by the near-hegemonic deployment of the language of 'victim-centrism' in international and domestic transitional justice thinking and practice (McEvoy and McConnachie 2012a, 2012b). The UN system and the EU, for example, have adopted a 'victim-centred' approach across many of their policies oriented towards dealing with the legacy of past atrocities. Such an approach seeks to ensure that victims are guaranteed a role 'in the design and implementation of transitional justice processes and mechanisms' (Robins 2017: 43).[1]

As a consequence, victims have been increasingly consulted over the design of transitional justice mechanisms and afforded spaces for dialogue with armed actors in contexts of war to peace transitions, as the 2014 Havana press communiqué demonstrated. Moreover, the consolidation of the victims' turn has been crafted through the progressive hardening of the normative framework for victims' rights in international human rights law, international criminal law and international humanitarian law. The UN, for example, has issued victim-centred standards, through its Basic Principles and Guidelines on the Right to Remedy and Reparation, which set up core principles to establish, ensure and promote victims' rights.[2] Victims' rights have consequently become increasingly codified through normativization and legal categorization, a process that has played a key role in facilitating political opportunities for claims making by survivors. These claims are now broadly perceived as morally and legally legitimate, as the decision to incorporate victims directly at Havana talks demonstrated (Garcia-Godos and Knut Andreas 2010: 515). Significantly, in the case of Colombia, victim inclusion demonstrated not only the legitimate role of victims and survivors in determining the nature of accountability mechanisms, but also the way in which transitional justice concerns have become increasingly relevant to the political and moral rationale determining liberal peacemaking and peacebuilding.

The contention of this book is that the decision to adopt diverse and sequenced mechanisms of victim participation in the Havana talks, including the victims' forums and the subsequent delegations, represented a context-specific manifestation of both the so-called local turn in peacemaking, as discussed in Chapter 3, and the victims' turn. In other words, Colombia's victim-centred process represented the convergence and culmination of both the local turn in peacemaking and the victims' turn in transitional justice.

---

[1] In 2005, the UN adopted guidelines and principles on the right to remedy and reparation for victims, and in 2012, established Resolution 18/7 of the Human Rights Council, which required a Report of the Special Rapporteur on the promotion of truth, justice, reparation and guarantees of nonrecurrence.

[2] General Assembly, Resolution 60/147. 16 December 2005. Furthermore, the Principles establish the principal categories of state obligations pertaining to victims' rights to truth, justice and specific forms of reparation, such as compensation, restitution, rehabilitation, satisfaction, and guarantee of nonrecurrence.

From such a point of departure, what is of central importance to the following chapters is an analysis of whether and, if so, to what extent these mechanisms facilitated the meaningful participation of survivors of atrocity and placed victims and their demands at the centre of the talks, as the negotiating parties claimed. This book explores whether and, if so, how victim inclusion mattered. The analysis developed is situated in broader discussions of whether victim-oriented transitional justice permits the effective exercise of victim agency, the incorporation of victims' demands and the representation of victims' self-defined needs, as policy makers have maintained. Widespread scholarship continues to dispute these claims, as discussed in the Introduction to this book. For example, McEvoy and McConnachie (2012a, 2012b) contend that 'victim-centeredness' is, in large part, habitually shaped by a quest for self-legitimation by government, state and international actors, and is, in fact, characterized principally by the instrumentalization of victims, an argument common across much of the literature. Empirical evidence drawing on the cases of Nepal and Northern Ireland has demonstrated how, even in spite of their apparent 'victim-oriented' focus and despite key innovations facilitating victim participation, transitional justice processes have failed to achieve their 'victim-centred threshold' (Sajjad 2016: 26).

However, the following chapters contend that the Colombia experience suggests a more nuanced argument. Based on interviews with those who participated in and organized the victims' forums and delegations, this research contends that the Colombia case poses a partial corrective to scholarship that, at best, refutes and, at worst, negates the capacity of victims as political actors within victim-centred transitional justice, framing victims therein as uniquely instrumentalized and lacking meaningful agency. The book argues that Colombia's forums and delegations were not exclusively depoliticizing mechanisms. Both empowerment/agency and disempowerment/instrumentalization/revictimization occurred, as will be demonstrated in the next four chapters. The contention of this book, then, is that, in the case of Colombia, we should resist a sweeping narrative that victim-oriented transitional justice is paralysing and merely instrumentalizes victims' narratives/experiences or, on the contrary, that it is solely transformative and empowering. As a consequence, the research presented here proposes an *instrumentalization–empowerment* spectrum, showing that both phenomena may occur simultaneously across diverse fields and levels during inclusion initiatives.

The victims' forums

The first specific mechanism oriented towards victims' inclusion, the Victims' Forums, was implemented in the immediate aftermath of the second round of elections in 2014. The Victims' Forums were mandated to receive and document civil society and, particularly, victims' proposals for Point Five, during mass public summits. All proposals were then sent to the negotiating parties in Havana, with the aim of guiding discussions over the accountability mechanisms. Given their subnational orientation, the forums were aimed towards documenting and acknowledging more localized agendas and proposals. The process was framed within the ten principles on victim participation previously consecrated within the joint statement, in particular the recognition of the rights and dignity of victims of the conflict. The forums were also guided by eight specific principles agreed upon by the negotiating parties and the organizers, principles that would influence the framework guiding the subsequent victims' delegations:

- ensure balanced and plural participation;
- prioritize the participation of direct victims;
- guarantee the participation of victims of state agents, guerrillas and paramilitaries;
- ensure representation of victims of the principal victimizing events of the armed conflict;
- guarantee the representation of victims from the most victimized sectors of the population;
- promote the participation of local victims' organizations;
- guarantee that participation be oriented towards the submission of proposals pertinent to the satisfaction of the rights of the victims of the armed conflict;
- assume a gender approach and ensure that 50 per cent of the participants were women.

The forums were held in strategic cities across the country in recognition of the impact of the armed conflict at the subnational and local levels, and of the importance of building 'territorial' peace out of the proposals made by conflict-affected populations themselves.[3] According to a member of the Organizing Committee: 'The forums represented a political and legal gesture towards peace, explicitly and publicly acknowledging the contribution that victims could make to the content of the conversations in Havana and the norm that the peace agreements should respond to victims appropriately and effectively.'[4]

---

[3] The rhetoric of 'territorial peace' had been employed persistently by government and international actors throughout the peace process, using the original Spanish term *paz territorial* (territorial peace).

[4] Interview, Bogotá, Colombia, April 2015.

In July 2014, the first three victims' forums were held in Villavicencio, Barrancabermeja and Barranquilla, with a final forum taking place in Cali, southern Colombia, during the first week of August. The forums in Villavicencio, Barrancabermeja and Barranquilla brought together more than 400 participants each, while the Cali forum, which was characterized as a national platform, gathered over 1,200 individuals from across the country. While the general themes of victimization and victimhood framed all four forums, each individual meeting addressed a specific thematic issue. The focus of the Villavicencio forum was linked to the protection of social leaders, while in Barrancabermeja, proposals related to sexual violence were brought to the fore. In Barranquilla, the issue of reparations was central, including corruption as an obstacle to victim reparation and the theme of psychosocial reparation as key to peacebuilding.

The four forums brought together representatives from all social sectors (see Box 4.1), a majority of whom were female victims, and included victims of all armed groups and individuals who had been subject to a diverse range of violations, including by multiple actors. As such, while forging a space to facilitate dialogue between victims, the forums simultaneously aimed to build a framework for and publicly acknowledge a 'universe of victims', a term that would gain currency during the subsequent victims' delegations (see Box 4.1).

The employment of mass forums aimed at gathering proposals was not new to the Havana talks, nor was it, in fact, considerably innovative. Beginning in 2012, the UN and the NUC had been mandated by the negotiating parties to organize civil society forums. These spaces were arranged to allow civil society organizations to present their proposals for the preceding three agreements as they were being negotiated. These forums, held between 2012 and 2014, were in large part a response to years of local and national-level mobilizations demanding inclusion within the formal political sphere and, subsequently, in the negotiations. These first forums resulted in thousands of proposals being sent to the negotiating parties in Havana, in relation specifically to those agreements signed during the first two years of the Havana talks. This *indirect* participation was compounded by an electronic portal, established in the 2012 Framework Accord, to which 9,306 proposals had been submitted; both mechanisms were ostensibly symbolic.

The 2014 Victims' Forums represented the first moment during the peace talks that victims had been specifically mandated *as victims* to participate collectively in the peace talks, albeit indirectly. According to a member of the Organizing Committee from the NUC: 'Having been invited as a university to organize the forums jointly with the UN represented our first connection to the negotiating table … our first initiative, through which, in

Box 4.1: Sectors invited to participate in the forums

1. Guilds and private sector organizations
2. Peasant organizations and movements
3. Indigenous populations and organizations
4. Afro-descendant populations and organizations
5. Women's organizations
6. Trade union organizations
7. Political parties with legal status
8. Political and social movements
9. Human rights organizations
10. Development and Peace Programmes and National and Territorial Peace Initiatives
11. Churches
12. Academic sector, universities and research centres
13. Children and adolescents
14. Youth organizations
15. LGBTI+ organizations
16. Organizations of Raizales, Palenqueros and Roma (racial organizations)
17. Environmental organizations
18. Media

our opinion, we were authorized to support the negotiating table without making any compromises.'[5]

The decision by the negotiating parties to delegate the organization of the mechanisms for victim inclusion (framed within the Joint Declaration) to third parties was unprecedented. After having been kept at arm's length by the Santos government during the first two years of the Havana talks, the invitation to the UN and the NUC to organize the forums was significantly important. The invitation formalized the participation of both institutions in the peace process and established the precedent for their subsequent role in organizing the victims' delegations.

By selecting the NUC – with its academic expertise on the armed conflict and accompanying patterns of victimization – and the UN – with significant experience in mediation, victim support and human rights, as well as financial clout – the negotiating parties sought to achieve a balance between national and international support. In so doing, it is likely that the parties were signalling that the discussions over accountability were

---

[5] Interview, Bogotá, Colombia, April 2015.

not being handed over to international experts, but rather would be a partnership in which national expertise and knowledge were integral. By subsequently bringing the Catholic Church into the partnership for the organization of the victims' delegations, the parties incorporated a second national institution with considerable geographical reach, moral legitimacy and knowledge of patterns of victimhood and victimization related to the armed conflict.

In the words of one of the organizers:

> From the beginning it seemed to me that it was a good decision to have chosen a national and an international institution to organise the forums. It ... struck an important balance. It seems to me that having later added the Episcopal Conference of the Catholic Church [to organize the delegations] – which is one of the institutions here that has the most legitimacy – was very important.[6]

In prioritizing the participation of victims and their organizations from the subnational and local levels, the 2014 Victims' Forums sought to give voice to the most vulnerable sectors. While effectively a top-down, formal inclusion mechanism, by prioritizing the participation of local actors, the forums were situated in and emphasized the everyday territorial realities of participants, rather than taking place in inaccessible and remote locations. Consequently, the forums, at least on paper, ensured that inclusion mechanisms were not irreconcilable with or peripheral to the everyday experiences of victims, or isolated from the sites where many violations had taken place, as other mechanisms had been.

The testimonies – both individual and organizational/collective – gathered from over 2,400 participants at the forums mapped a generalized pattern of victims' demands, experiences and claims. These testimonies brought a specific, evidence-based dimension to diverse victims' experiences that demonstrated the massive scale and forensic horror of the violence perpetrated by the negotiating parties. The massivity of victimization and the sheer extent of testimonies pertaining to sexual and gender-based violence and widespread denunciation of violence against LGBTI+ populations became increasingly apparent as the forums were held sequentially.

At the same time, the forums, particularly in Cali, highlighted ongoing divisions and tensions within the victims' movement. In the final forum in Cali, victims of the FARC-EP staged a powerful protest, claiming that their experiences as victims were not being taken into account or acknowledged adequately by the UN and the NUC. According to the interviewees, the

---

[6] Interview, Bogotá, Colombia, April 2015.

Cali Forum showed the serious polarization between victims of distinct armed actors. A victim of the FARC-EP, who took part in the forums and subsequently participated in the victims' delegations, stated how they had 'not been given satisfactory visibility by the organizers at previous forums and that, as such, their demands and perspectives had been marginalized'. In their words, 'as victims of the FARC-EP we felt underrepresented. There were approximately 1,700 people invited to the forum, and we counted 284 victims of the FARC-EP. This was absurd, especially when a peace negotiation is being carried out with the FARC-EP'.[7]

After the forums had come to a close, the UN and the NUC formulated a series of recommendations to the negotiating parties. The recommendations drawn up were sustained meticulously by empirical data gathered during 32 panels held over the four meetings. In direct response to the proposals gathered from victims, perhaps the key recommendation from the UN and the NUC was that the negotiating parties expand the parameters of whom they considered to be a victim for the subsequent selection process for the victims' delegations. The recommendation to broaden the definitional parameters of who was considered a victim – particularly with respect to gender-based violence, violence against LGBTI+ populations and victims of the FARC-EP – was subsequently incorporated as a core element of the selection process for the victims' delegations to Havana, as will be discussed later on.

In general, the forums generated important lessons. Taking place prior to the victims' delegations, they set a precedent for the thematic issues that the delegations would subsequently address in Havana, while demonstrating the importance of incorporating a broad and inclusive spectrum of victims and their experiences within participation mechanisms. Moreover, the divisions within the victims' movement that emerged during the forums signalled to the negotiating parties and the organizers of the delegations that mechanisms should be put in place to address polarization between victims. Furthermore, the forums highlighted a fundamental issue that would subsequently determine the configuration of the delegations. The data pertaining specifically to sexual and gender-based violence (SGBV) that were gathered from participants during the forums demonstrated that it was indispensable that the victims' delegations adopt a gendered and differential approach – and specifically address SGBV – if they were to respond meaningfully to widespread patterns of victimization. In this regard, by establishing relevant guidelines for the delegations that would occur in their wake, the forums demonstrated the significance of sequential and mutually reinforcing phases of victim inclusion during peacemaking and

---

[7] Interview, Bogotá, Colombia, April 2015.

transitional justice interventions. In fact, by preceding the victims' delegations with the forums, the inclusion of a complex mosaic of context-specific victim and survivor-driven 'pre-existing agency and organization' – what has been defined elsewhere as an 'ecosystem of participation' (Evrard, Mejía Bonifazi and Destrooper 2021: 43) – was, in part, facilitated. This point will be revisited later on.

Framing victim inclusion in the Havana talks

Engagement with the concerns of transitional justice during the Havana talks was not, in principle, pioneering or exceptional. In fact, since the mid-1990s, at the global level, approximately half of all signed peace agreements have addressed transitional justice concerns (Jamar 2018: 9). Provisions have focused on both retributive and restorative justice mechanisms – truth recovery, institutional reform, reparations, victim support and rehabilitation, humanitarian assistance and the exchange and return of dead bodies. However, despite the increasing adoption of transitional justice measures within peace agreements – and with the exception of a minority of cases such as Colombia, Nepal, Sierra Leone, Liberia and Uganda – the participation by survivors and victims of political violence in their design and implementation has been restricted. Where victim inclusion has occurred, its nature and scope has varied considerably, ranging from direct participation – where victims have assumed a seat at the negotiating table – to consultation with victims during specific rounds of peace talks, such as in Colombia. In the case of Liberia, for example, victims participated as part of the negotiating teams, with the latter nominating victim representatives within their respective delegations. The Liberia case echoes, in part, the inclusion mechanism adopted during the Guatemalan peace process, when, from 1994, at a generic level, civil society actors, including victims' organizations, were formally mandated through the Civil Society Assembly (ASC) to send proposals to the negotiating parties for the substantive peace agreements. The ASC led to explicit civil society influence on specific peace accords, although it was ultimately limited in its transformative capacity (Brett 2008). From a different perspective, during the 2003 Sierra Leone peace talks, victims did not negotiate directly, but rather were incorporated indirectly as observers and advisors. As had been the case, at least in part, in Northern Ireland during the 1990s, in Sierra Leone, the negotiating parties consulted civil society, religious leaders and victims' organizations with respect to the issue of victims' rights. During the Ugandan negotiations in 2008, the Juba talks were, in contrast, less explicitly victim-centred, with victims being excluded from direct negotiation or from advising the negotiating parties, and instead consulted at isolated points during the negotiations.

In this context, what was innovative about the Colombia experience was how, in response to victims' historical demands for participation in peace negotiations, the parties mandated variegated inclusion provisions. Beyond the more symbolic web portal and civil society summits, the victims' forums and victims' delegations ultimately provided mass indirect participation and select direct participation respectively. The incorporation of said mechanisms in 2014 aimed to respond meaningfully to the specificities of the Colombian context – in particular, the consolidated domestic presence of victims as political actors and their growing capacity to influence the peace agenda, and the protracted pressure from the international community for victim recognition and inclusion. Both factors locked the negotiating parties into providing mutually reinforcing channels through which to address victims' individual and collective demands. The approval of both inclusion mechanisms also represented an acknowledgement of evolving international norms relative to victims' rights since the end of the Cold War, while, in all likelihood, demonstrating a learning process on the part of domestic and international actors engaged with and leading transitional justice interventions. According to one member of the Organizing Committee:

> I think it is relevant that the issue of victims is on the agenda. This is a demonstration of how history has changed, because victims have been affirmed as a political subject in Colombia over the last five or six years. Victims in Colombia have special recognition. Today there cannot be a peace agreement without addressing this issue, given the evolution of international jurisprudence and the fact that, compared to 20 years ago, international norms and regulations are much more explicit in openly acknowledging victims in the construction of peace.[8]

However, in spite of evolving international norms and gradually more inclusive practices, victims have continued to claim that the promotion of their demands, satisfaction of their needs and guarantee of their rights have remained subordinated to the interests of state actors, illegal armed groups and heavyweight international actors (Sajjad 2016; Robins 2017). Victims' demands have, in this respect, been outranked by the prerogatives and interests of elite-level actors and subordinated to the pacts – and provisions therein – invoked to maintain the stability and impetus of fragile political transitions and negotiations. These trade-offs, of course, demonstrate the ongoing imbalance in scale and power between victims of political violence and the elite-level actors who often determine the trajectory of transitional justice mechanisms and profess to lobby on their behalf (Baker and Obradovic-Wochnik 2016).

---

[8] Interview, Bogotá, Colombia, April 2015.

As the research presented here will demonstrate, the Colombia case is not entirely an exception to this tendency, given that, as will be argued later on, in the end, victims' demands were included in the final transitional justice provisions within Point Five and the broader peace agreement only when they aligned with the interests of the negotiating parties.

Nevertheless, the centrality and treatment of transitional justice concerns to the Santos–FARC-EP negotiations from their inception compels a somewhat more nuanced approach to our analysis of the way in which engagement with the themes of truth, justice, reparation and nonrecurrence evolved during, shaped and, in turn, was shaped by the peace talks. Assessing the treatment of victims' concerns over the course of the talks as having been merely outranked by other thematic discussions, related strategic decisions and elite actors' interests alone fails to elucidate a complete story of the role victims played during the negotiations. In other words, the Colombia story is one defined by both empowerment and instrumentalization.

Why victim inclusion in Havana?

Discussion over and public debate concerning the matters at the core of the transitional justice paradigm – and, in particular, the controversies pertaining to possible provisions of amnesty or penal justice for perpetrators and the truth behind the violations committed – had been prominent from the outset of the peace talks in Cuba. Nevertheless, the significance of transitional justice concerns logically grew after June 2014, once negotiations for Point Five had commenced and the visibility of victims on the national and international public stage had been amplified through the victims' forums and subsequent delegations to Havana. According to one of the organizers, it was at this stage that victims 'irreversibly' asserted their 'importance' as a political actor, due both to their political prominence and to the escalation in their forms of collective organization. In this interviewee's words:

> although the victims, especially of the paramilitaries, were organized through a configuration of very important organizations, above all by actors such as the Movement of Victims of the State, what the process allowed was that not only could paramilitary victims organize themselves, but also that the victims of the FARC-EP could organize themselves.[9]

The 'well-established norm' of victim inclusion, as Méndez (2016: 2) has described it, consequently came to assume pivotal relevance to the Havana

---

[9] Interview, Bogotá, Colombia, May 2015.

talks. The delegations would become central protagonists in the design of the accountability mechanisms at the heart of the peace talks. At the same time, the mandate assumed by victims within the formal context of the talks came to give voice to an increasingly broad spectrum of actors, meaning that victims of state, paramilitary and insurgent groups became progressively visible on the public stage. Beyond compliance with international normative standards relative to victims' rights, direct victim participation in the talks brought the legitimization and recognition of victims and their demands a step closer, one of the core objectives of the initiatives. According to a member of the Catholic Church who played an instrumental role in the organization of the delegations, 'the arrival of the victims in Havana represented a qualitative leap in the peace process … and transformed it'. Referring to the attitude of the negotiating parties, the interviewee stated:

> I saw a process evolve in them. Especially when the victims began to speak, they [the negotiating parties] first thought that they had made political mistakes, after this that they had made military mistakes and finally they recognized that they had made human mistakes and that by making human mistakes they themselves had been affected. I saw that – thanks to the victims – the parties opened up to a type of conversation that was impossible beforehand … [and] that the way they behaved towards the victims was going to show how far [their] moral values were alive.[10]

Opening up the negotiating table to their victims had been understood by the negotiating parties as a 'moral imperative', according to one member of the Catholic Church. However, it was also a 'politically very important assumption of risk', in the words of one organizer.[11] Why were the parties willing to take such a risk, giving their victims a voice on perhaps the most controversial topic of the peace agenda and, in all likelihood, subjecting themselves as a consequence to public accusations concerning the moral and juridical rectitude of their conduct during the armed conflict, accusations that would bear very real legal repercussions?

Formalized interaction and dialogue between victims and perpetrators over the content of accountability mechanisms has, over the past decade, increased, as is discussed at length throughout this book. Transitional justice entrepreneurs, states and armed actors have responded to the claims and critiques of victims and survivors by accordingly seeking to reinforce the capacity of transitional justice interventions to represent victims'

---

[10] Interview, Bogotá, Colombia, April 2015.
[11] Interviews, Bogotá, Colombia, April–May 2015.

voices and demands. In this regard, a predominant goal of victim-centred transitional justice has been to strengthen the legitimacy of transitional justice interventions by building them on victims' perceptions of justice and international norms relative to victims' rights, including the right to victim participation and recognition, the recognition of responsibility by perpetrators, and the satisfaction of the rights of victims to truth, justice, reparation and nonrecurrence (Lundy and McGovern 2008: 265–266).

The Colombia case was no exception to the evolving tendency of elite actors to seek to legitimize transitional justice initiatives through victim participation. According to one interviewee involved in the Havana talks, in 2014:

> The peace process was seen as distant, as something abstract by much of the Colombian population. Moreover, the process itself was controversial in Colombia, with many feeling that it was legitimizing a terrorist group. So I think the need was felt [by the parties] to open up the process ... to give a greater legitimacy. In that sense inviting victims ... was a way of signalling the importance that the parties were giving to the victims themselves and ... of giving substance to the words of ... negotiators that the whole point of the process was to provide satisfaction to victims.[12]

Former President Juan Manuel Santos has echoed this argument, stating that the inclusion of victims through both the forums and the delegations represented an effort to 'repay the historical debt owed to victims',[13] an assertion reiterated in his 2021 autobiography, *The Battle for Peace*. The extent to which this perspective was common among the negotiating parties in 2014 remains unclear. However, one of the primary objectives of the delegations, which will be discussed in detail in the following chapter, was to ensure victim recognition. From this perspective, the delegations sought to demonstrate 'in its most generic sense, a reflection of the pain of Colombian society ... the will and need to ensure that society has an understanding of what this painful experience has represented and in some way the cultural change' required to overcome it.[14]

Critiques of victim-centred transitional justice have rightly contended that the practice has been ostensibly driven by the quest of governments, armed actors and policy makers to confer legitimacy upon top-down processes, as they pursue 'larger political or social goals' (McEvoy and

---

[12] Interview, Bogotá, Colombia, May 2015.
[13] Interview, University of Notre Dame, US, September 2022.
[14] Interview, Organizing Committee, Bogotá, Colombia, April 2015.

McConnachie 2012b: 490). In other words, the moral imperative towards victim recognition, as emphasized by former President Santos, has not habitually been the predominant driver of victim-centred interventions. Rather, by incorporating victim experience and knowledge within formal processes that endorse victim participation and acknowledgement and confer a role upon victims in transitional justice design, elite actors have aimed to reframe top-down processes as morally legitimate and politically inclusive – a quality that such processes often lack. The imperative towards the inclusion of survivors of political violence in the Colombian peace process may, to a certain extent, be seen through this lens; however, it does not tell the whole story.

Interviews with members of the three institutions that organized the victims' delegations – the UN, the NUC and the ECCC – highlighted a broad consensus around the notion that, in the words of one official, 'the visits came as a means to give credibility to the process and particularly to give greater credibility to the idea that it was in the service of the victims'.[15] However, according to the interviewees, more than an end in itself, the pursuit of credibility was tied to the perceived necessity of drafting a peace process that would adhere to international norms relative to victims' rights, while simultaneously being responsive to the demands of Colombia's organized mass victim constituency. As such, characterizing as premeditated instrumentalization the quest to gain credibility for the peace talks explicitly with respect to how accountability mechanisms would reflect victim experience and promote victims' rights – is a somewhat reductionist interpretation of the initiatives.

On paper, the negotiating parties and the organizers sought to satisfy the moral imperative for victim inclusion in the peace process through the establishment of diverse and sequenced mechanisms for participation. In the words of one official/organizer, 'this specific space for victims' participation is intended primarily as a form of recognition ... we do not want to reduce their participation to an almost symbolic act', but rather 'work with the victims through the recognition of their dignity'.[16] Similarly, another organizer stated how, by opening a space for encounter between victims and their perpetrators in Havana, the delegations had explicitly aimed to facilitate victim recognition. The delegations, in their words, were 'a means for the parties ... to assume responsibility, overcome denialism, acknowledge and, in the agreements, adopt measures so that the rights of the victims are satisfied ... Victims are not "decorative figures", nor are they going to legitimize the process with a photograph'.[17]

---

[15] Interview, Organizing Committee, Bogotá, Colombia, April 2015.
[16] Interview, Bogotá, Colombia, April 2015.
[17] Interview, Bogotá, Colombia, April 2015.

Another member of the Organizing Committee similarly stated how:

> From a human rights perspective, one of the most serious elements in this conflict has been [perpetrators'] denial on both sides ... The fact of taking 60 people of flesh and bone who attested to atrocity, is a way of overcoming denialism. This implies ... recognition ... consequences. And of course the consequence that should be derived from this is justice. It means to stop thinking that there are ... justifications. ... thousands of people have suffered and a small group [the delegations] came to materialize this at the negotiating table. The courage of these people ... looking into the eyes of their perpetrators or those who represent them is admirable. It is very powerful to see the courage and then the faith of these people in peace that this should not happen again.[18]

Beyond the ethical argument that inclusion sought to engender victim acknowledgement and the inclusion of those most affected, the organizers, as a whole, connected the moral imperative for participation to wider arguments regarding the efficacy of peace settlements. Accordingly, the organizing institutions were explicit in signalling how the inclusion of victims in the talks aimed to strengthen the efficacy of an eventual political settlement between the government and the FARC-EP, a contention frequently made in academic scholarship. According to one official:

> A peace process that doesn't somehow take into account the aspirations, the recommendations of victims, especially when there is such a large number of civilian victims, will be much more difficult to implement, and its sustainability threatened ... precisely because these victims have, by definition, suffered more than others ... they have the legitimacy in terms of promoting peace that few others have ... They can convince, they can become unique voices in contributing to reconciliation.[19]

Awareness of and respective discussions concerning the potential charge of victim instrumentalization was acute, and emerged frequently during interviews with both the organizers and participants in the delegations. Officials frequently contended that to use instrumentalization as the sole explanatory factor both belied victim agency and derided the importance of the evolution in recent decades of the normative framework relative to victims' rights and the obligations that states and international actors had

---

[18] Interview, Organizing Committee, Bogotá, Colombia, April 2015.
[19] Interview, Bogotá, Colombia, May 2015.

assumed therein. At the start of 2015, this sentiment was shared by many participants in the delegations that had recently returned from Havana.

For the organizers, then, and in particular for members of the ECCC, the moral question of recognition and acknowledgement represented the principal justification for why victims had been afforded a formal role in Havana. According to one representative who played a considerable role in accompanying the delegations, the victims were 'witnesses of human reconstruction'; each individual had been able to 'rebuild after being torn to pieces'.[20] From his perspective, the delegations held the potential to have a significant impact on the perpetrators, given that that their presence extended:

> an invitation for the perpetrators to do the same, to begin reconstruction work ... because they had dehumanized themselves with everything they did ... So the testimony of the victims can also help them, to know what they have to overcome ... the perpetrators have not opened up and they will have to reach the same level [as the victims]: to open up, to express the drama they have inside and that has to lead them to in-depth change.[21]

As will be seen in the following chapters, one of the consequences of the victims' delegations was, in fact, to precipitate a relational change in Havana, in many cases dyadically between victims and their perpetrators, although also arguably between the victims themselves and between the negotiating parties. This relational dynamic was complex, shaped in itself by the process of moral engagement and recognition that the delegations gradually engendered. However, the impact that the delegations came to have on the negotiating parties would not have been possible without the extraordinary generosity that the participants in the delegations showed towards their perpetrators in Havana, a point which will be returned to later on. According to a member of the Catholic Church:

> The victim experiences in herself ... the bestiality and barbarity of which the human being is capable, the ignominy, the capacity for destruction. Because it is not just that they shoot you, they want to annihilate you, they want to erase you, they want to fill you with shame about yourself, they want to make you feel that you have no right to live.[22]

---

[20] Interview, Bogotá, Colombia, May 2015.
[21] Interview, Bogotá, Colombia, May 2015.
[22] Interview, Bogotá, Colombia, May 2015.

The members of the victims' delegations were, from the beginning, deeply generous, both to the negotiating parties and, more broadly, through their shared demand that the war should end in order to prevent other individuals suffering what they themselves had suffered. According to one female participant: 'We don't want other people to suffer, we don't want more families to be touched by violence, we don't want to see more mothers cry.'[23] In the words of one interviewee from the Organizing Committee: 'You see the mother of a victim of the FARC-EP and the mother of a victim of the military, united in a single pain, stating that no matter where the bullets come from, there should be no more deaths.'[24] According to an official involved in the Organizing Committee, as a consequence of this relational dynamic, the presence of the victims and their harrowing narratives immediately asserted a significant impact upon the negotiating parties. As a result of participants' testimonies, the discussions that took place in Havana once the delegations began to arrive 'were not just political discussions', but rather demonstrated an evolving process of reflection. In her words:

> When they tell you about their experiences ... a woman who had to leave her land and leave her husband dead, had suffered sexual violence ... when they [the parties] hear the consequences that this has had in their lives ... those powerful moments are capable of humanizing the process.[25]

A member of the Organizing Committee mandated to accompany the talks echoed this perspective. They reiterated how the 'unprecedented' decision taken to establish the victims' forums and to invite the delegations to Havana had been driven by the imperative towards victim recognition. The interviewee testified to how the victims' delegations assumed a 'strategic character', as the hearings transformed the perspectives of the negotiating parties, both towards their victims and towards their own actions. The delegations, in their words, strengthened the 'will of the negotiators' towards acknowledgement of their victims and towards eventual agreement on the provisions of Point Five:

> one thing is that the victims participate ... that they be listened to, that the victims be able to look their perpetrators in the eye. Another thing is that their interlocutors, the actors at the negotiating table,

---

[23] Interview, Bogotá, Colombia, April 2015.
[24] Interview, Bogotá, Colombia, May 2015.
[25] Interview, Bogotá, Colombia, May 2015.

recognize that there can be no reconciliation, that there can be no peace, without [inclusion of] the issue of victims.[26]

The issue of instrumentalization and agency will represent a key thread in the following chapters, as we hold up the Colombia case to widespread critiques sceptical of the extent to which victim acknowledgement and meaningful response to victim claims making sit at the core of so-called victim-centred transitional justice. As was discussed in detail in previous chapters, scholars have contended that these processes are, in fact, driven by the needs of the state and other elite actors, and ultimately instrumentalize subaltern voices, fail to respond effectively to victims' demands, shy away from transforming relations of power and restrict victims' agency. The upbeat perspectives of the organizers are perhaps unsurprising, given the preponderance of critiques signalling the depoliticizing nature of victim-oriented interventions (Grewal 2016) and the former's role in this component of the peace talks. The following section draws on the experiences of the members of the victims' delegations themselves, in order to contrast the organizers' perspectives on inclusion with those of the participants.

The perspectives of the members of the victims' delegations

A core objective of this book is to comprehend the capacity of top-down, victim-centred peacemaking and transitional justice initiatives to permit the assertion of survivor/victim agency. A recurring theme in the following chapters is how we understand and, if appropriate, recalibrate the prevailing perspectives concerning victim recognition, instrumentalization and empowerment through drawing on the testimonies of participants in Colombia's victim-centred intervention. As a point of departure, a fundamental theme emerging from the data in this regard is that those who participated, for the most part, did not –at least initially – feel themselves to have been solely instrumentalized or disempowered *when they themselves had been acknowledged by their own perpetrator*. However, when perpetrators rejected their status as victim and, in turn, failed to acknowledge them, participants felt revictimized and instrumentalized, a point which will be revisited in later chapters. Such revictimization was experienced by victims of both negotiating parties, including a mother whose son had been killed extrajudicially by the military and a former policeman who had been held captive by the FARC-EP for 11 years in the jungle. In the words of this mother:

---

[26] Interview, Bogotá, Colombia, May 2015.

I believe that we are here so that the Colombian state recognizes that its army, police, ESMAD [riot police] ... violate human rights ... grab women by the hair, drag them, torture them. Here I am representing the families of extrajudicial executions, I am not a victim ... of any group outside the law, I am a victim of a Colombian state, of an indifferent and indolent state that kills our children to present positive results to the government.[27]

Participants across all five delegations were deftly and strategically able to navigate their relationships with their perpetrators while in Havana. Moreover, numerous participants were insistent that their agency had been generative of wider transformative processes and, in many cases, of the ways in which they themselves came to perceive that they had been dignified ('dignificados') through their participation. The data presented in the following chapters accordingly contend that instrumentalization and empowerment are not Manichean, mutually exclusive phenomena, but rather can occur across diverse fields and levels, at times simultaneously. As such, they have complex consequences. What the Colombia case attests to is therefore an *instrumentalization–empowerment* spectrum rather than a dichotomous field where victims are either uniquely disempowered or empowered.

A further relational consequence of the everyday, intimate politics that shaped both their (albeit temporary) encounters in Havana and the forms through which victims and perpetrators navigated their shared space therein pertains to how participants in the delegations moved gradually towards acknowledging a unifying, multidimensional victim identity based on the recognition of collective suffering. Victims of opposing armed actors moved beyond seeing each other as an extension of the armed conflict and came to acknowledge their mutual grief and affliction. A female victim of paramilitary and state violence explained how the delegations represented an 'exercise to erase hatred, to heal the wounds of war'[28] by bringing diverse victims together to face their perpetrators. A female survivor of an armed attack by the FARC-EP similarly described the delegations as 'the manifestation of pain, anguish and tragedy, that we victims express to the people who caused it'. In this interviewee's words, the delegations 'helped them [the perpetrators] to disarm their hearts ... to humanize'.[29] One participant who had lived in protracted exile after suffering state repression further clarified the factors that reinforced the

---

[27] Interview, Bogotá, Colombia, April 2015.
[28] Interview, Bogotá, Colombia, April 2015.
[29] Interview, Bogotá, Colombia, April 2015.

capacity of the delegations to forge a collective sense of victimhood and, in part, of trust:

> The validity of this initiative has to do with one thing: with situating the true country within a group of 60 victims. They brought together a fractured, divided, conflictive country, eroded by mistrust ... within the same space. The delegations made us look each other in the eye, acknowledge one another and understand that the war had touched us all in a way and that, in overcoming the violence, we were very similar.[30]

This process of transformation – the permanency of which cannot be assumed – demonstrates an aspect of empowerment that has not always been systematically identified in the literature on victim inclusive processes. While the Northern Ireland and Nepal cases have coherently demonstrated victim instrumentalization in nominally victim-centred processes, the Colombia case suggests the importance of crafting a more nuanced consideration of the critique of instrumentalization and of our understanding of victim agency and empowerment. In other words, what is key here is that we give credence to the experiences of those who participated in the victims' delegations during (process) and in the aftermath of (outcome) the delegations (Jones et al 2023). In this respect, it is important to understand how they enacted and conceptualized agency, recognition and empowerment and, in turn, to ask how the Colombia case stands up to previous critique. How did the participants understand the rationale for their inclusion within the Havana talks and how, if at all, did they feel instrumentalized?

A first relevant theme here is that a wide range of the participants in the victims' delegations echoed the organizers' claims that inclusion had, in fact, been fundamental for reinforcing the legitimacy of the Havana talks. According to a female survivor of sexual violence:

> Beyond legitimacy – *which I think is the fundamental point* – it is impossible to talk about nonrecurrence if we do not [include] those who have suffered the greatest damage ... Being able to incorporate the vision of those who have had to suffer the greatest damage, *in addition to legitimacy*, gives [the talks] a roadmap, embeds the process. (Emphasis added)[31]

What this statement – and others like it – demonstrate is how participants were intuitively capable of identifying the complexities associated with the

---

[30] Interview, Bogotá, Colombia, May 2015.
[31] Interview, Bogotá, Colombia, May 2015.

question of legitimacy. Victims, in this regard, were neither oblivious nor inattentive to wider relations of power, nor were they duped unmindfully into participating in and, in turn, into legitimizing a top-down process. Rather, participants were able to navigate their path through complex mechanisms and relations of power during the delegations. Moreover – and, in fact, echoing the perspectives of the organizers – many victims understood legitimization not as a mere end in itself, but rather as being integral to the wider objectives of guaranteeing the moral recognition of victims and strengthening the effectiveness of the peace process.

We should then be mindful not to characterize the participants in the victims' delegations as solely passive objects, appropriated unwittingly to legitimize the Havana talks. Interviewees who had been victim of state, guerrilla and paramilitary violence widely shared the opinion that, given the talks' hitherto elite, top-down nature, the negotiations in fact urgently *required* a deeper legitimacy. Participants were unequivocal that victim inclusion represented the crucial path towards achieving this goal. According to a male victim of both state and guerrilla violence:

> What a peace process like ours seeks is precisely to resolve a conflict that is deeply rooted … Only by listening to the testimony of victims can the damage be understood, and above all, within this dimension of damage, can measures be determined: specifically, reparation, true justice, guarantees of nonrecurrence. So listening to the victims is important because the measures that are taken have to be consistent with their testimonies and the damage caused, otherwise history repeats itself.[32]

Explaining the victim-centred mechanisms as having emerged solely as a top-down mechanism of inclusion, according to several participants interviewed, belied the fact that the space itself had been fought for and ultimately secured through the collective struggles of victims on the ground. As such, inclusion, for one participant, demonstrated how 'victims have won a political space in Colombia as subjects of rights: they no longer want to be seen as objects, but as citizens who actively participate in the construction of peace'.[33] According to one survivor of guerrilla violence, the parties' agreement to mandate participation was, at once, a fundamental achievement and an act of recognition in this respect. In her words: 'Law 1448, the Victims' Law, empowered us and made us visible to the world.' For this participant, her visit to Havana was a consequence of decades of

---

[32] Interview, Bogotá, Colombia, April 2015.
[33] Interview, Bogotá, Colombia, May 2015.

struggle: 'Within all the peace processes carried out in this country, victims had never been named, never ... At this moment, victims are empowered, victims have been recognized.'[34]

Another participant shared the perspective of naming and making victims' visible. This participant clarified how the decision to mandate victim inclusion had been directly influenced by victims' collective organization. In their words:

> There was great pressure from the victims demanding to be heard. We must bear in mind that victimization in Colombia has been immense ... What seems interesting to me is that the parties understood that victims from all sides should participate, which was not very well understood or accepted in public opinion and, above all, by those not in favour of the process.[35]

However, a participant whose father had been killed by the state also demonstrated restraint and, in part, scepticism, explaining how victim participation did not confer credibility automatically upon the peace process. In her words: 'Participation up to a certain point gives [the talks] credibility. But it will confer legitimacy only when we see our proposals incorporated [into Point Five]. If our proposals are not incorporated, then inclusion was nothing more than a salute to the flag and [the process] will lose legitimacy.'[36]

A complex nexus linking empowerment, legitimization and participation emerged as a thread across many of the testimonies given by participants in the victims' delegations. According to one male victim of state atrocity, participation was mandated by the negotiating parties 'as a repudiation of the suffering and pain of the victims, of the negative, disastrous consequences of the armed confrontations'.[37] However, it was, for one participant, the delegates themselves who were able to appropriate the inclusion mechanisms and shape them according to their own interests. For one survivor of paramilitary and guerrilla violence, his participation was significantly empowering and for him represented 'the most important step in history'.[38] This perspective was echoed by a female participant who had suffered repeated episodes of political violence. In her words, participation was core to her empowerment and was 'part of my growth as a political subject. As

---

[34] Interview, Bogotá, Colombia, April 2015.
[35] Interview, Bogotá, Colombia, April 2015.
[36] Interview, Bogotá, Colombia, April 2015.
[37] Interview, Bogotá, Colombia, April 2015.
[38] Interview, Bogotá, Colombia, May 2015.

a woman I think this is important'.³⁹ Another female participant, victim of guerrilla violence concurred:

> It is women that have been the most affected by the conflict. Women have lost our children, our husbands, women have had to take care of entire families when displacement occurs ... Women have a lot to contribute to this process. We women have borne the brunt of all the pain of this conflict, even the mothers of armed actors, those mothers also suffer for their children ... life for these women ... was not easy. So the participation of women is key ... because we women have to contribute a lot to this peace process.⁴⁰

Concluding remarks

This chapter has further developed the core question at the heart of this book, namely the role that Colombia's victims' delegations played in the Havana peace process. It began by detailing the antecedents to direct victim participation in the Santos–FARC-EP negotiations, with a discussion concerning the victims' forums of 2014. It then addressed the rationale for victim inclusion in the Havana talks by drawing on the perspectives of those who organized and those who participated in Colombia's victim-centred initiative.

The chapter has proposed a framework for unpacking the discussions relating to the strengths and weaknesses of victim inclusion, including specifically with respect to the themes of empowerment and instrumentalization. The contention that a complex, nuanced and context-specific understanding of participation should be adopted when evaluating victim inclusion will be further developed in the following chapters. This chapter has argued that instrumentalization was not the only outcome of Colombia's victim-centred approach, but rather that diverse forms of empowerment also resulted from the participation of the victims' delegations at the Havana talks. As such, an instrumentalization-empowerment spectrum is helpful in unpacking how the phenomena were not mutually exclusive, but rather occurred across diverse fields and levels, at times simultaneously during the delegations and in their aftermath.

The following chapters will explore how 'the mere presence of more actors is not sufficient' as a means through which to precipitate meaningful transformation (Paffenholz 2015: 88–89). The outcome of the assertion of victim agency across the instrumentalization-empowerment spectrum

---

³⁹ Interview, Santa Marta, Colombia, April 2015.
⁴⁰ Interview, Bogotá, Colombia, April 2015.

will be shaped by the degree to which victims are able to navigate and negotiate relations of power linked to elite political, economic and military/armed actors. In this regard, the degree to which victims might mould spheres of peacemaking and transitional justice mechanisms, rather than merely delivering moral, pragmatic and political legitimacy for states and international actors, will be contingent upon their strategic capacity to withstand and shape wider structures and relations of power (Jamar 2018). However, it will also be dependent on whether and, if so, to what extent formal mechanisms themselves are susceptible to the re-allocation and redefinition of relationships of power, including across and between genders (Bell and McNicholl 2019), and between dyadic groups, such as victims and perpetrators.

With this in mind, the following chapter now turns to a detailed examination of the empirical data, focusing specifically on the selection process for the victims' delegations and the consequences for those that took part, in turn linking such questions to the dynamics of representation.

5

A Participatory Process? Victim Inclusion and Representation in Havana

Introduction

The previous chapter addressed the antecedents to direct victim participation in the Santos–FARC-EP peace negotiations – documenting the victims' forums of 2014 and building into this a wider discussion of the rationale for victim inclusion in the Havana talks from the perspective of the participants in and organizers of the delegations. The chapter contended that a complex, nuanced and context-specific understanding of participation should be adopted when evaluating victim inclusion in peacemaking and victim-centred transitional justice initiatives. From this perspective, the chapter proposed the employment of an *instrumentalization–empowerment spectrum*, which allows for an approach that recognizes that instrumentalization and empowerment are not necessarily mutually exclusive phenomena, but rather may be experienced by victims across diverse fields and levels, at times simultaneously, during and in the wake of participation interventions. It was argued that *instrumentalization* and *empowerment* are contingent upon whether and, if so, to what degree victims are able to navigate and (re)negotiate relations of power exercised by elite political, economic and military/armed actors. The strategic assertion of individual agency by individual and collective victims as they seek to (re)negotiate power within the framework of formal inclusion mechanisms or peace talks plays a key role in this regard. However, the capacity of victims to assert their agency is not an isolated phenomenon, but rather is, in turn, itself contingent upon the extent to which the mandate of formal inclusion mechanisms allows for the re-allocation and redefinition of relationships of power and, of course, the degree to which perpetrators respond to the assertion of victim agency. In other words, although agency may be asserted innovatively and strategically, as it was during the Havana talks, the mandate of inclusion mechanisms will play a key role in setting the parameters for what victims – whether individual or collective – may or may not be able to achieve.

Within this framework, the following chapter examines the process through which participants were selected for the victims' delegations, drawing upon interviews with members of the delegations and other relevant actors in the peace talks. What is of particular interest in this chapter is how the selection process – which was designed and led by elite national and international actors – addressed the fundamental issues of representation and gender. In short, given that the organizers had been mandated by the negotiating parties to invite 60 victims out of an approximate total of nine million registered victims, a core question framing the victims' delegations – and critiques of them – was the extent to which such limited participation was morally justifiable, politically effective and able to provide a meaningful, representative reflection of historical patterns of political violence and victimization. Minimal numerical inclusion in Havana, of course, signified the mass collective exclusion of victims who did not go to Havana. Of crucial importance in this regard were the principles of inclusion developed by the organizers and, relatedly, their envisioning of a so-called 'universe of victims'. This chapter will propose that the framework employed was, in part, innovative and able to redress some of the critiques of the delegations' limitations, given that it placed emphatic focus upon the inclusion of female victims, victims of sexual and gender-based violence, victims of diverse crimes and of multiple armed actors and victims who had themselves been perpetrators. The chapter begins by situating briefly the discussions around victim agency and representation within broader debates pertaining to transitional justice, before addressing the specific themes of selection and gender in the context of victim inclusion in the Colombia peace talks.

Some thoughts on representation and selection

In a similar vein to the charges levied against the liberal peacebuilding paradigm (Mac Ginty 2012), transitional justice has been critiqued as an internationally led, top-down and Western-biased paradigm, which favours a state-centric, universalist rights-based agenda (Sriram Lehka 2007; Lambourne 2009; Andrieu 2010; Sharp 2013). Rather than facilitating and supporting broader political processes and transforming relations of power, state-led transitional justice interventions, it has been argued, have tended to exclude victim and civil society groups from their design and implementation, while obscuring 'the power relations that permeate a given context' (Gready and Roberts 2017: 258), in particular with respect to the leverage – or the lack thereof – that victim and civil society groups hold in relation to state and international actors. Furthermore, the paradigm's state-centrism and strict legalism reinforces its exclusionary character, in turn distancing interventions from individuals and communities affected directly by violence, and reifying and fixing victim and perpetrator identity (Andrieu 2010).

As discussed in previous chapters, in response to critiques of the mainstream transitional justice paradigm, the victims' turn was shaped by and further consolidated the increasing hardening of the normative framework for victims' rights in international human rights law, international criminal law and international humanitarian law, as well as in domestic legal regimes. The accompanying codification and normativization of victims' rights through victim-centred standards and legal categorization have, over time, come to represent important juridical instruments that have ushered in further legal and political opportunities for claims making by survivors (Garcia-Godos and Knut Andreas 2010: 515). As engagement with victims' rights has gradually become a core component of peacemaking and peacebuilding, so interventions have sought to guarantee victim inclusion and facilitate interaction and dialogue between victims and perpetrators (Sajjad 2016; Robins 2017), with the ultimate aim of constructing accountability mechanisms undergirded by victims' perceptions, demands and understandings of justice (Lundy and McGovern 2008).

Despite such developments, explicit engagement with the theme of victims during peace processes – and victim participation therein – has seen only a moderate increase in recent decades. As was discussed earlier, while approximately half of all peace agreements signed since the mid-1990s addressed transitional justice matters, only 195 provisions were, in fact, directly related to victims. Related provisions have nevertheless been innovative. Frameworks have provided broad mechanisms for addressing and redressing victims' rights to truth, justice, reparation and nonrecurrence.

Over time, then, peace agreements have included an increasingly broad spectrum of stipulations directly related to victims and their rights. However, as was noted earlier, the role of survivors and victims of political violence in the design and implementation of these provisions has remained limited. Rather, with few exceptions, it has been negotiating parties and/or state and international actors that have determined the mandates of the majority of transitional justice mechanisms drawn up in the context of peace negotiations.

While drawing upon the generic principles of victim participation and the guarantee of victims' rights, the mandates of inclusion mechanisms to date have been shaped by the context in which the respective negotiations have taken place, eschewing, in this respect, a one-size-fits-all model. Of course, context-specific frameworks hold the advantage that they are not standardized models, but rather respond to particular environments and patterns of victimization and victimhood. However, what has remained relatively absent in the policy sphere is the development of a more focused discussion at the national and international levels with respect to what inclusion mechanisms might look like and how they might effectively represent victims, specifically with regard to victim diversity and patterns of victimization and victimhood. Despite the significant evolution of international norms and trends in transitional justice and peacebuilding practices towards victim participation, there are few, if any, explicit guidelines determining what victim inclusion might look like or what specific principles it should follow beyond, in general, satisfying international standards pertaining to victims and, in particular, guaranteeing their rights to inclusion and representation.

Meaningful representation of complex narratives and patterns of victimization and victimhood is at the heart of discussions concerning the mandates of transitional justice mechanisms, whether mainstream or victim-centred. Historically, mechanisms have habitually emphasized demographic attributes such as gender, age, individual perpetrator, race, and ethnic or group membership, often not taking into account the wider political tensions, contradictions and structural factors shaping victims' experiences and how victims are defined/self-define (Jamar 2018). Mechanisms frequently present dichotomous, irreconcilable narratives of vulnerable victims alongside inveterate, irredeemable perpetrators and have rarely acknowledged either how power shapes victimhood under such circumstances or the dual condition where individuals may embody *both victim and perpetrator* (Theidon 2010). Accordingly, transitional justice initiatives have failed to reflect complex realities on the ground, where the line between victim and perpetrator may, at times, be blurred, as has been the case in Colombia. Furthermore, mechanisms have constructed victims as helpless, as lacking agency or as inherently marginalized (Sajjad 2016: 26), perspectives which may ultimately edify or strengthen existing power imbalances (Jamar 2018).

A meaningful approach to effectively representing patterns of victimization and victimhood within victim-centred peacemaking and transitional justice would consider not only individuals' demographic attributes but also, and significantly, wider context-specific debates pertaining to victim identity in situ. Core principles based upon which victims might be selected to participate in inclusion mechanisms would be both *intersectionality* – taking into account the articulation between gender, ethnicity, sexuality, race, socioeconomic background and so forth – and a *context-specific analysis* of the causes, manifestations and consequences of patterns of victimization.

In the case of Colombia, as will be seen, the organizers developed specific criteria for selecting the 60 individuals who would participate in the delegations that sought to consolidate such an approach. The organizers endeavoured to represent diverse demographic groups, while also overcoming binary narratives and responding to complex patterns of victimization and victimhood on the ground. The selection criteria aimed to incorporate victims whose condition of victimhood reiterated the widespread causes and consequences of political violence, the complex factors shaping victims' identities and the multiple forms of often mutually reinforcing violence that determined victimization. Nevertheless, while seeking to demonstrate the intersectional heterogeneous experience of victims, the delegations, in part, replicated previous processes that have either directly or indirectly depoliticized and instrumentalized victims. At the same time, the mechanism reiterated elements of the Burundi experience, which arguably led to the embedding of power imbalances between victims (Leebaw 2008) – what Gready and Roberts (2017: 956) term a 'competitive politics of division' – points which will be revisited in the following chapters.

A final point of reflection relevant to this initial brief discussion of the selection criteria mandated by the negotiating parties and employed by the organizers to determine who would take part in the victims' delegations relates to the number of participants selected. From the outset, appointing only 60 individuals to participate in the Havana talks was justifiably an issue of concern and contention, given the massivity of victimization during the conflict. Of course, the specific number of participants within an inclusion mechanism has a bearing on the degree to which inclusion may ultimately be meaningful and do justice to broader issues of representativity, through how it incorporates diverse voices and experiences. Nevertheless, we might also be mindful not to assume that a higher number of participants equates consequentially to better quality and more meaningful participation (Paffenholz 2015; Vogel 2016; Brett 2017b). In a context such as Colombia, where there are over nine million registered victims, if all victims cannot participate, then how many victims would it be ethically and politically efficacious to incorporate in an inclusion mechanism? How would such a number be calculated? In the end, the number of participants is important; however, it is less so than the nature of participation and the degree to which participation engages with relations of power and speaks accurately to patterns of victimization and victimhood.

Of course, bringing diverse sets of actors to the negotiating table has the potential to broaden the thematic focus of the negotiations and is thus significant, as cases such as the Guatemalan peace process have shown. Broader participation during peace negotiations is by no means tantamount to transformation. Rather, inclusion becomes meaningful when it guarantees the empowerment of participants and establishes channels through which to transform relations of power and the structural causes and consequences of conflict, rather than merely delivering pragmatic, political and moral legitimacy for states and international actors (Brett 2017b; Jamar 2018). As was mentioned earlier, with reference to the inclusion of women in peacemaking initiatives, Bell and McNicholl (2019: 4) cogently contend that engagement with gender should move beyond 'integrating women's concerns into policies and programmes, towards an approach that tries to understand the ways in which policies connect to questions of power relations between men and women'. The argument that inclusion from a gender perspective should be driven by the goals of re-allocating power and redefining relationships of power between men and women is of relevance for the development of a victim-centred approach and pertinent for the Colombia case. As such, this discussion of the numerical scope of inclusion should consider how including greater numbers of victims and, specifically, of women, for example, is not uniquely a benevolent good in itself. Rather, inclusion should be framed as a means through which to recalibrate power relations between victims and perpetrators, including the state and armed groups, and to forge a 'new political settlement or social contract' (Bell and McNicholl 2019: 2).

The victims' delegations: selection and composition

In June 2014, the negotiating parties formally mandated the UN, the NUC and the ECCC to organize the victims' delegations during the latter half of the same year. The decision to bring together two national institutions and one international institution to constitute the organizing body was astute. Each organization brought with it acknowledged degrees of trust, legitimacy and credibility, although not without controversy, and was able to demonstrate in-depth knowledge of the armed conflict and of the realities faced by its victims. Favouring national over international actors tipped the scales on the side of Colombian institutions, with the aim of shielding the process from criticism that the controversial discussions concerning transitional justice measures were being imposed and led by international actors. As a member of the organizers stated in an interview: 'The goal was that this would be seen as a process for Colombians, by Colombians.'[1]

With respect to the national institutions, both the NUC and the ECCC are, in general, recognized as enjoying high levels of credibility throughout the country. The National University of Colombia – *La nacional* – retains a prominent presence as a key educational and political pillar of Colombian society. The NUC is acknowledged as one of the highest-ranking universities in the country and has contributed significantly to national and international scholarship, including (although not limited to) analysis and understanding of the country's history of violence and peacemaking. In fact, Colombia's so-called *violentologists*, including figures such as Gonzalo Sanchez, have been globally recognized for their considerable contribution to the theorization of political violence. At the same time, the fact that the NUC has historically been stigmatized as an establishment peopled by scholars close to the political left, and where, allegedly, insurgent recruitment has recurrently taken place may also have played a role in the decision to include the NUC within the

---

[1] Interview, Bogotá, Colombia, March 2015.

delegations' mandate. In other words, just as Cuba had been selected as the site for the peace talks as a measure to build trust and confidence with the FARC-EP, so the NUC – beyond its academic prowess – may have been selected as a member of the Organizing Committee for a not unrelated reason, although this was not corroborated by interviewees.

The incorporation of the ECCC echoed cases elsewhere where the Church has been brought formally into peacemaking processes, in part both to legitimize talks and to represent a moral voice and authority therein. For example, during the Guatemalan peace process, the Catholic Church was mandated with a role to support dialogue between the formal negotiating parties and the wider civil society during the early stages of talks, while subsequently engaging within the so-called Civil Society Assembly. The perspective that the Church represented a moral voice during the visits to Havana was shared by an official from the ECCC who had accompanied the delegations in order to provide psychological support, if required. In their words:

> The church provides neutrality. I think [participation] gives a message of security and reassurance to the public that there is someone like the church that can represent a moral authority as a neutral player. The reputation of national institutions in this country is very low; [however] the latest survey shows that the church is one of the most credible institutions in the country.[2]

The Catholic Church remains a key pillar of Colombian society and, simultaneously, has had considerable direct experience of and proximity to the armed conflict. Many dioceses are situated in conflict-affected zones and their priests have been threatened or assassinated by armed actors. Moreover, victims and survivors of violence have often sought support from and refuge within the church. Colombia, of course, remains ostensibly a practising Catholic country, and many (although not all) participants in the delegations were themselves practising Catholics. In this case, the ECCC's presence brought spiritual solace and support, as well as heightening participants' feelings of trust in the process, particularly given that the ECCC was present from the start of the process, while later assuming a fundamental role during the delegations' visits to Havana. According to one of the members of the victims' delegations: 'On the day of our audience with the negotiating parties, at seven in the morning, a mass was given by members of the ECCC. For me, and for others, this was a moment of great spirituality.'[3] In the words

---

[2] Interview, Bogotá, Colombia, April 2015.
[3] Interview, Bogotá, Colombia, March 2015.

of another delegate who survived a massacre perpetrated by the guerrilla in the early 2000s, from the beginning of the visit to Havana,

> the church's role was very important. The priests were there accompanying us. We prayed together ... it was very good to see how this strengthened the group's unity [and generated] ... the feeling that regardless of whether we were victims of one or another armed actor, or even came from different categories of victimization, there was a lot of solidarity [among us].[4]

Such positive evaluations regarding the role of the church were not shared by all participants. Other interviewees stated how the 'religious aspect of the delegations was excessive'. Nevertheless, despite this, these interviewees did not deny the overall importance of the Church's participation in this process and its capacity to generate trust and solidarity among many of the participants and between them and the negotiating parties.[5]

The perspectives of members of the ECCC show how the institution itself contemplated its own role in supporting the delegations. According to one official:

> It is obvious that our country, after 50 years of war, has become dehumanized. If there is anyone who has become dehumanized not because they themselves have perpetrated violence, but because they have been on the receiving end of it – it has been the victims. [During this process] We have been by their side, supporting with great sensitivity, profoundly listening to them, from heart to heart. This is ... what we have tried to do.[6]

The NUC and the ECC were selected to reflect two historical and ideological key pillars of Colombian society, which, it was hoped, would legitimize and build trust in the process, while generating deeper societal appropriation of the talks. In the case of the single international institution selected to support the victims' delegations, the UN was brought in due to its long-term expertise on Colombia's armed conflict, its protracted institutional presence throughout the country and its in-depth comparative experience of transitional justice, peacebuilding and international standards relative to victims' and human rights. Up until this point, the UN had been kept at arm's length, in a process in which the government aimed to

---

[4] Interview, Bogotá, Colombia, March 2015.
[5] Interview, Bogotá, Colombia, May 2015.
[6] Interview, Bogotá, Colombia, May 2015.

maintain strict control and project an image of a nationally led peace process supported by key regional actors (Cuba, Venezuela and Chile) and neutral parties (Norway). Similarly, the negotiating parties likely believed that the incorporation of the UN would legitimize the discussions concerning Point Five, both nationally and internationally and, in particular, in the face of significant contemporary critique of victim-centred processes elsewhere. The UN has a consolidated territorial presence throughout Colombia, working closely with state and governmental institutions, although it has historically faced significant resistance from the military and political right-wing, as discussed in Chapter 4. The UN has also developed important strategic programmes supporting civil society actors with economic resources and technical capacity building throughout the country, and, from the perspective of the participants, enjoyed their trust.[7] A final objective of bringing in the UN system was to guarantee security and protection for the delegates both in Havana and on their return. However, while the security of participants was guaranteed in Havana, a significant number in fact faced severe security threats, including death threats, on their return to Colombia, as will be discussed further later on.

Selecting the participants

In June 2014, with a formal mandate from the negotiating parties to organize the victims' delegations, the NUC, the ECCC and the UN – through ten UN agencies[8] – established a working group tasked to clarify the criteria as to which the delegates would be selected and the selection process carried out. National victims' organizations did not participate directly in the organizing body, according to interviewees in order to facilitate 'the independence and impartiality' of the selection procedure.[9] However, the NUC, the ECCC and the UN formulated their selection criteria in consultation with diverse national organizations, including the National Participation Forum, Colombia without Wounds, Visible Victims, the Movement of Victims of the State, the Development and Peace Programmes and the Pastoral Sector of the Catholic Church. These organizations represented a wide spectrum of victims, including from diverse regions of the country and, most significantly, victims of all armed actors. According to interviewees, the incorporation of victims' organizations within the selection process was

---

[7] For example, the Reconciliation and Development Programme (REDES) mandated under the auspices of the UN Development Programme.
[8] Including the United Nations Development Programme, UN Women, the Office of the United Nations High Commissioner for Human Rights, the United Nations High Commissioner for Refugees and the United Nations Children's and Emergency Fund.
[9] Interview, Bogotá, Colombia, May 2015.

crucial. By collaborating with recognized national movements, the organizers had aimed to craft a broad alliance to support the process and embed it within national structures and consciousness, while 'capitalizing on the knowledge, capacity and experience of victims' organizations'.[10] According to one of the organizers: 'A crucial element of our work was the significant support we received from many victims' groups, organizations and platforms, including within the human rights movements. I believe they provided us with a substantial number of potential candidates.'[11]

The selection criteria agreed upon by the organizers aimed to balance a series of intersectional components: (a) diverse forms of victimization (including victims of distinct crimes and forms of violence as framed through national law and international norms); (b) victims from diverse geographical zones, covering local, subnational and national levels; (c) victims from distinct sectors of the population (women, men, minors, peasant farmers, indigenous people, Afro-Colombians, trade unionists, journalists, the military, the guerrilla, justice operators and the private sector, among others); and (d) victims of all armed actors, including, in numerous cases, victims of multiple armed groups. Delegates were simultaneously selected to reflect the most paradigmatic violations perpetrated during the conflict, including massacre, disappearance, forced displacement, kidnapping, torture, sexual and gender-based violence and homicide. The criteria sought to adhere to the negotiating parties' recommendation that the delegations be plural and balanced, guaranteeing demographic, gender, ethnic, ideological and philosophical diversity across all modalities of victimization.[12] Notably, over half of the participants selected were female, in recognition of the disproportionate impact the conflict has had on women and girls.

With the support of national victims' movements, the organizers had aimed to more faithfully represent patterns of victimization and victimhood on the ground. As such, the parameters decided upon, albeit to a limited degree, began in part to challenge reductionist narratives of victim–perpetrator binaries, a consistent critique of mainstream and so-called victim-centred transitional justice mechanisms. Accordingly, two former members of the security forces – a police commander and a former soldier – a young woman forcibly recruited into the FARC-EP as a child, an imprisoned FARC-EP guerrilla, and a male who had been forcibly incorporated into the paramilitaries as a minor were invited to participate in the delegations. By selecting these five individuals as participants, the organizers took an important step in acknowledging the complexity of patterns of victimization

---

[10] Interviews, Bogotá, Colombia, March–May 2015.
[11] Interview, Bogotá, Colombia, March 2015.
[12] Interviews with organizers, Bogotá, Colombia, March–April 2015.

and victimhood precipitated by Colombia's armed conflict. However, the presence of these individuals caused significant controversy and tension in Havana, which, in one case, led to the revictimization of one participant when the FARC-EP refused to acknowledge them as a victim, a point that will be revisited subsequently.

The organizers were, of course, obligated to follow the protocol agreed upon by the negotiating parties. In the Joint Press Communiqué of June 2014, the parties had indicated that the participants in the delegations should be individual victims and not representatives of collective victims or victims' organizations. The parties had also declared that participants must be victims of acts of political violence perpetrated during the length of the armed conflict and throughout the entire country. Finally, the negotiating parties had imposed three criteria upon which participants should be selected: *balance, pluralism* and *synderesis*. It was these last three elements that would act as determinant principles for bringing together the entire collective of 60 victims.

The organizers formally interpreted the three criteria and, in turn, applied them as practical parameters in the selection process. In response to the principle of 'balance', the organizers argued that the selection of participants should be as inclusive as possible in order to reflect the complex dynamics and forms of victimization associated with the Colombian armed conflict. In this regard, the organizers aimed to guarantee the participation of: (i) victims of all forms of victimization; (ii) victims of all types of affectation; (iii) victims of all armed actors; (iv) victims from across the national territory; and (v) victims from all affected social sectors, with an emphasis on populations disproportionately victimized, and with the employment of a gender and differential approach.

In response to the criterion of 'pluralism', the organizers aimed to guarantee that the delegations would reflect diverse ideological and philosophical perspectives (although not on partisan lines), while reflecting an intersectional approach, incorporating individuals from distinct gender, social, racial, class and ethnic groups. Finally, the organizers interpreted the requirement of the religious and philosophical principle of 'synderesis' as the ability of victims to understand and enact the moral order. In other words, the individuals selected were expected to demonstrate moral rectitude and righteousness, and to be able to express their own pain, while also having the capacity to transcend pain in order to show how their personal experience could be emblematic and representative of other cases of victimization.[13]

By consulting organizations that represented victims of all armed groups – specifically, the state, the paramilitaries and the FARC-EP – the organizers

---

[13] Interview with organizer, Bogotá, Colombia, May 2015.

sought to reach an equilibrium that would be perceived as legitimate by both negotiating parties. According to one national official involved in organizing the delegations:

> From the very first meeting, with the organizers we tried to interpret the criteria mandated by the negotiating parties, given that each [of the five] delegation had to fulfil all of these criteria. In our first joint press conference, we gave an explanation regarding how we interpreted this. In the final press conference, we explained how we believed we had achieved all proposed criteria ... The consultations with victims' organizations have been important ... we agreed that we should consult three or four [victims'] platforms, where we asked for names, and we began to build our own lists according to these proposals. This included the National Victims' Dialogue Table (Mesa Nacional), established through the Victims' Law of 2011 ... and the Movement of Victims of the State (MOVICE) ... then [consultations] with groups that represented victims of the FARC-EP, specifically two platforms, Victimas Visibles (Visible Victims) and one from Colombia sin Heridas (Colombia without Wounds).[14]

Consultations were carried out not only with victims' organizations, but also within the three organizing bodies and their own networks, including with their subnational offices or headquarters across Colombia. According to one of the organizers:

> Internally we carried out an exercise with our subnational offices saying 'there is this mandate, we are part of the organizers and we need you to identify key emblematic cases in your regions that we can take to Havana'. They sent us very interesting cases, several of whom actually went to Havana ... There were hundreds of solid cases ... [the idea was that] those who were most representative would go. We began to receive many cases, and we made a database precisely to cover the following criteria: name, region, victimizing event, age, date of the events, place, description.[15]

The selection of 60 victims – out of an approximate total of nine million – was, of course, a sensitive and controversial task, particularly given that the designated number of participants derided Colombia's mass, complex and systematic levels of victimization. In order to develop a practical

---

[14] Interview, Bogotá, Colombia, March 2015.
[15] Interview, Bogotá, Colombia, April 2015.

decision-making mechanism to facilitate the painstaking decision of identifying 60 out of nine million victims, the organizers and supporting actors drew up an internal document setting the initial specific parameters for including diverse forms of victimhood and victimization. The document established a framework that aspired to guarantee that victims of the most significant and emblematic acts of violence perpetrated during the conflict would be included. Employing their agreed-upon criteria and interpretations, and in consultation with their subnational offices, national civil society organizations and the negotiating parties, the organizers established a series of databases including thousands of potential participants. The databases themselves were built on consultation with approximately 130 victims' organizations incorporated into the UN Transitional Justice Fund and with the subnational offices of the Office of the UN High Commissioner for Human Rights. According to interviewees, the UN Office of the High Commissioner for Refugees and the UNDP also prepared their own databases that were consulted in tandem with all other databases. Conversations were also continually held with the network of Programmes of Development and Peace, situated in diverse regions of the country. Out of these conversations, and with the support of the NUC, the ECCC and the UN with respect to legal categorization, gender focus and definitions of victimization, a solid idea of what the collective of 60 individuals might eventually look like was developed. According to one member of the organizers, 'when you put all of this into a database, it gave us the ability to analyse who [which victims], what [which crimes] and which areas of the country were missing'.[16]

Once equipped with this framework, the working group held prolonged meetings during which they discussed the potential candidates for each 12-person delegation identified in their databases. A delegation was approved once there was a consensus among all those present.

Time was not on the organizers' side: the time allocated for arranging each delegation was extremely brief, a matter of weeks at most, with a delegation set to visit Havana approximately once a month during the second half of 2014. According to interviewees involved in the organization of the delegations, the process to select individuals for each delegation was protracted and debates over whom to select raised diverse tensions. The task itself was understood by the organizers as one of extreme difficulty:

> We departed from two very clear points where there was consensus. First, it was impossible to select 60 people from a universe of at

---

[16] Interview, Bogotá, Colombia, May 2015.

least eight million registered victims – and many more are not even registered. Second, the task that we were given was impossible. Starting from that baseline, we tried to interpret the criteria and seek the best solution ... There I think something fundamental united us and this was the fact that we represented three institutions with a very clear commitment to making this country a better place. This perspective shored up how we understood and how we carried out our task. Obviously the work isn't perfect, but I believe we really did the best we could do. Every time we made a selection there was anguish: it was a heavy responsibility and burden. It was a very stressful process, when we had our discussions, but fortunately the balance was very satisfactory in the end. It was very good teamwork and I think the result was good too.[17]

Once agreement upon all 12 potential candidates for each delegation had been reached, and usually with only very little notice prior to departure for Havana, candidates were advised by telephone of their having been selected. The majority of candidates did not accept the invitation immediately and were given a maximum of two days to confirm their participation. In some cases, individuals did not have passports and so expedited requests had to be made to distinct government/state agencies with the support of the organizers. Due to potential security risks, candidates were asked not to share the information concerning their selection with anyone except immediate family, which was a problematic request, not least given the emotional impact of the potential encounter and the fact that many selected candidates belonged to victims' organizations with which they were obliged to consult about their potential participation. Many interviewees stated that, in reality, they did not adhere to this request, precisely because they had to talk through their participation with colleagues, to seek approval in some cases from their organizations, and felt that not doing so would be morally and politically untenable.

The participation of 60 individuals was inadequate in numerical terms, and ethically and politically problematic given the exclusion of more than 99 per cent of the country's registered victims in the mechanism. Such curtailed/symbolic participation remains a core criticism of so-called victim-centred peacemaking and transitional justice. From the perspective of the negotiating parties and the organizers, the composition of the delegations sought to craft a meaningful vision of Colombia's universe of victims and complex patterns of victimhood and victimization. Neither the organizers nor negotiating parties intended that the delegations directly represent the

---

[17] Interview, Bogotá, Colombia, March 2015.

country's nine million victims. As indicated in the final report published by the organizers in 2014 in the wake of the final visit, 'a limited group of sixty victims cannot be representative of all the victims of the Colombian armed conflict, given the levels of victimization in Colombia and the diversity of perpetrators and forms of victimization' (UN, NUC and ECCC 2014). The majority of interviewees who had participated in the delegations strongly criticized the decision to include such a low and arbitrary number of victims. For one participant, the 60 who were selected failed to include many others who, from her perspective were 'the most forgotten victims ... the most invisible ... they have neither voice nor representation. They have had to suffer considerably, with minimal support, [they are] the most abandoned'.[18]

Nevertheless, the constellation of victims that the delegations ultimately included, based as it was on an intersectional approach to selection, achieved the effect of providing a meaningful picture of Colombia's complex mosaic of egregious victimization and mass victimhood. In interviews, while critiquing the number of participants invited, members of the delegations voiced their widespread support for the composition of all five delegations in terms explicitly of their diversity and representative nature. The majority of delegates, in fact, stated that the pragmatic process and outcome had been successful, even in spite of what was the problematic minimal number of individuals invited.[19]

The remaining chapters will argue that the delegations ultimately punched above their weight, in the end having a significant impact, including in terms of individual episodes of empowerment. However, it will also be contended that the success of the delegations was simultaneously limited, given that significant instrumentalization/depoliticization/retraumatizaion took place.

The five delegations evidenced the following characteristics:

- *Gender*
  - 36 women
  - 24 men
- *Age*
  - Victims between the ages of 19 and 78
- *Victims from 25 departments of the country, including:*
  - Valle del Cauca, Cauca, Antioquia, Cundinamarca, Huila, Nariño, Santander, Caquetá, Bolívar, Chocó, Magdalena, Meta, Norte de Santander and Tolima
  - ten victim representatives at the national level (Bogotá)

---

[18] Interview, Bogotá, Colombia, April 2015.
[19] Interviews, Bogotá and Santa Marta, Colombia, March–May 2015.

- *Acts of victimization, including:*
  - violation of the right to life (including homicide, extrajudicial execution, massacre, forced disappearance)
  - forced displacement
  - threats
  - hostage taking and kidnapping
  - sexual and gender-based violence
  - victims of anti-personnel mines
  - victims of the recruitment of children and adolescents into armed groups
  - victims of violations of freedom of opinion and expression (including journalists).
- *Victims from diverse populations, including:*
  - victims or relatives of human rights defenders
  - politicians from different sectors and regions of the country
  - Afro-descendants
  - indigenous people
  - peasants
  - journalists
  - teachers
  - trade unionists
  - private sector
  - members of the security forces
  - LGBTI+ population
  - victims from religious groups
  - judicial operators
  - civil servants
  - social and community organization leaders
  - cattle ranchers
  - young people who were minors at the time of their victimization.
- *Victims of a wide range of perpetrators, including:*
  - the state
  - paramilitary groups
  - the FARC-EP
  - the ELN
  - victims of multiple armed actors.
- *Of those who participated, there were a total of:*
  - 53% victims of the state and paramilitary forces
  - 47% victims of the FARC-EP.

The challenge of perpetrator identity

Critics of victim-centred transitional justice and inclusive peacemaking interventions have questioned the degree to which their practices and objectives align with the rights, equity and justice-based narratives often undergirding inclusion initiatives. As was discussed in previous chapters, scholars have contended that 'victim-centred' mechanisms have habitually been established at the behest of state and armed actors engaged in peace negotiations or directing transitional processes, and of those international custodians who frequently oversee such processes, as they seek to secure their own requirements and interests (McEvoy and McConnachie 2012a; Robins 2017). From this perspective, elite actors instrumentalize victims as they pursue wider objectives inherent in 'pragmatic deal making', such as the achievement of a political settlement, limiting penal sanctions for perpetrators, the consolidation of the rule of law or the institutionalization of mechanisms through which to deter future criminal acts and violations (McEvoy and McConnachie 2012b: 500). The argument that, under such conditions, victims do not participate on their own terms, but rather are objectified and instrumentalized, has significant relevance for specific elements of Colombia's victim-centred experience, although it fails to tell the whole story, as was proposed in previous chapters.

A considerable challenge that the organizers faced was how they would balance numerically the victims of the principal armed groups (state, guerrilla and paramilitaries) across the spectrum of the 60 individuals set to visit Havana. This challenge was further complicated by the fact that, since the early 2000s, a vocal sector of Colombians had propagated the perception that the guerrilla represented the only actor that should be obligated to confront its victims and face criminal prosecution for its actions, a narrative that had been exacerbated by former President Uribe's demonizing political rhetoric and the severe polarization that his presidencies had sculpted. Those opposing the talks, in particular former President Uribe, his political supporters and other influential actors, such as the cattle-ranching sector, initially contended that only victims of the guerrilla should participate in the delegations. The proposal gained little political traction. However, Uribe and his supporters' rhetoric heightened further political and public debates concerning the selection process and politicized the victims who visited Havana. Echoing Uribe and his constituents' declarations, Colombia's Procurator General, the ultra-conservative Alejandro Ordoñez, consistently criticized the initiative during 2014, making several public statements that only FARC-EP victims should go to Havana and, when this claim became untenable, that the number of victims of the FARC-EP in Havana had been inadequate.[20]

---

[20] See https://www.eluniversal.com.co/colombia/procurador-insiste-en-que-solo-deben-ir-cuba-las-victimas-de-las-FARC-EP-170448-FUEU265132 and https://www.elespectador.com/politica/a-la-habana-solo-deben-ir-las-victimas-de-las-FARC-EP-procurador-article-533282/ (accessed 5 May 2023).

Under significant public pressure domestically, the organizers faced the challenge of balancing the number of victims of each conflict party: state forces, guerrilla forces and paramilitaries. Undergirding demands for greater numbers of victims of either the FARC-EP or the state and paramilitary forces was a zero-sum mentality, treating the victims as an extension of the conflict. According to one interviewee: 'The delegations were perceived of as a type of popular tribunal through which the parties would be able to achieve moral ascendancy by maximizing the number of *accusers* their adversary would have to face.'[21] Therefore, across the media and in the minds of many Colombians, there existed the perception that the number of the victims of each party showed the degree of their relative responsibility for the violations perpetrated during the conflict. Prior to the visit of the first delegation, both the state and the FARC-EP had publicly denied responsibility for all violations and abuses; the composition of the delegations and the individual stories of horror and suffering they brought, of course, belied such denial. The zero-sum mentality held firm until the visits of the delegations in 2014 gradually began to bring about a cumulative transformation in the minds of the negotiating parties, which broke down perpetrator denial, as will be discussed in the following chapter. According to one member of the organizers:

> The process was difficult on many levels, especially given that we were still in the midst of the armed conflict. The question of what should have been the balance between victims as seen from the perspective exclusively of their perpetrators was seen by some actors as a judgement call regarding the degree of responsibility for the violence perpetrated during the conflict. In the eyes of many, in making the selection, we were pointing a finger, we were attributing responsibilities for the suffering. And we did not want the selection process to be perceived as a signal, as pointing a finger.[22]

In a context in which victim inclusion was interpreted as an indication of criminal responsibility, the organizers sought to play down the accusatory implications of the composition of the five delegations, both to the negotiating parties and the wider public. In press communiqués and public statements, the organizers clarified how the selection criteria responded to demographic factors, such as ethnicity, region, gender and type of violation, among others, rather than being focused uniquely on perpetrator identity. With the aim of legitimizing their choices and as a bulwark against further criticism of the composition of the delegations, the organizers referred in

---

[21] Interview, Bogotá, Colombia, April 2015.
[22] Interview, Bogotá, Colombia, May 2015.

their statements to how the selection criteria had been imposed by the negotiating parties. In the face of criticism of the process from diverse sectors – and with particular respect to demands for greater numbers of FARC-EP victims – the organizers received support from the government's chief negotiator, Humberto de la Calle. After the first delegation in August 2014, de la Calle publicly stated:

> The victims will be selected based on the criteria established by the negotiating parties that permit the reflection of all victimizing events and of the diversity of sectors and populations and parts of the country in such a way that the delegations are inclusive, plural and balanced. We do not understand the criteria of addition and subtraction.[23]

Nevertheless, logically, the number of victims selected from each armed group became an issue of fundamental significance, with the negotiating parties and wider interested sectors monitoring not only each perpetrator's victim count within the delegations, but also the type of crimes that the participating victims themselves embodied.[24] Therefore, the 60 Colombians who visited Havana were frequently treated as the personification and embodiment of criminal liability rather than as the victims of egregious human rights violations and abuses. As a consequence, the participants, in particular, and the inclusion mechanism, in general, were instrumentalized and politicized in part by the negotiating parties and systematically by those vocal actors opposing the peace talks in their efforts to assign responsibility and to ridicule the negotiations, as will be discussed later on.

In the words of one individual who worked closely with the organizers and the delegations:

> I believe that the organizations in charge of the selection process were qualified, were probably the organizations with the greatest competence, and in that sense, one has to agree, they did it rigorously, seriously, with absolute responsibility, and tried to be as objective as possible ... I believe that they fulfilled their role well and it seems to me that they made the appropriate selection ... in more than one of these selections, there were complaints that [the parties] ... did not agree with the selection made ... however there was the ability to adapt and achieve the final purpose.[25]

---

[23] See https://www.elcolombiano.com/historico/de_la_calle_confirma_viaje_de_otras_48_victimas_y_cuestiona_criticas_a_visita-DGEC_307499 (accessed 5 May 2023).
[24] See Annex 1 for a breakdown of the victims' delegations in terms of crimes and perpetrators.
[25] Interview, Bogotá, Colombia, May 2015.

Perhaps the most significant point of public controversy and tension between the negotiating parties, the organizers and the invited victims occurred with respect to the decision taken by the organizers to include a former high-ranking police officer within the third delegation.[26] The individual concerned had been kidnapped by the guerrilla on 1 November 1998, during the FARC-EP's seizure of the town of Mitú (in the Vaupés department), along with 60 other police officers. The then Colonel was held in captivity in the jungle for 11 years, 7 months and 13 days under infra-human conditions. He was liberated on 13 June 2010 as a result of Operation Chameleon. Kidnapping/prisoners of war (*secuestro*) was one of the emblematic crimes carried out by the FARC-EP during the conflict, and a clear contravention of international humanitarian law. As such, the inclusion of victims of kidnapping within the victims' delegations was crucial.

The delegate initially rejected the organizers' invitation to visit Havana, particularly given the FARC-EP's public rebuke of his participation.[27] Given the FARC-EP's position that members of the security forces could only be categorized as perpetrators and not as victims, the invitation and his subsequent presence in Havana levied acute tension between the negotiating parties and victims, prior to, during and after the visit of the third delegation. In the wake of his visit to Havana, the FARC-EP continued to oppose the organizers' decision, stating publicly that the individual had never been a victim, given his role in the state security forces. For the individual concerned, the experience was 'disturbing, heavy'. In his words, the guerrilla's attitude:

> was to disqualify my presence in Havana ... I believe that they didn't see me there as a victim, but as an enemy. But I was there as a victim. I made my approach [to the negotiating parties] as a victim and they, on the contrary, directed their approach [to me] as the enemy. In other words, they saw me as being on the other side ... that I was and would continue to be the enemy.[28]

The episode led to the individual's revictimization, highlighting the limits to the potential capacity of victim-centred transitional justice and inclusion mechanisms, as will be discussed in the following chapters.

---

[26] See https://www.eltiempo.com/archivo/documento/CMS-14622975 and https://www.eluniverso.com/noticias/2014/08/03/nota/3319111/FARC-EP-piden-que-tambien-se-considere-victimas-sus-combatientes (accessed 5 May 2023).

[27] See https://www.eltiempo.com/archivo/documento/CMS-14622975 (accessed 6 May 2023).

[28] Interview, Bogotá, Colombia, April 2015.

In the wake of the third delegation, the guerrilla remained resolute in its position that members of the security forces should not be treated as victims. In an attempt to levy equilibrium, in August 2014, the FARC-EP made a public statement demanding that wounded, fallen or detained combatants be considered victims.[29] The organizers' response was supportive and, in a following delegation, an imprisoned FARC-EP combatant presented his testimony to the parties in Havana via video link from prison. Unsurprisingly perhaps, the inclusion of this individual precipitated a similar degree of polemic in the media, particularly from those who opposed the talks. Nevertheless, the tensions that resulted from the inclusion of these two participants, and that of a former female FARC-EP combatant and former AUC member both recruited as children, did not derail the victims' delegations, but arguably strengthened their inclusivity. As will be discussed further later on, the inclusion of victims/perpetrators within the delegations in fact showed a demonstrable advancement in comparison with other victim inclusion measures elsewhere, given that the organizers had attempted to move beyond a simplistic victim–perpetrator dichotomy and represent the complexity of patterns of violence on the ground.

Gender as a lens for the selection criteria

As was discussed in previous chapters, critiques of inclusive peacemaking and victim-centred transitional justice have pushed back against simplistic proposals for increasing numerical levels of inclusion that equate participation with empowerment (Paffenholz 2015; Firchow and Selim 2022), yet fail to engage with or transform relations of power. From the standpoint of a gendered approach, this contention retains significant relevance, given arguments that effective inclusion within this framework should be driven by the goal of redefining relationships of and re-allocating power between genders and across other spheres such as the state, government, civil society and the private sector (Bell and McNicholl 2019).

The effective representation, participation and inclusion of women then have remained ongoing and unresolved problems within both the transitional justice and liberal peacebuilding paradigms. In recent decades, transitional justice provisions for women have been consecrated in approximately half of all signed peace agreements. However, the overwhelming majority of these agreements have not provided for the establishment of specific institutions to address women and gender in post-transitional polities and societies (Bell and McNicholl 2019: 41). Women's concerns have continued to be

---

[29] See https://www.eluniverso.com/noticias/2014/08/03/nota/3319111/FARC-EP-piden-que-tambien-se-considere-victimas-sus-combatientes/ (accessed 6 May 2023).

marginalized within transitional justice initiatives, while the paradigm has set up a 'gendered notion' of conflict. In short, women are commonly incorporated into truth and justice commissions predominantly as 'innocent victims', including particularly of gender-based violence. Moreover, women's 'relationship to conflict is primarily as 'third party' victims through male relatives', with the exception of specific provisions for women prisoners (as combatants) and references to sexual violence. Furthermore, women tend to be included at later stages of peace negotiations and are less likely to be incorporated into the implementation framework (Bell and McNicholl 2019: 41–43).

Transitional justice and liberal peacebuilding initiatives, then, have historically shared a 'gender-blind' approach, excluding the 'gender-specific interests and needs of women in transitional settings' (Bell and McNicholl 2019: 41–45). Even with the formalization of Resolution 1325 of the UN General Assembly on the Participation of Women in Peace Processes and the policy framework that it has provided, 'gender justice and equality in (post-)conflict settings remain largely unachieved' (O'Reilly 2016: 419; 424). For O'Reilly (2016: 419), transitional justice in particular has lacked a 'gender-equitable distribution of material and symbolic resources', which has signified that the participation of women as agents of transitional justice processes has been severely limited.

Despite such ongoing setbacks, the likelihood that settlements include a gender perspective is approximately five times greater in peace agreements signed after 2015 compared to those accords signed in the 1990s (Bell and McNicholl 2019: 32–35). Moreover, and of relevance to the Colombia case, the thematic inclusion of women and gender is significantly more likely if the UN has been involved as a signatory, although this is the case only in the aftermath of the ratification of Resolution 1325. A germane issue arising here is what a meaningful gender-inclusive mechanism might look like and what we might expect from it. The case of Colombia provides a degree of innovation in this respect, given that both the peace process and the victims' delegations incorporated a paradigmatic gender perspective, a subject that will be discussed next.

From the commencement of the Havana peace talks in 2012, the UN System in Colombia – with the crucial support of UN Women – promoted a strategy to guarantee the equal participation of women during the civil society forums held in 2012 and 2013. This demand was subsequently reiterated as a key aspect of the selection criteria for the victims' delegations in 2014. The UN's policy was a response to the historical claims of women's organizations on the ground in Colombia, while it was also a strategy through which to adhere to international norms relative to women's rights and peacebuilding, such as Resolution 1325. From the outset, foremost in the minds of the organizers was to overcome the ongoing challenge of underrepresentation of women in peace processes, despite significant provision enshrined in Resolution 1325 to guarantee the right and duty of women to participate directly therein.

According to one of the organizers:

> In the case of Colombia, what we saw, in 2013 when information concerning the peace talks began to emerge, was this enormous absence ... that the normative framework [concerning women's rights and participation] was clearly not being complied with. But we also saw the impact of the conflict on women. We collaborated with other cooperation mechanisms to generate documentation and evidence regarding what this [participation] meant from a gender perspective ... In the face of such a flagrant absence, what we developed was a process of listening very clearly to the demands of women's organizations.[30]

The work carried out by the UN and, emphatically, by UN Women in support of a gender-focused approach during the negotiations was levied on diverse levels and during distinct stages, and particularly so once the parties had mandated the UN to organize the civil society and victims' forums, in 2012 and 2014 respectively, and, in their wake, the victims' delegations. From 2012, the UN provided political and technical advice to the negotiating parties, which was augmented by the logistical and political support provided to and selection and accompaniment of the delegations to Havana. Furthermore, UN Women spearheaded the elaboration of a policy document that brought together the proposals of women's organizations in line with the different points on the negotiating agenda (Brett 2017a).

The UN's support to the parties prior to the delegations culminated, in October 2013, in the National Women's Summit for Peace. Bringing together 500 women from 30 departments of the country and stemming from 20 social sectors, the summit was financed by five donor countries and supported by the UN System, with a central role assumed by UN Women. The summit was given prior governmental approval and the FARC-EP negotiators were notified of the process, which aimed to facilitate a dialogue between civil society, government and the private sector to discuss the role that women and their organizations might play in the negotiations.

In the summit's closing public statement, the participants demanded the formalized participation of women in the Havana talks at a binding level, the incorporation of a gender and women's rights perspective within and

---

[30] Interview, Bogotá, Colombia, March 2015.

throughout the peace agreements and the immediate de-escalation of violence against women. The summit's declaration, in part, established a precedent upon which the organizers built their later stipulations for a gendered approach during the ongoing negotiations and within the victims' delegations. At the same time, the declaration, in turn, echoed the wider demands of women's movements and adhering to obligations enshrined in international law.

Three weeks after the summit, the negotiating parties signed the Partial Agreement on Political Participation, which established a series of gender prerogatives and provisions and clarified that these principles would be taken into account for the remaining agreements. Moreover, a month after the summit, two female plenipotentiaries were appointed by the government to its negotiating team in Havana. In parallel, the FARC-EP delegation began to carry out internal reflections concerning the participation of female guerrillas in the talks, subsequently appointing female negotiators to their Havana team. Arguably, then, the preparatory work that culminated in the summit, and the summit itself, influenced both the peace agenda and the dynamics of the negotiations. The gradual construction of a broader gendered approach framing the negotiations was reinforced by an increasingly productive dialogue between UN Women and the negotiating parties, which ultimately led to a crucial mechanism – the Sub-commission on Gender – in which women belonging to both parties and diverse sectors discussed issues relevant to the peace agenda (Brett 2017a), which will be discussed in more detail later on.

With the announcement by the negotiating parties in June 2014 which formalized the victims' delegations, the NUC, the ECCC and the UN, and UN Women in particular, assumed an important role in shaping the gendered approach adopted within the peace negotiations and, specifically, with regard to the transitional justice provisions therein. A central prerogative of the organizers was to incorporate a gender lens as a central organizing principle of the selection criteria for the victims' delegations, in recognition of the disproportionate levels of victimization against women and girls during Colombia's armed conflict and in response to the claims and demands of women's organizations. Across the country at the national, subnational and local levels, women's organizations – such as CISMA Mujer, Ruta Pacifica and Casa de Mujer – have historically levied a public role as peacebuilders, shaping informal processes by mobilizing against patterns of direct and structural violence and influencing public policy, national legislation, Constitutional Court rulings and public debate relative to women's rights and gender issues. Beyond their context-specific platforms often pursuing rights-based demands, many women's organizations have, over recent decades, simultaneously demanded formal participation in peace talks. As a consequence of such widespread mobilization – frequently carried out with the support of international actors – diverse platforms and national summits have taken place over recent decades, reinforcing the visibility of women's movements as political actors. The gender focus of the delegations simultaneously acknowledged the core achievements of Colombia's women's organizations and the egregious impact that historical political violence has had upon women and girls.

The decision to prioritize a gendered approach within the selection criteria was made collectively by the organizers, with significant expertise provided by UN Women. The development of the gender framework came ultimately to have significant repercussions both for the victims' delegations themselves and, more broadly, for the dynamics of the negotiations and the content of the peace accord, in the latter case in the form of the mainstreaming of gender provisions across all agreements, a task assumed by the Sub-commission on Gender (Peace Accords Matrix 2023).

According to one female participant in the victims' delegations, the participation and incidence of women remained a constant during and up until the closure of the Havana talks, having initially commenced in 2013 and developed impetus during the regional forums. In her words:

> The sector of female victims has been a sector that has been organizing around spaces for dialogue and forums for citizen consultation. These two processes have been linked not only to women victims, but also to women peacebuilders. There was between 40 per cent and 60 per cent representation of women in all these forums and this meant that the issue of women, in general, and female victims, in particular, began to be much more crystallized around the proposals [of women] as a sector of the population, in addition to indigenous and Afro-Colombian [women].[31]

As they sought to apply a gendered approach to the selection process/criteria, the first immediate step taken by the organizers was to impose a gender quota on the delegations, aimed at guaranteeing that a minimum of 50 per cent of participants were women. In the end, 36 of the 60 victims were women. In the words of one of the organizers, this approach aimed to be 'intersectional' by taking into account not only the gender identity of the participants, but also by ensuring: 'That the women [selected] were not only victims of one form of human rights violation, but also that there was a wide representation of the diverse violations of the human rights of

---

[31] Interview, Bogotá, Colombia, March 2015.

women, ranging from sexual violence to [female victims of] intimidation, massacre and homicide.'[32]

According to the organizers, the gender focus sought to move beyond a 'thermometer for categorizing the nature of violations perpetrated against women' in order to 'narrate untold histories, evidence the impact of the conflict upon women and open a space within which it would be possible to launch proposals related to the transformation of the state and wider society towards a more equal, equitable and progressive country' (Brett 2017a: 35). However, the degree to which the latter objective was achieved has been limited, as will be discussed later on.

The extent to which the specific demands and proposals of the female delegates were incorporated into Point Five and whether these provisions represented a mandate to re-allocate relations of power will be discussed in the following chapters. However, at this stage, it is germane to signal that, as a result of the demands levied by the female participants in the victims' delegations and the broader pressure from female negotiators, Colombian civil society and international actors supporting the talks, two key outcomes were achieved. First, significant gender provisions and a gendered perspective were incorporated into Point Five and across the Final Agreeement. Second, the negotiating parties formally mandated the so-called Sub-commission on Gender to the talks in September 2014. The Sub-commission brought female negotiators from both parties together to discuss themes of relevance to them in a separate space for encounter; members could meet with visiting delegations in Havana, including the victims' delegations. The mechanism was mandated to review the remaining accords and guarantee that they would incorporate a gendered approach. As a consequence of the work of the Sub-commission, the Colombian accords have been assessed as the most sophisticated settlement to date in terms of their capacity to represent a gendered perspective (Peace Accords Matrix 2023). Augmenting the Sub-commission on Gender, three separate women's delegations were subsequently invited to Havana to provide expertise on the issues of women and gender. The first delegation arrived in December 2014 and included representatives from Iniciativas de Mujeres por la Paz, Ruta Pacifica, Corporación Colombiana de Teatro, Red nacional de Artistas, Asociación de Mujeres por la paz y los derechos de la Mujer (ASODEMUC) and Sisma Mujer y Casa de la Mujer. This delegation was followed by two further delegations in 2015.

Describing the overall impact of the gender framework, one female participant in the delegations stated how:

---

[32] Interview, Bogotá, Colombia, March 2015.

Most of the victims who arrived in Havana were women ... a series of women's issues were proposed, and in the process, the creation of the Sub-commission on Gender has been important. I think there has been positive evolution within the parties themselves ... Ask some of the women's organizations, how did they find their first meeting with the delegations in Havana? What [the FARC-EP] say is that the women in particular had a great impact on them ... which I think is historical. The Sub-commission is working, it meets frequently. And, in this way, the previous [signed] agreements are under the process of review, so that the language and framework of gender undergirds them. It will be important to include gender issues in the accords that will be agreed upon later.[33]

At the same time, according to one female interviewee, a participant in the delegations, the formal participation of women in Havana also fed back into the process of women's grassroots organizing. In her words:

For the women of the delegations of victims, their participation in Havana was so significant that they began to generate a cascade effect from what happened in Havana with their grassroots bases or even with their peers. From the point of view of those female delegations from women's organizations, this was even more the case, because they were there representing an organizational experience [perspective] and had the experience of having had a voice [in Havana]. This generated high expectations for them to transmit that voice later on.[34]

In interviews, the female members of the delegations acknowledged the significance of their participation. According to one female indigenous leader, a victim of paramilitary violence, going to Havana:

gave me the opportunity to be in a scenario like that because we ourselves have struggled ... we have resisted ... the persistence of our struggle for justice, for the truth, for the return [after displacement] for me as a woman, as a mother and as a victim who has suffered in her own flesh. I felt like a woman forging peace ... It's been the women who have put our faces, our bodies, who have received the blows, the hunger we have suffered, thousands of difficulties. It's been us, the women.[35]

---

[33] Interview, Bogotá, Colombia, March 2015.
[34] Interview, Bogotá, Colombia, February 2015.
[35] Interview, Bogotá, Colombia, March 2015.

A female participant from the mountainous central region of Colombia, who had been victim of multiple armed actors, stated:

> There has been equity in the participation of women in Havana, why? Because women have been the most affected by the conflict. Women have lost our children, our husbands. Women have had to bring entire families when displacement occurs. We women have borne the pain of this conflict. Even the mothers of armed actors. So the participation of women is key in this peace process.[36]

Other female participants discussed their perspectives on the significance of visiting Havana and facing their perpetrators. An Afro-Colombian woman from Cauca, who had been a victim of the military, reiterated a similar perspective, stating how: 'It was very important that we were given the opportunity. Many times here in Colombia, women are the ones who have the least opportunities. It was important that, as women, we are given the space to be there, to be able to share what we know [and have experienced].'[37] A woman whose family had suffered multiple violations perpetrated by the armed forces, which included the forced disappearance of various relatives, recognized that women had been disproportionately affected by the conflict. For this individual, the participation of women in the delegations was 'a vindication of women's historical struggles', a reflection that echoes the original objectives as defined by the organizers. In her words: 'Women have contributed to the recognition of rights, to the legitimacy of these struggles and to advancing respect and gender equality as a consequence of their participation in the delegations.'[38]

When asked about her experience in Havana and why she felt that the adoption of a gender perspective had been so urgent for the Havana talks, a survivor of violence perpetrated by the military and paramilitaries commented:

> I spoke for women victims of sexual violence. I have to focus on that. I am aware that I am participating myself, but I am doing it for a country, for women. This is the first step: going to speak [in Havana]. From now onwards, it will be a very long continuous struggle, because, as a survivor, I'm not going to settle for going there to bare my soul to them and then nothing happens afterwards. In other words, the issue of sexual violence either remains on the negotiating agenda

---

[36] Interview, Bogotá, Colombia, April 2015.
[37] Interview, Santa Marta, Colombia, April 2015.
[38] Interview, Bogotá, Colombia, May 2015.

or it remains on the negotiating agenda and, if it does not, then we already have the path open to the International Criminal Court ... In a peace process, where there's been a war, an armed conflict, it is impossible to talk about nonrecurrence without taking into account those most affected, because otherwise those speaking are just the ones who have had the power of weapons ... but you would never include those who have suffered the greatest damage. I think that being able to include the vision of those who have had to bear the greatest damage, as well as giving legitimacy, gives you the path, a blueprint, it guides the process.[39]

Echoing the previous comments regarding the role that women should play in peace negotiations, a female participant from the second delegation stated: 'As a woman, the achievements that we women have been having for many centuries, of our rights, of giving voice; now, a peace process without women is not a peace process, because as some say, we do not give birth to children for war.'[40]

One female participant from the Atlantic coast, a victim of multiple violations, including sexual violence, homicide and forced displacement perpetrated by all armed actors (the armed forces, paramilitaries and the guerrilla), commented on how the process leading to participation in Havana had been a protracted one. From her perspective, the path to Havana had begun ten years previously with the approval of Law 975, the Justice and Peace Law. It had been at this moment that her own process of empowerment and individual politicization had begun. From her perspective, the inclusion of victims was a recognition of her own struggles and those of other female participants, again highlighting one of the original objectives of the delegations. In her words:

In 2006 we began filing complaints for women victims of sexual violence, because one day we had sat down to talk over a coffee and we realized that not only had we been displaced [as women] and that not only had some of us seen our husbands murdered, but also, there were some women who, in the midst of their displacement, had been victims of sexual violence.[41]

According to interviewees, the vindication of women's historical struggles and recognition of the egregious violence perpetrated against women during

---

[39] Interview, Bogotá, Colombia, May 2015.
[40] Interview, Bogotá, Colombia, April 2015.
[41] Interview, Santa Marta, Colombia, April 2015.

the conflict were identified as common factors precipitating the gendered approach assumed during the Havana talks. For one survivor of violence perpetrated by the armed forces and the paramilitaries:

> In the forums we began to participate, we had already been working with women in the theme of justice for sexual violence. There was a great debt with respect to the women who have been affected, especially in [terms of] justice because these are the crimes for which there is greatest impunity ... It is important to highlight how the voice of the victims is there [in Havana] and how women have played a very important role in the peace process.[42]

Female delegates also commented on how their participation had resulted in the significant consequence of experiencing 'great moments of solidarity' with the other female participants during the traumatic process of facing their perpetrators in Havana. A mother whose son had been the victim of extrajudicial execution perpetrated by the army in the so-called *False Positives* cases – a paradigmatic example of the contravention of humanitarian law by the military – told how a FARC-EP delegate had approached her. In her words, the female FARC-EP combatant expressed how: 'We admire you because you are a woman who defends her rights and who defends the rights of this country. Your political advocacy is notable because you are not afraid to name these people and put faces on them.'[43]

The identification of an evolving dynamic between female victims and female negotiators was a further common theme that emerged during the interviews with participants. Interviewees commented on how important it had been for them to be able to talk with the women from both negotiating parties and how such moments precipitated important moments of recognition between both victim and perpetrator. One participant from Cali whose family member had been executed by the paramilitaries explained her meeting with some of the members of the Sub-commission on Gender:

> We were able to talk. In that interaction, you no longer saw the person for their function or for having the brand of the government or the brand of the FARC-EP, or for being a victim. Rather, it was a relationship of equals, as human beings ... Due to various experiences that I had [in Havana], I saw how we demystified each other ... After lunch, we were able to talk with the women who wanted to go [to the Sub-commission]. For me it was key to have [a female combatant]

---

[42] Interview, Bogotá, Colombia, May 2015.
[43] Interview, Bogotá, Colombia, May 2015.

by my side, no longer as the character of [a female combatant], but as a woman who was interested in the issues of life, in this country. As someone who shares the same concerns. So how is it possible that we see each other as human? To be able to talk and not only denounce what we did or what we did not do? But rather to recognize that we have to heal? To be able to share lunch ... it really caught my attention that the victims, the FARC-EP, the UN ... those of the National University and the Episcopal Conference could sit at the same table ... and have an informal conversation.[44]

Ultimately, a female victim of the guerrilla from Cali summarized this emergent solidarity between female victims and members of the negotiating parties, an issue that will be explored further in the following chapter, given its relevance to gradual processes of acknowledgement between victims and perpetrators in Havana. In her words: 'We were sitting at the table with the women victims, the negotiators, and the international community. At some point I looked around, and I had forgotten who was who, and who had done what to whom. I realized that we were only women, talking about peace.'[45]

Concluding remarks

Of the core justifications for inclusive peacemaking and victim-centred transitional justice, two perhaps stand out. The first is the moral imperative to guarantee that those most affected by political violence play a role in the construction of a shared, post-accord future. The second is the contention that including victims' proposals will sculpt a more legitimate and representative political settlement and accountability mechanisms that may, in turn, lead to broader societal buy-in and, ultimately, a more sustainable post-accord scenario. As the establishing principle of the victims' delegations, the invitation to only 60 out of a total of approximately nine million victims to present their proposals and testimonies to the negotiating parties was, on first sight, ethically bereft and likely to be politically ineffectual. Such a parsimonious number of participants failed to do justice to any meaningful attempt to redress the moral catastrophe that has been Colombia's armed conflict. On the surface, it also did little to satisfy the moral imperative of incorporating those most affected by the violence in the design of the accountability mechanisms at the heart of the accord. The restricted number of participants appeared to be unlikely to craft a representative reflection

---

[44] Interview, Cali, Colombia, April 2015.
[45] Interview, Bogotá, Colombia, April 2015.

of historical patterns of political violence and victimization. As such, the mechanism initially appeared to be little more than a symbolic gesture to legitimize the peace process and the transitional justice provisions consecrated therein, suggesting that the victims' delegations would, in all probability, lead to the instrumentalization of those victims invited to participate in the Havana talks.

In addressing these themes, this chapter has explored how the organizers of the victims' delegations developed and practically applied the criteria established by the negotiating parties through which to select the 60 individuals to visit Havana in the latter part of 2014. The institutions selected to organize the delegations – the UN, the NUC and the ECCC – sagely balanced national and international actors, a decision likely aimed at dispelling widespread concerns that the controversial theme of accountability lay in the hands of international actors. While national victims' organizations were excluded from this triumvirate, the organizers drew considerably upon the experience and knowledge of national victims' organizations during the process of selecting the participants in the delegations.

This chapter has addressed how the UN, the NUC and the ECCC interpreted the framework dictated by the negotiating parties – that the victims visiting Havana embody balance, pluralism and synderesis – in order to demonstrate a so-called universe of mass and systematic victimizing acts and historical patterns of victimhood. It initially explored the selection criteria that aimed to constitute this universe of victims. The latter part of the chapter turned to how the organizers approached the theme of gender, documenting how the UN, the NUC and the ECCC sought to guarantee a gender perspective within the peace negotiations in general and the victims' delegations in particular through the deployment of diverse mechanisms and forms of support during distinct phases of the peace talks.

There is no convincing counterargument to the charge that the inclusion of only 60 individuals was, at best, ethically untenable. The get-out clause employed by the negotiating parties and the organizers had been that the delegations were not meant to be 'representative' of Colombia's mass victimizing events and patterns of victimhood. However, at the same time, the parties and the organizers developed a framework through which to envision a so-called 'universe of victims' that constituted an image of complex patterns of victimhood and victimization. In other words, the victims' delegations were meant to be representative without being representative. In this endeavour, the organizers crafted a meaningful framework that facilitated an intersectional approach to inclusion that, in the end, depicted a representative image of Colombia's mass and egregious patterns of victimization and victimhood.

In this regard, the delegations brought together victims from diverse populations, such as Afro-descendants, indigenous people, human rights defenders, politicians, peasants, journalists, teachers, trade unionists, the private sector, members of the security forces and illegal armed groups, the LGBTI+ population, victims from religious groups, judicial operators, civil servants, social and community organization leaders, and who had been minors at the time of their victimization. One in 12 (five) of the victims who visited Havana had also previously been a member of an armed group (legal and illegal), a detail that sought to demonstrate the complexity of patterns of violence on the ground. The participants were victims of the most emblematic crimes perpetrated during Colombia's armed conflict by the state, paramilitary groups, guerrilla (the FARC-EP and the ELN), and, in many cases, victims of multiple armed actors. Those who spoke before the negotiating parties in Havana were, in this respect, victims of the violation of the right to life (homicide, extrajudicial execution, massacre, forced disappearance), forced displacement, threats, hostage taking/ kidnapping, sexual and gender-based violence, anti-personnel mines, the recruitment of children and adolescents into armed groups and of violations of freedom of opinion and expression. In various cases, individuals were victims of multiple crimes. Through this framework and the testimonies of 60 individuals, the organizers were to show a web of mutually reinforcing victimizing events and patterns of victimhood that had, in distinct ways, directly affected approximately nine million people, the embodiment of the Western hemisphere's worst moral and human rights catastrophe in the 20th and 21st centuries.

One significant consequence of the limited number of participants that could not be remedied was the fact that such massive exclusion of victims inevitably restricted the number of diverse voices pertaining to the core transitional justice themes of accountability and justice, as will be discussed in the following chapters. This was particularly the case with respect to the exclusion of individuals and collective groups that demanded strict penal sanctions for human rights violations and abuses, evidencing a clear division within the victims' movement. While the numerical dimensions of the victims' delegations were inadequate, even in spite of these constraints, the selection criteria employed by the organizers got it right. In the end, the selection criteria crafted a valid and accurate representation of the effects of over five decades of savage cruelty and moral aberration wrought in the name of freedom by state and nonstate actors alike.

As was discussed earlier, the organizers endeavoured to demonstrate how Colombia's armed conflict had not been characterized uniquely by narratives of vulnerable victims and inveterate perpetrators, but rather how certain individuals embodied the condition of both victim and perpetrator. Five participants in the delegations personified this circumstance: a former police commander, an ex-soldier, an imprisoned insurgent, a young woman forcibly recruited into the guerrilla and a young man who had been forcibly incorporated into the paramilitaries, in both cases when they were children. The participation of these individuals precipitated significant polemic from and tension between the negotiating parties and, emphatically, from powerful elite actors opposing the Havana talks. As was noted earlier, in the case of the former police commander, a victim of the FARC-EP's emblematic strategy of hostage taking, the individual was publicly revictimized and instrumentalized.

This case of instrumentalization compounded the more general instrumentalization of the participants in the victims' delegations that took place consistently over the latter half of 2014, as the negotiating parties and those opposing or questioning the rationale for and legitimacy of the talks publicly treated the victims as an indication of criminal responsibility and, in turn, as an extension of the conflict. The following chapter will discuss further how episodes of politicization, revictimization and instrumentalization against participants wrought significant impact upon some individuals both during and in the aftermath of their visit.

This chapter has also examined how the organizers attempted to influence the victims' delegations and the wider Havana talks through the adoption of a gendered approach. From the beginning of the public phase of the negotiations, the organizers employed a series of mechanisms that sought to acknowledge the egregious harm against women and girls during the conflict, to respond to the demands of women's organizations in Colombia and to adhere to international norms relative to gender and women's rights. Drawing on testimonies from the participants and the organizers, the chapter has argued that the latter were able, in large part, to achieve these three goals effectively. The incorporation of the Sub-commission on Gender during 2014 ensured that all accords were revised in order to permit the mainstreaming of gender provisions throughout the peace agreements, an unprecedented achievement.

However, the degree to which the inclusion of a gender perspective in Point Five led to the re-allocation of power and redefinition of relationships of power between genders and across state, government and society more broadly is questionable and will be addressed in the following chapters. In this regard, despite the drafting of innovatively gendered agreements and the unexpected relational transformation between female victims and perpetrators that the approach precipitated, power relations between victims and perpetrators and across genders have not been recalibrated or a new social contract forged as a result of the victims' delegations.

In concluding this chapter, it is pertinent to reiterate how the selection criteria employed during Colombia's inclusive peacemaking and victim-centred experience considered individuals' demographic attributes, as well as wider context-specific factors shaping victim identity. In other words, the organizers employed the principles of intersectionality and a context-specific historically informed analysis of the causes, manifestations and consequences of patterns of victimization in the country.

Given this, the proposition of a sweeping narrative that articulates the logic that victim-oriented transitional justice solely instrumentalizes victims and, in turn, collapses spaces for agency, contestation and resistance remains problematic for the case of Colombia. Rather, the Colombian experience suggests the importance of affirming the micro- (personal) and macro- (political) level consequences of victim inclusion in relation to empowerment, while simultaneously acknowledging the evident limitations and challenges that such processes may face.

The following chapter will explore how the participation of the victims' delegations sculpted a relational impact on and between victims and their perpetrators in Havana. In this regard, it will explore the role of victims as peacebuilders. It will examine how their presence in Havana gradually influenced the perspectives of those negotiating peace, ultimately leading to the breakdown of the historical wall of perpetrator denial, a process in turn linked in numerous cases to victim empowerment and acknowledgement. As such, the chapter will further promote the contention in this book that an *instrumentalization–empowerment spectrum* is useful in analysing the degree to which victim inclusion mechanisms enable the exercise of victim agency. In this regard, the following chapter will argue that the delegations were, in part, an emancipatory project, while also documenting and analysing episodes of depoliticization, retraumatization and revictimization.

6

Victims as *Peacebuilders*: The Relational Impact of the Victims' Delegations

The preceding chapter addressed the theme of representation, exploring the criteria employed by the Organizers to select the 60 participants who would present their proposals and testimonies to the negotiating parties in Havana. The argument proposed was that, despite the restricted number of individual participants in the delegations, the organizers' interpretation of a so-called universe of victims and victimizing events and their deployment of a gendered approach crafted a meaningful portrayal of the dynamics and humanitarian consequences of Colombia's complex, protracted armed conflict. By demonstrating an ostensibly accurate depiction of patterns of victimhood and victimization embodied in a literal sense through 60 individuals, the delegations curbed, although by no means expunged, the moral predicament derived from what was, in quantitative terms, the unquestionably inadequate dimensions of victim participation in Havana. Furthermore, it was argued in the previous chapter that the presence of only 60 individuals simultaneously exercised a pejorative effect with respect to claims of representation. By excluding, in general, the perspectives of those diverse individual and collective victims who had been more sceptical of the application of the transitional justice paradigm, and who had demanded, in its stead, the imposition of heavier penal sanctions for perpetrators, the delegations failed to do justice to the diversity of victims' voices, experiences and demands.

The previous chapter also considered the relevance of the composition of the organizing body – the coalition of the NUC, the ECCC and the UN – to wider debates concerning victim inclusion. The mandate conferred by the negotiating parties upon the organizers explicitly tipped the balance towards national actors, the latter outnumbering international actors by two to one. Given the antagonism towards and distrust of international actors demonstrated by certain domestic sectors in recent decades – particularly of the UN – this decision had aimed to consolidate the national character of the victims' delegations and to anticipate criticism of international interference from those opposing or sceptical towards the Havana talks. The organizers' decision to collaborate closely with national victims' organizations during the selection process and the subsequent hearings in Havana reinforced these efforts to sculpt the homegrown *local* character of the victim-centred mechanism. Therefore, when evaluating the relative strength or weakness of victim-centred approaches, we might be mindful not only of the extent, scope and breadth of victim participation that they facilitate, but also of which actors are responsible for the selection process and how this may have a bearing on the wider representative nature of inclusion mechanisms.

A related, overarching theme in this book has been the degree to which victim-centred initiatives instrumentalize and restrain victim agency or allow for victim empowerment. Chapter 5 argued that in some instances, the negotiating parties treated the participants in the delegations as an extension of the conflict, particularly with regard to their adversary's victim count. Throughout the peace talks, powerful political and economic actors opposing the negotiations, including former President Uribe and the Procurator General, Alejandro Ordoñez, also explicitly instrumentalized and politicized the 60 victims who visited Havana, in certain cases precipitating repeated incidences of revictimization and, potentially, of retraumatization.

In this chapter, this theme is further considered. The visits of the victims' delegations to Havana did indeed lead to politicization and revictimization. However, the chapter contends that the delegations also had a considerable impact on the negotiating parties. The research presented here argues that alongside instrumentalization, politicization and, in some instances, revictimization and retraumatization, the delegations, in fact, dramatically transformed the historically embedded perspectives held by the negotiating parties, in particular with respect to their attitudes towards their victims and, in general, to their own role as perpetrators. Such an unprecedented shift in perception and attitudes, precipitated by the cumulative presence and the impact of the victims' delegations, had a significant effect, leading, it will be contended, to victim acknowledgement and the breakdown of the wall of perpetrator denial and contributed to strategic decisions by the negotiating parties to de-escalate.

The chapter argues that victim acknowledgement by the negotiating parties was at the heart of this transformation chain: victim recognition, in turn, ushered in episodes of conciliation between victims and perpetrators. Such moments did not signify unfettered reconciliation, nor did they travel extensively beyond Havana; in fact, what happened in Havana principally stayed in Havana. Nevertheless, despite their geographically constrained nature, the fact that such episodes of conciliation took place at all suggests we might be more circumspect in our promotion of critiques of victim-centred transitional justice as solely disempowering. Rather, what is of interest here is how and, if so, to what extent victim-centred initiatives may, in fact, provide a space for encounter where dialogue and conciliation between victims and perpetrators might take place and, in turn, what such processes may signify for victim instrumentalization and empowerment.

In the end, the research presented in this chapter develops further the argument that victim instrumentalization and empowerment may occur across a spectrum. In other words, the phenomena are not mutually exclusive, but may instead take place across diverse fields and levels during inclusion initiatives and in their aftermath. The chapter will therefore explore how, in the case of Colombia, the assertion of victim agency was shaped by the extent to which they themselves were able to navigate and negotiate relations of power asserted and embodied by elite actors in Havana. As such, the chapter addresses the degree to which the delegations represented, in part, a politicizing and emancipatory project, while also being characterized by episodes of depoliticization, retraumatization and revictimization.

The chapter begins with a brief discussion of the question of reconciliation. Drawing on the interviews with the participants from the victims' delegations, it subsequently explores, in sequential order, the extent to which the visits of the victims' delegations levied change across three levels: (i) the individual level; (ii) the intragroup level; and (iii) the intergroup level (victims-perpetrators; and perpetrators-perpetrators). While only a limited number of excerpts from the interviews could be included in the discussion given space constraints, the citations aim to be emblematic of the range of perspectives that emerged during the research.

The discussion addresses the scope of and limits to these transformations, drawing on interviews carried out with participants in the victims' delegations and members of the organizing body. The discussion aims to present a nuanced account with respect to how we might define the changes crafted in Havana as a result of the inclusion of the victims' delegations. The chapter ultimately provides further evidence for the broader argument presented in this book that instrumentalization and empowerment may occur simultaneously across a spectrum in the context of victim inclusion mechanisms.

Thinking about the possibilities for intragroup and intergroup encounter

As discussed in the introduction, the study of reconciliation has, over recent years, undergone somewhat of a resurgence and is increasingly an area addressed by practitioners and policy makers through explicit post-accord interventions. In academic debates and strategic initiatives, scholars and policy makers emphasize distinct dimensions within and across which reconciliation may occur, including at the interpersonal (individual), intergroup (communal) and institutional levels (Hamber 2009; Prieto 2012; Aiken 2013; Hughes 2018), and across dyadic relationships, such as between victims and perpetrators and between violent adversaries (Bar-Tal 2014).

Reconciliation is pre-eminently understood as a process through which, in light of new knowledge, individuals and collective groups redefine or reinterpret what they consider real, possible and desirable regarding their relationships with the outgroup or their adversary (Lederach 1997, 2010). A transformation of the antagonistic relationships and the psychological orientation that determine intergroup relations is then at the core of reconciliation (Bar-Tal 2000), although this is, in turn, contingent upon a shift in perceptions and beliefs held by the ingroup towards its own members. Such changes may, of course, occur at both the individual and the collective levels. It has been argued that the path towards sustainable peace may ultimately be wrought if the beliefs that undergirded the rationalization for, psychological investment in and cultural foundations of violent conflict are permanently transformed and replaced by new learning and understanding (Brett 2021a). In this sense, intergroup and interpersonal reconciliation will be contingent upon the transformation of the ideologies, beliefs, narratives and perceptions that shape individual and collective identity, both internally towards members of the ingroup and externally towards the outgroup and its members.

Of course, changes at the individual, interpersonal level do not necessarily imply or engender transformation at the intergroup level or across dyadic relationships. As such, the question of scale is crucial when it comes to identifying the scope of reconciliation processes; interpersonal or isolated, episodic processes are not easily scaled out or scaled up, as the Colombia case will illustrate. As will be seen, in fact, in the case of the changes ushered in by the contact between victims and perpetrators that the visits of the victims' delegations to Havana engendered, significantly important shifts at the interpersonal level and across the dyadic relationship between victims and perpetrators did not foster wider changes at the interpersonal or the intergroup level, or between victims and perpetrators in Colombia. Therefore, episodes of interpersonal conciliation and wider intergroup reconciliation may not consequentially precipitate intergroup reconciliation.

While scholarship emphasizes diverse attributes and drivers of reconciliation/conciliation, there is consensus that the transformation of the identitarian and ideological frameworks that shape ingroup identity and mould beliefs about the outgroup is fundamental. In other words, the possibilities for and extent of reconciliation will be influenced by the degree to which outgroup stereotyping narratives are recalibrated and outgroup members are, in turn, rehumanized, repersonalized and relegitimized. These processes, in part, took place in Havana as a result of contact between the participants in the victims' delegations and the negotiating parties. At the same time, the extent to which the ingroup is willing to reflect on and overcome its own historical self-glorification narratives – narratives that simultaneously demonized its adversary – will play a determinant role in opening up a path towards or closing down reconciliation processes. The argument ultimately goes that by overcoming the historical narratives that bred antagonism and by generating mutual respect and recognition (Adler and Bartlett 1998; Shnabel, Halabi and Noor 2013), new interpersonal and intergroup relationships may be forged that ideally *acknowledge* the outgroup's narrative, *recognize* that it no longer represents a threat to the ingroup and *craft* a belief in a common history and identity shared by both the ingroup and the outgroup.

Of course, approaches differ as regards the scope of reconciliation. A spectrum from minimalist to maximalist interpretations of reconciliation exists (Hamber 2009), the former characterized by 'peaceful coexistence' and the latter by widespread 'harmony' between social groups (Seils 2017). Minimalist accounts, so-called 'thin reconciliation', encompass the cessation of political violence, respect for the rule of law and a basic level of intergroup coexistence within a shared political community. A maximalist approach or 'thick reconciliation' would further include redress of the structural causes of conflict, marginalization and discrimination, and the restoration of victims as rights bearers (Seils 2017). In a similar vein, reconciliation can be both negative – 'nonlethal coexistence' and 'rapprochement' between former adversaries – and positive – characterized by intergroup harmony, cooperation and trust (Crocker 2002).

Lederach (1997) contends that intergroup reconciliation requires truth (understanding the past), mercy (forgiveness), justice (restitution and new social structures) and peace (the vision of a common future based on wellbeing and security for all). Emotions understandably play a significant role in shaping the consolidation of these requirements, as Brett et al (2022) posit. For example, mercy and truth and intergroup trust may emerge as a result of the recognition of the suffering of individuals belonging to the adversary group (Davis, Nsengiyumva and Hyslop 2019; Brett et al 2022). Goman and Kelley (2016: 80) claim 'that understanding forgiveness as a process that has intrapersonal and interpersonal components enables us to define it as a response to traumatic events'. In so doing, survivors of political violence may be able both to 'manage the emotional impact and search for meanings of the trauma, while at the interpersonal level also helping determine the future of the relationship' (Goman and Kelley 2016: 80). Such components are of direct relevance to and help us understand the impact of the albeit limited relational changes that occurred as a consequence of the visits of the victims' delegations to Havana, as will be seen later on. This is not to say that reconciliation occurred in Havana, but rather that important first steps to conciliation across interpersonal and dyadic relationships were ushered in by the victims' delegations.

A final theme of relevance to the broad debates pertaining to intergroup contact concerns those factors signalled as instrumental to building (or, indeed, to impeding) reconciliation. Across the literature, a wide range of potential reconciliation drivers has been identified, including the extent to which the guarantee and satisfaction of victims' rights is achieved (Seils 2017); whether the impact of legacies linked to deep structural cleavages remains ongoing (Hughes 2018); the degree to which an inclusive political community has been constructed (Murphy 2010); and whether and, if so, to what level the dignity and moral value of both former enemies and their victims has been acknowledged (Lederach 1997; Androff 2010).

While scholarship and practice have developed significant insights into the preceding themes, less is known about how, if at all, victim inclusion mechanisms deployed during peace negotiations or transitional justice initiatives might precipitate such changes at the interpersonal, intragroup and intergroup levels and across the dyadic relationship of victims and perpetrators. A core issue here pertains to the question of agency and, specifically, whether victims are able to assert their agency during episodes of participation or, on the contrary, whether they are instrumentalized.

If we approach victim inclusion in transitional justice mechanisms as defined pre-eminently by instrumentalization, a common proposition in the scholarship as discussed previously, then how can we accurately explain or understand whether and, if so, how victim participation may also occasion profound attitudinal changes? The case of Colombia suggests that such attitudinal changes may occur and, in turn, influence wider conflict dynamics – such as in the parties' decision to push forward de-escalation measures – as well as shaping the content of the peace accords with respect to accountability mechanisms.

If we presume that only numbers are determinant – in short, that the quantity of participation has more significance than its quality – then we would likely scoff at the argument that 60 individuals were able to precipitate a meaningful impact during what was no more than five days of direct participation in Havana. However, the Colombia case suggests we think beyond such reductionist logic. This is not to say that victim participation is a benevolent good in itself – it is not – or that numeric indicators of inclusion do not matter. Rather, the argument proposed here is that the terms on which participation takes place count a great deal towards shaping the degree to which victims may be able to transform relations of power inherent in conflict dynamics and conflict narratives. Numbers are important, then, but they are not the sole determinant factor.

As previously argued, and as this chapter ascertains, certain limited intragroup and intergroup transformations took place in Havana.

Recognition of victims' narratives and their role as rights bearers resulted from the visits of the victims' delegations. Furthermore, fundamental shifts in intergroup and intragroup relations were occasioned. Changes in the negotiating parties' perceptions of and beliefs concerning their victims (the outgroup), as well as those directed towards themselves (the ingroup) occurred. These were concurrent with the negotiating parties' progressive acknowledgement of victims' narratives, demands, rights and experiences. Such changes evidenced the development of an albeit fragile relationship of trust between those negotiating peace and some participants in the victims' delegations. At the same time, many (although not all) participants in the victims' delegations took steps in shifting their beliefs about and perceptions of the negotiating parties (their perpetrators). These changes were gradually reinforced by the emergence of a partial peace vision, as both victims and perpetrators in Havana systematically expressed their mutual will to reach a political settlement based on shared propositions and principles. As the data presented in this chapter will demonstrate, a noticeable transformation in how both victims and perpetrators comprehended the country's history of the conflict, its impact and its rationale also occurred. Nevertheless, the transformations laid out earlier did not travel beyond Havana, as this book demonstrates; the peace vision forged between some members of the victims' delegations and the negotiating parties was not immediately scaled up or scaled out. As such, no discernible shift in wider collective identititarian narratives evolved in Colombia, as will be discussed later on. Despite their significance, the changes wrought by the victims' delegations were, in the end, limited spatially and temporally.

Transformation at the individual level

The five victims' delegations travelled to Havana consecutively during the latter half of 2014, with the final visit occurring in December. Each 12-person hearing lasted a day, during which the participants were given 15 minutes to present their testimony and proposals for the transitional justice agreement, Point Five. Six delegates offered their testimonies before and six after lunch, while a coffee break took place halfway through the morning and afternoon sessions.

In coordination with the negotiating parties, the organizers set out and implemented a framework to regulate the hearings. Delegates were advised before attending that they would not receive a direct response from the parties to their specific, individual cases. They were informed that they could not represent collective victim groups, but could only discuss their specific individual episode of victimization. The negotiating parties were not authorized to respond to the participants' petitions during the hearings, and were permitted only to communicate a formal intervention at the beginning and end of each day. Under such conditions and with moderation provided by the organizers, the parties were obligated to listen, respectfully and in silence, to each individual participant. Consequently, direct interaction between the representatives of the government and the FARC-EP and the victims' delegates could only take place during the lunch and coffee breaks. According to members of the victims' delegations and the organizers, the lunches and coffee breaks came unintentionally to assume important significance for intergroup dialogue, ultimately providing regulated, safe spaces for encounter between participants and the negotiating parties. Numerous episodes of intergroup dialogue between participants and their perpetrators took place within these spaces, as will be illustrated further later on. The negotiating parties, the organizers and representatives of the guarantor and accompanier countries were present throughout the hearings. A therapist employed by the organizers was also in attendance in the event that participants required such support.

Acceptance of the invitation to visit Havana and the delegates' subsequent attendance at the peace talks understandably provoked a complex emotional reaction for all invitees; the courage of those who participated should therefore be underlined. For the members of the victims' delegations, participation in Havana generated feelings and emotions such as profound fear, anger, anxiety and pain. As such, the therapist's presence was important in this regard. Some delegates explained how, when they received the invitation from the organizers, the idea of meeting 'their perpetrator' in person had instantaneously precipitated feelings of dread. Other interviewees stated how, before going to Havana, they were concerned that the meeting could lead to further acts of violence against them. Fear and distress were commonly compounded by feelings of distrust towards the negotiating parties.[1]

The invitation from the organizers and the potential encounter with the negotiating parties in Havana itself therefore carried a significant risk of revictimization and retraumatization. Many delegates recounted how the feelings of fear, pain and anger precipitated in anticipation of their presence at the hearings were, in their words, similar to those they had experienced during and in the wake of the original victimizing event. One delegate expressed how she felt she was going 'back into the past to the event that I had sought to overcome'.[2] According to another delegate, participation in Havana was severely challenging on an emotional level: 'On arriving in Havana it was very strange, because I broke down from first the moment when we all met. I went into terrible shock, I cried and cried.'[3]

---

[1] Interviews, Bogotá, Santa Marta and Cali, Colombia, March–May 2015.
[2] Interview, Bogotá, Colombia, April 2015.
[3] Interview, Bogotá, Colombia, May 2015.

According to a participant in the fourth delegation:

> I actually crumbled in Havana before I gave my testimony, and I thought I was not going to be able to express what I was feeling. After I came back from Cuba, you know, I have felt that I have got over these crises, and they haven't returned ... For me, it was a healing process. It won't bring back my loved ones, but I reconciled with myself and with my life.[4]

Given the fear and pain that the idea of meeting their perpetrators had provoked, from the outset, the majority of interviewees approached their visit to Havana with anxiety and trepidation. The prospect of directly contributing to the peace talks in some way tempered these feelings, as did the possibility of conveying their testimony to their perpetrator, of disclosing their lived experiences of violence to the party that had caused them harm. Participants in the delegations also drew inspiration and strength from their own experiences of victimization and solidarity. For one mother whose son had been disappeared:

> If I tell you how, behind me, there are 876 women crying for their disappeared children ... [in Havana] I remembered them. When they realized I was in Havana, they said hopefully ... [I will] bring them news ... I felt the pain of my women and cried ... . But that was my own condition as a victim. A woman who has 13 people missing and dead in her family. So it was hard for me ... The dialogue with [the FARC-EP] gave me great joy.[5]

Another participant similarly referred to their family as providing the strength and motivation to go to Havana: 'My mother told me that you have to go talk to those gentlemen, and I told her yes, I have a debt, to the memory of my father and my loved ones who have fallen in this conflict, but I also have the authority to tell the armed actors that we don't want this anymore.'[6]

The decision to take part in the victims' delegations was far from a straightforward one for participants to take, given the acute emotional response that many experienced. Feelings of individual isolation, trauma, stress and pain were widespread, demonstrating the possibility for revictimization and retraumatization that participation in the inclusion mechanism brought about. In spite of the challenges that their visit imposed, interviewees narrated

---

[4] Interview, Bogotá, Colombia, April 2015.
[5] Interview, Bogotá, Colombia, April 2015.
[6] Interview, Bogotá, Colombia, April 2015.

how their participation represented a critical opportunity for them to take part in what they saw as 'a historical process',[7] a petition that, in some cases, they had been demanding for decades.

According to one delegate, the hearings were 'unique', given that they provided: 'The opportunity for each victim to look their perpetrator – or the representative of the actor responsible for directly causing them harm – in the eyes, narrate their suffering, and make concrete proposals for the peace agreement.'[8] A survivor of sexual and gender-based violence expressed similar sentiments, stating: 'My heart changed and rested when speaking. When facing the perpetrators, you rest ... Looking at their faces and eyes. They stayed crouched down, just like the reaction you have when you say things to express the pain you have felt and been caused.'[9] Diverse participants reiterated this experience, describing how being seated opposite 'my perpetrator' ('mi victimario') on an equal footing and with a formal mandate to contribute to the peace talks was transformative. In this regard, the fact that the participants were able to confront those responsible for their suffering under conditions of parity, and that the latter were obliged to listen to and consider the delegates' statements respectfully and *in silence*, arguably represented a step towards addressing the inherent power differential between the negotiating parties and their victims. In a reversal of historical roles, the formalized hearings literally gave voice to the victims of the conflict, while temporarily muting the voice of the perpetrators.

Despite the suffering that the encounter brought with it then, many delegates identified their participation as a crucial 'step towards their own individual recovery',[10] a point that has not been frequently emphasized in characterizations of victim inclusion as uniquely instrumentalizing. Numerous testimonies from victims of diverse violations perpetrated by all armed groups show how, for them, inclusion in the peace talks came to represent a *before* and *after* moment, specifically in terms of participants' mental health, physical wellbeing and their attitudes towards their perpetrators. Experiences of individual level transformation suggest a corrective to scholarship that solely emphasizes how inclusion mechanisms disempower victims.

Of the over 52 delegates interviewed, approximately 40 responded that they had returned from Havana a different person, due to the transformative experience they had undergone. Such transformation reflects Minow's (1998: 72) insight that 'speaking in a setting where the experience is acknowledged can be restorative ... Acknowledgment by

---

[7] Interview, Bogotá, Colombia, March 2015.
[8] Interview, Bogotá, Colombia, March 2015.
[9] Interview, Santa Marta, Colombia, April 2015.
[10] Interview, Santa Marta, Colombia, April 2015.

others of the victim's moral injuries is a central element of the healing process' and may contribute to the re-establishment of 'a moral framework, in which wrongs are correctly named and condemned'. Several delegates expressed how the encounter with 'their perpetrators' felt 'like an exorcism'. Others explained that 'the nightmares have stopped' and that the experience brought a key shift in their perceptions of those who had directly caused them harm.[11]

What is notable is that the instances of individual-level transformation in perceptions and beliefs that resulted from participation in the hearings occurred across a broad range of delegates, including in those cases where individuals had departed for Havana with little idea that such transformation would be likely:

> Before going to Havana ... I felt in my heart that once I saw them, I was not going to be able to forgive them, that the hatred would always be there. I went with hatred and bitterness because they destroyed my family. But when I was there, sitting there in front of them all, and I told them what I had to say, and they told me what they had to say, in my heart there was peace. And I said to myself, there is such a thing as reconciliation, forgiveness does exist.[12]

The rules of engagement in Havana played a key part in generating changes and empowerment at the individual level, as well as, arguably, laying the foundations for intergroup transformation. Being listened to respectfully and in silence by their perpetrator engendered a feeling of recognition for many delegates. According to a peasant farmer who had suffered multiple episodes of victimization perpetrated by diverse armed groups:

> I left my anger there [in Havana] ... we were not going to get angry and crash there, but rather to make a problem visible ... to demand that there be a will for peace ... we were not going in the plan to clash with them [the parties], but rather to show them that we are victims and that there was a need for a commitment and political will from both sectors to define a peace process that, for us, was very necessary. So I left contented ... I didn't come away angry; on the contrary, I think I came away satisfied with having been able to express everything that I had to express as a peasant farmer.[13]

---

[11] Interviews, Bogotá and Cali, Colombia, March and April 2015.
[12] Interview, Bogotá, Colombia, April 2015.
[13] Interview, Bogotá, Colombia, April 2015.

Another female participant expressed similar feelings, adding how her participation in Havana had led to an even stronger commitment in her own peace activism: 'My anger and pain stayed in Cuba. For me it was like an exorcism ... and today I continue to work harder for peace, I continue with more enthusiasm. Hearing other victims' stories in this regard was especially moving, filling one with admiration.'[14] Such a statement uncovers perhaps a further element of empowerment linked to victim participation, an aspect that numerous delegates identified – specifically, many individuals returned from Havana, in their words, 'strengthened' and 'more committed' to the peace process. For one mother whose son had been killed by the FARC-EP, her return to Colombia came with a commitment for greater responsibility in building peace: 'I understood that I was going to Cuba to plant a seed for peace... and [now] what else can I do ... but to carry out actions that bring that awareness to those 46 million Colombians.'[15]

A sense of empowerment brought by their inclusion in the victims' delegations was signalled by many participants in Havana. For one young woman, a human rights lawyer whose father had been executed decades before:

> I came back more committed, I have always been committed to the issue of peace, my entire life, above all because I understood my historical role. The fact of having been privileged – because it is a privilege that among 8 million victims you're chosen – this signifies a greater commitment to the country.[16]

Importantly, this change in perception was notable not only in those delegates who had supported the peace process from the outset, but also in participants who had initially travelled to Havana with scepticism towards the peace process. In all but one of these cases, these individuals returned to Colombia convinced of the value of the peace process. In fact, on their return, many who had been critical of the talks subsequently assumed an advocacy role, informing their communities, organizations or the general public about the negotiations and aiming to replicate the effect that their own participation had had on them. Some individuals immediately assumed a public role in this regard. For one delegate, a victim of the FARC-EP, whose own networks were critical of the peace process, 'telling the story of the Havana talks [and my experience] to these people was tuning in with

---

[14] Interview, Cali, Colombia, April 2015.
[15] Interview, Bogotá, Colombia, May 2015.
[16] Interview, Bogotá, Colombia, May 2015.

other victims'.¹⁷ Similarly, a delegate whose brother had been murdered by the Colombian state expressed how she:

> came back changed ... with another concept ... was not alone anymore ... I used to say that the peace talks were just a party, they're swindling us, that's what I thought . When I arrived back ... I said to all [my family and other victims], how this is a serious process; how this is not going to be easy ... but it can be achieved, because there is the will of the parties ... [this new perception] ... has brought me into conflict with people.¹⁸

Consequently, for various participants, their visit to Havana transformed the beliefs and perceptions they had of the negotiating parties, and generated important change at the individual level, bringing a deeper commitment to the peace process, a perception that, in many cases, they acted upon once they arrived back in Colombia. A member of the Afro-Colombian community from the Pacific coast, after the visit, returned 'with a different consciousness, with a change of attitudes, beliefs, positions, because ... how they treated me and received me, I arrived in Colombia with a commitment to continue contributing to peace. I give that message in the communities'.¹⁹

Beyond demonstrating a perhaps veiled form of empowerment, a further theme emerging from this discussion – and which will be revisited later on – relates to whether and, if so, how the formal participation of victims at the national level might hold the potential to deliver impact at distinct levels, including the subnational and community levels, and within family, political and victims' networks. As was discussed earlier, many of the 60 sought to replicate, to scale up and to scale out their own transformative experience and to convince their peers and the wider Colombian public of the importance of and advances made in Havana. The fact that many delegates, on returning to Colombia, began to engage significantly with their community, organization, trade union or family and friendship network suggests that inclusion initiatives may represent a first step in the wider scaling up and scaling out of transformative processes elsewhere.

However, the extent to which such change was possible was ultimately limited, given that no mechanisms through which to formalize any such process were developed in Colombia by the government or the organizers. Moreover, while some participants may have returned to contexts in which the peace process was supported more broadly – through local victims'

---

¹⁷ Interview, Cali, Colombia, April 2015.
¹⁸ Interview, Barranquilla, Colombia, April 2015.
¹⁹ Interview, Bogotá, Colombia, May 2015.

organizations, for example – the country itself remained deeply divided on the issue of whether the talks should be taking place, with powerful spoiling actors opposing the negotiations and demanding the guerrilla be either militarily defeated or surrender. Moreover, approximately one quarter of those who took part in the delegations paid the price for their participation, receiving threats on their return, a point that will be revisited later on. Under these conditions, in large part what happened in Havana stayed in Havana.

Intragroup transformation

Beyond changes at the individual level, the visits of the victims' delegations to Havana also generated important incidences of intragroup transformation, specifically with respect to victim identity.

The first collective encounter of the participants in each delegation took place in Bogotá, on the night before their departure to Havana, in a hotel arranged by the organizers. Many of the delegates arrived already shouldering complex emotions; the meeting with the other individuals taking part in their delegation initially generated further concern and worry. Given that delegates were victims of opposing armed groups in a context in which the armed conflict remained active, some explained how they had felt anxiety at meeting victims of the other armed group. According to one delegate:

> When we arrived at the hotel in Bogotá, I saw ... many of my companions were victims who were currently being attacked, under threat, their lives in danger ... The work we did was carried out without much anaesthetic ... without knowing each other you unclothed the whole truth. There was a very big risk here because you didn't know what would happen afterwards. So the big questions for me were what was going to happen and who were my colleagues? ... [in the end] everyone was very mature and nothing negative happened ... there was a lot of respect.[20]

A delegate who had been forcibly recruited into an armed group as a child felt initially concerned about meeting the other victims, given that some may have been victims of paramilitary atrocities. In his words, meeting the other delegates was:

> hard and shocking since I had belonged to that group, although not because I had wanted to, but because I had had to live that life ... so

---

[20] Interview, Bogotá, Colombia, April 2015.

I felt very emotionally charged. I arrived at the airport and I told [the other delegates] 'I have to talk to you, I feel very guilty, I didn't choose that life, but now with everything you have told me I feel worse even than before I accepted to go to Havana' … and … when I heard the stories of rapes, deaths, I asked myself, when did this happen … I cried a lot … but [other delegates] understood and told me that I was also a victim, because I was a child and they had taken advantage and used me … This brought us closer.[21]

Another participant, whose father had been executed by the state, observed how participation:

was a life lesson, to a large extent, [seeing] people who have lived and suffered very terrible things, some that I can say are much worse than what I myself had to live. They have an impressive generosity and willingness to think about the need to solve the conflict. I think this is one of those reasons why one can always believe in humanity.[22]

Indeed, the generosity of those victims who took part in the Havana process, a point mentioned earlier, deserves further discussion. Without exception, those who took part demonstrated extraordinary generosity both to the negotiating parties and the other members of their delegations. The capacity to empathize with and acknowledge the suffering of their fellow delegates played a crucial part in generating a cumulative sense of solidarity and, ultimately, in engendering a wider, inclusive sense of victim identification and identity, regardless of their perpetrator. As one delegate stated: 'At the moment when everyone told their story, no one reproached anyone.'[23] For another delegate:

When I arrived in Havana, I thought that my own pain was really a tragedy. But when I sat down with my comrades and was able to listen to 11 other testimonies, I realized my pain is not the only pain here. That transforms you, because you begin to recognize and also to value the sacrifice that others make. So that … has united us with the victims in the delegations. After returning from Havana, the victims who participated are much more united.[24]

---

[21] Interview, Bogotá, Colombia, April 2015.
[22] Interview, Bogotá, Colombia, April 2015.
[23] Interview, Bogotá, Colombia, April 2015.
[24] Interview, Bogotá, Colombia, April 2015.

A female delegate, who had been a victim of the FARC-EP, reiterated this perspective, stating how:

> When one has experienced pain, one feels immense respect for the other victims and it doesn't matter who the perpetrator was. As I said in conversations ... 'we didn't choose our perpetrator'. It's so curious how sometimes, when I meet a fellow delegate, who they were a victim of has already been erased for me. That issue moved to a secondary plane. For me, the real difference between the people is those who are against the process and bombard it from one side or the other: they haven't been victims.[25]

From a similar perspective, on understanding that the participants in the delegations were to be victims from all armed groups, one delegate stated:

> when I started to listen to the victims, to the level of their suffering, [to witness] their greatness, their dignity ... I realized that the perpetrator was not important. What was important was the pain. And when I saw the level of their commitment to peace, I said ... we don't have to ask them by whom they are victims. What I have is to feel very honoured that they have chosen me to be part of this group.[26]

The emergence of a collective, shared intragroup identity among the victims who went to Havana and the manner in which membership in this albeit small group came to be perceived as emancipatory and empowering was emphasized by all interviewed participants. This phenomenon evidences further how victim-centred inclusion processes may indeed precipitate unanticipated forms of victim empowerment. The words of one delegate, a victim of state crime, illustrate this point coherently: 'There was a lot of pain, the pain of each one of us was a single pain, the pain of the country ... lived in different ways. It was as if, at that moment, we had been chosen to represent bonds of brotherhood, to be a chain, to unite more links throughout the country.'[27]

In the end, the crucial point here is how the delegates had initially travelled to the talks as victims of a defined, specific armed group, and yet, in the majority of cases, had returned as collective victims of the armed conflict. This shared, collective identification as victims then either stood alongside or, on occasion, supplanted delegates' self-identification as victims of specific

---

[25] Interview, Bogotá, Colombia, April 2015.
[26] Interview, Bogotá, Colombia, May 2015.
[27] Interview, Bogotá, Colombia, April 2015.

actors. This transformation evidences how, according to interviewees from both the victims' delegations and organizers, a collective victim identity emerged across the delegations that overcame the Manichean categorization of victims according to their perpetrators. In the words of one of the organizers from the ECCC:

> In each delegation ... they always went as the victims of the FARC-EP, the victims of the State, victims of the paramilitaries. And in the five groups, and without exception, there was a recognition as 'victims of the Colombian armed conflict' ... [which] helped them to commit themselves as ambassadors of peace ... The victims are no longer alone. They left as victims of a particular group, and returned as victims of a single armed conflict.[28]

Furthermore, while individual participants articulated diverse proposals according to their own specific circumstance, all delegates commonly demanded, as a priority, the cessation of the armed conflict. One survivor of a massacre perpetrated by the FARC-EP had stated to the negotiating parties that the way that they would repay part of their debt to the victims was that they 'do not get up from this table until there is peace in Colombia'.[29] Regardless of the identity of their perpetrator and the nature of the act of victimization perpetrated against them, all participants insisted on 'the need and urgency to rebuild the social fabric together'.[30] To achieve this objective, participants demonstrated extraordinary generosity, placing the collective pursuit of peace alongside and, habitually, above their own victimhood and demands to resolve their own specific case. One woman whose brother had been executed by the FARC-EP stated:

> Well, if my brother was able to forgive, I cannot be inferior to his legacy and what I have to do is to fight for peace. I can't get my brother back, he's already gone. The only thing I can do is to make sure that his death wasn't in vain. And the only way it won't be in vain is by trying to prevent other families from experiencing what I went through. What prolonging the war does is to increase the likelihood of other kidnappings, so my decision is not revenge, my decision is to try to help Colombia get out from this vicious circle of war.[31]

---

[28] Interview, Bogotá, Colombia, April 2015.
[29] Interview, Bogotá, Colombia, April 2015.
[30] Interview, Bogotá, Colombia, April 2015.
[31] Interview, Bogotá, Colombia, March 2015.

When reflecting on her experience both as a victim and as a participant in Havana, one female interviewee who had been held in captivity by the FARC-EP for almost a decade, stated how:

> I took the decision to support the search for reconciliation ... I always said we could find an inclusive, respectful, equitable Colombia ... when faced with forgiveness, there are people who do not understand the position of the victims when we support this process. It is difficult for them to understand why, because people believe that we were subjected to so many violations of all our rights, and so we have to harbour feelings of hatred, rejection, and resentment. But I have my own way of seeing things. Today I defend freedom more than ever, but freedom in its entirety, and hence the position that I have assumed in solidarity with the peace process. Because I say if I consent to feelings of resentment, I am not going to be free, I am going to be tied to negative feelings that are going to determine many attitudes and that are not particularly convenient for me in my life ... And I tell people why I defend this process ... because I did live through the war and I know what it is like to run through the jungle away from a bombardment seeking to escape possible death. I know what it's like to have rifles ... against my neck ... so when people speak for me, I tell them ... I cannot want war for Colombia.[32]

A further dynamic that accompanied the consolidation of an intragroup victim identity was the development of a subgroup, based on solidarity and identification between female victims across the diverse delegations. According to one of the delegates who had suffered episodes of victimization from diverse armed groups: 'In our delegation we got very close ... there were more women than men, so we supported each other ... there were no quarrels ... we all always said that we were victims, regardless of the group.'[33] Another female participant stated how:

> As I learnt about other pains [of women], this had a great impact on me ... the impact of sexual violence, the impact of the woman [who had been raped by armed actors] ... all these perturbing life stories helped me to overcome my pain ... and gave me strength. I felt ... courage to speak to the guerrillas, to them ... my life ... when I commented on all my pain, I had a life-changing [experience] ... when I got to

---

[32] Interview, Bogotá, Colombia, May 2015.
[33] Interview, Bogotá, Colombia, April 2015.

Havana] I felt a lot of anger ... but when I was able to have them close, I changed my attitude ... I returned totally different when I left Cuba.[34]

The development of important bonds of solidarity based upon female delegates' shared experience in Havana gradually also began to affect female members of the negotiating parties, culminating in the establishment of the Sub-commission on Gender, as discussed earlier. Commenting on her dialogue with female members of the negotiating parties, a member of the fourth delegation explained how: 'I met women who were nothing more than women, who have their beliefs, who are defending what they believe to be their rights. In my case I say that they thought that the solution was to take up arms. For me the solution is dialogue.'[35]

According to another delegate, who had been a victim of violations perpetrated by both the paramilitaries and the guerrilla:

> The female FARC-EP negotiator grabbed my hand and told me 'the story you told was heartbreaking ... what happened with your family was very painful. If the organization made a mistake ... I apologize'. So I told her 'it is still a crime against humanity'. And there were no more words, because at that moment. What my heart felt, and what she felt. And I gave her a hug, we hugged. I felt she was an ordinary woman ... the hug for me was conciliation.[36]

Changes at the intergroup level

With the arrival of the victims' delegations, relational transformation also gradually began to take place at the intergroup level in Havana due, in large part, to the harrowing nature of the testimonies delivered by the delegates. One by one, the participants narrated their experiences of egregious violence, for which the negotiating parties had been, in many cases, directly responsible. It was this dynamic during the hearings that conferred a hitherto absent moral authority and humanity upon the peace talks, according to both delegates and organizers. Under such conditions, participants' testimonies obligated the parties to confront the 'human face of suffering' and to witness the human cost of their violence.[37] After taking off his prothesis and placing it on the table in front of him as he spoke, one victim of a FARC-EP landmine, for example, delivered an agonizing testimony.

---

[34] Interview, Bogotá, Colombia, April 2015.
[35] Interview, Bogotá, Colombia, March 2015.
[36] Interview, Bogotá, Colombia, May 2015.
[37] Interview, Bogotá, Colombia, April 2015.

From his and other participants' perspectives, his words, which shone a bleak light upon the insurgency's systematic practice of sowing minefields across rural Colombia and its human impact, precipitated a collective response of grief and acknowledgement from all present, particularly the negotiating parties: 'I lost my life's project. You're left quite destroyed by everything ... because not only is it about falling on the landmine, but also about accessing state services.'[38]

After all the delegations had visited Havana, announcements were made by the negotiating parties relating to specific obligations under international humanitarian law, including explicitly to demining and the forced recruitment of minors. From the perspective of one of the organizers, in general, 'the delegations had a significant impact on the process of the de-escalation of the conflict'.[39] In reference to this point, another member of the Organizing Committee stated: 'If I remember correctly, the negotiating parties made explicit reference to the victims when they announced their commitment to move towards de-escalation.'[40] Delegates contended that the participants had influenced the perspectives of the negotiating parties in relation to two aspects of international humanitarian law: the forced recruitment of minors and anti-personnel mines. According to one male delegate, 'around 15 or 20 days after our delegation visited Havana, the FARC-EP stated [formally] that they were not going to recruit children younger than 17 ... I think [our] proposals are being adopted. The guerrilla is listening and they are complying'.[41] Both delegates and members of the organizing institutions contended that the testimony given specifically by the survivor of the landmine cited earlier had had a significant impact on the parties and that its emotional force had contributed directly to the FARC-EP's decision to craft an agreement on demining.[42]

As each delegation visited Havana during 2014, their cumulative presence began to weigh increasingly heavily upon the negotiating parties. Arguably the beholding of the human tragedy and suffering caused by their violence progressively transformed the parties' understanding of the humanitarian dimensions of the conflict. Interviewees stated how hearing the testimonies of those present contributed to recalibrating both the negotiating parties' perspectives of their own actions and their perceptions of those who had suffered from the egregious violence that the parties had meted out. According to numerous interviews with delegates, representatives

---

[38] Interview, Bogotá, Colombia, April 2015.
[39] Interview, Bogotá, Colombia, April 2015.
[40] Interview, Bogotá, Colombia, April 2015.
[41] Interview, Santa Marta, Colombia, April 2015.
[42] Interviews, Bogotá and Santa Marta, Colombia, March to April 2015.

of Colombian institutions, guarantor countries and the organizers, this experience brought about a significant transformation due to the parties' 'unavoidable proximity to human pain and suffering' and evident physical and emotional upset.[43] According to one of the organizers, the presence of the delegates led to the 'softening of their [perpetrators'] hearts'.[44] One member of the ECCC stated how the parties consequently underwent a process of maturation: 'in almost all of them, an imprint, a mark, remains. A memory, a reminder of what made them grow and develop'.[45]

According to the participants, one factor that explained their transformative experience was the respect with which, in general, they were treated by the negotiating parties. In the words of one male delegate:

> It seemed to me that the hearing was very respectful, I saw an attitude of receptivity on both sides ... [there was] indifference from some state officials, and, in some of the guerrillas I think ... when the hearing commenced. But when we began to listen to the testimonies, I felt that everyone was quickly copying everything we said into their notebooks and it seemed to me to be a very important space, I think for everyone.[46]

One mother, whose son had been executed extrajudicially by the military, similarly characterized the negotiating table as a 'space for reflection ... a space of great respect, of great dignity, but ... a space of much pain, of shared pain ... not only individual pain but ... the pain of other mothers and families'.[47] In this regard, and as diverse participants signalled, hearing the testimonies of their fellow delegates and witnessing their suffering represented a crucial transformative step both for themselves and for the negotiating parties, which ultimately crafted a common 'victim identity' and led to acknowledgement between victims and from their perpetrators, as will be discussed later on.

Therefore, what emerged from the interviews was a shared perspective that the negotiating parties had shown – in general, although not in all cases – great respect and restraint towards their victims during the hearings. While such respect was not evident across all cases, when it did take place, it laid the foundations for the development of trust between delegates, and between the negotiating parties and the delegates; it also brought with it the acknowledgement of the latter's pain and suffering. Reflecting on his

---

[43] Interview, Bogotá, Colombia, March 2015.
[44] Interview, Bogotá, Colombia, April 2015.
[45] Interview, Bogotá, Colombia, April 2015.
[46] Interview, Bogotá, Colombia, March 2015.
[47] Interview, Bogotá, Colombia, April 2015.

encounter with members of the FARC-EP in Havana, a former paramilitary who had been forcibly recruited as a child stated how:

> After my intervention I was approached by a member of the FARC-EP. He explained to me that he had joined the FARC-EP at 16 or 17 and that we had things in common. He had been shot and wounded at the time, and had become tired of the war too. It was an informal conversation, but you begin to realize. I think they had been victims too.[48]

Significantly, in those cases where the negotiating parties willingly acknowledged their victims, and where the latter similarly recognized their perpetrator, a mutual process of (re)humanization began gradually to occur – what in Colombia is often referred to as the *deconstruction of the enemy*. This transformation had its roots in the environment in which the delegations took place as much as in their design. The majority of delegates identified how the treatment that they had received from the organizers and, in many cases – to their surprise – from the negotiating parties had, in fact, been one of respect, kindness and recognition. The support given by the organizing institutions played a central role therein: delegates were made to feel protected, respected and acknowledged by the organizers. However, the generosity and general openness shown by those attending the hearings to move beyond their anger, fear and mistrust played the crucial role in this process of change. In the words of one of the delegates: 'The interaction we had [during breaks] was central: I no longer saw this or that person as being from the government or the FARC-EP, a perpetrator, nor did I see myself as victim. What we created was a relationship between equals, as human beings.'[49]

For another participant, who as a child had been forcibly recruited by the paramilitaries, contact with the negotiating parties and the latter's willingness to listen respectfully to the delegates were instrumental in shifting his attitudes towards the FARC-EP. In his words: 'I changed a lot. I saw the FARC-EP from another perspective. I was trained to fight them, to eliminate them. Sharing time with them ... [during the hearing] made me think how those of us here are all children of peasants, we are the same.'[50] A female delegate, who had suffered multiple violations from diverse armed groups, offered a similar perspective:

---

[48] Interview, Bogotá, Colombia, April 2015.
[49] Interview, Bogotá, Colombia, April 2015.
[50] Interview, Bogotá, Colombia, April 2015.

When the testimonies of the victims were finishing and there was a break, members of the government and the FARC-EP approached several of us and we were able to talk together. In that interaction you no longer saw the person for having a function or having a government brand or a FARC-EP brand or a victim brand. But rather there was now a relationship of equals, as human beings.[51]

Another delegate commented on the important encounters that took place during the lunches and coffee breaks:

At the end, there was a lunch [on my table] … We had [a police commander] and a [negotiating] commander of the FARC-EP. It seemed to me that one wouldn't even imagine this in the movies, a FARC-EP commander sitting at the table with a police commander. And we the victims were there. They weren't shooting at us, but talking to us and sharing lunch. It wasn't a military dispute, but rather the sharing of rice and fish. Very good! Well, that's the country that we want, in the midst of our differences … the country that … talks … and that, in the end, reaches an agreement.[52]

Another delegate offered a similar insight concerning the (intergroup) changes that she witnessed with respect to the negotiating parties' mutual perceptions of one another. For this participant, seeing two adversaries taking seriously the challenge of how to deal with the past and build peace was inspirational. In her words:

When I saw the Colombian military official shaking hands with the FARC-EP, greeting each other, I never imagined that … seeing that had a lot of impact on me … I had tears and hope in my soul … [for] peace. My eyes watered then the way they water now. I didn't tell anyone anything. But lately, I've been commenting a lot … that.. respectful, decent greeting between two Colombian men who deserve to build a different country, really influenced me. A country at peace and without weapons, without uniforms.[53]

Despite the traumatic emotions and experiences they generated, the formal and informal encounters between victims and perpetrators that represented the central axis of the inclusion mechanism in Havana also gradually broke

---

[51] Interview, Bogotá, Colombia, March 2015.
[52] Interview, Bogotá, Colombia, April 2015.
[53] Interview, Bogotá, Colombia, March 2015.

the isolation of victims and temporarily positioned them at the centre of the process. By the time the fourth delegation visited Havana and the negotiating parties had witnessed almost 40 testimonies, their acknowledgement of their victims and recognition of the moral catastrophe precipitated by the conflict had reached a point of irreversibility. According to one member of the organizing institutions, who would later play a central role in the country's transitional justice architecture:

> There is a moment in which the FARC-EP say something that deeply impressed me ... [referring to the violence] they say 'this cannot be repaired, the drama we have caused, the horror that we have brought cannot be repaired, the only thing we can offer is to help to build a different country for the future'.[54]

A member of the Organizing Committee commented on this transformation in the perspectives and attitudes of the negotiating parties. In his words:

> Both the guerrilla and the government were initially very defensive, very afraid that they would throw all the dirt concerning the war onto those two groups ... but after meeting with the victims that defensive attitude changed. The FARC-EP were very clear in acknowledging that they have caused many people to suffer, and the government was also very clear in acknowledging that it had not done what it should have done to defend the population ... there was a process of maturation in their attitudes.[55]

As such, the visits of and testimonies given by the victims' delegations precipitated significant attitudinal change in Havana, crafting as they did evident relational transformation between the delegates themselves, the negotiating parties and the organizers and other supporting actors in Havana. As one survivor of violence perpetrated by the paramilitaries described it:

> those 60 interventions, I think they managed to soften the hearts of the negotiators. The perspective they held about victims is indisputably not the same as it was before the victims arrived ... because I think they fully understood the dimensions of committing to ... the victims. Before they saw us as 'poor things, six million victims'. But when you feel the weight of 60 testimonies, so close up [they] move you.[56]

---

[54] Interview, Bogotá, Colombia, May 2015.
[55] Interview, Bogotá, Colombia, March 2015.
[56] Interview, Bogotá, Colombia, May 2015.

Another female delegate characterized the impact on the negotiating parties she perceived the delegations had precipitated in Havana. During one coffee break, she was approached by one of the lead FARC-EP negotiators, who accompanied by a member of the government, who wished to speak to her. According to this participant, the exchange was of fundamental importance. With the government representative as his witness, the FARC-EP commander began:

> 'What I want to tell you is that everything you said was true, what you told about your father was true and I thank you for the sincerity of your words, what happened with your brother should never have happened.' I told him, 'well the only thing I hope is that you are sincere, that you are honest'. He told me 'yes, I am honest'. And I said to him: 'Well, then don't leave the negotiating table until this is signed, because it is the only way to vindicate the memory of my brother.' And he responded: 'We are not going to leave.' And that was what I talked to him about. So let's say that to a certain extent what I hoped for was achieved, which was to sensitize them and make them realize that they have made a serious mistake and that this cannot continue to be repeated and that the only way to guarantee non-recurrence is to demobilize.[57]

As was discussed previously, it is important to clarify that the negotiating parties were not interviewed within the remit of this study; however, former President Juan Manuel Santos was interviewed during the writing-up phase in September 2022. The former President concurred with the conclusions proposed in this chapter that the visits of the delegations strongly shaped the perspectives of the negotiating parties. Notably, the deep effect that the delegates' testimonies had on the negotiating parties was signalled by the participants, organizers and other supporting actors, although it was not confirmed systematically by the negotiating parties. In the words of one organizer:

> the victims brought reality to the negotiating table ... [being present] was a very powerful experience, regardless of who was a victim, and who was not. The negotiating parties were affected, yes, but so was everyone else: the guarantors, the UN, the organizers. It was formidable, because up until that point, only very technical issues had been discussed, and then suddenly the victims arrived with their stories of suffering and violence.[58]

---

[57] Interview, Bogotá, Colombia, April 2015.
[58] Interview, Bogotá, Colombia, April 2015.

One female delegate confirmed how she:

> felt the parties were very affected ... there had been some tremendous statements [from the participants] ... one negotiator approached one of the victims and said to her 'I don't know exactly how much, but I know that we have caused so much damage ... and I don't know how we are going to be able to remedy this'.[59]

Another delegate, whose family were victims of state and paramilitary groups, stated how, after his testimony, 'several people from the government ... came out crying and hugged me ... they were deeply touched by my testimony, as were several members of the FARC-EP'.[60] Such a perspective was shared by one female participant, who had been a victim of the FARC-EP. In her words, the negotiating parties were increasingly moved by their victims' testimonies, given that the latter represented 'the manifestation of pain, anguish and tragedy ... expressed to those who committed the crimes'.[61]

What these interviews broadly demonstrate is how a crucial consequence of the victims' delegations was an incipient acceptance of responsibility over their crimes by the negotiating parties. In the words of one male victim of state crimes: 'To a large extent, the [delegations] ... challenged the repudiation of the suffering and pain of the victims ... [illustrating] ... the negative, disastrous consequences of armed confrontations.'[62] Such a change is of great significance. Prior to the visits of the victims' delegations, the negotiating parties had continually rejected the accusation that they themselves had caused harm or had been instrumental in the perpetration of violations. However, as the delegations successively visited Havana, this denial was gradually worn away. One female victim of sexual violence perpetrated by the state confirmed how the parties began to assume responsibility for their crimes and how, in her case, the consequence was a commitment by both parties to collaborate on reparatory measures. The participant indicated how, during one of the breaks, she was approached by representatives of both the government and the FARC-EP: 'some gentlemen from the FARC-EP and some from the government sat with me ... they met and said they would collaborate since I was in a very bad situation. Both parties were there with me, and they said they were going to help me, that they were not going to leave me alone'.

---

[59] Interview, Bogotá, Colombia, March 2015.
[60] Interview, Bogotá, Colombia, April 2015.
[61] Interview, Bogotá, Colombia, April 2015.
[62] Interview, Bogotá, Colombia, April 2015.

In the words of one delegate, the will and capacity shown by the negotiating parties to assume responsibility was 'amazing to see ... particularly at a time when many Colombians are screaming at each other and sending messages of hate and intolerance, aggression and stigmatization'.[63] However, according to the interviewees, the negotiating parties' level of aperture towards the victims' delegations and their proclivity to assume responsibility fluctuated, reaching a particular low in the immediate wake of the third delegation, given the opposition generated by the FARC-EP due to the presence of a former police commander. While the waxing and waning of aperture towards the participants was determined closely by the parties' perceptions of their victims' legitimacy, it was very likely also a natural phenomenon, driven by negotiation and emotional fatigue. By holding the hearings only once a month, the organizers were able, in part, to mitigate more widespread emotional fatigue associated with the emotional impact of the delegations. The political will of the parties and the organizers themselves should be signalled here as a further factor keeping the process on track. Despite these temporary setbacks, the diverse forms through which the negotiating parties ultimately demonstrated their assumption of responsibility in Havana – as a result of listening to and interacting with their victims – cannot be underestimated. From direct admissions of responsibility to expressions of contrition and acknowledgement and private acts of apology (later followed by public apologies), both parties evolved significantly with respect to their role as perpetrators. One delegate – who had survived an attack carried out against the LGBTI+ population – stated how 'in the hearing [the FARC-EP] said ... we promise to compensate the LGBTI+ victims. For me, the truth meant that a weight fell from my shoulders'.[64]

As discussed throughout this book, such contrition and admission represent cornerstones of any transformative, reparatory and (re)conciliatory process. In combination with the acknowledgement of their victims, the evident evolution in the negotiating parties' perspectives and beliefs challenges, once more, the reductionist perspective that victims are solely instrumentalized in the context of victim-centred inclusion mechanisms. As one of the organizers stated:

> From the perspective of human rights narratives and practice, one of the gravest aspects of the conflict has been the denial from both sides that they had caused suffering and harm to non-combatants ... The fact that 60 people in their flesh and bones directly attested to the

---

[63] Interview, Bogotá, Colombia, April 2015.
[64] Interview, Cali, Colombia, April 2015.

atrocities represented a central mechanism through which to overcome this denial.[65]

A further theme pertinent to the capacity of the delegations to effect individual and intragroup/intergroup transformation relates to the issue of the negotiating parties' admission of responsibility and asking for forgiveness. Prior to the visits of the victims' delegations, the attitudes of the negotiating parties had been unequivocal, characterized by a generalized denial from both the government/military and the FARC-EP with respect to their responsibility for violations perpetrated and damage caused. In the case of the FARC-EP, for example, during the installation of the government–FARC-EP dialogues in 2012, Jesus Santrich, a FARC-EP commander, had cynically intoned the words 'Perhaps, perhaps, perhaps' when asked by a journalist whether the guerrilla would ask for forgiveness from its victims.[66] Rejection of victims' testimonies and narratives had similarly been the position assumed systematically by successive governments and the armed forces prior to and during the first two years of the Havana talks. In fact, even in the immediate wake of the victims' delegations, the government remained reticent to admit public responsibility, continuing to deny its role in causing massive human rights violations, as was the case, for example, in 2015, when it rejected the report published by Human Rights Watch on the false positives scandal.[67]

However, as has been discussed in this chapter, delegates stated that in Havana, both the guerrilla and government negotiators gradually began to admit responsibility for some of the specific violations they had perpetrated, particularly during conversations with the victims' delegates during the breaks and lunches. As the delegations visited the talks, and arguably as the negotiating parties began to feel the weight of the testimonies, so the latter began to approach individual victims in order to express contrition for their actions and, in some cases, to offer private apologies. According to one delegate:

> When I finished the testimony ... I was very dismayed ... a military negotiator approached me ... He said that he had no words to say I'm sorry ... and that they were going to keep reviewing the case. He told me 'perhaps you don't think I'm feeling a lot about what happened to

---

[65] Interview, Bogotá, Colombia, April 2015.
[66] Seven years later, as a parliamentarian, Santrich himself apologized to the victims of the armed conflict from the Colombian congress. See https://www.semana.com/nacion/articulo/las-disculpas-de-santrich-con-las-victimas-por-el-quiza-quiza-quiza/620334/ (accessed 31 July 2023).
[67] See https://elpais.com/internacional/2015/06/24/actualidad/1435172484_324109.html?event=go&event_log=go&prod=REGCRART&o=cerrado (accessed 31 July 2023).

you' ... later the FARC-EP guerrilla also approached me and told me 'very sorry for what had happened ... unfortunately, in this conflict, there were many errors of war'. I told him 'the life of a human being is not a mistake of war ... a human being cannot be called a mistake of war' ... It was very sad, there was a lot of fatigue, there was a lot pain ... when he was about to retire that afternoon, he turned and approached me ... [he said] it also caused them a lot of pain, that everything they had done ... had undoubtedly generated many difficult situations in which many people had fallen.[68]

The willingness of the negotiating parties to demonstrate contrition privately further showed how their perceptions of their victims and their attitudes regarding victimization had begun to evolve from outright denial to the assumption of responsibility for a range of violations committed and damage caused. Significantly, over time, these private conversations with individuals in Havana gave way to acts of public apology in the aftermath of the visits of the victims' delegations. It was this initial process of encounter, acknowledgement and recognition in Havana, which had, in turn, led to individual-level admissions, that was arguably instrumental to wider public institutional and organizational level acts. According to one survivor of a massacre perpetrated by the guerrilla:

the FARC-EP negotiators approached, around eight of them ... and told me 'we want to talk to you ... about the situation of the Bojayá massacre, because it is the case that we are clearer about concerning our responsibility ... And we would like to apologize to you ... we want first to know if you will give us a moment to listen to our request for forgiveness'. I thought, my God, what is happening. I told him, 'well the only thing I can do is to take your message to the community'. But at that moment, different things come to mind. You get confused. Of course, it was totally unexpected ... After that we returned to Bojayá, and with the victims we told them that ... an armed actor would like to apologize to the community. Would you give us the space to listen to them? That was the question, and most of the people there said yes.[69]

Several key public apologies for grave violations followed from the negotiating parties, victims of whom had been part of the victims' delegations. In December 2015, after a long-term process of dialogue, with the agreement of the community of Bojayá, the FARC-EP visited the town and offered a

---

[68] Interview, Bogotá, Colombia, May 2015.
[69] Interview, Bogotá, Colombia, April 2015.

formal public apology for the massacre perpetrated there.[70] Similarly, as head of state, from 2016, President Santos offered a series of public apologies. Santos gave a public apology on behalf of the state for the extermination and disappearance of the political party the Patriotic Union (UP).[71] He also offered a public apology acknowledging the 'moral debt owed [by the state] to victims and relatives' of those killed and disappeared during the sacking of the Palace of Justice in 1985.[72]

In response to their participation in the Havana talks and the episodes of contrition and apology that subsequently materialized, interviewees from across the five delegations often spoke of the question of forgiveness, although the theme was not a line of inquiry followed directly during interviews, given the sensitivity of the subject. The overall, common perspective that emerged was that 'forgiveness was the individual choice of the victim',[73] '[it] is my personal decision ... cannot be collective ... [or] imposed by decree'.[74] In the words of one victim of the guerrilla: 'The fact that [the FARC-EP negotiator] apologizes is relevant ... As a human being this is a very significant thing ... As I told you at the beginning, it has been a very long process. So much work ... I can't say that I've forgiven them and that's it. But I don't feel hate or resentment. Forgiveness is a process.'[75]

A crucial insight on this matter was offered by another delegate, whose perspective reflects the earlier discussion concerning victim acknowledgement. When mutual, acknowledgement and recognition, it was contended, has the potential to lead to victim empowerment and establish an important step towards conciliation. However, as the case of the police commander who had been a FARC-EP captive illustrates, an encounter may retraumatize and revictimize when a perpetrator denies a victim's narrative and condition, leading to a 'second injury'. One delegate proposed that forgiveness was contingent upon whether the perpetrator offered an apology or, more broadly, on perpetrators' attitudes. In their words:

> When I talk about forgiveness, I always say for this to happen there must be a two-way street ... they have not said 'forgive us'. But they

---

[70] See https://www.centrodememoriahistorica.gov.co/descargas/FARC-EP-perdon-boj aya/FARC-EP-pide-perdon-por-masacre-de-bojaya.pdf (accessed 31 July 2023).
[71] See https://centrodememoriahistorica.gov.co/presidente-pide-perdon-por-genocidio-de-la-up (accessed 31 July 2023).
[72] https://www.dailymotion.com/video/x3cr58s (accessed 31 July 2023). Santos' apology was given within the framework of the resolution passed by the Inter-American Human Rights Court on the case of the genocide of the UP.
[73] Interviews, Bogotá, Cali and Santa Marta, Colombia, March–May 2015.
[74] Interview, Bogotá, Colombia, May 2015.
[75] Interview, Santa Marta, Colombia, April 2015.

dared to hear us, they dared to meet us face to face. I don't know what the other delegations must have been like, but all of us in one way or another, with one language or another, told each other a lot of things ... I think it was also a catharsis for victims and perpetrators and I have seen that as positive.[76]

Several delegates stated how to forgive was an individual act isolated from wider acts or decisions of other parties. Nevertheless, there was a clear consensus shared by the interviewees that 'any position that a victim assumes deserves all the respect and all the consideration'.[77] This latter point was of key relevance, given that a number of delegates had, on their return to Colombia, been publicly berated by individuals opposing the Havana talks, who accused them of betrayal for meeting with the negotiating parties, as will be discussed subsequently.

Limits to individual and intergroup transformation

However, not all delegates were treated with the same level of respect and recognition by the representatives of the party that had victimized them. In such cases, both individual-level and intergroup transformation and empowerment were constrained. Victims of both the state and the FARC-EP were subjected to rejection, denial and severe criticism from the negotiating parties, leading to their revictimization and, in some cases, possible retraumatization. On several occasions, when obliged to face victims of specific violations they perpetrated, both the government and the FARC-EP rejected a participant's condition as victim, failed to evidence remorse or contrition for the violence perpetrated and undermined their legitimacy. Under such conditions, the encounter did not bring with it a restorative or transformative effect for the individual concerned. Walker's work on revictimization provides important insight here:

> If the community or authority ignores the victim, challenges the victim's credibility, treats the victim's complaint as of little import, shelters or sides with the perpetrator of wrong, or worse, overtly or by implication blames the victim, the victim will feel abandoned and isolated. That abandonment is a 'second injury'. (2006: 83)

During the visit of the first delegation to Havana, according to one participant, who had been victim of a crime perpetrated by the Colombian

---

[76] Interview, Bogotá, May 2015.
[77] Interview, Bogotá, May 2015.

state, the government's negotiating team initially closed down any possible recognition of state crimes. Such a statement immediately put into question their condition as victim. In their words:

> [the government] opened by ... saying: 'We recognize that some state agents have made mistakes, have committed crimes. But we give full support to the security forces and we are not going to recognize that there have been state crimes.' Of course that was very powerful to hear ... I feel that it was something against ... my testimony ... Although I have to recognize that both the government and the FARC-EP were still very respectful ... [a government negotiator] said to me 'your speech was very dignified ... we took careful note' ... After all the very painful interventions, at the end [a different government negotiator] ... made a very interesting intervention saying: 'How are we not going to recognize that the state committed crimes against trade unionists? How can we not recognize that the state has committed forced disappearance?'[78]

Despite having characterized the encounter that took place during the hearing as respectful, as was cited earlier, another victim of state crime, whose son had been executed during the so-called false positives scandal, was sceptical of the government's response to her testimony. In fact, she felt it to have been injurious. In her words:

> I was there representing the families, the women of extrajudicial executions ... my perpetrator is the Colombian state, the Colombian government and the military leadership ... [after my testimony] there was the intervention of the government. Their words were mechanical, cold words, words that hurt. They hurt me, they caused me a lot of damage, I cried throughout [their] speech ... because they wanted to silence me, they don't want me to tell the truth. My eldest [surviving] son has received death threats, because it's the way they want to shut me up. But my son said 'no mother, you continue [your struggle]'.[79]

The negative experience that some victims of state crime underwent in Havana was echoed in the case of certain victims of the FARC-EP. Several FARC-EP victims of sexual and gender-based violence faced opposition from the guerrilla. According to one participant, a member of the FARC-EP delegation directly stated to her that:

---

[78] Interview, Bogotá, Colombia, May 2015.
[79] Interview, Bogotá, Colombia, April 2015.

the FARC-EP did not rape women. Telling someone this in her face – that 'we didn't do this' – was hard to hear, but ... it was ... my word against his. I was a victim of that act and he couldn't tell me that I wasn't, because I was the one who had lived through that moment. Well this happened in the hearing, but then something happened outside the hearing. I gave him a book that we had published with many testimonies in it. I told him 'I give you this book on behalf of the Colombian Women's Initiative for Peace'. He received it from me.[80]

As was discussed earlier, an emblematic example of the FARC-EP's repudiation of one of its victims was the case of a former police commander held in captivity ('secuestrado') for over a decade in one of the FARC-EP's most paradigmatic crimes. The FARC-EP persistently questioned the organizer's selection of this individual and, in fact, formally and publicly rejected his condition of victimhood, issuing a number of press communiqués disqualifying him due to his membership in the state security forces. The antagonistic stance of the guerrilla in this case caused the individual to suffer severe anxiety and revictimization. In his words: 'I think they did not see me there as a victim but as an enemy. But I attended as a victim, I made my statement as a victim and they, on the contrary, made a statement to me as the enemy.' For him, 'their reaction was similar to their [treatment] when I was held in captivity; that is ... aggressive, dismissive ... arrogant, that was the feeling I got in Havana'.[81]

Nevertheless, what is of significance in this case is how the individual involved – who himself suffered considerably as a result of his participation – in fact positively evaluated the strategic decisions taken by the FARC-EP in the wake of the visit of his delegation to Havana. While the specific dynamic between the participant and the FARC-EP had itself been damaging, his own individual participation – and the demands he had made – arguably did have an effect on the guerrilla's negotiating position, despite the insurgency's mistreatment of the individual. In his words:

In the days that followed, there were pronouncements that I see as positive and that at the time I told them that they should demonstrate with true acts of peace. The months passed and in December they declared a unilateral truce ... later they decided to stop the recruitment of children under 17 years of age ... And the last point

---

[80] Interview, Bogotá, Colombia, April 2015.
[81] Interview, Bogotá, Colombia, May 2015.

is that steps were already taken a few days ago on the agreement for demining.[82]

Concluding remarks

This chapter has explored the relational impact of the visits of the victims' delegations to Havana in 2014. The research set out in the chapter has documented how transformation took place across three dimensions: the individual, intragroup and intergroup levels.

The relational changes wrought by the delegations affected the perspectives and beliefs held by the negotiating parties and by victims of all armed groups, as well as the relationships between them, a remarkable outcome given the very restricted number of participants who took part in the delegations. The chapter has illustrated how the victims' delegations were far more than the sum of their parts. Representing a universe of victims and victimizing events, the individual participants brought to Havana the catastrophic humanitarian impact of Colombia's brutal armed conflict and its tragic, differential consequences. In so doing, the delegations occasioned a progressively profound and arguably unprecedented shift in the dynamics between the negotiating parties, generating a recalibration of their perspectives on the armed conflict.

This chapter has illustrated that while the numerical extent of participation remains a relevant factor in determining the impact of victim inclusion, it is the terms under which participation takes place that ultimately shape the degree to which victims may be able to transform relations of power inherent in peace negotiations, conflict dynamics and conflict narratives. In this regard, the data presented challenges approaches that characterize victim inclusion mechanisms as defined uniquely by instrumentalization and the numerical breadth of victim participation.

Drawing on a broad range of interviews with participants and organizers, this chapter has explicitly demonstrated how the visits of the delegates led to significant changes in the perspectives of the negotiating parties regarding recognition of their own role in the conflict, the beliefs they held with respect to their own and their adversaries' victims, and the impact of the violence they perpetrated. Changes in the negotiating parties' perceptions of and beliefs concerning their adversaries and their victims (outgroups), as well as in their perceptions of their own group's actions (ingroup), were concurrent with the negotiating parties' progressive acknowledgement of victims' narratives, demands and experiences.

---

[82] Interview, Bogotá, Colombia, May 2015.

The hearings themselves did not afford 'new information' to the negotiating parties – a factor that scholars have often been keen to indicate as instrumental for transforming antagonistic intergroup relations. On the contrary, victims' and human rights organizations have been documenting and making public human rights violations and abuses against civilians in Colombia for decades. However, their protestations have been rejected by the armed actors and victims have, more often than not, been intimidated and left voiceless.

Yet, what was new about the delegations was the rules of engagement that determined how victims and perpetrators interacted with one another. Perpetrators' voices were silenced during the hearings, when the parties were obliged to listen respectfully and without comment to each participant. It was this mandated, formalized shift in victim–perpetrator power dynamics that contributed to what gradually became a transmission chain of impact. The informal encounters between victims and perpetrators during the lunches and coffee breaks compounded this process, assuming a fundamental significance as safe, regulated spaces for intergroup dialogue. Together, both formal and informal spaces for encounter facilitated the conditions within which the negotiating parties gradually came to comprehend differently the country's history of conflict, its impact and its rationale. Victim acknowledgement emerged progressively from these victim–perpetrator encounters, and became central to the widespread evolution in intergroup and intragroup relations, in turn ushering in episodes of limited conciliation between individual victims and perpetrators. Therefore, in Havana, it was the procedures and regulations governing the victim inclusion mechanism rather than the nature of the information provided to the parties that were instrumental in levelling the playing field and balancing predominant historical relations of power, at least temporarily.

According to many delegates, the cumulative consequence of this transmission chain of impact was that participation broke down the historical wall of perpetrator denial, ultimately contributing to decisions by the negotiating parties to de-escalate their military strategies, including with regard to the use of anti-personnel mines, the recruitment of minors and wider military actions. Such a transformation chain was contingent upon the negotiating parties undergoing a process of maturation with respect to their understanding of the individual and collective damage caused by the armed conflict. In the words of one delegate: 'I would say that, for me, the most important element was that both the state and the guerrillas saw the degree of degradation that the war has reached.'[83]

---

[83] Interview, Bogotá, Colombia, March 2015.

The data presented in this chapter have sought to interrogate how, if at all, victim inclusion mechanisms deployed during peace negotiations or transitional justice initiatives might precipitate changes at the individual, intragroup and intergroup levels, including across the dyadic relationship of victims and perpetrators. A core issue here pertains to the question of whether victims are able to assert their agency during episodes of participation or, on the contrary, whether they are merely instrumentalized. Delegates were mandated to provide specific guidelines to the negotiating parties as regards Point Five. At the individual level, inclusion afforded a critical, emancipatory opportunity for delegates to take part in a historical process, consolidating the satisfaction of victims' rights to participation and representation as it did so. The experiences of the delegates illustrate how the recognition, opportunity to confront their perpetrators and, in some cases, the individual apologies offered led to an improvement in participants' mental health and physical wellbeing. At the same time, at the group level, inclusion precipitated the emergence of a collective, common intragroup identity among the victims who went to Havana. For many of those who took part, the assumption of a shared collective identity was signalled as empowering, with participants stating how they no longer felt alone. Many participants, in fact, returned to Colombia with an even stronger commitment to peace activism and to the peace talks. Once back home, many sought to scale out and to scale up their experiences, although with limited degrees of success.

While the visits of the victims' delegations to Havana led to forms of empowerment, this chapter contends that the delegations also brought about profoundly disturbing experiences for some delegates. In these specific cases, both the government and the FARC-EP rejected claims made by the delegates, denied them their condition as victim and delegitimized their participation, leading to incidences of instrumentalization, politicization and revictimization and, in some cases, of retraumatization. Compounding the feelings of fear, anger, anxiety and pain that individuals had already experienced in the run-up to and during their visits to Havana, when the negotiating parties failed to acknowledge their victims, (re)humanization did not, logically, occur. Given these experiences, this chapter provides further supporting evidence for the argument made throughout the book that victim *instrumentalization* and *empowerment* are not mutually exclusive and may occur across a *spectrum*, taking place within and across distinct fields and levels during inclusion initiatives. Nevertheless, in the case of the Havana talks, victims were able, in part, to navigate and renegotiate relations of power, despite clear incidences of disempowerment.

A final point of significant interest to this research relates to the degree to which the victims' delegations were able to engender dialogue and (re-) conciliation across dyadic relationships. Ingroup–outgroup stereotyping narratives were recalibrated and outgroup members were, in large part, rehumanized, repersonalized and relegitimized. At the same time, both negotiating parties in Havana showed a significant degree of willingness to reflect upon and overcome elements of their own historical self-glorification narratives, as evidenced through their apologies. Moreover, victims and perpetrators, particularly at the individual level, showed a strong willingness to forge relationships that acknowledged the outgroup's narrative, to recognize that it no longer represented a threat to the ingroup and to craft a belief in a common history.

Despite the unprecedented developments that took place between the negotiating parties and their victims at the talks, what happened in Havana ostensibly remained in Havana. As will be discussed later on, the scope (and outcome) of intergroup dialogue processes was limited. The significant changes at the individual, interpersonal, intragroup and intergroup levels did not amount to reconciliation: with few exceptions, participants were careful not to refer to having reconciled with their perpetrators. The processes in Cuba were brief and systematic follow-up in the wake of the delegations was not offered. Delegates returned to a divided, polarized country. While the changes in Havana were significant, they were also restricted, taking place as isolated, episodic and restrained processes that were not scaled out or scaled up. As such, what happened in Havana across the dyadic relationship between victims and perpetrators did not foster wider transformation at the interpersonal, intragroup or intergroup level between victims and perpetrators, or indeed across other dyadic groups or, more broadly, across Colombian society. In this regard, a broad peace vision was not forthcoming and did not take root beyond the actors who participated in the Havana talks who had themselves been able to transform their antagonistic relationships and the beliefs that undergirded the rationalization for, psychological investment in and cultural foundations of violent conflict.

The following chapter will continue this discussion, analysing the degree to which, beyond orchestrating relational changes between those actors in Havana, the victims' delegations were able to shape the content of the peace agreement in general and Point Five in particular. In this respect, it analyses the degree to which, beyond acting as peacebuilders, the participants in the victims' delegations also acted as peacemakers.

7

The Impact of the Victims' Delegations: Victims as *Peacemakers*

Introduction

The previous chapter explored the degree to which the participants in the victims' delegations played a role as peace and peacebuilders. It elaborated further the core argument developed in this book that victim inclusion at the Havana peace talks led, on the one hand, to *empowerment* and, on the other, to *instrumentalization*. The data presented highlighted how such phenomena are not mutually exclusive, but rather, in the case of Colombia's victim-centred peacemaking and transitional justice initiative, occurred across a *spectrum* within distinct individual and collective dimensions and levels.

With reference to the unique interviews carried out with participants, it was contended that the delegations wrought changes at the individual, intragroup and intergroup levels. At the individual level, inclusion and the recognition it engendered led, in diverse cases, to improved physical and mental health for delegates. Participation simultaneously fostered an inclusive, intragroup victim identity for those delegates who visited Havana, leading many participants to signal how they no longer felt alone or isolated. Inclusion also transformed a range of perspectives and beliefs held by the delegates themselves and by the negotiating parties, facilitating significant relational changes among and between them. Relational changes occasioned a progressively meaningful shift in the dynamics between the negotiating parties. This shift allowed for a reconfiguration of the parties' perspectives on the armed conflict and widespread incidences of acknowledgement that resulted from the recalibration of ingroup-outgroup stereotyping narratives and episodes of rehumanization, repersonalization and legitimization. In turn, acknowledgement led to the breakdown of perpetrator denial with respect to some crimes and, subsequently, to public apologies by the armed actors and, arguably, to the introduction of de-escalation measures. Notably, it was both the generosity of those who participated and the modus operandi itself of the inclusion mechanism – including how perpetrators were literally silenced during the hearings – that allowed for this partial renegotiation of power relations in Havana.

However, when the negotiating parties failed to acknowledge their violent actions or rejected victims' narratives, inclusion occasioned instrumentalization, politicization and revictimization and, in some cases, retraumatization. Compounding these profoundly disturbing episodes, the limited nature of inclusion and, in particular, the lack of systematic follow-up in the aftermath of the visits meant that the episodic, isolated processes that were begun in Havana were not scaled out or scaled up. What happened in Havana ostensibly stayed in Havana.

As outlined in this book, the negotiating parties faced considerable challenges as they sought to tread a path that adhered to international standards relative to victims' rights, while simultaneously bringing an end to the conflict and satisfying the petitions of the conflict parties for (partial and conditional) amnesty. The hostility to the talks and opposition to transitional justice provisions allowing for a reduction in penal sanctions for the FARC-EP asserted by powerful actors – such as Uribe and his political cadres, cattle ranchers, sectors of the military, and veterans – and by the wider public further complicated this undertaking.

In this chapter, we explore the degree to which, beyond orchestrating unprecedented relational changes between the actors in Havana, the victims taking part in the Havana talks also played a role as peacemakers. In this regard, this chapter addresses whether the delegations were able explicitly to shape the specific content of Point Five.

The delegations permitted participants to table demands reflecting their individual and collective condition of victimhood and experiences of victimization. In Havana, according to interviewees, many participants advocated a shift away from an exclusively retributive approach to justice and supported an integral framework that aimed to achieve a balance between the rights to truth, justice, reparation and nonrecurrence. This general tendency towards an integral approach to victims' rights coincided with and, ultimately, came to legitimize the negotiating parties' own position that retributive justice should be balanced with restorative justice if talks were to continue and a political settlement were to be reached. In other words, participants' generous acknowledgement of the integrality of and balance between restorative and retributive justice coincided with the petitions from the negotiating parties that penal sanctions for human rights violations and abuses be limited. It is precisely this issue that explicitly shines a light on the question of instrumentalization, as will be discussed further later on.

Given the preceding discussion, this chapter will argue that, for the case of the role of *victims as peacemakers* during the Havana talks, a delicate balance exists between victim empowerment on the one hand and instrumentalization on the other. This assertion supports the overall argument of the book that *instrumentalization* and *empowerment* are not mutually exclusive, but rather may occur across a spectrum in the context or as a consequence of victim inclusion mechanisms. However, the extent to which victims played a decisive role as peacemakers during the Havana talks was more closely articulated with and subordinate to wider structural factors and relations of power than was their capacity to wield interpersonal and, in part, intergroup relational transformation in Havana, as was noted in the previous chapter. A key issue in this respect relates to the nature of participation and whether it is ultimately meaningful for victims. Specifically, what is of significance in this regard is the degree to which, in regulating participation, an initiative's mandate limits or permits the capacity of victims to become 'stakeholders in, and active agents of change' (Lundy and McGovern 2008: 267). Moreover, what is of crucial importance is the extent to which this mandate affords ownership and control over processes that enable a transferal of power from elites to subordinated actors (Firchow and Selim 2022), as will be further discussed subsequently.

The agreement – signed on 12 December 2015 – established the so-called *Comprehensive System for Truth, Justice, Reparations and Non-recurrence*. This framework, based on international standards relative to victims' rights and the principles of a victim-centred approach, established three interrelated bodies: a truth commission – The Truth, Coexistence and Non-Recurrence Commission – a special body to investigate cases of forced disappearance – the Unit for the Search for Persons Presumed Disappeared in the context and by reason of the Armed Conflict (the UBPD in its Spanish acronym) and a tribunal, the so-called Special Jurisdiction for Peace (the JEP in its Spanish acronym). This chapter demonstrates how, even despite the powerful opposition to and competing demands affecting the negotiations, the proposals made by the victims' delegations were, in large part, incorporated by the negotiating parties into the *Comprehensive System for Truth, Justice, Reparation and Non-recurrence* consecrated within Point Five and more widely across the Final Agreement. As such, the Final Agreement came to incorporate many demands tabled by participants during the hearings in Havana.

However, an important caveat exists here. Victims' petitions were incorporated only when they converged with and reflected the interests of the negotiating parties. For example, although the agreements included significant provisions aimed at addressing rural development and patterns of land use,[1] they did not establish a system for integral land reform, a demand made repeatedly by individual participants in Havana, which

---

[1] See specifically the provisions included in *Towards a New Colombian Countryside: Comprehensive Rural Reform; Political Participation: A Democratic Opportunity to Build Peace; Solution to the Illicit Drugs Problem*.

reflected historical causal drivers of the conflict and its accompanying violence. Similarly, a further proposal made by delegates was that the JEP should include within its mandate the investigation of so-called 'third parties' – groups, such as the private sector, that had enabled and, in some cases, directly supported the armed actors. This provision would have been of crucial significance given the widespread support to paramilitary groups that came from certain elements of the private sector (Hristov 2016). While the provision was included within the final draft of Point Five, it was subsequently expunged by the Constitutional Court during the revision of the peace agreements. The exclusion of land reform and, in fact, more broadly of security sector reform, and the post-facto removal of such a core component of the JEP represent examples of how the transformative capacity of Colombia's victims' delegations as peacemakers was constrained and subordinated to the prerogative of powerful actors.

Drawing on interviews with participants from the victims' delegations and with direct reference to their individual proposals, this chapter addresses the extent to which the visits to Havana shaped the final content of Point Five. The discussion begins by setting out some of the core debates related to the capacity of victim participation to shape transitional justice mechanisms and formal peace initiatives. It then turns to a discussion of the specific petitions made by the participants in the victims' delegations. Discussion of delegates' demands is framed according to how the proposals converged with formal norms relative to victims' rights to: (i) truth; (ii) justice; (iii) reparation; and (iv) nonrecurrence. In order to allow for an assessment of the degree to which formal inclusion occasioned the incorporation of victims' demands, the chapter closes with a discussion of the final content of Point Five and the wider Final Agreement.

Thinking about the scope of transitional justice and participation

Colombia's victims-centred peacemaking experience was shaped by the principles inherent to liberal peacebuilding and transitional justice thinking and practices. Both paradigms have historically been critiqued for their association with liberal and neoliberal norms, values and governance structures, a factor which, it has been argued, plays a role in disciplining them into conformity with the international system (Richmond 2004; Sriram Lehka 2007; Paris 2012; Baker and Obradovic-Wochnik 2016) and limiting their emancipatory capacity. For the specific case of transitional justice, the paradigm's origin story situates it within an ideologically (neo)liberal and predominantly Western-biased sphere that eschews transformative politics (Sharp 2013; Brinton Lykes and Murphy 2023). A core characteristic of this Western-centric bias can be found in transitional justice's foundation within the human rights framework. A considerable challenge in this regard has been that the paradigm has inherited the 'longstanding legalistic bias towards civil and political rights' and towards the (state and individual) actors privileged by these rights configurations, to the detriment of an approach grounded in collective rights or more diverse rights frameworks, including socioeconomic rights (Sharp 2012: 158; Santamaría et al 2020).

What has been intrinsic to critiques has been the discussion over whether, beyond direct violence, transitional justice mechanisms should address forms of structural violence, a debate reflecting wider deliberations over the limitations of liberal peacebuilding to transform the root causes of violent conflict and effect meaningful socioeconomic transformation (Miller 2008; Sharp 2012; Waldorf 2012). In fact, debate over the scope of the mandates of transitional justice initiatives has been one of the paradigm's historic terrains of contention. Transitional justice has accordingly been defined as a 'definitional project' and 'function of a power apparatus', which serves to 'voice and silence tolerable structural violence and intolerable physical atrocity ... delineating who may ... speak ... deciding what and who will be punished' (Miller 2008: 267).

In response to such critiques, scholars and practitioners have argued that transitional justice mechanisms should move beyond their more restricted engagement with the causes and consequences of physical atrocity and engage with socioeconomic rights and the structural causes of political violence. By situating violations of economic and social rights as core to its mission, transitional justice would, it is argued, no longer depict poverty and inequality solely 'as the landscape against which murder, disappearance, torture and other gross human rights violations are committed' (Miller 2008: 272). Former UN High Commissioner for Human Rights Louise Arbour promoted this discussion, identifying the legal, intellectual, moral and political arguments concerning how and why transitional justice should adopt a more holistic approach to justice. In her words: 'A comprehensive strategy for transitional justice would ... address the gross violations of *all* human rights during the conflict as well as the gross violations that gave rise to or contributed to the conflict.' In this way, the paradigm could 'serve as a springboard for the systematic anchoring of economic, social, and cultural rights in the political, legal, and social structures of societies in transition' (Arbour 2006: 26). By so doing, transitional justice interventions, it was contended, might have the potential to contribute more meaningfully to transformative processes challenging the relations of power and structural exclusion driving violent conflict. It would thus be both backward- and forward-looking, reactive and preventive.

In parallel to these debates, and of direct relevance to the Colombia case, there has been a considerable disjunction between survivors' habitual prioritization of demands for housing, employment and basic needs satisfaction, and the more conventional themes undergirding transitional justice, such as truth, justice and reparations for past crimes. In fact, empirical data has evidenced how the range of often complex and context-specific demands articulated by victims and survivors (Jacoby 2015), such as the fulfilment of basic needs, the restitution of economic and social rights, transformation of the structural causes of conflict, are rarely prioritized in transitional justice interventions (Robins 2017).

The progressive mainstreaming of victim-centred approaches – including in UN and EU policy for dealing with the past – has sought to close this gap between victims' context-specific demands and conventional transitional justice thinking by affording 'meaningful participation' to victims 'in the design and implementation of transitional justice processes and mechanisms' (Robins 2017: 43). Accordingly, over the past two decades, transitional justice initiatives have progressively incorporated frameworks through which to engage with socioeconomic violence. For example, the truth commissions in Chad (1990–1992), Sierra Leone (2002–2004), East Timor (2002–2005), Ghana (2003–2004), Liberia (2006–2009) and Colombia (2017–2022) demonstrated significant advancement with respect to the manner in which socioeconomic violence might be addressed.

This chapter shows how participants in the victims' delegations fielded a broad range of proposals to the negotiating parties situated in both conventional transitional justice matters and wider issues relevant to delegates' context-specific experiences of structural/indirect and direct violence. However, the task of making transitional justice more transformative undoubtedly goes beyond the inclusion of provisions addressing structural injustice and socioeconomic rights in transitional justice mandates. In order for transitional justice initiatives to effect long-term change, they require forms of participation that both empower victims/survivors and recalibrate historical relations of power. A core proposition in this regard has been to reconsider transitional justice interventions as integral to peacebuilding and to the longer-term processes embedded in the transformation of 'economic and political structures and relationships' required for sustainable peace (Lambourne 2013: 20). Within this framework, scholars have contended that 'transition' should no longer be conceptualized narrowly as a 'neat interregnum' between 'conflict' and 'post-conflict'. Rather, transition might be framed as a less neatly bounded process, during which accountability for individual and collective culpability is sought, at the same time as the causes of longer-term violence are dismantled, diverse forms of justice are guaranteed and sustainable peace is consolidated (Nagy 2008; Andrieu 2010). From this standpoint, some scholars have posited that in order for accountability mechanisms to play an effective role in peacebuilding, the concept of justice undergirding them should be 'transformative' rather than solely transitional (Lambourne 2013).[2] Key requisites to transformative justice have been identified as local participation and empowerment (Lambourne 2013), two themes central to this book. This broader, more ambitious gambit framing justice as transformative is as much about dealing with and moving on from the past as it is about establishing the 'conditions and structures to ensure justice in the present and the future' (Lambourne 2013: 23).

Of course, expecting transitional justice to address socioeconomic and structural violence, tackle wider injustices, deliver victim empowerment and forge stable peace places yet heavier burdens on a paradigm that already 'struggles to deliver on its original promises of truth, justice and reconciliation' (Waldorf 2012: 172). Waldorf, for one, is reluctant to advocate for a broader, more 'transformative' mandate for what are, in his words, 'already over-stretched and under-funded' mechanisms. Waldorf (2012: 179) contends instead that remedying economic injustices represents part of a long-term, 'post-transitional' political project, and proposes that the focus of transitional justice should remain 'short-term, legalistic and corrective', oriented towards 'accountability for gross violations of civil and political rights'.

Such caution is, in part, well placed: imposing yet further burdens on transitional justice mechanisms may indeed be ill-advised, given the destabilizing effect that the negotiation of even limited transitional justice provisions has on fragile, conflict-affected transitioning societies. However, the transitional moment indisputably affords significant opportunity, even while it represents a highly complex terrain where struggles for power between competing social, political and military actors occur and where the parameters determining their historical rectitude, or the lack thereof, may be defined. In this respect, it would be prudent to keep discussions as uncomplicated as possible. It is difficult enough already to negotiate basic justice and truth provisions in conflict-affected societies; demands for even greater and more complex commitments from the state and illegal armed actors may be likely to perpetuate the killing and prolong or even derail negotiations. Notwithstanding this, it would also be ill-considered not to take advantage of the transitional moment and at least to seek to recalibrate social, economic and political power and relations as broadly as possible. In this respect, the proposition that transitional justice should be conceived as 'as a tool of conflict prevention' (Gready and Roberts 2017), in which

---

[2] Lambourne (2013) conceptualizes transformative justice as grounded in six core principles: symbolic/ritual and substantive aspects of justice; prospective (future-oriented, long-term), contemporaneous and historical justice (dealing with the past); local ownership and capacity building; structural transformation and institutional reform; relationship transformation and reconciliation; and holistic, integrated and comprehensive justice. See also Lambourne and Gitau (2013).

economic violence should be incorporated yet expectations tempered, perhaps represents a more appropriate alternative.

The full ramifications of these ideas will emerge in the later discussion of the extent to which the delegations shaped the specific content of the accountability provisions incorporated into the final rendering of Point Five (and the wider peace agreement). Engagement with socioeconomic rights and structural violence was, in the end, relatively limited, despite victims' demands to incorporate wider rights frameworks and mechanisms for redress. Given such limited purchase in this regard, and the fact that the Colombia experience of victim inclusion has represented one of the most comprehensive and progressive to date, how realistic is it for us to expect mechanisms to deal with past violations, while establishing an effective framework for conflict prevention?

Scholarship on civil society and victim participation in formal peace negotiations has interrogated the degree to which inclusion may lead to more durable and sustainable peace settlements and agreements. As was discussed in previous chapters, the rationale for victim inclusion is twofold: first, victim inclusion is framed as the morally correct thing to do; and, second, victim participation, it is argued, leads to more sustainable peace settlements by bringing more diverse themes to the negotiating table, broadening the peace agenda (McKeon 2004; Bell 2019: 13) and increasing the potential to hold the parties accountable (Paffenholz 2014: 73–74). As such, wider participation may empower marginal populations (Kew and Wanis St John 2008), while making agreements more robust and durable by increasing their legitimacy (Nillson 2012) and transparency, and facilitating greater public ownership (Hirblinger and Landau 2020). Inclusion, it has also been contended, may have a relational impact by building positive relations between adversary groups and social constituencies (Hirblinger and Landau 2020), an argument that was developed in the previous chapter.

Similarly, scholarship has interrogated the degree to which victim inclusion in peace processes and victim-centred transitional justice initiatives empowers victims and legitimizes processes/mechanisms (Mendes 2019), while addressing longstanding inequalities and structural drivers of conflict. Although, of course, inclusion 'may make consensus harder to achieve', scholars have contended that, once reached, 'an inclusive consensus will have much higher potential to build sustainable peace' (Mendes 2019: 275).

Merely increasing the numerical extent of participation is widely perceived as inadequate, a discussion supported by the data presented in the previous chapter. Rather, it is commonly contended that it is the nature of inclusion that is decisive. From a normative perspective, dynamics of victim participation, it is contended, should aim to transform dominant power relations, echoing insight that the participation of women and inclusion of a gender perspective within peace negotiations should aspire to re-allocate power and redefine power relations to forge a 'new political settlement or social contract' (Bell and McNicholl 2019: 3–4). How might mechanisms of participation be designed in order to move beyond merely symbolic participation and victim instrumentalization?

Scholars contend that meaningful participation is made more likely when mechanisms are grounded in local processes, experiences, knowledge and demands, an assertion that is of relevance to the Colombia case. At the same time, it has been proposed that inclusion is more transformative when it guarantees decision-making capability to victims and civil society actors, both during and as an ongoing commitment after talks (Lundy and McGovern 2008). In short, an effective participatory approach would allow for a 'transfer of power' and would recategorize participants as 'stakeholders in, and active agents of change', during and after negotiations (Lundy and McGovern 2008: 278–280). Participation is thus meaningful when it constitutes more than a seat at the table, by precipitating elite actors' acknowledgement of victims and excluded groups, and permitting the exercise of the latter's agency and influence within the respective process. What is fundamental is that initiatives permit groups habitually excluded from formal negotiations to access and to shape talks directly (Aulin 2019). More than *quantity*, it is the *quality* of participation that more profoundly then determines whether mechanisms may hold the potential to be transformative.

The demands of the victims to the negotiating parties in Havana

The discussion now moves on to examine the proposals tabled to the negotiating parties in Havana by the participants in the victims' delegations. Rather than engaging, in detail, with each specific demand made by the 60 participants – which is beyond the scope of this chapter – proposals are clustered by their convergence with the framework of victims' rights to truth, justice, reparation and nonrecurrence. The objective of this chapter is to decipher whether victim inclusion empowered participants by enabling the delegations to contribute effectively to the content of Point Five or, on the contrary, whether participants were ultimately instrumentalized as a result of their participation.

As discussed throughout this book, the so-called victims' turn in transitional justice emerged as policy makers and scholars sought to respond to victims' claims that transitional justice mechanisms and institutions were failing to represent their experiences and self-identified needs and demands. What has increasingly followed have been interventions progressively incorporating survivors and victims within purportedly 'victim-centred' practices, including processes of consultation, initiatives allowing for victim–perpetrator dialogue and, more recently, direct engagement in peace-making processes and in the design, planning and implementation of transitional justice mechanisms.

With respect specifically to participation in peace negotiations, Paffenholz (2014, 2015) has identified distinct 'modalities of inclusion', such as *direct representation* (at the negotiation table), observer status, official consultative forums running in parallel to formal negotiations, less formal consultation processes, inclusive post-agreement mechanisms, high-level civil society initiatives, public participation, public decision making and mass action.

The victims' delegations were mandated in the latter half of 2014 to allow participants to offer their individual testimonies to the negotiating parties and make specific proposals for the accountability mechanisms to be incorporated into Point Five. Significantly, the mandate regulating the victims' delegations had been decided upon pre facto in Havana by the negotiating parties. Victims were not given a say in the design of the mechanism itself, which emerged out of an elite pact (Mendes 2019). Their participation was, in this regard, limited by and subject to parameters that had been previously established; therefore, victims had no say in the design of the inclusion mechanism in which they subsequently participated.

Viewed within Paffenholz's framework, the delegations combined diverse forms of inclusion. The initiative temporarily afforded victims a direct seat at the negotiating table, although without binding decision-making capability; rather, and above all, the delegations enjoyed a consultative status. However, as previously discussed, the victims' delegations contributed to the subsequent establishment of the Sub-commission on Gender, a significantly important high-level consultative body running in parallel to the official negotiations. Moreover, as was discussed in Chapter 4, the so-called Victims' Forums, which preceded the delegations, were a public consultative body created to provide guidance for the content of Point Five. The Victims' Forums aimed, at the same time, to engender a dialogue, at the very least across civil society and between victims of all armed groups. Finally, with respect to wider inclusion in the Havana talks, the General Framework Agreement, signed in 2012, had consecrated other forms of participation to be deployed during the talks, such as the e-portal and initiatives allowing consultation with political representatives in Colombia. The diversity of the inclusion mechanisms incorporated within the wider framework of the negotiations demonstrates how distinct forms of inclusion are not necessarily mutually exclusive, but rather may occur sequentially or simultaneously (Paffenholz 2015).

In this context, what was unique specifically about Colombia's victims' delegations was their hybrid nature. Victims were mandated to participate directly in the broader *peacemaking* apparatus (the talks) and consulted with respect to the design of the accountability framework at the centre of the Santos–FARC-EP peace agreement. Victim participation was directly aimed at crafting a victim-centred transitional justice practice that sought to place victims' rights at the heart of the transitional justice/accountability provisions. It is to the delegates' proposals concerning specific rights to (i) truth, (ii) justice, (iii) reparation and (iv) nonrecurrence that the focus now turns in order to assess the degree to which the mechanism facilitated the inclusion of victims' experiences and self-defined needs and demands.

Demands for the right to truth

On paper, the primary objective of victim inclusion in Havana was to place the satisfaction of victims' rights at the core of the peace agreement, allowing, in theory, the parties to craft the talks and eventual peace agreement around victims' rights to truth, justice, reparation and nonrecurrence. One tenet of the victims' delegations in this regard was to guarantee the right of victims to truth. In accordance with international norms, the right to truth encompasses the verification and full public disclosure of all facts associated with those specific crimes suffered by victims or their relatives (Klinkner and Davis 2021).[3] In order to ensure that the accountability mechanisms incorporated within Point Five fulfil this right, provisions were to be aimed at ensuring that the full and complete truth concerning violent events would be known, including the circumstances in which they took place, the nature of those acts, the reasons driving perpetrators to commit acts of victimization and the full data concerning those who participated in them. For cases of forced disappearance, the whereabouts of individuals represented a key claim made by victims' relatives.

A pervasive demand made by participants in the victims' delegations was that Point Five should incorporate explicit provisions to allow for the establishment of a comprehensive truth commission.[4] One mother, whose son had been the victim of a FARC-EP operation, demanded that Point Five include a truth commission that enjoyed 'an institutional mandate, budgetary and administrative autonomy'.[5] Many of the 60 participants

---

[3] See also UN, https://www.un.org/en/observances/right-to-truth-day (accessed 2 October 2023).
[4] According to some participants in the victims' delegations, there was an element of confusion over whether the delegations were a truth-seeking mechanism in themselves, despite the guidelines given to them by the organizers stating the contrary. Participants in some cases had hoped that they would hear the 'truth' from the negotiating parties about their specific case. According to one participant: 'I had certain expectations that I would be able to see those responsible for all these deaths in my family. Well, I had that expectation that I was going to be able to encounter the truth, the truth of what had happened to my entire family and that really perhaps this was going to help so that this would not happen again.' However, the delegations were not a truth commission and, as such, they did not guarantee the victims' immediate right to the truth, leading in numerous cases to disappointment and frustration. Interviews, Bogotá, March–May 2015.
[5] Interview, Bogotá, Colombia, April 2015.

demanded that the mandate of a truth commission for the Colombia case should include provision to focus not only on direct perpetrators, but also on the role of so-called 'third parties' – in other words, civilian actors who had supported (and in some cases bankrolled) armed groups, particularly paramilitary organizations. Delegates were aware that a truth commission represented only one single element of a broader framework that aimed to establish conditions for accountability and peace. One female delegate, whose brother had been assassinated by the FARC-EP, described how she had proposed a truth commission 'not as a panacea ... [as] we are starting from the fact that the whole truth is not going to be known ... nor is what they [perpetrators] say necessarily 100 percent of the truth'. Rather, for this participant, the establishment of a truth commission represented 'a process that helps heal the victims'.[6]

Other participants reiterated the perspective on the centrality a truth commission for healing individual victims. Accordingly, one survivor of conflict-related sexual violence perpetrated by military and paramilitary forces offered a significantly important reflection on what truth meant in the context of the transitional justice arrangements consecrated in Point Five. In her words:

> my expectation [of the victims' delegations] is that they can clarify to the parties the impact that this war has had on women. They [the parties] have to understand it, and not so they all end up in prison. They have to understand it so that it doesn't happen again. They have to understand it so that women are told the truth. They have to understand the impact because they can't give us anything back, nothing ... for what they did to us ... for our marked bodies, that you see every day in the mirror ... nothing can repair this. But to know that there is going to be truth, that they are going to tell you it this happened for this or that reason. And [to know] that you are also going to work so that it doesn't happen again to any other woman ... I think this already represents a journey. A path. And I will at least continue working on that.[7]

A number of delegates suggested that a truth commission could play a fundamental role in ushering in collective reflection across Colombian society and state concerning more than five decades of atrocious violence. According to one participant, a truth commission represented a way of constructing 'monuments ... out of our memory ... that are part of [belong

---

[6] Interview, Bogotá, Colombia, April 2015.
[7] Interview, Bogotá, Colombia, May 2015.

to] the nation'. For this delegate, an institutional mechanism to acknowledge the truth would legitimize and formalize victims' struggles, as they had been 'working with our nails to maintain and rebuild' Colombia.[8]

Participants' demands for a truth commission – or the specific components that might characterize it – were not uniform, but rather were shaped by and read through the lens of their particular experience of victimization. As such, individual proposals for a truth commission aimed to satisfy a participant's own self-defined needs and demands. Nevertheless, the solidarity that was built between victims in Havana also meant that participants appealed to peers' experiences of victimization and suffering. In their proposals, then, participants often referred to and supported the demands for truth that other delegates had made. The collective demand for truth was greater than the sum of its individual parts in this regard, ultimately representing a broad petition that sought to satisfy diverse victim constituencies. In other words, the value of truth was recognized by all participants as central to dealing with the past. In the words of one female victim: 'I told them that ... it was unjust that they murdered my brother ... because he did not allow himself to be recruited. I told them ... we need to know why they did this, why they harmed *our families, why they took the land from us.*'[9] According to one Afro-Colombian leader, a survivor of violence perpetrated on distinct occasions by all armed groups:

> Getting to the real issue, my proposals were that *we, as Afros, as black Colombians*, need to know why they made us move from our original lands, why they murdered the leaders who defended our human rights, why they stripped us of our resources and our territories, why they brought violent conflict to our territory.[10]

Relatives of the disappeared – including those disappeared by the Colombian state in the 'false positives' scandal – demanded that a truth commission should lead to the disclosure of the whereabouts of their loved ones. These proposals were bolstered by their explicit demands for a commission to search for the bodies of the disappeared. In the words of one mother, 'from mass graves, they [the disappeared] are screaming, wanting to come back, to be returned to their relatives. We are here with open arms waiting for them to return, so that they can die with dignity'.[11] Another mother, whose son had

---

[8] Interview, Santa Marta, Colombia, April 2015.
[9] Interview, Cali, Colombia, May 2015.
[10] Interview, Bogotá, Colombia, April 2015.
[11] Interview, Bogotá, Colombia, April 2015.

been disappeared by paramilitary operatives, stated how, for her, knowing the truth was linked to justice. From her perspective:

> Prison for forty or fifty years isn't going to bring back my son, and nor will a check from the government for millions of pesos. I base my vision of justice on knowing the real truth and the facts of what happened, knowing what they did, knowing the real truth about the facts of what happened, who did it, why they did it and who benefited from it.[12]

Beyond the satisfaction of each victim's individual right to truth, participants interviewed described how a truth commission potentially represented a mechanism to provide perpetrators with the forensic truth about the impact of the violence they had committed. In this respect, some interviewees envisioned a truth commission as a body that was crucial for securing their right to nonrecurrence, by showing the grotesque nature of the violence and its wider individual and societal consequences. Interviewees argued that knowing how the violence they perpetrated affected victims could lead the negotiating parties to a *never again* moment. Accordingly, one male participant described how delegates had emphasized 'the importance of truth, of a complex and complete truth ... [to] guarantees of nonrecurrence'. As such, victims' testimonies had, for this delegate, sought to address the issue of truth 'in its entirety, including truth and reparation processes and measures to ensure nonrecurrence' as integral.[13] In the words of one of the organizers, it was precisely this assemblage of '[t]ruth on many different levels' that represented the 'most urgent demand' tabled by the delegates.[14]

Demands for the right to justice

During the hearings in Havana, within their proposals and recommendations to the negotiating parties, participants in the victims' delegations simultaneously prioritized demands for justice. According to the Joinet/Orentlicher Principles, the right of victims to justice consecrates their right to 'receive a fair and effective remedy, including the expectation that the person or persons responsible will be held accountable by judicial means and that reparations will be forthcoming' (Sisson 2010: 12). Integral to the right to justice are the obligations of the state to 'investigate violations, to arrest and prosecute the perpetrators and, if their guilt is established, to punish them' (Sisson 2010: 13). Services providing justice for victims should

---

[12] Interview, Bogotá, Colombia, March 2015.
[13] Interview, Bogotá, Colombia, May 2015.
[14] Interview, Bogotá, Colombia, May 2015.

enhance the rule of law and must be fair, timely, accessible, transparent, effective, nondiscriminatory and accountable.[15] Of course, as was discussed in earlier chapters, the conceptualization of justice as framed within the paradigm of transitional justice allows for and promotes other mechanisms through which to attain justice, including nonjudicial mechanisms, while recognizing the integral, mutually reinforcing nature of victims' rights to truth, justice, reparation and nonrecurrence.

Interviews with participants drew out the multilayered, complex nature of their demands for justice and the constitutive connection between demands for the right to justice and other correlative rights. To begin with, the approach adopted by the delegates was pragmatic and, it must be underscored, deeply generous. All participants demanded the closure of Colombia's armed conflict as a priority. Delegates, who had experienced the embodied consequences of suffering due to egregious violence, advocated the immediate cessation to hostilities. 'No More Victims' ('*Ni una víctima más*') became the slogan of the victims' delegations. Echoing statements by other delegates, a mother whose son had been killed in Bogotá by a FARC-EP bomb stated how she 'did not want another mother to have to go through what she had gone through'.[16]

All delegates interviewed demanded that justice provisions be incorporated within the framework for Point Five and that sanctions be imposed on perpetrators. Participants identified diverse forms of sanction, including the application of penal sanctions for perpetrators. Many participants highlighted the need for the full and integral satisfaction of all their rights, including to justice, truth, reparation and nonrecurrence, as will be discussed further later on. While prioritizing the satisfaction of the right to justice, delegates were conscious that they might have to accept a reduction in prison time in exchange for information concerning violations, as had previously been the case during the 2005 agreement crafted with the AUC. Many interviewees stated how they had been willing to take such a step in order to guarantee other rights and to bring an end to the country's armed conflict. In the end, it was how participants envisioned the scope and nature of justice provisions, including of penal sanctions, that differed, embedded as it was in participants' individual experiences of victimization.

Interviewees who had been victims of both and sometimes multiple armed groups explicitly proposed criminal investigation and penal sanction for those found responsible. For example, victims linked to the UP political party, victims of state crime, described how justice for them required state recognition of and sanction for its role in the genocide of the UP. In the

---

[15] See https://www.ohchr.org/en/transitional-justice (accessed 3 October 2023).
[16] Interview, Bogotá, Colombia, May 2015.

words of one delegate, 'if there is no recognition there is nothing, especially with such obvious facts clarified in the statements of paramilitary leaders pointing to the complicity of the state [in the genocide]. What we demand is truth, justice and reparation'.[17]

One survivor of sexual violence perpetrated by both military and paramilitary groups stated how, for her, recognition by the armed groups of their responsibility represented only the minimum for achieving justice. In the absence of such acknowledgement, the delegate pointed to international justice mechanisms as potentially playing a role in guaranteeing accountability for these crimes. In her words, the parties were in 'a strong position ... to talk about the issue of sexual violence ... if you don't [do so] here at this negotiating table, there is the International Criminal Court and we will get there'.[18] A victim of the FARC-EP reiterated the importance of the armed groups' recognition of their crimes as central to the pursuit of justice. In her words:

> I think that acknowledgement of the victims and the damage caused must occur ... I think there must be recognition of the damage caused and obviously in that context they have to demonstrate regret ... they have to ask for forgiveness, offer guarantees of nonrecurrence ... the process has to take place even if the whole truth is not told, even if all justice is not applied, even if everything isn't acknowledged ... These processes have to occur so that the peace process is legitimate and so that later the International Criminal Court doesn't intervene.[19]

A mother from Bogotá, whose son had been extrajudicially executed by the state, similarly signalled how truth and justice were linked and mutually reinforcing:

> Victims have the right to know where their relatives are, so that they can recover them to be able to mourn with dignity ... I am a victim of a Colombian state, of an indifferent and indolent state that does not mind killing our children so it can present significant military results ... I am a mother who did not give birth TO a son ... for a war ... there are many mothers who have not been able to recover their children, there are many wives who have not been able to recover their husbands, there are many sisters who have not been able to recover their brothers ... allow them to receive [the bodies] from the mass graves that exist

---

[17] Interview, Bogotá, Colombia, May 2015.
[18] Interview, Bogotá, Colombia, May 2015.
[19] Interview, Bogotá, Colombia, April 2015.

throughout the country so that we can all grieve with dignity [have] ... a dignified and true peace process ... with social justice.[20]

What was significant during interviews with participants was how they had demanded that retributive justice be balanced with restorative justice and that the right to justice must be bolstered by the satisfaction of other rights. As such, the proposition that victims merely required the maximum from criminal justice (penal sanction) was questioned by numerous delegates. One delegate referred to the importance of rethinking the penal approach so as not to impede the peace process. In her words:

> I am fully aware that the FARC-EP is not going to sit down to negotiate to end up in jail. But then, in this regard, if there is to be transitional justice, there must also be a judicial process, with some alternative sentencing ... I am aware that justice cannot be an impediment to the peace process, but a process without justice is not legitimate either, we must reach a middle ground ... for this process to be legitimate.[21]

A survivor of the massacre of Bojayá echoed these sentiments. According to this delegate:

> The justice we seek as victims is not an unmovable righteousness that hinders the peace process ... Everyone is demanding bars, prison time. I don't know why ... maybe because of how the idea of justice has been sold in Colombia? So we said, as victims of Bojayá, we are not in a position to allow the need for justice to truncate the peace process and the desire for peace. However, we must also maintain a delicate balance. We cannot attain a level of justice so low that it impairs the dignity of the victims. In that sense, there are minimums that must be met ... we in the Afro community have been developing internal measures and regulations ... Social punishments, for example, community work, community service, messages in favour of peace, that sort of thing. In essence, justice has to be restorative ... because if we impose an eye for an eye and a tooth for a tooth, then we will damage this country and the world.[22]

During the hearings, individual delegates also tabled proposals for culturally sensitive justice-seeking mechanisms that were contingent upon and

---

[20] Interview, Bogotá, Colombia, April 2015.
[21] Interview, Bogotá, Colombia, April 2015.
[22] Interview, Bogotá, Colombia, April 2015.

acknowledged their specific ethnic, racial and cultural contexts. Reflecting the perspective of the delegate from Bojayá, one indigenous leader, a victim of diverse armed groups, similarly advocated that the accountability mechanisms consecrated in Point Five should recognize the capacity of indigenous communities to apply their own internal regulations with respect to justice for victims of political violence. They demanded that 'indigenous people ... be able to exercise their right to self-government ... within that sphere, it is our ethnic territorial entities who can [administer] justice [so] ... the victims can have serious, real and effective access'.[23]

Returning to the issue of balancing restorative and retributive justice, a male participant whose son had been kidnapped and disappeared, most likely by paramilitary groups, offered an important reflection on the integral operationalization of justice:

> It seems to me that even if one of these criminals lasts for another 40 or 50 years, he will not return my son to me. Nor will the government return him to me by giving me a check for 100, 500 or a million pesos. Today I base my justice on knowing the real truth of the facts concerning what happened, who did it, why they did it and which individuals or group benefited from what happened.[24]

Delegates' proposals for an approach that sought an equilibrium between retributive and restorative justice were very generous and implied that scholars should be mindful of how individual victims and survivors may make nuanced claims in the context of inclusion mechanisms. Moreover, such a reflection may have a bearing on how we evaluate empowerment and instrumentalization, and this will be discussed in the final section of this chapter.

Significantly, the tendency to appeal to an integral approach to victims' rights ultimately converged with the demands and statements made by the negotiating parties, who, from the beginning of the Havana talks, had clarified how they were determined not to face prison time. The negotiating parties were, in the end, able to refer/defer to the proposals made by the victims' delegations as a point of moral and pragmatic reference to legitimate their own demands for alternative sentencing, pardon or amnesty. For those opposing the talks, the fact that the demands of the FARC-EP and the government ultimately coincided with specific proposals made by the victims' delegations was at best problematic and, at worst, delegitimized the talks yet further. Under such conditions, the imposition of transitional justice

---

[23] Interview, Bogotá, Colombia, May 2015.
[24] Interview, Bogotá, Colombia, April 2015.

for perpetrators, and particularly for the guerrilla, further exacerbated the perceptions of spoiling actors (such as former President Uribe) and sectors of the public that the agreement was illegitimate. Arguably, their vehement public rejection of the victims' delegations was heightened precisely because participants' demands had coincided with calls for amnesty, particularly by the guerrilla.

One member of the organizers offered an important reflection on this issue:

> many ... are afraid of the victims because, as we have always said, the parties may feel that justice is a thirst for revenge. I believe they have to understand that justice does not equal thirst for revenge ... I was tremendously surprised that [many] participants ... said we are willing ... that [perpetrators] do not pay a day in jail as long as they tell the truth, the complete truth, not just pieces of what happened, as long as there are true guarantees for nonrecurrence, as long as there are levels of real reparation ... [the victims] are willing to turn the page in favour of peace ... From the outside people believe that the victims want total punishment, in fact many people said 'I don't understand how they go and shake hands with those criminals ... forgive them'. There are people who have not experienced the consequences [of violence] but want to see [the perpetrators] rot in jail.[25]

The statement of one participant, a former police commander who had been a prisoner of war held in captivity for over a decade by the FARC-EP, was also illustrative with respect to the significance of an integral approach to justice as demanded by the victims. The individual had been rejected by the FARC-EP and he had been revictimized in Havana, as was discussed in previous chapters. Nevertheless, his perspective on the importance of balancing restorative and retributive justice was enlightening. The participant proposed to the parties that all prisoners of war held hostage be returned, including the remains of those who had died in captivity. Echoing proposals by other participants, he also demanded that accountability provisions in Point Five must establish a mechanism to guarantee the search for, location and return of the remains of disappeared persons. Offering an approach that recognized the integrity of victims' rights, he stated how:

> We are waiting for what ... will be in Point Five ... when those points ... are made known, we will know if our expectations are met. Whether our rights are going to be guaranteed. Because what is being asked for is truth to find all those kidnapped and disappeared. That there is

---

[25] Interview, Bogotá, Colombia, May 2015.

justice, even if it is transitional justice. That there are reparations, of course. That there is rehabilitation according to the standards of the Inter-American Court/Commission. That compensation is given. That guarantees of nonrecurrence be given and there we insist that for there to be guarantees of nonrecurrence, weapons must be delivered ... that [will be] our guarantee.[26]

The right to reparation

As consecrated in international norms, the right of victims to reparations refers to those measures aimed at redressing human rights violations through the provision of a range of material and symbolic measures to victims or their families, and, where appropriate, to affected communities or populations. Reparations mechanisms must be easily accessible to victims and measures must be adequate, effective, prompt and proportional to the gravity of the violations perpetrated and the harm suffered by victims and survivors.[27] According to the UN *Basic Principles and Guidelines on the Right to a Remedy and Reparation for Victims of Gross Violations of International Human Rights Law and Serious Violations of International Humanitarian Law*, reparations must incorporate four elements: restitution; compensation; rehabilitation; and satisfaction. Compensation applies to a series of damages, including physical or mental harm, lost opportunities (including employment and education), material damages and loss of earnings, moral damage, and legal costs and other services.[28]

There has been significant academic and policy debate concerning the fact that reparations have been traditionally conceived as a mechanism to restore the victim of the gross violation to their original condition (restitution) (Brett and Malagón 2013). Pablo de Grieff, the former UN Special Rapporteur on Truth, Justice and Reparation, advocated a perspective on reparations that would go beyond such basic restitution through the satisfaction of individual rights claims and, instead, aim to build social solidarity and recognition (de Grieff 2006). Uprimny Yepes

---

[26] Interview, Bogotá, Colombia, April 2015.
[27] See the 2005 United Nations *Basic Principles and Guidelines on the Right to a Remedy and Reparation for Victims of Gross Violations of International Human Rights Law and Serious Violations of International Humanitarian Law*, https://documents-dds-ny.un.org/doc/UNDOC/GEN/N05/496/42/PDF/N0549642.pdf?OpenElement). See also https://www.ohchr.org/en/transitional-justice/reparations#:~:text=Victims%20have%20a%20right%20to,as%20well%20as%20affected%20communities (accessed 5 October 2023).
[28] See UN *Basic Principles and Guidelines on the Right to a Remedy and Reparation for Victims of Gross Violations of International Human Rights Law and Serious Violations of International Humanitarian Law*, Article 20 (p 7).

(2009) has similarly challenged conventional framings of restitution, positing that the aim of reparations to restore victims to their original position is inadequate, given that, prior to the violation, many victims already lived in conditions of indirect and structural violence. Brett and Malagón (2013: 260–261) have argued that, as a consequence, reparations programmes must simultaneously redress fundamental human rights violations and grievances of civil and political rights, while redressing 'those rights that speak to the socio-economic and structural roots of conflict'. From their perspective, the most relevant path to crafting responsive measures is an inclusive process that responds to the self-defined needs and demands of collective and individual victims.

These principles and debates are of relevance to the claims made by the participants in the victims' delegations. Interviewed participants explained how, in their proposals to the negotiating parties, they had eschewed mere monetary compensation as an adequate framework for reparations policies. Instead, participants stated how they had conceived (and demanded) reparations measures as both a compensatory mechanism and a future-oriented intervention through which to transform the embedded structural conditions and antagonistic social relationships shaping the evolution of violent conflict. Participants saw no benefit in being *returned to their original condition*, but instead believed that reparations needed to be transformative if they were to play any role in guaranteeing nonrecurrence. While proposals tabled by the delegates were contingent upon individual experiences of victimization, victims' demands for individual, collective, economic and symbolic reparation were, in this regard, commonly undergirded by claims for socioeconomic rights.

A ubiquitous demand tabled by delegates in this respect pertained to access to, control over and title to land, conditions that, for many, had been at the heart of their own experiences of victimization, as well as a central causal factor driving the country's violent conflict. One female participant, a victim of multiple armed groups, proposed that 'the return of land and its restitution' should be at the centre of the reparations framework.[29] Over a quarter of those interviewed explained that they had proposed comprehensive agrarian reform. In the words of another female delegate, essential to reparations had to be:

> The right to land, an agrarian reform. For victims from rural areas, and in general for people living in situations of forced displacement, the possibility of return in conditions of dignity and safety is a central aspect. The reconstruction of the countryside: agrarian reform that

---

[29] Interview, Bogotá, Colombia, May 2015.

meets the needs of those in the countryside and the families that live off the land. I made a call to address these structural causes of the conflict.[30]

According to one participant, forcibly recruited into an armed group as a minor, a comprehensive programme of land reform was a fundamental requisite to guarantee their and their community's rights to reparation and nonrecurrence. From their perspective, such a programme had to be linked to a policy of institutional strengthening in rural areas:

> There are parts [of the country] where the abandonment by the state is absolute. So the proposal to the government/state was that it take responsibility, not only by compensating, but also by providing guarantees to the people living in these areas, where there still remains no presence of the state security forces and where people reside without any protection.[31]

According to another participant, a victim of multiple armed groups, the presence/testimonies of the victims' delegations in Havana in fact provided an apposite point of departure from which the government could begin to craft an effectual, inclusive agrarian policy. From his perspective, it was imperative that the negotiating parties take into account victims' demands for agrarian reform as a central pillar, in general, of the accountability mechanisms consecrated in Point Five and, in particular, of a meaningful reparations programme: 'The proposal that I made [in Havana] was that peasant organizations be listened to on the agrarian issue ... I don't understand how an agrarian policy can be built by armed actors ... without taking into account victims who are really the ones in need of a process of agrarian reform.'[32]

Another participant supported this statement, clarifying how he had proposed an explicit, practicable strategic framework to the negotiating parties:

> a proposal entitled *Interlocution and Dialogue Space*. That proposal includes everything related to the peasant economy, food security, recuperating local seed traditions, looking after our territories, how to defend the territory, how to prevent the expansion of monocultures ... [it was] a very complete proposal. In that sense, the proposal was that we [the rural farmers] represent the axes of the construction of a territorial peace. Because we know that if it is done in any other way,

---

[30] Interview, Bogotá, Colombia, April 2015.
[31] Interview, Bogotá, Colombia, April 2015.
[32] Interview, Bogotá, Colombia, April 2015.

it will not be anything more than other previous processes ... that have already been done [and failed].³³

Drawing on the wider configuration of socioeconomic rights, one male participant, a victim of the FARC-EP, similarly proposed a series of specific recommendations for reparations. His demands were undergirded by three principles: 'income generation, housing and administrative reparation for victims'. According to him, what should be central to the accountability mechanisms incorporated into Point Five should be the construction and implementation of a framework for '[g]eneration of income through sustainable projects with technical support for a value of no less than 30 million pesos [approximately £6,000) per family unit'. This delegate acknowledged that reparations of such a dimension would be costly. However, from his perspective, 'just as we got into debt to wage war, I believe that we are going to have to go into debt for peace, to be able to live together in peace as Colombians'.³⁴

Proposals for mutually reinforcing reparations mechanisms – referring to the restitution of land, effective agrarian reform and the consolidation of the rural economy – were supported by a key prerequisite. Given the humanitarian catastrophe that mass displacement in Colombia had precipitated, many of those interviewed referred to the safe return of refugees and displaced persons as central to the reparations measures incorporated into Point Five. In the words of one male participant, 'a fundamental issue must be that those people who are outside their territory can have the security of returning'.³⁵ Without such safeguards, many argued that any reparations would be meaningless.

Other participants linked the question of agrarian reform and rural development to the broader framework for socioeconomic rights. For one female participant, a victim of multiple armed groups from the Montes de María region, the armed conflict had left villages and towns 'desolate': high schools and health centres had been destroyed, as had the rural economy. In addition to the restitution of lands and agrarian reform, then, as central to reparations for victims, she proposed 'programmes for generating income, productive projects, education, training to access employment'.³⁶ For this participant and many others, the guarantee of the right of access to health represented a fundamental tenet of their demands for reparations.

---

³³ Interview, Santa Marta, Colombia, April 2015.
³⁴ Interview, Bogotá, Colombia, April 2015.
³⁵ Interview, Santa Marta, Colombia, April 2015.
³⁶ Interview, Bogotá, Colombia, May 2015.

Demands for socioeconomic rights as central to reparations provisions represented a prevalent proposal by those who participated in the victims' delegations. One female delegate, whose brothers had been disappeared and executed by the Colombian state, had proposed that the reparations programme should guarantee 'the right to education, work, housing and health'.[37] The words of another female participant, a victim of sexual and gender-based violence by diverse groups, provide a coherent summary of the nexus between socioeconomic rights, reparation and transformation. In her words:

> Reparation is education, health, housing, land. We do not focus on money ... Comprehensive reparation is that I can enter university, that my children can enter university ... In the issue of public policy [reparation is] participation and that those who represent us are women who have gone through this pain. On the topic of health, we have already said ... [reparation means] health has to be public health system.[38]

A male victim of a FARC-EP landmine similarly proposed the right to health as a core aspect of reparations programmes. For him, the reparations measures in Point Five should incorporate 'public rehabilitation centres for physical and psychological health. At least one per department or region to address the specific needs of victims with disabilities'.[39]

A further common proposal made by participants in Havana framed as central to reparative measures pertained to the question of stigma. Individuals explained how the dynamics of the armed conflict had left communities broken and divided, and how certain groups had often ended up severely stigmatized by their having been associated, frequently wrongly, with armed groups. One participant described how, under such conditions, 'the relations of solidarity, the social fabric of the communities ... had been broken during the war'. This delegate proposed that reparatory measures should include programmes aimed at overcoming the embedded stigma within specific communities and populations. In her words, 'the stigmatization that exists now in certain communities is very great ... reparations measures that the majority of the [residents] want is that their good name be restored, that their tainted dignity be repaired'.[40]

---

[37] Interview, Bogotá, Colombia, May 2015.
[38] Interview, Santa Marta, Colombia, April 2015.
[39] Interview, Bogotá, Colombia, April 2015.
[40] Interview, Bogotá, Colombia, April 2015.

Finally, another participant proposed that the negotiating parties should incorporate specific provisions that address reparations for exiled Colombians. In order for such provisions to be developed, this individual proposed to the negotiating parties that they 'create a sub-committee at the negotiating table that would be led by the UN High Commissioner for Human Rights and the International Organization for Migration'. The subcommittee, from their perspective, 'would link organizations and experts on the issue of exile and victims and ... make structural recommendations on how to resolve the issue of exile at the negotiating table'.[41]

The right to nonrecurrence

The right to nonrecurrence, or nonrepetition, was incorporated as one of the 'four pillars' of the transitional justice paradigm in 2011, with the establishment of the UN Special Rapporteur for the Promotion of Truth, Justice, Reparation and Guarantees of Non-recurrence. The inclusion of nonrecurrence built on the measures recommended by Joinet in his impunity principles, aimed at preventing victims from facing repeated violations (Davidovic 2021). Guarantees of nonrecurrence are incorporated into the principles for effective reparation, as set out in the UN *Basic Principles and Guidelines on the Right to a Remedy and Reparation for Victims of Gross Violations of International Human Rights Law and Serious Violations of International Humanitarian Law* (Articles 19–23).[42] As such, these provisions connect closely to composite elements that undergird the right to reparation and

---

[41] Interview, Bogotá, Colombia, May 2015.

[42] See UN, *Basic Principles and Guidelines on the Right to a Remedy and Reparation for Victims of Gross Violations of International Human Rights Law and Serious Violations of International Humanitarian Law*. Specifically, *guarantees of nonrecurrence* should include, where appropriate: (a) ensuring effective civilian control of military and security forces; (b) ensuring that all civilian and military proceedings abide by international standards of due process, fairness and impartiality; (c) strengthening the independence of the judiciary; (d) protecting persons in the legal, medical and healthcare professions, the media and other related professions, and human rights defenders; (e) providing, on a priority and continued basis, human rights and international humanitarian law education to all sectors of society and training for law enforcement officials as well as military and security forces; (f) promoting the observance of codes of conduct and ethical norms, in particular international standards, by public servants, including law enforcement, correctional, media, medical, psychological, social service and military personnel, as well as by economic enterprises; (g) promoting mechanisms for preventing and monitoring social conflicts and their resolution; (h) reviewing and reforming laws contributing to or allowing gross violations of international human rights law and serious violations of international humanitarian law. See https://www.ohchr.org/en/instruments-mechanisms/instruments/basic-principles-and-guidelines-right-remedy-and-reparation (accessed 13 November 2023).

were closely reflected in the claims made by participants in Havana in this regard, as was demonstrated in the previous section.

Measures designed to ensure nonrecurrence usually fall into three categories: first, general guarantees of nonrecurrence; second, guarantees directed towards legislative reform (to *revoke* previous legislation); and, third, guarantees oriented towards institutional reform, such as DDR, reintegration or reincorporation of armed groups and so on. While the scope of measures for nonrecurrence continues to evolve (Davidovic 2021), in general, provisions tend to be articulated at three levels: institutional (DDR, SSR and so on); societal (support to civil society and the empowerment of marginal and legally underprotected groups); and individual (education and memorialization).

The multilevel focus and widespread scope of guarantees of nonrecurrence was echoed in the diverse set of demands and proposals made by the participants in the victims' delegations. Delegates urged the parties to ensure that the peace agreement, including Point Five specifically, would take into account mechanisms for nonrecurrence across distinct levels and spheres. Individual delegates made explicit proposals for measures to guarantee nonrecurrence. Others also directly identified how the satisfaction of the rights to truth, justice and reparation were integral to and essential for nonrecurrence. In other words, they were clear about the mutually reinforcing and integral nature of victims' rights. Accordingly, one female victim of the FARC-EP proposed that 'the acknowledgement by both sides of their victims, of the damage caused' should be central to the accord and the accountability mechanisms consecrated therein; such acknowledgement could only be manifest through the adherence by the negotiating parties to the peace agreement and the implementation of wider provisions oriented towards the satisfaction of victims' rights.[43]

All participants demanded that the negotiating parties cease all armed actions and introduce a bilateral ceasefire in order to prepare the ground for measures for nonrecurrence. Numerous delegates demanded that the FARC-EP must assume an organizational commitment to cease the practice of sowing anti-personnel mines and stop the recruitment of children and minors. These participants also proposed measures to improve the effectivity of the government's anti-personnel mine programmes, including providing greater resources to respective state institutions. With respect to children, one participant, who had been forcibly recruited into an armed group as a minor, described how current reintegration programmes suffered institutional 'weakness', leaving boys and girls 'vulnerable'. She demanded that the government must improve the technical capacity of officials, including by

---

[43] Interview, Bogotá, Colombia, May 2015.

guaranteeing proper training programmes for officials. This participant called for 'improvements in the processes of disengagement of young children and adolescents from armed groups by using trained officials ... [because] unfortunately, sometimes officials are not prepared'.[44]

Within the institutional sphere, participants tabled proposals that reflected their and their peers' experiences of victimization. Numerous victims of state crime proposed reforming the state's national security doctrine, which had been established in the 1960s. These participants also called for wider security sector reform as key to guarantees of nonrecurrence. One female participant had proposed 'that there be a total and definitive closure of the conflict, with the dismantling of paramilitarism and with reforms that put an end to the anti-insurgency policy and the dirty war in the country. Nonrecurrence before everything else'.[45]

A male participant, whose father had been executed by state security forces, demanded security sector reform. For him, abolition of the national security paradigm was fundamental to nonrecurrence:

> More than compensation, we are asking for institutional reform, transformation of the public security forces, of the security doctrine. In a postconflict country, there is no counter-insurgent force. Today there remain 16 counter-insurgent battalions. This ... should not be. We say that there should be no paramilitary practices ... in collusion with the military.[46]

Another delegate referred specifically to the ESMAD, the anti-riot special forces. He demanded 'the need to reformulate the repressive attitude of the state with the ESMAD as its spearhead. I did so, above all, arguing that these are the provisions that the entire country needs as measures of nonrecurrence'.[47] A young woman, whose father had been executed by the state and who had herself been the victim of state and paramilitary intimidation, similarly referred in her proposals to the requirement to transform the state's overriding security paradigm in order to establish the minimum possible conditions to guarantee nonrecurrence. She proposed:

> the need for the repressive attitude of the state to be dismantled ... the purging of the military forces and state agencies ... [is fundamental].

---

[44] Interview, Bogotá, Colombia, May 2015.
[45] Interview, Bogotá, Colombia, May 2015.
[46] Interview, Bogotá, Colombia, April 2015.
[47] Interview, Bogotá, Colombia, April 2015.

The issue of the declassification of intelligence files. My father was in the intelligence files: from there, the list of who to assassinate was put together ... we have been able to prove how this takes place ... [you find] in the intelligence files ... not only the internal enemies of the state, but also, us, human rights defenders ... we are considered enemies of the government. We will not be able to move on, unless this internal enemy mentality is changed and national security doctrine is dismantled.[48]

Many participants tabled proposals that aimed to transform societal practices and attitudes that had become deeply embedded as a consequence of decades of violent conflict. A starting point for this set of demands was the tendency of participants to propose mechanisms aimed at overcoming stigmatization of populations, organizations, individuals and communities. Many such communities and groups continued to suffer from dehumanization, delegitimization and depersonalization, attitudes and beliefs shaping the violence they had suffered. For numerous participants, only by creating programmes to combat stigmatization could the satisfaction of the right to nonrecurrence become a possibility.[49]

Referring to the over nine million victims of the armed conflict, one participant stated how her proposal to the parties had revolved around demanding 'guarantees for the victim population, given that, when the postconflict moment arrives, we need this agreement between the government and [the] FARC-EP to hold ... that's the most important thing'.[50] Another female delegate proposed to the parties that the state develop specific measures for nonrecurrence that 'erase hatred, to heal the wounds of war ... because we all have war wounds and heroes'.[51] Another young female participant explained how, in her intervention, she had argued that:

In terms of guarantees of nonrecurrence, obviously ... stigmatization cannot continue ... neither against trades union members nor against human rights defenders ... They stigmatize us before they murder us. I have experienced this ... in my capacity as a human rights defender. I have been called an enemy of the country directly by the former president.[52]

---

[48] Interview, Bogotá, Colombia, May 2015.
[49] Interviews, Bogotá, Santa Marta, Colombia, April–May 2015.
[50] Interview, Bogotá, Colombia, April 2015.
[51] Interview, Bogotá, Colombia, May 2015.
[52] Interview, Bogotá, Colombia, May 2015.

The majority of participants proposed that the accountability mechanisms consecrated in Point Five should establish specific guarantees of nonrecurrence referring to conflict-related violence against women and girls. Delegates called, in general, for the recognition that sexual violence had been employed by the armed actors, often systematically, 'as a weapon of war'. The vast majority of participants demanded that the peace accord incorporate a gendered approach throughout and across all five agreements, a demand that ultimately became a significant achievement with the support of the Sub-commission on Gender, as was discussed in previous chapters. In the words of one delegate: 'Sexual violence has been invisible in war. Therefore, the women victims have demanded their recognition, the need to establish the truth of what happened through in-depth and rigorous investigation, as well as guarantees of nonrecurrence.'[53] For many delegates, sexual and gender-based violence had been a 'continuum', existing before and during the conflict. It would exist afterwards, they argued, unless specific measures for nonrecurrence were adopted in this regard. Such insights reflect wider scholarship that addresses the continuum of sexual and gender-based violence against women and girls in diverse war and postwar contexts (Wood 2014).

One participant called for the establishment of nonrecurrence measures oriented towards the violations perpetrated against the LGBTI+ population. In an interview, she stated how 'the LGTBI victim population is making itself much more visible every day so that the Colombian state, the armed groups, must realise that we are also human beings ... that our rights should not be violated, that our lives should be respected'. She proposed that the peace accord should include mechanisms of recognition in this regard and develop nonrecurrence measures aimed at constructing effective norms and ethical codes of respect within both wider society and state institutions. After her statement, she was approached by one member of the negotiating parties, who declared explicitly 'we are committed to compensating the rights of the [LGBTI] victims'. In her words, 'I felt like a weight had fallen off my shoulders'.[54]

Victims' demands and the framework for accountability

Drawing on the interviews carried out with members of the victims' delegations and the organizers, this chapter has explored the proposals made by participants at the Havana talks. As discussed throughout the book, the

---

[53] Interview, Bogotá, Colombia, April 2015.
[54] Interview, Cali, Colombia, April 2015.

so-called victims' turn in transitional justice emerged in response to critiques by survivors and victims that their experiences, demands and interests had been excluded from conventional transitional justice interventions. In this context, the justification for the emerging victim-centred model has been twofold: first, that there is a moral imperative for inclusion – we should not exclude those most affected by conflict from discussions about accountability and peacebuilding mechanisms; and, second, that there is a transmission chain that links inclusion with efficacy and sustainability. Inclusion, from this perspective, brings to the negotiating table alternative perspectives based on the self-defined demands and needs of conflict-affected populations, moving the negotiations beyond those themes prioritized by the parties. These processes, it has been argued, lead to the acknowledgement of victims and their claims and identify 'unseen' patterns of victimization. These links, in turn, generate wider legitimacy and foster broader societal appropriation of peace talks and accountability mechanisms. The result, so the argument goes, are post-accord settlements that are more resilient to recidivism and poor-quality peace.

However, widespread empirical evidence has demonstrated that the claims made by 'victim-oriented' transitional justice practices have rarely been upheld. Inclusion is often restricted in numerical and proportional terms (the number of victims) and in temporal terms (the extent of participation in terms of days or weeks, let's say). Critiques also point to the limited impact of such mechanisms. As such, victim-led processes rarely reach the 'victim-centered threshold' (Sajjad 2016: 282), signifying that, in the end, the victims' demands and priorities have habitually remained excluded from formal transitional justice mandates. Whether victim-led processes are, in fact, more resilient remains a largely unproven question; the Colombia case contributes insights to this debate, as will be discussed in the final chapter, although conclusions can only be partial given the limited time since the signing of the accord. Scholars have consequently charged that inclusion is frequently tokenistic (Firchow and Selim 2022) – used to rubber stamp ostensibly top-down processes – and ultimately objectifies, disempowers and instrumentalizes victims (McEvoy and McConnachie 2012a; Robins 2017).

Colombia's Final Agreement, comprised of five separate thematic accords, was unprecedented in terms of its comprehensive nature. Across all five agreements, there are a total of 578 stipulations, as identified by the Peace Accords Matrix based at the Kroc Institute for International Peace Studies, University of Notre Dame. Of these provisions, a total of 167 stipulations focus explicitly on the rights of victims. These specific provisions are distributed across the entire Final Agreement, although the largest concentration of stipulations relative to victims and their rights can be found in Point Five (Peace Accords Matrix 2022: 6).

Point Five, *Agreement Regarding the Victims of the Conflict*, was signed on 12 December 2015. The Agreement established the so-called *Comprehensive System for Truth, Justice, Reparation and Non-recurrence*. The preamble to the Agreement recognized the 'resolute participation' of the victims, 'their noble testimonies and their proposals, without which it would not have been possible to construct this Agreement'. Moreover, the preamble states how the parties 'hope that with the implementation of this and all of the Agreements, the dignity of victims will be restored, justice will be done, and the foundations will be laid to bring an end, once and for all, to the violence of the conflict in the country, and to ensure that nobody in Colombia ever becomes a victim again'.[55] As such, the preamble reiterates how nonrecurrence would be contingent upon the implementation of all provisions within the agreements signed and the integral satisfaction of all victims' rights.

The specific content of the *Agreement Regarding the Victims of the Conflict* was unparalleled in terms of the explicit provisions incorporated with the intention of satisfying victims' rights to truth, justice, reparation and nonrecurrence. As discussed throughout this chapter, the 60 individuals who participated in the delegations proposed to the negotiating parties a series of core demands referring to victims' rights and other related content. These demands and proposals are summarized in Table 7.1, alongside a summary of the final provisions included in the accord.

As mandated by the negotiating parties, delegates' proposals were framed within the principles of victims' rights as enshrined in international law and norms, including victims' participation and recognition, and their specific rights to truth, justice, reparation and nonrecurrence. In general, participants proposed demands linked to their individual experiences. However, at the same time, many delegates also proposed measures for redress for wider patterns of victimization affecting diverse constituent victim groups and populations. As detailed in this chapter and in Table 7.1, proposals explicitly demanded a truth commission, a mechanism to search for the disappeared, a comprehensive reparations programme, mechanisms aimed at obtaining retributive and restorative justice, and measures for nonrecurrence.

Even despite initial reticence on the part of the negotiating parties, powerful opposition to the Havana talks and the limited numerical scope and temporal dimensions of victim inclusion, the inclusion mechanism punched above its weight. Beyond the key relational changes discussed in the previous chapter – and their subsequent impact – the proposals tabled by the victims' delegations were, in large part, incorporated by the negotiating parties into Point Five

---

[55] See https://www.peaceagreements.org/viewmasterdocument/1845 at p 135 (accessed 9 October 2023).

Table 7.1: Proposals of the victims' delegations and related Final Agreement provisions

Proposals from the victims' delegations	Content of Point Five (and the Final Agreement)
Right to justice: • Retributive justice – including penal sanction – for some human rights violations and abuses • Restorative justice mechanisms – to accompany and complement retributive justice mechanisms • Recognition of responsibility by perpetrators • Acknowledgement of victims • Recognition of conflict-related sexual violence as a crime • Populations and communities to be mandated to administer justice	**Right to justice:** • Special Jurisdiction for Peace – sanctions balance retributive and restorative justice • Access to special and alternative sanctions require recognition of responsibility by perpetrators and acknowledgement of victims • Conflict-related sexual violence recognized as a crime • Populations and communities in part able to administer forms of restorative justice and spaces for dialogue and reconciliation
Right to truth: • Establishment of a truth commission • Commission mandate to allow for recommendations • Third parties to be investigated	**Right to truth:** • Truth, Coexistence and Non-recurrence Commission (CEV) for three years • Commission mandated to offer formal recommendations • Third parties to be investigated (post facto expunged by Constitutional Court)
Right to reparations: • Individual and collective reparations to be guaranteed • Full institutional support for satisfaction of socioeconomic rights, including to health, education, housing and employment • Compensation for loss of land, income, employment and goods • Measures adopted to overcome stigmatization of specifically targeted populations and communities (women and girls; human rights defenders; members of political parties; trade unions; Afro-Colombian and indigenous people)	**Right to reparations:** • Individual and collective reparations guaranteed • Final Agreement mandates institutional mechanisms to guarantee socioeconomic rights, including to health, education, housing and employment (across diverse accords) • Compensation for loss of land, income, employment and goods consecrated in Final Agreement • Measures adopted to overcome stigmatization of specifically targeted populations and communities incorporated into Point Five, and Final Participation Agreement
Right to nonrecurrence: • Security sector reform – abolition of national security doctrine • Individual and collective reparations to be guaranteed	**Right to nonrecurrence:** • No provision for security sector reform – no revision of national security doctrine • Individual and collective reparations supported

Table 7.1: Proposals of the victims' delegations and related Final Agreement provisions (continued)

Proposals from the victims' delegations	Content of Point Five (and the Final Agreement)
• Full institutional support for the satisfaction of socioeconomic rights, including to health, education, housing and employment • Compensation for loss of land, income, employment and goods • Measures adopted to overcome stigmatization of specifically targeted populations and communities (women and girls; human rights defenders; members of political parties; trade unions; Afro-Colombian and indigenous) • Agrarian reform • Better-resourced state institutions (including those mandated to address reincorporation) • Specific mechanisms oriented towards LGBTI+ population • Establishment of a subcommission to address exiled populations • Institutional mechanism to search for disappeared persons	• Final Agreement mandates institutional mechanisms to guarantee socioeconomic rights, including to health, education, housing and employment • Compensation for loss of land, income, employment and goods consecrated in Final Agreement • Measures adopted to overcome stigmatization of specifically targeted populations and communities incorporated into Point Five and two further accords: End to Conflict and the Political Participation Agreement • No support for agrarian reform • Commitment to better-resourced state institutions • Specific mechanisms oriented towards LGBTI+ population approved • Establishment of a subcommission to address exiled populations • Special Unit for the Search for Persons deemed as Missing in the Context of and Due to the Conflict

and, broadly, the overall agreement. As such, the provisions in both Point Five and the wider Final Agreement ultimately came to reflect many of the demands made by the members of the victims' delegations in Havana.

Point Five explicitly addressed a series of crucial proposals made by the individual delegates during the latter half of 2014. In terms of general principles, Point Five committed the parties to guarantee a series of demands that delegates had, in many cases, proposed specifically in Havana:

- to guarantee recognition of victims;
- to guarantee acknowledgement of responsibility;
- to guarantee the realization of victims' rights;
- to guarantee victim participation;
- to guarantee historical clarification of the truth;
- to guarantee reparations to victims;
- to guarantee protection and security;
- to guarantee nonrecurrence;

- to guarantee the principle of reconciliation;
- to guarantee a rights-based approach.

As a means of conforming to these principles, the parties committed to the so-called *Comprehensive System for Truth, Justice, Reparation and Non-recurrence*. This mechanism was constituted by three core institutions: the *Truth, Coexistence and Non-Recurrence Commission* (CEV); *the Unit for the Search for Persons Presumed Disappeared in the context and by reason of the Armed Conflict* (UBPD); and the *Special Jurisdiction for Peace* (JEP) (see Table 7.1).

With respect to the right to truth, the CEV was given a formal mandate for three years as an extrajudicial, independent and impartial mechanism tasked with uncovering 'the truth about what has happened', 'the human and social impact of the conflict on society' and the 'collective responsibilities' for the violence perpetrated and the damaged caused. The CEV was mandated to 'foster an environment of dialogue' and 'establish forums for restoring the dignity of the victims ... for strengthening people's respect for and trust in each other, cooperation and solidarity, social justice'. Working from an intersectional, gender-based approach, the CEV was authorized to carry out popular education programmes, as well as writing a formal report and, therein, tabling a series of recommendations. All the preceding components had been directly proposed by participants during the victims' delegations.[56]

Delegates had also articulated explicit recommendations for the establishment of a mechanism through which to institutionalize the search for and location of disappeared and missing persons. In this regard, Point Five consecrated the UBPD. The Unit was tasked with collecting 'all information necessary to establish the universe of people deemed as missing in the context of and due to the armed conflict ... and ... to coordinate and conduct processes to search for, identify, locate and provide for the dignified return of remains'.[57] The Unit's mandate closely resembled the core proposals tabled by the participants in the victims' delegations with respect to the search for and location of disappeared persons.

With respect to the highly contentious issue of the right to justice, Point Five established the so-called JEP. In its capacity to administer both retributive and restorative justice, the JEP was, in the end, a Solomonic feat of highly complex institutional engineering. The JEP was mandated with the overall task of ensuring 'the dignity and respect of victims – especially women, LGBTI persons, and ethnic communities – and the appropriation of a

---

[56] See the *Agreement Regarding Victims of the Conflict*, https://www.peaceagreements.org/viewmasterdocument/1845 (accessed 9 October 2023).

[57] See https://www.peaceagreements.org/viewmasterdocument/1845 (accessed 9 October 2023); *Agreement Regarding the Victims of the Conflict*.

restorative justice model'.[58] The tribunal came into force in 2017 and since then has been developing a series of emblematic juridical cases, including by opening (at time of writing) ten so-called macro-cases and charging high-level perpetrators with war crimes and crimes against humanity (Bries Silva 2024).

The JEP's mandate also included the assessment of applications and petitions for amnesty and pardon. In this respect, petitions have since been approved, including for political and other related crimes (rebellion). In line with international normative standards, those crimes ineligible for amnesty have included crimes against humanity, genocide and violations of international humanitarian law committed as part of a systematic attack. In this respect, the JEP, of course, treads a controversial path, given that the crimes of hostage taking, torture, extrajudicial execution, forced disappearances, rape and conflict-related sexual violence, forced displacement and the recruitment of minors have been perpetrated to differing degrees, and often systematically, by all armed actors during the country's protracted armed conflict (Björkdahl and Warvsten 2021).

As consecrated in Point Five, the tribunal seeks to guarantee 'the restoration of the damage caused and reparations for the victims affected by the conflict' through 'a holistic approach that guarantees justice, truth and guarantees of non-recurrence'. In this respect, in line with its objective of balancing victims' rights to truth, justice, reparation and nonrecurrence, in operative terms, the JEP's mandate represents a highly sophisticated approach to sanctioning perpetrators. Sanctions for specific crimes – which aim to incorporate both a retributive and restorative justice dimension – are determined according to the degree of acknowledgement of responsibility and truth offered by an individual (see Table 7.2); a similar framework was also employed in the Justice and Peace Law in the mid-2000s regulating the AUC's DDR programme.

The general objective of the *Comprehensive System for Truth, Justice, Reparations and Non-recurrence* was 'to guarantee legal certainty in order to promote a stable and lasting peace'.[59] Working as an integrated system, the mechanisms aim to overcome some of the core challenges of the so-called peace versus justice debate discussed in previous chapters. This general principle of the System then closely echoed the sentiments expressed by many participants, who had demanded justice and accountability for human rights violations and abuses, while at the same time voicing concern over the

---

[58] See https://www.peaceagreements.org/viewmasterdocument/1845 (accessed 9 October 2023); *Agreement Regarding the Victims of the Conflict*.

[59] See https://www.peaceagreements.org/viewmasterdocument/1845 (accessed 9 October 2023); *Agreement Regarding the Victims of the Conflict*.

Table 7.2: Path of possible sanctions by the Special Jurisdiction for Peace

Individual	Type of sanction	Features
'Most responsible' individual who acknowledges exhaustive, complete truth and accepts full responsibility (before the Judicial Panel for Acknowledgement of Truth and Responsibility)	Special sanction	• 5–8 years of restriction of liberty and work, activities and actions with reparative content *or* • 2–5 years of restriction of liberty and work, activities and actions with reparative content (restorative)
Persons who acknowledge truth and responsibility prior to ruling by the First Instance Chamber	Alternative sanction	• 5–8 years of imprisonment *or* • 2–5 years of imprisonment in cases of less responsibility (retributive)
Persons who do not acknowledge either responsibility or truth (at any stage and lose an adversarial legal proceeding)	Ordinary sanction	• 15–20 years of imprisonment

Source: Adapted from Sandoval et al (2022: 483)

termination of the armed conflict, the satisfaction of wider victims' rights and the prevention of further violence.

The comprehensive reparations measures established in Point Five similarly incorporated a broad spectrum of provisions that closely reflected the proposals tabled by participants in the victims' delegations, as previously discussed in this chapter. Rather than focusing predominantly on measures for economic compensation, the provisions in Point Five aimed to induce wider processes of acknowledgement, coexistence, nonrecurrence and peacebuilding, a focus that many delegates had themselves proposed. The provisions in Point Five specifically included diverse constituent elements, which directly reiterated participants' demands, including:

- material and symbolic measures to address harm (dignification, commemoration and infrastructure);
- measures aimed at coexistence and reconciliation (promotion of coexistence within communities, reincorporation of armed groups; strengthening trust between the public authorities and communities);
- a specific settlement in the pending case at the Inter-American Commission on Human Rights concerning the UP;
- emotional recovery measures (individual level);

- psychosocial rehabilitation plans;
- creation of spaces for community dialogue and collective mourning (to address individual and collective suffering);
- local initiatives focusing on reconciliation, dignity and acknowledgement;
- collective processes of return of displaced persons and reparations to victims abroad;
- land restitution.

Finally, with respect to guarantees of nonrecurrence, *The Agreement Concerning Victims of the Armed Conflict* made explicit reference to how nonrecurrence would be contingent upon the 'coordinated implementation' of all measures within Point Five. As such, nonrecurrence was defined as being dependent on the implementation of the final report and the recommendations of the CEV, the work carried out by the UBPD, the effective conferral of individual and collective reparations and the longer-term results of the JEP. Point Five also stipulated that nonrecurrence was contingent upon the implementation of 'all the items of the Final Agreement and ... of the additional measures of nonrecurrence' agreed upon in the specific accord dedicated to closing the armed conflict, the so-called *End of Conflict Agreement*.[60]

As Table 7.1 makes clear, the proposals tabled by the victims' delegations and the final provisions of Point Five (and, more widely, the Final Agreement) closely resembled one another. In this regard, victim inclusion was, in part, successful. The victims' delegations arguably contributed to the crafting of a peace agreement and accountability mechanisms that were more responsive to and representative of victims' experiences and demands. This assertion was held up by many participants, who stated how their participation had led them to feel 'empowered', even before they had seen the final content of Point Five.[61] In follow-up interviews, former participants in the victims' delegations stated that, given the content of the final peace agreement, they had been, in general, satisfied with the impact of their participation. For one, it was precisely the participation of victims that had 'shaped the content

---

[60] In this respect, Point Three (*End of Conflict Agreement*) explicitly identified a broad spectrum of measures aimed at guaranteeing nonrecurrence, which included preventing repetition of 'the paramilitary phenomenon' and 'dismantling of criminal organizations and behaviours responsible for homicides and massacres and systematic violence, particularly against women, or which attack human rights advocates, social movements or political movements, or which threaten or attack persons participating in the implementation of the accords and the construction of peace'. See https://www.peaceagreements.org/viewmasterdocument/1845 (accessed 9 October 2023); *Agreement Regarding the Victims of the Conflict*.

[61] Interviews, Bogotá, Cali, Santa Marta, Colombia, April–May 2015.

of Point Five'.⁶² While it may be difficult to prove direct causality here, the close resemblance between the proposals made by the participants and the content of the Final Agreement suggests, at the very least, convergence between victims' demands and the interests of the negotiating parties. However, other participants also explained how their invisibility after Point Five had been signed led them to feel 'used',⁶³ a point that will be revisited in the closing chapter.

Significantly, two specific proposals tabled by the majority of participants in the victims' delegations were excluded from the final provisions consecrated in Point Five and the Final Agreement: land reform and security sector reform. As was discussed previously in this book, from the commencement of the Havana talks, President Santos had stated repeatedly that Colombia's economic and political models and its security paradigm and military doctrine were not up for negotiation. His red lines were likely established in order to keep both the private sector and the Colombian military onside during negotiations, and also because the Colombian political, economic and military elite were never going to negotiate away their historical pillars of privilege and power. Of course, Santos' red lines also conformed to the predominant principles of liberal peacebuilding. Accordingly, the Havana talks were never likely to usher in a radical transformation of the structural causes of Colombia's armed conflict, nor, by eschewing security sector reform, were they likely to establish basic conditions for nonrecurrence. In this respect, any radical transformation of the structural causes of the armed conflict or a meaningful recalibration of the predominant relations of power in Colombia was stillborn even before the Havana talks had ended.

The exclusion of agrarian reform and security sector reform from the Final Agreement echoes insights from other cases elsewhere, such as Nepal, where victims were, in large part, instrumentalized, given that their core demands remained unaddressed and excluded from formal transitional justice mandates (Sajjad 2016: 22). The Colombia case then further demonstrates the incapacity of inclusion mechanisms to lead to the incorporation of victims' demands when these contradict or fail to align with the predominant interests of state and other elite actors. As such, Colombia's experience of victim-centred peacemaking and transitional justice shows how inclusion mechanisms are limited in their capacity to transform power relations and redistribute power.

Nevertheless, it should also be noted that, while not straying from the liberal peacebuilding playbook, the Final Agreement did incorporate explicit

---

⁶² Interview, Bogotá, Colombia, May 2018.
⁶³ Statements made during a workshop to disseminate the author's report written for the UN on the impacto of the Victims' Delegations, *La voz de las víctimas en la negociación: sistematización de una experiencia*, Bogotá, April 2017 (Bogotá: United Nations 2017).

reference to wider rights configurations, including of socioeconomic rights, many of which had been directly proposed during the victims' delegations. While only Point Five had been mandated to receive direct victim participation, the principle guiding the Havana talks that 'nothing was agreed until everything had been agreed' meant that the negotiating parties were able to revise specific elements of the agreement, where necessary or appropriate, in the wake of the delegations' visits. Experts have suggested that this principle allowed the parties to recalibrate certain elements of the entire agreement based on the proposals of the victims' delegations, including specific content of relevance to victims and their rights and the transversal issues of gender and intersectionality.[64]

For example, the agreement on rural reform, *Towards a New Colombian Countryside: Comprehensive Rural Reform*, consecrated provisions to address rural development; provide universal coverage in health and education, housing solutions and subsidies; usher in formalization of the labour market; and guarantee land titling and access to land – in this case, through a loans programme. The accord focusing on *Solution to the Illicit Drugs Problem* incorporated a range of further provisions to address rural reform, including crop substitution plans, local development plans formulated with local participation, public health programmes and land titling. These agreements went some way towards addressing, on paper, the humanitarian crises affecting rural areas of Colombia and, in part, institutionalizing measures to acknowledge the causes and consequences of the armed conflict.[65] However, and significantly, they did not establish a system for integral land reform, but rather established a neoliberal policy framework as the response to the structural causes of Colombia's historical violence.

The accord addressing *Political Participation: A Democratic Opportunity to Build Peace* incorporated a series of provisions demanded by participants in the victims' delegations. These measures included comprehensive security guarantees for political participation and protection mechanisms for social organizations and leaders and for human rights defenders. The accord also established wide-ranging and innovative provisions dedicated to promoting coexistence, tolerance and reconciliation and overcoming stigmatization, themes that had been repeatedly proposed by numerous delegates in Havana. Moreover, echoing the demands of participants, the accord, explicitly referenced nonstigmatization measures directed towards

---

[64] Interviews, Kroc Institute for International Peace Studies, University of Notre Dame, August 2022–May 2023.

[65] See specifically, for example, the provisions included in *Towards a New Colombian Countryside: Comprehensive Rural Reform*; *Political Participation: A Democratic Opportunity to Build Peace*; and *Solution to the Illicit Drugs Problem*.

vulnerable or discriminated groups and those most affected by the armed conflict, such as trade unions, women, ethnic communities, the LGBTI population, youth, the elderly, disabled persons, political minorities and religious groups.[66]

Concluding remarks

This chapter has addressed the extent to which, beyond precipitating what were unprecedented relational changes between the negotiating parties and their victims in Havana, the victims' delegations assumed a role as peacemakers. In short, the chapter has explored the extent to which the delegations shaped the specific content of Point Five.

Participants offered a set of explicit demands and proposals to the negotiating parties for Point Five, which emerged out of their individual and collective condition of victimhood and their experiences of victimization. In interviews, delegates forensically detailed their proposals. Many explained how the unprecedented opportunity of being able to present their proposals directly to the negotiating parties led to their feeling empowered. Of course, when the interviews took place in 2015, the final content of Point Five had yet to be agreed upon. However, measuring up the Final Accord to the content of the proposals made by the delegations reveals a fascinating picture of assemblage: the agreement in itself reiterates, at times almost to the letter, the demands and proposals that victims themselves had made during their visits to Havana.

Whether it was uniquely the proposals of the victims' delegations that shaped the content of Point Five (and, more broadly, the Final Agreement) is open to question, although, in the final instance, it is unlikely. Wider conditions, including pressure from the international community, legal norms and restrictions pertaining to amnesty for perpetrators and justice for victims, the preferences of the negotiating parties and the simple gradual direction of travel in peacebuilding and transitional justice – towards more locally focused, bottom-up paradigms – likely played a role in shaping and formalizing the content of the agreements. However, the presence of the victims' delegations played a crucial role in this wider enabling environment. Participants' harrowing testimonies, their extraordinary generosity and their highly sophisticated proposals were crucial in transforming the beliefs and attitudes of the negotiating parties and making visible to them solutions that may have initially appeared improbable. In short, in a wider national context where intergroup and interpersonal relations remained entrenched

---

[66] See *Final Agreement to End the Armed Conflict and Build a Stable and Lasting Peace*, https://www.peaceagreements.org/viewmasterdocument/1845 (accessed 9 October 2023).

in a zero-sum perspective, the victims' delegations humanized the Havana talks, softened their perpetrators' hearts and brought to the table new visions of what could be possible. The silencing of the negotiating parties during the hearings also permitted new voices to be heard and unrecognized patterns of violence to be acknowledged.

These insights suggest that the participants in the victims' delegations were not uniquely instrumentalized, as has been evidenced for other cases elsewhere. Rather, drawing in detail on the experiences of delegates, and juxtaposing their own demands to the content of Point Five and the Final Agreement, allows us to tell a more nuanced story. Victims did play a role as peacemakers, shaping both the accountability mechanisms and the wider provisions agreed upon in Havana. These provisions drew upon and closely reflected victims' local experiences, their cultural memory banks and their self-defined strategic and tactical solutions to the causes and consequences of embedded violent conflict. This side of the story narrated by many participants – one of empowerment – should not be lost to reductionist analyses characterizing victims and their role within inclusion mechanisms as solely depoliticizing and disempowering, subject irreversibly to instrumentalization.

However, other elements demonstrate how aspects of the Colombia experience echo the cases of Nepal, Guatemala and Northern Ireland, where victims were instrumentalized and politicized. The delegations were indeed preceded by other inclusion mechanisms and forms of participation, including the Victims' Forums, civil society forums and the online portal. In general, these mechanisms allowed victims (and wider civil society) to enjoy a combination of direct participation and consultative status (Paffenholz 2015). However, victims' direct participation and representation in Havana were limited across both numerical and temporal dimensions: only 60 individuals took part during a total of five days in a negotiation in which their proposals were not binding. Moreover, participants had not asserted any role in shaping the mandate of the inclusion mechanism in which they participated (Mendes 2019).

Under such conditions, a key theme developed in this chapter has been with respect to the conditions under which participants' specific proposals were incorporated into Point Five and the Final Agreement. As has been demonstrated, a considerable range of those proposals offered by participants was reflected in the final rendering of Point Five. One substantial aspect in this regard was the way in which victims' demands for and acknowledgement of the need to balance restorative and retributive justice approaches ultimately represented a central tenet undergirding the final accountability mechanisms agreed upon. Of course, victims' perspectives clearly coincided here with public statements and petitions from the negotiating parties that penal sanctions for perpetrators should be restricted and subject to special and alternative sanctions. In such a context, victims' proposals were perceived as legitimizing the demands and interests of the negotiating parties for limited prison time. We cannot know whether delegates' proposals would have been incorporated in the same way had participating victims called, instead, for longer and more strict penal sanctions for perpetrators. However, it is unlikely that they would have. What we do know is that when participants' other more radical proposals, such as demands for land reform and security sector reform, failed to align with elite interests, they were excluded from the agreement. In the end, this issue raises critical questions pertaining to debates on participation: what participatory practices mean for distinct actors, how participation addresses and transforms relations of power (if at all), how participation might permit (or limit) agency, and whether participation leads to empowerment or instrumentalization.

Broad academic scholarship has confronted these questions, including the literature on victimhood, victimization and participation already addressed in this book. Other scholars have addressed the theme of participatory development, exploring how participation may lead to either 'tyranny or transformation' (Cooke and Kothari 2001; Hickey and Mohan 2004), how participation might be understood differently by diverse actors (Cornwall 2008), and whether participation is, in fact, employed by elite actors to legitimize top-down decisions that have already been taken (Kapoor 2004). These questions will be revisited in the final chapter of this book. However, the role of victims as peacemakers in the Havana talks led to both empowerment on the one hand and instrumentalization on the other. This assertion supports the overall argument of the book that *instrumentalization* and *empowerment* are not mutually exclusive, but rather may occur across a spectrum during inclusion mechanisms.

With respect specifically to the role of victims as peacemakers, participants' capacity to precipitate change was subordinated to and paralysed by wider relations of power, which ultimately constrained victim agency. A key insight developed in this book is that the role of victims as peacemakers was more constrained and contingent upon external factors than was participants' capacity to wield interpersonal, intergroup and, in part, intergroup relational transformation in Havana. In the sphere of peacemaking, then, victims were less able to assert 'ownership and control' over the Havana talks, and were more limited in their capacity to enable a 'transfer of power' away from the historical interests of elite powerbrokers (Firchow and Selim 2022). The limited capacity of the victims' delegations to impose their interests onto the Final Agreement – with specific relation to agrarian reform and security sector reform – ultimately supports claims that, as a paradigm, transitional justice continues to remain limited in its capacity to transform wider relations of power. Victim inclusion mechanisms then continue to reiterate and re-enact the historical tendency of the wider transitional justice paradigm to embed and institutionalize a perception of structural violence as tolerable and physical atrocity as intolerable (Miller 2008: 267).

In the final chapter of this book, I will draw together the insights and conclusions developed in response to the Colombia case, building further the notion of an *instrumentalization–empowerment* spectrum and thinking about the implications of this for policy.

Conclusions

Since the 19th century, Colombia has experienced a mosaic of complex and intersecting conflicts at the local, subnational and national levels, characterized by mutually reinforcing expressions of political and criminal violence. Callous violence has been committed by state and nonstate actors alike in the name of state security, liberty and emancipation. The most recent manifestation of such organized barbarie has been the country's more than five decades of internal armed conflict, which began in 1964 and remains ongoing at the time of writing. This barrage of killing, maiming and carnage has left the country with over nine million victims (National Centre for Historical Memory 2012; Peace Accords Matrix 2023).

Amid enduring war and atrocity, victims and survivors of political violence in Colombia have crafted innovative strategic initiatives aimed both at withstanding and putting an end to egregious violence, and redressing the causes and consequences of protracted military, partisan and ideological confrontation. Moreover, since the early 2000s, victims of political violence have forged an increasingly visible role as political actors at the local, subnational and national levels (Rettberg 2015), leading them to participate in formal peacemaking processes, such as the Caguan negotiations and, more recently, the Havana peace talks. This book has sought to understand how those who have survived the atrocious violence perpetrated within the confines of Colombia's protracted and aberrational Cold War narrate and make sense of violent conflict and endeavour to build peace by shaping the accountability mechanisms structured within formal peacemaking processes.

The research presented here has focused on the Santos–FARC-EP peace negotiations (2012–2016) and, specifically, on the formal role played therein by victims and survivors of political violence. As discussed throughout this book, at the behest of the negotiating parties, five delegations of victims travelled to Havana in 2014 to present their individual testimonies and proposals for Point Five, *the Victims' and Transitional Justice Agreement*. On paper, the objective of Colombia's victim-centred initiative was to place victims of the armed conflict at the centre of the peace talks and, in turn, to satisfy victims' rights by guaranteeing participants a role in crafting the transitional justice and accountability provisions consecrated within the accord.

The participation of the victims' delegations within the Santos–FARC-EP peace talks was significant for a series of reasons that speak both to the context of Colombia and to broader debates pertaining to peacemaking/peacebuilding, transitional justice, and the practices and theories of conciliation/reconciliation.

Specifically, the Colombia experience evidences concretely how the transitional justice paradigm has evolved, since the 1990s, towards its gradual embeddedness within the broader enterprises of peacemaking and peacebuilding, and as part of the repertoire of liberal peacebuilding. As such, the Colombia case illustrates explicitly how transitional justice matters have, in this regard, become progressively intrinsic to how states and international actors negotiate and build peace. Beyond demonstrating the increasingly entrenched articulation between transitional justice and liberal peacemaking/peacebuilding, the Colombia case illustrates a further aspect of the evolution of the transitional justice paradigm: the gradual consolidation of a so-called victim-centred transitional justice approach. Framing Colombia's victims' delegations as a context-specific manifestation of victim-centred practices, the research has examined the degree to which victim inclusion shaped both the dynamics and the content of the Havana peace talks. Finally, the Colombia case provides detailed insights into the relationship between peacemaking, victim-centred transitional justice and the broader concept and practices of conciliation and reconciliation. As such, the book has explored, first, how victims and survivors of political violence contribute to peacemaking, second, how they shape accountability frameworks and, third, what the spaces for contact and encounter between victims and their perpetrators established within victim-centred initiatives may ultimately mean for interpersonal, intragroup and intergroup relations and wider conflict dynamics. These are the core points that have been developed throughout the book, and to which the conclusion will be dedicated.

Understanding Colombia's victims' delegations as a context-specific manifestation and culmination of both the so-called local turn in peacebuilding and the victims' turn in transitional justice, this book has addressed the degree to which the delegations effectuated the meaningful participation of victims in the Havana talks. Explicitly, the research has explored the extent to which victims were *empowered* or *instrumentalized* during their participation in the victims' delegations. This question has been at the core of the research presented here, given that, as has been widely documented for cases elsewhere, such as Northern Ireland (McEvoy and McConnachie 2012a, 2012b) and Nepal (Sajjad 2016), despite its nominal focus on victims, the claims made by 'victim-oriented' transitional justice have rarely been borne out in practice (Robins 2011, 2017). In this final chapter, we further promote the central argument of the monograph, proposing that a binary reading fails to do justice to the nuanced, multidimensional – and at times overlapping – forms and expressions of empowerment and instrumentalization that characterized the Colombian experience. As such, the book has advocated that a more accurate victim/survivor-led approach is required, which does justice to victims' experiences within inclusion mechanisms in terms of both process and outcome. The book identifies *instrumentalization* and *empowerment* as occurring along and across a *spectrum*. This approach allows for the acknowledgement of subtle gradations in experience rather than imposing a Manichean, reductionist reading of individual and collective victim experience and participation as solely disempowering and depoliticizing.

Referring back to the academic debates and empirical data presented in previous chapters, the conclusion discusses participants' lived experiences of *empowerment* and *instrumentalization* from two perspectives: *victims as peacebuilders* and *victims as peacemakers*. In this regard, the conclusion returns us to the question of whether victim inclusion in the Santos–FARC-EP peace talks mattered, focusing on two complementary realms. First, the conclusion explores the extent to which the space for victim–perpetrator encounter facilitated by the delegations transformed the dynamics of the Havana talks by bringing about relational changes between the negotiating parties and the participants (peacebuilding). Second, the discussion addresses the degree to which the victims' delegations shaped the formal peace process, in terms of the explicit content of Point Five and of the Final Agreement (peacemaking). The third section will return to broader questions, making it possible to bring together these diverse insights to offer lessons learned for policy from the Colombia case with respect to victim inclusion mechanisms. As mentioned previously, with the exception of President Santos, interviews were not conducted with the negotiating parties directly. A such, the analysis will remain limited and only partial in this regard, suggesting that future research should address and engage with the experiences not only of the victims' delegations and the organizers, but also of those sitting at the negotiating table.

Victims as peacebuilders: empowerment and instrumentalization

As a collective expression of victimhood and victimizing events – a *universe of victims* – the victims' delegations were far more than the sum of their individual parts. During 2014, their cumulative visits to Havana brought to the negotiating parties the embodied testament of the human pain and catastrophic humanitarian impact of the armed conflict, suffering that, at least until the latter half of 2014, the negotiating parties had, for the most part, denied causing. Under such conditions, the presence of the delegations in Havana yielded significant transformation at the individual, intragroup and intergroup levels for both the participants and the negotiating parties.

In this regard, the Colombia case offers important insights in terms of whether contact between survivors and victims of political violence and their perpetrators may precipitate positive outcomes and forge a path towards conciliation and reconciliation (Aiken 2013; Druliolle and Brett 2018). At the individual level, inclusion – and the opportunity that it gave participants to confront their perpetrators in a safe, regulated space – led, for many delegates, to what they perceived as their empowerment. Facing the negotiating parties, who were authorized only to comment during the opening and closing sessions of the hearings, levelled the playing field, meaning that delegates felt they were on an equal footing. Many signalled how the visits had resulted in improvements to their physical and mental health. For victims of both armed actors, interaction precipitated a process of individual recovery – in some cases of healing – for many of those interviewed. Some delegates explained how they had in fact returned from Havana not only with a less severe physical and psychological burden, but also 'strengthened' and 'more committed' to the peace process and to peace activism. In the words of one female participant:

> no one more longs not to feel a gun to the head, or to feel threatened, or to feel stalked than someone who has suffered the violence. I have to walk with bodyguards every day. I ride in an armoured car and my big dream is to be able to go out and take the bus one day and I can only do that if this country ends this conflict. What meaning does it have or what benefit does it have that I viscerally hate the perpetrators. In the midst of that nightmare that I have to live every day, what do I get out of filling myself with that anger? If that anger makes me sick, it burdens me with more pain, it doesn't make sense. [1]

Participants in the delegations identified a further expression of empowerment that resulted from their inclusion in the delegations. All interviewees – including both delegates and organizers – stated how participation had fostered an inclusive, intragroup victim identity for those who visited Havana. Many participants commented on how, when they had initially travelled to Havana, they had defined themselves as victims of a specific armed actor, a factor that, in part, had been intrinsic to their identity. Some interviewees explained how they had, in fact, travelled to Havana feeling, in part, wary

---

[1] Interview, Bogotá, Colombia, May 2015.

of individuals who were victims of the opposing group. However, after their visits, all participants indicated how they had returned to Colombia seeing themselves as collective victims of the armed conflict, assuming, as such, a superordinate shared victim identity. Their collective experience during the inclusion process then led to a sense of shared identification, which frequently supplanted delegates' self-identification as victims of specific armed actors. What became a collective victim identity – regardless of the perpetrator – mitigated the impact of potential expressions of competitive victimhood among delegates. This shared sense of collective victimhood was accompanied and reinforced by feelings of empathy, compassion and solidarity between participants, which, in their words, encouraged them to make proposals and advocate on behalf of other victim groups, while shifting their view of the dynamics and consequences of the armed conflict towards a *collective* tragedy. In the words of one male participant:

> I went to tell a story, a personal story and finally the story of all of Urabá. Of how we have suffered, of how we have continued to maintain ourselves resilient. Of a peaceful form of peasant civil resistance. Of telling the armed actors that we do not want them to involve us in their war. I think it was the most important step our history.[2]

Beyond empowering transformation at the individual and intragroup levels, the delegations also instigated significant change across the dyadic, intergroup relationship framing victim–perpetrator interaction. In the majority of cases, recognition of their victims by the negotiating parties sat at the core of what became a transmission chain of relational transformation and empowerment. This transmission chain was a process rendered, in the first instance, by victim acknowledgement, which, in turn, led to changes in the beliefs and perceptions regulating dyadic intergroup interaction, rehumanization, repersonalization and relegitimization of the outgroup.

As discussed in previous chapters, as the negotiating parties sat across from their victims and listened to their testimonies and narratives of suffering, the organizers and the participants identified how 'their hearts softened'. The willingness of both victims and perpetrators to open up to and empathize with each other was a core factor here. In this respect, the human face of suffering that the delegates represented gradually facilitated the negotiating parties' increasing proclivity towards acknowledging their victims and, later, accepting responsibility for their crimes. Drawing on Staub's insights, as the negotiating parties opened up, so they began to 'assume responsibility for their share in the historical antagonism and violence' (Staub 1998: 255).

---

[2] Interview, Bogotá, Colombia, May 2015.

As one female participant explained, her participation led to 'the manifestation of pain, anguish and tragedy, which the victims express to those who perpetrated it ... the pain, the tragedy, the anguish ... I believe that this helps them to suddenly disarm their hearts ... this helps a little to humanize [them]'.[3]

Scholars have argued that sustained intergroup interaction may reduce prejudice and discrimination, an outcome of which may be the erosion of narratives of outgroup stereotyping. As such processes move forward, the perception of the outgroup as uniform and hostile – manifest through outgroup deindividualization, depersonalization and delegitimation – may gradually break down (Allport 1954; Aiken 2013: 34). As intergroup encounters lead to the breakdown of outgroup stereotyping narratives, so the development of mutual empathy and rehumanization and the acknowledgement of outgroup members may occur (Allport 1954; Staub 1998; Aiken 2013; Hughes 2017).

According to those interviewed, with victim acknowledgement in Havana came the recalibration of ingroup-outgroup stereotyping narratives: in many cases, this culminated in outgroup rehumanization, repersonalization and relegitimization. In Havana, changes in the perceptions and beliefs undergirding intragroup and intergroup narratives, relations and interactions were key to forging the acknowledgement of the outgroup's narrative, and, in some cases, to recognizing that it no longer represented an existential threat to the ingroup. Arguably, relational changes levied a progressively meaningful shift in the dynamics between the negotiating parties, as, according to the participants and organizers, the latter began to craft a belief in a shared future defined by the absence of the armed conflict. According to one of the organizers, the delegations meant that: 'The dynamics of the conversations in Havana changed ... by both actors recognizing that ... [they] have really been generators of violence ... recognizing the victims of the conflict ... this has been a very important step forward.'[4]

Recalibration of the negotiating parties' perspectives on the armed conflict and their own role within it, and the widespread overcoming of negative stereotyping narratives between dyadic groups, demonstrate important episodes of conciliation ushered in by victim inclusion in Havana.[5] Such moments of conciliation were not tantamount to reconciliation – a point that will be revisited later on. Nevertheless, conciliatory dynamics were closely linked to two further manifestations of victim empowerment.

---

[3] Interview, Bogotá, Colombia, March 2015.
[4] Interview, Bogotá, Colombia, May 2015.
[5] As stated previously, this perspective was offered by the organizers and participants and has not been corroborated by the negotiating parties, with the exception of President Santos.

First, as mentioned earlier, the transmission chain of transformation gradually led to the breakdown of perpetrator denial and, later, to de-escalation measures initiated by the negotiating parties. According to participants, as the delegations continued to visit during 2014, and in their wake early in 2015, the negotiating parties' attitudes towards their own acts of violence and victimization began to evolve from denial to the acceptance and assumption of responsibility for a range of violations committed and related damages caused. On various occasions, members of both negotiating teams had privately demonstrated contrition towards their victims in Havana. Over time, these privately expressed acts of admission in Havana evolved into public acts of apology, such as the FARC-EP's public apology in Bojayá. In the latter case, according to one participant, this was 'the first time that the FARC-EP recognized themselves as perpetrators and asked for forgiveness'.[6] At the same time, in the aftermath of the visits of the delegations, announcements were made by both negotiating parties related to specific de-escalation measures tied to key obligations under international humanitarian law, including to demining and the forced recruitment of minors. For many of those interviewed – both participants and organizers – the victims' delegations played a significant role in terms of ushering in this process of de-escalation.

Admission of responsibility over and the offering of public apologies for acts of victimization and the willingness to support de-escalation strategies shows how the negotiating parties came, at least in part, to demonstrate a degree of willingness to reflect on and overcome elements of their own group's historical self-glorification narratives. Moreover, these changes demonstrate how the negotiating parties gradually came to develop reasonable expectations of each other's future behaviour and to resituate their victims and each other within a common moral sphere. Such processes represent fundamental building blocks for peace (Lederach 1997; Staub 1998). Delegates were unequivocal in signalling how such processes left them feeling empowered.

Second, as discussed in previous chapters, the presence of the victims' delegations also played a role in imposing onto the peace agenda a series of egregious crimes that had been marginalized from discussions between and, in fact, initially rejected by the negotiating parties. As was discussed earlier, this outcome has been identified as one of the core justifications for victim inclusion in peacemaking and transitional justice initiatives (Lundy and McGovern 2008; Nilsson 2012; Bell 2019). The presence of female victims of sexual and gender-based violence and victims of violations perpetrated against LGBTI+ populations, for example, pushed the parties to begin both

---

[6] Interview, Bogotá, Colombia, May 2015.

to acknowledge the perpetration of these crimes, and, in some cases, to accept responsibility for them. An aspect of this process was the establishment of the Sub-commission on Gender, and the subsequent incorporation of intersectionality and a gender perspective throughout the Final Agreement. Numerous participants identified this as a significant consequence of the victims' delegations.

While the visits of the victims' delegations to Havana engendered forms of empowerment, they also led to diverse episodes and manifestations of victim instrumentalization, as documented in previous chapters. During the selection process and visits of the delegations to Havana, diverse actors – both endogenous and exogenous to the talks – treated the participants as an extension of the armed conflict. The negotiating parties initially perceived the victims' delegations as a form of tribunal. As such, the inclusion of higher numbers of their adversary's victims was taken to signify greater levels of relative responsibility for the violations and abuses committed, representing in part a moral victory that held potential legal repercussions for their adversary. The organizers sought to mitigate the negative impact of the delegations in this regard by balancing the overall number of victims of each armed group and releasing public statements to justify their decisions and support for the talks. However, public spats between the negotiating parties in the media concerning which victims were invited to Havana demonstrated instrumentalization, as the parties depersonalized and delegitimized specific participants.

This zero-sum mentality, which led delegates to be perceived as the embodied extension of the conflict, was replicated by other actors not participating directly in the talks. Across social media and other media platforms, politicians linked to Alvaro Uribe's political party, the Democratic Centre (CD), orchestrated public attacks against participants, particularly against victims of the FARC-EP. This initiative represented a pillar of their wider strategy aimed at destabilizing and delegitimizing the peace talks, which they opposed, particularly concerning the provision to the FARC-EP of transitional justice stipulations allowing for a reduction in penal sanctions. In a post on what was then Twitter, Maria Fernanda Cabal, a member of the CD, in fact insinuated that a female victim of the FARC-EP was suffering from Stockholm syndrome. In her words: 'She who greets the FARC-EP with a big smile is a representative of the victims? ... This "victim" who greets the FARC-EP very happily ... Stockholm syndrome?' The politician was subsequently investigated by the Deputy Prosecutor General Jorge Perdomo for the crimes of defamation, discrimination and aggravated harassment.[7] This

---

[7] See https://www.telesurenglish.net/news/Colombia-Congresswoman-Investigated-for-Revictimizing-Victim-During-Peace-Talks-20140820-0075.html (accessed 24 November 2023). The X/Twitter post has since been taken down.

form of instrumentalization, which publicly treated victims with contempt, was commonplace among those opposing the talks.

In numerous cases, both negotiating parties rejected the inclusion of specific individuals, arguing that they should not be categorized as victims. These incidences reflected cases where the respective conflict party reacted against the assignation of specific crimes (particularly sexual and gender-based violence, state crimes, crimes against humanity and violations of international humanitarian law). In such cases, including that of a former police commander and numerous victims of state-sponsored extrajudicial execution, the government and the FARC-EP publicly rejected the narratives and claims made by the individuals concerned and denied their condition of victimhood.

As was discussed earlier, in the run-up to their participation, and the face-to-face meeting with their perpetrator, many delegates experienced acute feelings of fear, anger, anxiety and pain, in some cases reliving the initial victimizing event. In those cases where the parties failed to acknowledge their victims, their public rejection and humiliation by the negotiating parties went beyond instrumentalization, leading to the victims' politicization and revictimization, and, in some cases, retraumatization. Such episodes were deeply disturbing for all members of the victims' delegations,[8] threatening, at best, to delegitimize victim inclusion and, at worst, to destabilize the wider peace process.

Victims as peacemakers: empowerment and instrumentalization

In large part, the *Agreement Regarding the Victims of the Conflict* (signed 12 December 2015) in particular and the *Final Agreement to End the Armed Conflict and Build a Stable and Lasting Peace* (signed 24 November 2016) incorporated a range of provisions that closely reflected the priorities, proposals and demands tabled by participants during the hearings in Havana. In this respect, the inclusion mechanism should be lauded as having empowered the delegates to sculpt the content of both Point Five and the Final Agreement.

A pervasive demand from participants was that Point Five should incorporate provisions for a comprehensive truth commission to be supported by an institutional mandate enabling budgetary and administrative autonomy. Participants proposed that the commission be tasked to investigate human rights violations and abuses by all parties to the conflict across the national territory, and that it be authorized to make recommendations to the Colombian state and negotiating parties. Many participants proposed that

---

[8] Interviews, Bogotá, Santa Marta, Cali and Barranquilla, Colombia, March–May 2015.

the truth commission should also investigate the role of 'third parties' who had supported (and in some cases bankrolled) armed groups, particularly paramilitary organizations.

Many delegates were relatives of persons that had been disappeared by the armed actors, including those disappeared by the Colombian state in the 'false positives' scandal. A preponderant demand from participants with respect to their rights to truth and justice in this regard was the establishment of a commission or independent agency tasked with searching for and locating their loved ones.

Participants' proposals for mechanisms to satisfy their right to truth were combined with the prioritization of provisions to guarantee victims' right to justice. A cross-cutting proposal made by participants was that armed actors' recognition of their responsibility and of the damage caused should represent the minimum for achieving justice. Many participants accordingly proposed mechanisms – such as tribunals – mandated to carry out criminal investigation and to guarantee, where appropriate, the application of penal sanctions for perpetrators. As such, the range of demands framing the satisfaction of victims' right to justice was sophisticated and broad, and ultimately included both retributive and restorative approaches.

Delegates situated their proposals across a spectrum, framing the right to justice as a requisite to the full and integral satisfaction of their rights as victims. Participants were pragmatic, conscious that they would likely have to accept a reduction in prison time in exchange for the guarantee of the end of the conflict, the truth concerning violations committed, and their access to reparations or the whereabouts of disappeared family members. Indigenous and Afro-Colombian participants proposed that their communities be mandated to apply their own internal regulations with respect to justice for victims of political violence, approaches that were, at their heart, restorative. From their perspective, the accountability mechanisms consecrated in Point Five should reflect Colombia's culturally diverse approaches to the administration of justice. Many participants thus acknowledged that the accord should achieve an equilibrium between retributive justice and restorative justice in order to satisfy victims' rights, in turn underscoring their integrality. However, participants made clear demands that the measures incorporated within Point Five should guarantee the dignity of victims and should not undermine it by stipulating only symbolic measures that would ultimately formalized amnesty for perpetrators. According to one male participant:

> Only by listening to the testimony of the victims can the damage be understood, and above all with that dimension of the damage, can measures be determined, precisely of reparation, of truth, justice, guarantees of nonrecurrence. A peace process like ours seeks precisely

to resolve such a deep-rooted problem of conflict ... So, in this process, it's important to listen to the victims, because the measures taken have to be consistent with the testimonies and the damage [we identify], because if not history repeats itself.[9]

With respect to the right to reparations, the 60 participants proposed a range of material and symbolic measures to be provided to victims or their families, and, where appropriate, to affected communities or populations. A common perspective shared by participants was that reparations provisions should not be contemplated as a means to restore victims of gross violations to their original condition, as the normative framework stipulates. There was similar consensus among participants that proposals for reparations programmes go beyond mere monetary reparation. Delegates accordingly proposed that reparations measures should combine immediately compensatory provisions in the short term, while also incorporating future-oriented stipulations aimed at transforming the embedded structural conditions and antagonistic social relationships that led to the onset of the armed conflict. Victims' demands for individual, collective, economic and symbolic reparations were, in this respect, undergirded by claims for a wide range of socioeconomic rights. Delegates, for example, proposed programmes guaranteeing land reform, income generation, housing, education, training to access employment and public rehabilitation centres for physical and psychological health.

Reparatory measures were articulated closely with the wider framework for establishing mechanisms to satisfy the right to nonrecurrence. In general, proposals for nonrecurrence measures sought to guarantee acknowledgement by the armed actors of their victims and of the damage caused. Participants proposed the programmes ensure, from the outset, the safe return of refugees and displaced persons. Numerous proposals were made to incorporate provisions to overcome the embedded stigma within communities and populations affected by the conflict. Delegates signalled the urgency of anti-stigmatization programmes particularly where communities had borne the brunt of counterinsurgent violence and had been dehumanized, delegitimized and depersonalized – including human rights defenders, trade unions, LGBTI+ communities, or communities where guerrilla groups had allegedly been present. Many participants identified programmes to combat stigmatization as essential for the satisfaction of the right to nonrecurrence.

All participants demanded the cessation of armed actions and the introduction of a bilateral ceasefire. They simultaneously proposed the parties begin de-escalation measures, including the cessation of the practices of anti-personnel mines and recruitment of children and minors. Guarantees of

---

[9] Interview, Bogotá, Colombia, May 2015.

nonrecurrence related to conflict-related violence against women and girls were proposed by the vast majority of participants. Finally, a key proposal aimed at guaranteeing the right to nonrecurrence – demanded particularly, but by no means uniquely, by victims of state crimes – was for security sector reform. Participants proposed the abolition of the state's national security paradigm as fundamental to nonrecurrence. Within this demand, individual participants called for a series of measures, including the decommissioning of the ESMAD, the anti-riot police special forces.

In the end, a total of 167 stipulations incorporated into the Final Agreement focused explicitly on the rights of victims. Closely reflecting the proposals made by the participants, Point Five established the so-called *Comprehensive System for Truth, Justice, Reparations and Non-recurrence*. Based on international standards relative to victims' rights to truth, justice, reparations and nonrecurrence and on the principles of a victim-centred approach, the accord established three interrelated bodies: a truth commission (the CEV), a body to investigate cases of forced disappearance and a tribunal (the UBPD) and the criminal tribunal (the JEP). To a forensic degree of detail, the content of Point Five was unparalleled in terms of both the accountability provisions incorporated with the intention to satisfy victims' rights and, significantly, the resemblance of these stipulations to the proposals made by participants in Havana (see Table 7.1). The provisions in Point Five then closely echoed a substantial number of proposals made by the 60 participants in the victims' delegations. Furthermore, and significantly, the Final Agreement incorporated a gendered and intersectional approach throughout and across all five agreements, a significant achievement attained with the support of the Sub-commission on Gender. This element had been a common proposal made by delegates in Havana.

Proposals by the victims' delegations were also consecrated within the Final Agreement more generally speaking. The accord addressing *Political Participation: A Democratic Opportunity to Build Peace*, for example, incorporated a series of delegates' proposals. It included comprehensive security guarantees for political participation, protection mechanisms for social organizations and leaders and for human rights defenders, and provisions dedicated to promoting coexistence, tolerance, reconciliation and overcoming stigmatization. Similarly, reflecting the specific proposals and demands made by numerous participants, the agreement on rural reform, *Towards a New Colombian Countryside: Comprehensive Rural Reform*, included diverse stipulations addressing rural development, universal coverage in health and education, housing solutions and subsidies, formalization of the labour market and the guarantee of land titling and access to land. These provisions were bolstered by mechanisms within the accord focusing on the *Solution to the Illicit Drugs Problem*, which incorporated crop substitution plans, local development plans, public health programmes and land titling.

The charge that victims were instrumentalized with respect to their mandated role and capacity to contribute to the crafting of the content of the peace agreement is one that requires consideration. As was summarized earlier and was detailed in previous chapters, victims' specific petitions were incorporated widely into the accords. However, a crucial point is that participants' proposals were only incorporated when they reflected and converged with the interests of the negotiating parties. While rural development, patterns of land use and ownership and land titling are addressed across the Final Agreement, no provision was established to introduce a system for integral land reform. As a key driver of Colombia's conflict, this proposal had been made repeatedly by individual participants in Havana; its incorporation was potentially decisive for guaranteeing the right of victims to nonrecurrence.

At the same time, delegates had demanded that both the truth commission and the JEP be mandated to investigate so-called 'third parties' that had enabled and often directly supported the armed actors. Such a power for the JEP would have been of fundamental significance in both mapping out and deciphering the causal drivers of the armed conflict, and in establishing mechanisms to guarantee accountability for perpetrators and their supporters. However, as was mentioned previously, the JEP's provision to investigate third parties was expunged by the Constitutional Court during the revision of the peace agreements.

The Final Agreement – in particular from the perspective of the right to nonrecurrence – was, in the end, severely limited, despite the centrality of these themes to victims' demands and proposals. While broader rights frameworks and configurations proposed by delegates were brought into the agreements, mechanisms for redress failed to reiterate participants' demands that directly challenged the economic and security foundations of the Colombian state. That the stipulations for socioeconomic rights included in the agreement addressed meaningful themes is not in question; they indeed did. However, what is problematic is that the accord failed to provide redress for perhaps the most significant socioeconomic issue of all: that of the urgent necessity for effective land reform in Colombia.

At the same time, and of equal concern and significance, the absence of provision for security sector reform and, specifically, of the state's ongoing reliance on its outdated Cold War national security doctrine signals a further acute weakness in the capacity of Colombia's victim inclusion mechanism to respond effectively to victims' demands and guarantee nonrecurrence. The disproportionate use of force by the Colombian state security forces and their reliance on a paradigm shaped by the National Security Doctrine remain significant threats to peace in Colombia, as the practices of the security forces during the 2021 national protests demonstrated.

In this regard, the Havana talks, and the victim inclusion mechanism incorporated therein, ultimately manifested a contextually specific iteration of the failed liberal peace and conventional transitional justice paradigms, wherein the fundamental causes of political (and, in this case, of criminal) violence are not given meaningful redress (Mac Ginty and Richmond 2007; Miller 2008). In this respect, the exclusion of land reform and security sector reform and the post facto removal of a core component of the JEP's mandate demonstrate how the transformative capacity of Colombia's victims' delegations as peacemakers was constrained and subordinated to the prerogative of powerful actors (Lundy and McGovern 2008; McEvoy and McConnachie 2012a). Moreover, this omission suggests that the effective guarantee of victims' rights to nonrecurrence is likely to be severely hampered in the future.

The Havana talks then represented, in the end, a hybrid of top-down, liberal peacemaking combined with diverse inclusion mechanisms aimed at putting victims' rights and participation at the forefront through a victim-centred approach to peacemaking and accountability provisions. Colombia's Final Agreement is, it should be acknowledged, innovative in terms of both its content and the inclusion mechanisms employed during the talks. Although in part an effort to 'telescope' the process of statebuilding (Krause and Jütersonke 2005), particularly in rural areas, it shied away from addressing the urgently necessary transformation of the security functions of the state, in deference to the country's powerful armed forces. At the same time, by eschewing meaningful engagement with socioeconomic rights and mechanisms to provide redress for structural violence, in deference to the economic and political elite, it reiterated the liberal peacebuilding paradigm's 'increasingly formulaic synthesis of Western-style democratization, good governance, human rights, the rule of law, and developed, open markets' (Mac Ginty and Richmond 2007: 491).

A further critical point pertaining to the issue of instrumentalization relates to the nature of the justice provisions consecrated within the Final Agreement. Participants recognized the integrity of retributive and restorative justice mechanisms, as was demonstrated earlier. Their perspective coincided, of course, with appeals from the negotiating parties to limit penal sanctions for human rights violations and abuses. Such petitions represented a core prerequisite for the talks: the armed actors had not gone to Havana in order to end up in a prison cell, as their repeated statements to the media made abundantly clear. Rather, the negotiating parties sought to consecrate provisions for special and alternative sanctions within the peace agreement, provisions that, by 2012, had become commonplace as a manifestation of an increasingly visible and globally dominant postconflict justice paradigm. In numerous cases, members of the victims' delegations concurred with this perspective, affirming the relevance of special and alternative sanctions and conditional reduction in prison time for perpetrators, as was discussed previously. Given the convergence between the negotiators' demands and many participants' recognition of the importance of an integral approach to victims' rights, the parties were ultimately able to defer to the victims' delegations as a point of moral and pragmatic reference. Such a reference point allowed the negotiating parties to legitimate their own demands for alternative sentencing, pardon or amnesty, a point strengthened by the fact that the perspectives of other victims' groups calling for more severe penal sanctions had been marginalized from the conversations in Havana.

A range of actors both endogenous and exogenous to the peace talks strategically employed victim instrumentalization, politicization and revictimization in pursuit of their political, economic and security objectives. Ultimately, the degree to which the victims' delegations were instrumentalized in their role as peacemakers in Havana was more manifest and simultaneously more closely articulated to broader structural factors and relations of power than was their capacity to craft interpersonal, intragroup and intergroup relational transformation at the talks. Reflecting cases discussed elsewhere (McEvoy and McConnachie 2012b; Robins 2012; Sajjad 2016), delegates' proposals were incorporated when they reiterated, converged with and/or legitimated the interests of the negotiating parties, and not when they ran contrary to the economic, political, security and juridical norms and concerns driving the prerogatives of the armed actors and their primary constituents (Robins 2017). When the demands of the victims' delegations conflicted with the interests of the negotiating parties – such as in relation to land reform, security sector reform and so forth – they were categorically excluded from the Final Agreement.

However, a caveat should be included here. Land reform and the reform of national security norms and doctrine had historically been demands of the FARC-EP guerrilla. In this case, even if the FARC-EP did agree with participants' demands in this respect, it lacked the capacity to levy such heavyweight influence in Havana. Rather, in true liberal peace fashion, the decision to exclude negotiation of the economic and security models of the state from the peace agenda was imposed by the Santos government as a prerequisite of the negotiation and was unlikely to have been overturned, with or without the inclusion of victims.

In the end, then, the Colombia case supports insight from the cases of Northern Ireland and Nepal, evidencing the instrumentalization of victims and the incapacity of inclusion mechanisms to effectuate the incorporation of victims' demands when these contradict or fail to align with the predominant interests of state and other elite actors (McEvoy and McConnachie 2012a, 2012b; Robins 2012; Sajjad 2016). As such, Colombia's experience of victim-centred peacemaking and transitional justice reiterates the challenges that inclusion mechanisms (and the wider transitional justice paradigm) face in their capacity to transform the structural causes of political violence or precipitate the meaningful recalibration of the predominant relations of power (Lundy and McGovern 2008; Firchow and Selim 2022).

The instrumentalization–empowerment spectrum

Building on Colombia's long tradition of mobilization and the gradual ascendance of victims as political actors, the victims' delegations mandated participants with a formal role to influence two of the parties responsible for the frenzy of horror characterizing Colombia's recent history. Drawing on interviews with the participants in and organizers of the victims' delegations, the research presented here has sought to give credence to how those who participated in the victims' delegations themselves recognized, experienced and enacted agency, instrumentalization and empowerment. In earlier chapters, it was argued that participants were neither oblivious nor inattentive to wider power relations, either in Havana or in Colombia. Many, in fact, consciously made the link between their participation and the legitimization of the Havana talks. Participants were, in this respect, cognizant of the potential their participation held for their empowerment and instrumentalization.

The contention that victims are instrumentalized and disempowered within victim inclusion and peacemaking processes led by the state or by international actors and their demands are sidelined is persuasive for other cases elsewhere, and, in fact, tells part of the story of Colombia's victims' delegations. Instrumentalization, politicization, revictimization and retraumatization did take place in Cuba and Colombia in the context of the victims' delegations, to severely pejorative effect. However, the research presented here does not prioritize this experience over other, transformative occurrences of bottom-up empowerment, dignification, acknowledgement and restoration narrated by participants in the victims' delegations. This book contends that the victims' delegations represented a space for encounter and the affirmation of political subjectivity that ultimately permitted participants to undergo individual transformation and to dispute and disrupt power – albeit with varying degrees of success. The consequence of this process was that victims who participated in the Havana talks wrote themselves into history. As they strategically asserted their individual and collective agency as victims, delegates were not duped into participation, nor did the organizers and negotiating parties view them from a static, one-dimensional perspective. In fact, the parties' perceptions of their victims evolved over time, as the participants urged forward what Heaney has described as 'the longed-for tidal wave of justice', when 'hope and history rhyme' (Heaney 2018).

As a result, this book has proposed an *instrumentalization–empowerment spectrum* as a tool to support the analysis of the experience of victims within inclusion mechanisms. Such an approach allows for the recognition that instrumentalization and empowerment are not mutually exclusive phenomena, but rather that both may be experienced by individual victims and collective groups across and within diverse fields and levels. Such processes may, at times, occur simultaneously and be in tension with one another, during and in the wake of inclusion mechanisms. In the case of Colombia, with respect to relational peacebuilding, participants' experiences tended to be situated further towards empowerment than instrumentalization, as was discussed earlier.

The Colombia case shows how a composite set of factors imposed considerable restraints on the delegates' capacities to shape the content of the Final Agreement. In this case, the limitations at play derived from what were ultimately the narrow scope of the wider peace process and, specifically, of the victim inclusion mechanism to allow for the reallocation and redefinition of relationships of power and the restricted dimension of participation, limited as it was temporally and in terms of thematic scope. In the end, then, participants in the victims' delegations were inhibited in their ability to navigate and (re)negotiate relations of power exercised by elite political, economic and military/armed actors. In the final instance, the capability of victims to assert their agency is not an isolated phenomenon, but rather contingent upon the parameters of the wider peace process (or transitional justice process) and, emphatically, whether these permit the reallocation and recalibration of power relations. In this sense, Colombia's formulaic liberal peacebuilding process worked against the aspirations of its victim-centred peacemaking mechanism.

A more sustainable peace?

Moving beyond the specific analysis of whether the victims' delegations occasioned victim empowerment or instrumentalization, a question emerging from the Colombia case pertains to whether victim inclusion crafted a more effective process and sustainable peace settlement in the wake of the 2016 agreement. Scholars have justified victim inclusion in peacemaking and transitional justice interventions in two ways: first, that a moral imperative drives inclusion – in short, those most affected by violent conflict should participate in discussions over the accountability mechanisms and peacemaking/peacebuilding initiatives to which they will, in theory, be subject (Garcia-Godos 2016); and, second, that inclusion also has a bearing on the efficacy of negotiations and the sustainability of the peace settlement. Victim inclusion, so the argument goes, brings alternative perspectives to the negotiating table. Participation identifies 'unseen' patterns of victimization and new visions necessary for structural change (Bell 2019), moving talks beyond the narrow themes habitually prioritized by parties.

Inclusion, in turn, engenders relational change, transforming dyadic victim–perpetrator and perpetrator–perpetrator relationships, and leading to the acknowledgement of victims and their claims (Hirblinger and Landau 2020). As a result, victim participation, it is argued, fosters wider legitimacy and broader societal appropriation of agreements and accountability mechanisms. The result are post-accord settlements that are more resilient to recidivism and poor-quality peace (Kew and Wanis-St John 2008; Lundy and McGovern 2008; Nilsson 2012; Paffenholz 2015; Bell 2019; Mendes 2019).

Evidencing causality in this regard is, of course, problematic. Scholars have identified a broad spectrum of factors that may both account for poor-quality peace and influence the likelihood of recidivism, including deficient DDR measures and the post-accord political exclusion of conflict actors (Call 2012), the absent or weak implementation of socioeconomic or rights-related provisions (Paris 2012; Gates, Mokleiv Nygård and Trappeniers 2016), economic stagnation after armed conflict (Cheng et al 2018) and the inadequate embedding of democratic structures within the everyday lives of those affected by political violence (Joshi and Wallensteen 2018). Accounting for the resilience of Colombia's peace settlement as solely conditional on the inclusion of victims in the negotiations would be ill-advised, given the wider phenomena at play. However, we can enquire whether victim inclusion contributed to the efficacy of the talks – as previously discussed – and the wider societal appropriation of Colombia's peace agreement.

The mandate of the victims' delegations came to an end in December 2014. Direct victim participation in the discussions around the victims' agreement had amounted to a total of five days over 18 months of negotiations. As was discussed previously, while diverse, sequential mechanisms had been established to facilitate third-party participation from the commencement of the talks, no direct participation was mandated during the negotiation of the other four agreements. As such, direct victim inclusion was limited temporally and in terms of its thematic scope. Victims were authorized only to participate directly in the negotiation of the agreement that took their name.

In the wake of their visits to Havana, direct victim inclusion ceased and the 60 participants enjoyed almost no visibility. Delegates were, on occasion, given the stage to accompany President Santos, including on National Victim's Day in 2015 and 2016. The five delegations also independently issued a series of joint press releases at key moments of the talks, breaking their invisibility to express their support for the process. However, the idea floated during the visits to Havana that the 60 delegates would assume a formal role as 'peace ambassadors' during the negotiations and in their wake failed to materialize.[10] Disenchantment with the process for some participants

---

[10] Interviews, Bogotá, Santa Marta, Cali and Barranquilla, Colombia, March–May 2015.

followed, and by 2017, during a closed-door online workshop to launch a UN report on the victims' delegations, several delegates expressed how they felt that they 'had been taken advantage of'.[11] In the words of one participant: 'There's no coherence between the policy and discourse for victims and our reality. It is not just that the government to gain prominence by saying that they took the victims to Havana. What did we get from there and what happened since? There hasn't been any change.'[12]

Between 2018 and 2022, victim participation in the hearings of the CEV, UBPD and the JEP was unprecedented, situating victims and survivors once again in the political spotlight and at the centre of the transitional justice interventions they themselves had helped to formulate. However, prior to this, between 2017 and 2018, during the drawing up and adoption in Congress of the legal framework to formalize the transitional justice mechanisms consecrated in the Victims' Agreement, victim participation was almost non-existent. According to interviews, with the exception of a minimal number of related hearings attended by victims' organizations within Congress, victims had been largely absent. Legislators were exclusively responsible for the adoption of the provisions into law, with victims' organizations marginalized from discussions over the content of legislation.[13]

The invisibility of the delegations post-Havana reinforced the experiences of victim instrumentalization that had occurred during the discussions over Point Five. A combination of insufficient budgetary and human resources designated by the organizers for follow-up and the negotiating parties' and organizers' narrow focus on the negotiation of the remaining provisions represents the likely explanation for their subsequent marginalization. However, victim exclusion after 2014 showed how the organizers' and negotiating parties' conceptualization of victim participation had comprehended inclusion as a restricted process relevant only during the peace talks. The victims' delegations then ultimately represented little more than an exceptional episode of inclusion during and in the aftermath of what was, in the end, an elite-led peace process framed within the liberal peacebuilding paradigm.

Polarization often increases during peace negotiations and, unsurprisingly after a five-decade-long conflict, Colombian society remained acutely polarized during and in the wake of the Havana talks. The country's cleavages were made further evident when, in October 2016, the signed Final Agreement was put to a national plebiscite. Abstention in the referendum was high: only 37.4 per cent of registered voters went to the polls. Of

---

[11] Online interviews with participants in Bogotá, Colombia, April 2017.
[12] Interview, Bogotá, Colombia, April–May 2015.
[13] Interviews, Bogotá, Colombia, May 2018.

those who voted, 50.2 per cent, a negligible majority akin to the majority Santos' had won in the 2014 elections, rejected the peace deal. The peace process consequently faced a national crisis, as social groups respectively called for the immediate reinstatement of the accord, or, on the contrary, for its complete revision. Talks resumed with both negotiating parties opening a space allowing the process' most vehement critics, such as former President Uribe and his supporters, to give input into the new agreement. In the end, on 24 November, after almost a month of shuttle diplomacy, a new accord was agreed, with the (second) Final Agreement incorporating a series of modifications, including around the rights of the FARC-EP to political participation.

The victims' delegations had necessarily incorporated a limited number of individuals. It was not feasible for nine million victims to take part, despite the unquestionable moral prerogative for them to do so. Moreover, given the objectives of the delegations, participation was also restricted to direct victims. Despite the unprecedented transformations at the interpersonal, intragroup and intergroup levels in Havana detailed earlier, the restricted, episodic nature of inclusion in Cuba and the lack of follow-up in the wake of the delegations ultimately meant that the achievements in Havana remained isolated from the wider Colombian society.

Scholars have argued that the success of contact processes between adversarial groups or across dyadic relationships is contingent upon whether negative stereotyping is diminished across and transformations can be generalized across all members of the ingroup (Adler and Bartlett 1998; Staub 1998, 2011; Aiken 2013). While in Havana, and upon their return, participants had proposed to the negotiating parties that spaces of encounter between victims and perpetrators should be established at the local, subnational and national levels in Colombia, to re-create their own positive experiences. However, the proposals were not taken forward,[14] meaning that the achievements in Havana enjoyed little chance of being replicated extensively in Colombia once the delegations returned. The unprecedented relational transformation in Havana was not, in the end, scaled out or scaled up: what happened in Havana, in large part, stayed in Havana. On the contrary, participants returned to a deeply polarized and violent country, living the final throes of the conflict with the FARC-EP. Under such conditions, over 25 per cent of those who returned after their participation in Havana received threats; many of whom were forcibly displaced as a consequence (Brett 2017a).

The plebiscite exposed Colombia's ongoing polarization and extant public mistrust in the peace talks and the Santos government. Voting patterns were

---

[14] Interviews, Bogotá, Colombia, March–May 2015.

complex. However, those most affected by the conflict voted appeared overwhelmingly to ratify the agreement, while, with the exception of the capital city, those in urban areas, perhaps less exposed to more recent violence, voted against the agreement (Herbolzheimer 2019; Mendes, Siman and Fernández 2020: 338).

The plebiscite was effectively instrumentalized by political elites opposing the Havana talks, including particularly former President Uribe and his political cadres and recalcitrant groups from the private sector (Matanock and García-Sánchez 2017: 153). Uribe and his followers had opposed the talks from their commencement, framing key aspects of the Final Agreement – particularly the transitional justice provisions – as unacceptable concessions (Matanock and García-Sánchez 2017: 153; DeMeritt et al 2019) that were tantamount to surrender to the FARC-EP. The plebiscite then highlighted the ongoing Santos-Uribe political cleavage in Colombia (Matanock and García-Sánchez 2017: 158), while at the same time demonstrating how large sectors of Colombia's population remained unconvinced by the peace process, particularly by what they felt to be leniency towards the guerrilla (Herbolzheimer 2019). On the other hand, those victims who had travelled to Havana and, according to voting patterns, many others who resided in conflict-affected regions were convinced by the process.

The factors shaping the outcome of Colombia's 2016 plebiscite shared characteristics with the Guatemalan national plebiscite held in 1999 over the constitutional reforms linked to the country's peace process (Brett and Delgado 2005). Both cases saw the successful instrumentalization by the 'Vote No' campaign of misinformation narratives that simplified the complex agreements, defining them as surrendering to and providing impunity for leftist insurgencies (Gomez-Suarez 2017). Both 'Vote No' campaigns also drew on and sought to stoke up anger, fear, deception and indignation (Gomez-Suarez 2017), including by engendering narratives that stated how the agreements promoted a 'gender ideology' that undermined traditional family values (Brett and Delgado 2005: 35; Gomez-Suarez 2017a). In the case of Guatemala specifically, ethnic divisions had played a key role in the anger and fear that the 'Vote No' campaign sought to provoke (Brett and Delgado 2005: 35). In both cases, moreover, the 'Vote No' campaigns outmanoeuvred the 'Vote Yes' campaigns, which operated on the assumption that the 'Yes' vote would be triumphant. In both Guatemala and Colombia, the 'Vote No' campaigns presumed no such thing, mobilizing at the national, subnational and local levels, using the Protestant Church and, in the case of Colombia, by systematically deploying social media to spread disinformation.

Despite the readiness of the Colombian government and the FARC-EP to negotiate peace – a condition often categorized problematically as *ripeness* – no equivalent, wider *societal ripeness* prevailed in Colombia. Large sectors of Colombia's population continued to live daily lives marked by the causes and consequences of the armed conflict, in contexts affected by ongoing egregious political violence, fear and intimidation, and ongoing systematic exclusion and poverty. For them, the peace talks were precisely that – just talk. Moreover, many people remained unconvinced by the peace process, particularly given the Caguán failure more than a decade before. In the run-up to the 2016 plebiscite, political, religious, military and economic elites opposing the peace negotiations – and the diverse, multilevel transformations that the accords, on paper, sought to occasion – took advantage of such conditions. Their 'Vote No' campaign instrumentalized pre-existing ideological cleavages, and mobilized gender and religious divisions, as had been the case in Guatemala two decades earlier.

As peace processes come to an end and in the wake of prolonged political violence, collective societal beliefs and perceptions change slowly, if at all (Brett 2021a). Moreover, norms and conflict identities remain sticky, continuing to hold currency sometimes decades after a conflict has formally ended (Verdeja 2009), particularly when the peace dividend is not delivered widely and structural inequalities continue to shape everyday lives (Theidon 2010). Under such conditions, a discrete dichotomy between the past and present is seldom experienced (Rosoux and Anstey 2017), especially by the victims and survivors of political violence. This is particularly the case when powerful groups strategically mobilize historical societal cleavages as they publicly oppose narratives of inclusion, economic and political reform and rights-based approaches consecrated within peace agreements, as the Colombia case illustrates.

Scholars have convincingly demonstrated how the outbreak and continuation of conflict is shaped by the development and persistence of perceptions, beliefs and motivations that determine the relationship between social groups and between victims, perpetrators and their constituencies (Bar-Tal 2000, 2013; Leader Maynard 2019; Castano, Muñoz-Rojas and Čehajić-Clancy 2020). Ideological and identitarian frameworks then play a significant role in atrocity onset, perpetration and ending, habitually shaping perpetrators' willingness to kill and influencing bystanders' support for and acceptance of their own group's strategies of violence through 'atrocity-justifying ideologies' (Leader Maynard 2019). As was discussed previously, the concept of the conflictive ethos provides insights into the psychological infrastructure that enables individuals and communities to comprehend, justify and cope with the protracted and vicious nature of violent conflict (Bar-Tal 2013).

For Bar-Tal (2000: 352), 'outbreaks of conflicts are dependent on the appearance of particular perceptions, beliefs, attitudes and motivations, all of which must change for conflict resolution to occur'. Logically, then, beyond the closure to hostilities and engagement with the structural drivers of violent conflict, the sustainable end to conflict would require the unfreezing of the conflictive ethos and the beliefs that undergird it. In this case, such beliefs include the justness of the ingroup's goals, the delegitimization and dehumanization of the outgroup, the dismantling of ingroup self-glorification narratives based on the attribution of positive traits, and the recognition that the ingroup is not the only victim and, perhaps, is also a perpetrator.

Many individual participants – and arguably representatives of the negotiating parties – underwent meaningful transformations as a consequence of the inclusion of the victims' delegations. These individuals were ready to support the peace talks unconditionally, having experienced significant forms of empowerment and having been given the opportunity to interact with their perpetrator. However, the remainder of the Colombian population, many of whom voted against the peace deal, had not been given this opportunity. While numerous regions affected by Colombia's armed conflict voted to support the peace deal, over half of those who voted in the plebiscite did so in order to reject it. In other words, victim inclusion in Havana did nothing to convince these voters to support the peace agreement. Moreover, since the Final Agreement was signed in November 2016, polarization and ongoing violence continue to sculpt daily life in Colombia. Dissident FARC-EP groups have returned to the armed struggle and paramilitary organizations maintain their reign of carnage throughout the countryside. Hundreds of social leaders and former FARC-EP combatants have been executed since the Final Agreement was signed. There also remain significant implementation gaps in the stipulations of the accords (Amaya-Panche 2021; Peace Accords Matrix 2023). Yet, at the same time, Colombians elected Gustavo Petro to the presidency in 2022, a leftist politician and former M-19 guerrilla. While it is beyond the scope of this book to analyse Colombia's electoral politics, it is likely that the closure of armed conflict with the FARC-EP played a game-changing role in facilitating the election of President Petro.

The Colombia case has demonstrated that victim inclusion may contribute positively to the efficacy of peace processes by precipitating relational transformation and shaping – albeit in a restricted manner – the agenda and outcome of peace negotiations. However, the contention that victim inclusion mechanisms may contribute to more sustainable peace should be treated with caution. Under conditions of acute militarization, ongoing poverty and entrenched societal cleavages, the expectation that victim inclusion may counter embedded, structural factors and generate wider appropriation of peace processes and accountability mechanisms is perhaps unrealistic.

The outcome of Colombia's 2016 plebiscite thus raises questions concerning the proposition that victim inclusion may facilitate public legitimacy or wider appropriation of peace agreements and transitional justice mechanisms (Herbolzheimer 2019). The data suggest we should be measured regarding our expectations that people living in societies emerging from atrocious violence should be willing quickly to reinterpret what they 'consider real, possible, and desirable – on the basis of new causal and normative knowledge' (Adler and Bartlett 1998: 43).

Nevertheless, as scholars, policy makers and practitioners, we should also be mindful not to impose sweeping narratives that engender the reductive logic of victim-oriented peacemaking and transitional justice interventions as uniquely paralysing and instrumentalizing processes. This book has aimed to pursue a more nuanced approach that, in response to victims' narratives and experiences, acknowledges both the limitations of formal mechanisms and the capacity of survivors and victims to appropriate inclusion mechanisms as spaces for contestation and resistance. In the words of one female participant:

> It's a historical fact that, during all the peace processes in this country, victims had never been named. At the moment, we victims have empowerment, we victims have acknowledgement ... visibility to the world ... if our participation is to be important, the government, state institutions and [international] actors have to give it greater meaning ... we are in the centre of this conflict ... and if there is no recognition of victims, then I believe that this process will be, in the end lame, null. The centre of these [peace] agreements must be us, the victims.[15]

Lessons learned and policy implications from the Colombia case

As a manifestation of the evolution of the transitional justice paradigm towards progressive victim-centredness and its greater proximity to the liberal peacebuilding repertoire, the Colombia case offers important lessons for victim inclusion in those interventions oriented towards bringing closure to and moving away from protracted violent conflict.

The following section asks what might an effective victim-centred peacemaking and transitional justice process look like in contexts of ongoing ubiquitous violence, mass victimization and continued polarization. A core qualification here is that context-specificity remains the fundamental guiding principle for any policy implications emerging from empirical research. In other words, the following recommendations are not provided as a formula for other cases elsewhere, but rather as points of departure. The victims' delegations were mandated to provide input into peace negotiations and were not, in this regard, uniquely tied to an existing transitional justice mechanism. Such specificity may not be the case elsewhere and said conditions, as well

---

[15] Interview, Cali, Colombia, May 2015.

as Colombia's wider political, institutional and historic context, represent a key caveat on the development of recommendations.

The nature of participation

A first theme of discussion deriving from the Colombia case relates to the nature of participation. No convincing argument may counter the charge that the inclusion of 60 victims – of a total of over nine million – was ethically untenable. The negotiating parties and the organizers argued that the diverse mechanisms of inclusion throughout the process (including the Victims' Forums) made up for the limited scope of participation in Havana. Moreover, both the negotiating parties and the organizers stipulated that the delegations were not actually meant to represent Colombia's incidence of mass victimization; the term 'representation' was, in fact, absent from official discourse (Mendes 2019). However, the parties and the organizers sought simultaneously to develop a framework of representativity through the deployment of the 'universe of victims', which rendered the picture of complex patterns of victimhood and victimization.

The 'universe of victims' was based on the general principles of pluralism, balance and rectitude. To guarantee these principles, the organizers employed explicit selection criteria defined by: (i) demographic attributes; (ii) victim identity; (iii) perpetrator identity; (iv) gender; (v) intersectionality; (vi) nature of violation; and (vii) a context-specific historically informed analysis of the causes, manifestations and consequences of patterns of victimization. As such, the delegations included victims of all armed groups from the entire country, victims of diverse and paradigmatic violations, individuals who had been victims and perpetrators, and victims of all genders, among others.

The 'universe of victims' as an operational framework represents a potentially replicable model that significantly punched above its weight by effectively embodying Colombia's egregious patterns of victimization and mass victimhood. By incorporating two national organizations (the NUC and the ECCC) and one international institution (the UN), the organizers balanced domestic and external actors, in part protecting the process from claims that it was being externally led. The nationally led aspect of the mechanism is worth highlighting for cases elsewhere. However, national victims' organizations played an informal role during the selection process. National victims' organizations should be more formally recognized and incorporated into victim inclusion processes, to build on local capacities and knowledge and to foster stronger legitimacy from victims' groups.

The inclusion of a disproportionate number of victims left the mechanism open to justified criticism. Moreover, the decision to select 60 individuals, rather than 100, or 500, appeared arbitrary. The limited inclusion of victims who were more vociferously critical of transitional justice as an adequate mechanism for achieving victims' rights – in particular of restorative justice and alternative sentencing – further delegitimized the process in some quarters. As a consequence, involved parties should work carefully to design relevant, comprehensible numerical parameters for victim inclusion that respond to context-specific and historical factors, while also guaranteeing the inclusion of more diverse victims' voices.

The procedures and regulations governing participation played an instrumental role in levelling the playing field between victims and their perpetrators. In this respect, prohibiting the negotiating parties from responding to or questioning their victims during the formal hearings was crucial in providing a safe and regulated space for victim testimony. Designing processes that address the power balance between perpetrators and their victims and guarantee safe, protected spaces is fundamental to prevent revictimization and amplify victims' voices and concerns.

Beyond the numerical dimension of participation, a core lesson emerging from the Havana process pertains to the degree to which victims' proposals were adopted by the negotiating parties and whether they contributed to the recalibration of relations of power. While broad victims' demands were included in the Final Agreement, those proposals that had the potential to transform the historical/structural pillars of Colombian state and society were excluded. In this respect, the quality of participation was poor, although, as discussed throughout this book, such limitations were not unexpected. It is worth discussing whether frameworks can be designed to permit victims greater ownership and control over victim inclusion mechanisms. By drafting initial prenegotiation agreements that, from the outset, give victims a seat at the table during the negotiation of *all* agreements, and permit victims a say in designing the mandate of future inclusion mechanisms, negotiating parties can bolster the inclusivity of processes.

What would be significant here as an innovation would be that parties design inclusion mechanisms that reach and connect distinct levels throughout the respective society. In short, networks could bind together: (a) direct inclusion in the negotiations from the commencement and across all accords (not just those nominally relevant to victims); (b) higher numerical inclusion of victims during the process by inviting groups to assume a seat during specific phases of negotiation or discussion; and (c) wider mechanisms established at the national, subnational and local levels, as was the case in Burundi (Nee and Uvin 2010). The widest range of actors at national, subnational and local should be incorporated into participation mechanisms. The charge that participation is employed by elite actors to legitimize top-down decisions that have already been taken (Kapoor 2004) could, as a consequence, be mitigated.

However, at the same time, thinking outside of the box also suggests that negotiators and, where relevant, mediators and accompaniers contemplate the possibility that victims should be conferred with a veto card for some instances and thematic issues under negotiation. The nonbinding nature of victims' proposals inevitably subordinates them to a secondary status.

When participation occurs

As discussed in previous chapters, informal encounters between victims and their perpetrators during the lunches and coffee breaks played a fundamental role as safe, regulated spaces for intergroup dialogue. The episodes of privately expressed contrition, discussion over specific cases and simple conversation over a meal that took place during such moments were imperative to the longer-term processes of trust building and victim acknowledgement, and the widespread evolution in intragroup and intergroup relations in Havana. Organizers and negotiating parties should contemplate the broader provision of such spaces during inclusion mechanisms, while maintaining their informal, nonhierarchical nature.

A further key aspect that emerged from the research was how victim participation was restricted to the visits to Havana. As such, despite accompanying participation spaces during the talks, in the end, victims were not protagonists during the negotiation of the other accords or in the wider peace process once they had returned to Colombia. They did not become 'peace ambassadors'. The delegates also played no role in the design and implementation of the legislation governing the transitional justice mechanisms established in the Final Agreement. Parties should mandate victim inclusion through the entirety of a process and the discussions over all accords by designing sequential, multilevel and multilayered initiatives, and should not limit inclusion to an episodic singular enterprise. By so doing, it may be possible to strengthen the process, while also building pillars to generate its broader appropriation and buy-in and pathways for upscaling and outscaling the inclusion process.

In this regard, formal mechanisms allowing for victim–perpetrator dialogue should be linked to widespread spaces for encounter established across and throughout the respective country. Of course, this will demand a hefty budget. However, articulating an infrastructure of spaces of victim–perpetrator encounter that lead from the community level all the way up to the national peace process or respective transitional justice architecture may have the possibility of replicating the significant level of individual, intragroup and intergroup transformation that took place in Havana.

Not all states/societies will be ready or willing to make such a commitment; this is understandable. However, many of the 60 delegates sought to replicate, scale up and scale out their own transformative experiences on returning from Havana. All too often, they returned to contexts that were hostile to them and rejected their proposals. Establishing a more interconnected infrastructure of victim-perpetrator-bystander spaces for encounter could, at the right moment, begin to articulate positively with transformations taking place within the more narrow sphere of formal, national-level talks and institutions. It could also begin to provide a countermeasure to the narratives propagated by powerful actors opposing the respective process. A final component necessary in this regard is that organizers and negotiating parties guarantee that inclusion initiatives adopt effective communication strategies in order, once more, to counter the narratives of spoiling actors opposing the process.

Contemplating such a network of victim-perpetrator-bystander spaces for encounter from the outset may, if and when the moment arrives, provide a path towards crafting the broader societal ripeness referred to earlier and, in the end, effectuate the beginnings of the transformation of antagonistic intergroup relations, prejudice and stereotyping. Ultimately, the incapacity to scale out and scale up limited experiences of positive intergroup transformation remains a key factor shaping the fragility of peace in post-accord societies, where polarization, lack of trust and intergroup violence and antagonism persist.

Protection measures

According to the interviewees, security in Havana was effectively provided. However, many delegates returned from Havana and faced death threats and other forms of serious intimidation. As such, it is incumbent on the parties and the organizers to guarantee that effective protection mechanisms should be provided to those individuals who participate in victim inclusion mechanisms. Victim safety is paramount in any initiative. Security mechanisms should be budgeted for and arranged prior to participation. They should be consulted with and agreed upon between participants, the respective government and, where appropriate, relevant international actors. Numerous participants who received threats once back in Colombia were, in fact, already under the protection of state security outfits. Security should therefore be guaranteed by trusted and effective providers, and, in particular, follow the recommendations of victims.

A further point here is that, as discussed earlier, spoiling actors opposing the Havana talks and, specifically, the victims' delegations employed systematic strategies on social media to humiliate, politicize and instrumentalize participants in the delegations. These episodes resulted in significant cases of revictimization and retraumatization. Prior to the commencement of public inclusion mechanisms, parties and organizers should develop an operational framework through which to hold such actors accountable. This may include reform of the penal code, or special alternative mechanisms, as well as a special office or unit to investigate related incidents. When and if they occur, these violations should be investigated and sanctioned immediately.

A final point here pertains to the importance of adopting further procedures to protect individuals participating in inclusion mechanisms. Many participants in the Havana process stated how the constant presence of a counsellor to accompany the delegations was of fundamental significance and support to them, given the profound fear and emotional upset they experienced. However, in the wake of the delegations, this support was no longer readily accessible for those who returned to their communities outside of Bogotá. The physical and mental health of participants must be taken seriously before, during and after their engagement with inclusion mechanisms. As such, adequate budget and resources should be provided by parties and organizers for all forms of protection, including mental health support, during and in the wake of victim inclusion mechanisms.

Did inclusion matter?

This book has narrated the story of Colombia's victim-centred peacemaking/transitional justice experience from the perspectives of those who took part in the process. The research has explored what inclusion in the victims' delegations signified for participants and, more generally, for peacemaking and transitional justice in Colombia and beyond. The book argues that when assessing the capacity of victim inclusion measures to deliver empowerment to or to instrumentalize victims, the claim that inclusion initiatives merely paralyse and instrumentalize victims, and, in turn, collapse spaces for agency, contestation and resistance is inadequate.

In the case of Colombia, the consequences of the victims' delegations were indeed complex. The mechanism precipitated experiences of depoliticization, revictimization, retraumatization and instrumentalization. However, the delegations also created paths for empowerment and politicization at the individual and, in part, collective levels, ultimately informing the dynamics and content of the Havana talks, albeit to a limited degree, as was discussed earlier. In the end, then, Colombia's victim-centred initiative did matter, although perhaps less than its supporters would contend and more than its detractors would charge.

The research presented here proposes that if we are to do justice to victims' and survivors' extraordinary courage and to acknowledge how they may leverage their agency, we should take seriously and be guided by victims' own perspectives and assessment of the process and outcomes of their inclusion. Given the complex and nuanced consequences of the victims' delegations, this book has advocated for the deployment of an *instrumentalization–empowerment spectrum* as an appropriate approach through which to understand the capacity of victims to effect change during and as a consequence of victim inclusion initiatives.

By drawing on the direct experiences of participants themselves, the book has crafted a context-specific understanding of what delegates experienced during and after their visit to Havana and whether they perceived participation as meaningful, beneficial and dignifying. Of course, such assessments are not static, but rather are linked to wider evolving structural factors and contingent upon ongoing individual and collective experiences of engagement and disengagement, inclusion and marginalization. In other words, people's perspectives on whether they experience empowerment and instrumentalization transform over time. The research for this book was carried out between 2015 and 2018. Since then, Colombia has elected a former M-19 guerrilla, Gustavo Petro, to the presidency. However, at the same time, implementation of the peace agreements has not been far-reaching, and the country continues to experience horrific forms of structural and direct violence and ongoing polarization. Given the dramatic and far-reaching impact of the politics of war, peace, violence and victimhood in Colombia's post-accord scenario, the perspectives of those interviewed within the confines of this investigation may well have changed over time. As such, further research is essential – including with those that negotiated in Havana – in order to trace how the relational and wider changes that the victims' delegations precipitated have fared over the past half-decade.

Colombia's victims' delegations embodied the potential for redemptive change. However, such transformation will remain elusive and their capacity to be replicated will remain limited while Colombia continues to tread a path in which armed conflict, criminality, violent development and peace are not anathema, but, rather, are co-constitutive of the country's Janus-faced polity and savage political economy. Under such conditions, led by those who bore the brunt of the violence, we must continue to and embolden ourselves to imagine effective mechanisms to transform relations of power and the structural drivers of conflict, to overcome the marginalization of subordinated groups and build social relations based on the recognition of mutual humanity.

ANNEX 1

Interview Format

The victims' delegations to Havana

Block 1. Biography and armed conflict

- Where were you born? Could you explain your family/neighbourhood/community/environment where you grew up?
- How has your life been during the armed conflict?
- What was the impact of the conflict on your life?

Block 2. Participation in the Havana talks

- Could you tell me why you think you were selected to be part of the victims' delegations to Havana?
- Why do you think the victims participated in Havana?
- What was the process of travelling to Havana like? Could you tell me about the trip and its events? What did you feel and think when they called you to be part of the delegation?
- What did you feel and think during the preparatory process for the meeting? And after it?
- Could you tell me about the claims and demands that you made to the negotiating parties?
- What were your expectations regarding the process of participation?
- Were your expectations met? Have your expectations changed?
- What was the process like of getting to know the other members of your delegation and, later, the other delegations?

Block 3. The day of the hearing

- When you were at the negotiating table presenting your testimony and listening to the stories of the other victims and your own story, what impacted you the most?
- What was the process of meeting the negotiators/perpetrators like? What was the impact of meeting them, of telling them your life story? How did they react? Had you met any of them before?
- Could you tell me how you felt on the day of the hearing?
- Could you tell me what you talked about at the hearing?
- How did the people in the government delegation and the FARC-EP react to you and to the delegation in general?

Block 4. Impact of the visit to Havana

- What was the impact of participating in the delegations for you?
- Did this visit have any impact on your family, neighbourhood or community environment?
- What – if anything – has changed in you as a result of participating in the delegations to Havana?
- Do you think it has had or will have an impact on your human rights (individual and collective)?
- Do you believe that your presence in Havana has had or will have impacts on your rights to truth, justice, reparation and nonrepetition?
- Do you think that your participation had an impact on the negotiating parties?
- Why was the participation of the victims' delegations in Havana important and significant?
- Do you think that your participation has had an impact on the content of the peace agreements and more generally on the peace process?
- What proposals should be taken into account in an eventual agreement on victims?
- What did you like least about going to Havana?
- Has your participation had an impact on your personal or collective security?

Block 5. Role of the accompanying countries

- What opinion do you have of each of the accompanying organizations: the UN, the NUC and the ECCC?
- How was your relationship with the members of the international community (UN, guarantor and accompanier countries)?
- How were you treated during this process?
- Do you think that your participation had an impact on the behaviour/perception of the members of the international community, the NUC and the ECCC?

Block 6. Expectations for the future

- Could you tell me about your expectations regarding the future, the post-accord scenario? What role do you and the other members of the delegations see yourselves playing?
- Do you think that this experience leaves open the possibility of new participation by victims?
- What were the notable aspects of the process of participating in the delegations to Havana? What were the negative aspects of participation?
- What aspects could be improved in the process of participating in the delegations to Havana?
- What have been the lessons learned during the course of this process?

The government and state institutions

Block 1. Biography and armed conflict

- Could you explain your current position/role?
- How has your lived experience of the armed conflict been?
- How did it affect your life?
- How has the current peace process evolved? What are its notable aspects?

Block 2. Participation of the victims' delegations in the Havana dialogues

- How and why did you make the decision to authorize the participation of the victims' delegations in Havana?
- What were your expectations regarding the inclusion process?
- Were your expectations met? Have your expectations changed?
- What was the process of getting to know the members of the delegations like?

Block 3. Impact of the visit of the delegations to Havana

- What impact did meeting the victims and listening to their life stories have on you?
- Have you changed as a result of the participation of the delegations?
- Do you think that the participation of the victims had an impact on the other members of the negotiating parties and on the dynamics of the talks?
- Do you think that this participation has had an impact on the content of the peace agreements and more generally on the peace process?
- Did you or your team change your position regarding victims, human rights violations or the conflict itself as a result of participation?

- Why was the participation of the victims' delegations in Havana important and significant?
- Do you think victim inclusion achieved its objective?
- Has participation had an impact on the personal or collective security of the members of the victims' delegations?

Block 4. Expectations for the future

- Could you tell me about your expectations for the future, the post-accord scenario?
- Do you believe that the members of the delegations to Havana should play a role in the post-accord scenario?
- What is the precedent that the participation of victims' delegations establishes for other peace processes in other contexts?
- What is the precedent that the participation of victims' delegations establishes for transitional justice in other contexts?
- Does this participation leave open the possibility of new participation by victims?
- What were the notable aspects of the victim inclusion mechanisms in Havana? What were the negative aspects?
- What aspects could be improved in the process of participating in the delegations to Havana?
- What have been the lessons learned during the course of this process?

The organizers (the UN; the NUC and the ECCC)

Block 1. Biography and armed conflict

- Could you explain your current role?
- How has the current peace process evolved?
- What are its notable aspects?

Block 2. Selection and participation of victims' delegations to Havana

- Could you tell me about the selection process to invite delegations of victims to participate in the Havana talks? Why did the delegations participate?
- How and why were the people selected?
- What was the role that you and your institution played in the process of incorporating the victims' delegations into the Havana talks?
- Does the participation of victims' delegations in Havana have precedents in other peace processes?
- Why was the participation of the victims' delegations in Havana important and significant?

- What were your expectations regarding victim participation?
- Were your expectations met? Have your expectations changed?
- What was the process of getting to know the members of the victims' delegations?

Block 3. Impact of the visit of the delegations to Havana

- What was the impact of meeting the participants, of listening to their life stories?
- What was the impact of listening to the delegations for you yourself?
- Has the participation of the delegations had an impact on you or your institution?
- Do you think that the participation of victims has had an impact on the content of the peace agreements and more generally on the peace process?
- Did you or your institution change position regarding victims, human rights violations or the conflict itself as a result of victims' participation?
- Do you think victims' participation had a negative impact in one way or another?
- Has participation had an impact on the personal or collective security of the participants?

Block 4. Expectations for the future

- Could you tell me about your expectations and those of your institution regarding the future, the post-accord scenario?
- Do you believe that the members of the delegations to Havana should play a role in the post-accord scenario?
- What is the precedent that the participation of victims' delegations establishes for other peace processes in other contexts?
- Does participation in Havana open up possibilities for other types of participation?
- What is the precedent that the participation of victims' delegations establishes for transitional justice in other contexts?
- What were the notable aspects of the inclusion process in Havana? What were the negative aspects?
- What aspects could be improved?

The accompanying countries

Block 1. Biography and armed conflict

- Could you explain your current role?
- What role have you played in the peace process?

- How has the current peace process evolved?
- What are its notable aspects?

Block 2. Selection and participation of the victims' delegations

- Why did the victims' delegations participate in the Havana talks?
- What was the role that you and your institution played in the process of incorporating the victims' delegations in Havana?
- Does the participation of the victims' delegations have precedents in peace processes?
- Why do you think the participation of the victims' delegations in Havana was important and significant?
- What were your expectations regarding the inclusion process?
- Were your expectations met? Have your expectations changed?
- What was the process of getting to know the members of the delegations?

Block 3. Impact of the visit of the delegations to Havana

- What was the impact of meeting the participants, of listening to their life stories?
- Has the perspective or behaviour of your institution changed at all as a result of the participation of the delegations?
- Do you think that your participation had an impact on the negotiating parties and on the dynamics of the conversations?
- Do you think victim participation had a negative impact in one way or another?
- Do you think that your participation has had an impact on the content of the peace agreements and more generally on the peace process?
- Have you or your institution changed your position regarding victims, human rights violations or the conflict itself as a result of victim inclusion?
- Has participation had an impact on the personal or collective security of the participants?

Block 4. Expectations for the future

- Could you tell me about your expectations and those of your institution or government regarding the future, the post-accord scenario?
- Do you believe that the members of the delegations to Havana should play a role in the post-accord scenario?
- What is the precedent that the participation of victims' delegations establishes for other peace processes in other contexts?
- What is the precedent that the participation of victims' delegations establishes for transitional justice in other contexts?

- What were the notable aspects of the process of victim participation in Havana? What were the negative aspects?
- What aspects could be improved?
- Does this participation leave open the possibility of new participation by victims?

ANNEX 2

Participation in the Victims' Delegations

First delegation

- Female
  Victimizing event: kidnapping/massacre.
- Male
  Victimizing event: homicide/torture.
- Female
  Victimizing event: homicide of a protected person, massacre and dispossession.
- Female
  Victimizing event: massacre and forced displacement.
- Male
  Victimizing event: homicide of a protected person/massacre.
- Female
  Victimizing event: forced disappearance.
- Male
  Victimizing event: forced displacement.
- Male
  Victimizing event: homicide of a family member.
- Male
  Victimizing event: massacre and forced displacement.
- Female
  Victimizing event: extrajudicial execution.
- Female
  Victimizing event: gender-based violence and displacement.
- Female
  Victimizing event: homicide of a protected person/displacement.

Second delegation

- Female
  Victimizing event: forced disappearance.
- Female
  Victimizing event: forced recruitment (as a minor) into armed groups.
- Female
  Victimizing event: homicide of a protected person.
- Female
  Victimizing event: forced disappearance.
- Male
  Victimizing event: forced displacement, threat and violation of personal integrity.
- Male
  Victimizing event: victim of the use of prohibited weapons (anti-personnel mine); forced displacement.
- Male
  Victimizing event: displacement; threats; discrimination, disappearances, selective deaths and acts of violence against ethnic groups in especially vulnerable conditions.
- Female
  Victimizing event: sexual and gender-based violence.
- Female
  Victimizing event: deprivation of liberty with violation of personal integrity.
- Female
  Victimizing event: homicide of a protected person.
- Female
  Victimizing event: homicide of a family member.
- Female
  Victimizing event: kidnapping.

Third delegation

- Male
  Victimizing event: kidnapping.
- Male
  Victimizing event: kidnapping.
- Female
  Victimizing event: undeclared.
- Female
  Victimizing event: victim of partisan attack.
- Male
  Victimizing event: homicide of a family member.

- Female
  Victimizing event: homicide of a protected person.
- Female
  Victimizing event: kidnapping.
- Female
  Victimizing event: homicide of a protected person; forced displacement.
- Male
  Victimizing event: homicide of a protected person.
- Female
  Victimizing event: homicide of a protected person.
- Female
  Victimizing event: homicide of a protected person.
- Female.
  Victimizing event: homicide of a protected person.

Fourth delegation

- Female
  Victimizing event: homicide of a protected person; forced displacement.
- Female
  Victimizing event: victim of sexual violence.
- Female
  Victimizing event: homicide of a protected person.
- Male
  Victimizing event: victim of threats; forced displacement.
- Female
  Victimizing event: homicide of a protected person; forced displacement.
- Female
  Victimizing event: homicide of a protected person; forced displacement.
- Female
  Victimizing event: victim of forced displacement and torture.
- Male
  Victimizing event: homicide of a protected person.
- Male
  Victimizing event: victim of prohibited weapons (anti-personnel mine).
- Female
  Victimizing event: homicide of a protected person; forced displacement.
- Male
  Victimizing event: victim of forced recruitment (as a minor).
- Male
  Victimizing event: victim of exile.
- Male
  Victimizing event: victim of violations of human rights as a detainee.

Fifth delegation

- Male
  Victimizing event: loss of several members of family in a massacre.
- Male
  Victimizing event: murder of a protected person.
- Female
  Victimizing event: victim of an attack by the FARC-EP guerrilla.
- Male
  Victimizing event: attack with explosives.
- Male
  Victimizing event: victim since 1988 of threats, displacement, arbitrary detention and attacks by multiple armed actors.
- Female
  Victimizing event: murder of a protected person.
- Female
  Victimizing event: displaced and has been the subject of frequent threats from criminal gangs.
- Male
  Victimizing event: victim of several attempts on his life; members of his family have been threatened and intimidated.
- Female
  Victimizing event: continues to receive threats from different groups opposing her political position.
- Event
  Victimizing event: kidnapped by the armed left along with her husband and her two children, aged 10 and 13.
- Female
  Victimizing event: murder of a protected person.

References

Adler, E. and M. Bartlett (1998) 'A Framework for the Study of Security Communities', in E. Adler and M. Bartlett (eds) *Security Communities*, Cambridge: Cambridge University Press, pp 29–66.

Aggestam, K. and A. Björkdahl (eds) (2013) *Rethinking Peacebuilding: The Quest for Just Peace in the Middle East and the Western Balkans*, Abingdon: Routledge.

Aiken, N. (2013) *Identity, Reconciliation and Transitional Justice: Overcoming Intractability in Divided Societies*, Abingdon: Routledge.

Allen, S., L. Hancock, C. Mitchell and C. Mouly (eds) (2022) *Confronting Peace: Local Peacebuilding in the Wake of a National Peace Agreement*, Basingstoke: Palgrave Macmillan.

Allport, G. (1954) *The Nature of Prejudice*, Cambridge, MA: Addison-Wesley.

Amaya-Panche, J. (2021) 'Implementing the Peace Agreement in Colombia: Challenges for Peacebuilding and Reconciliation', *Conflict Series*, 11, Luxembourg: European Union Institute for Security Studies.

Andrieu, K. (2010) 'Civilizing Peacebuilding: Transitional Justice, Civil Society and the Liberal Paradigm', *Security Dialogue*, 41(5): 537–558.

Androff, D. (2010) '"To Not Hate": Reconciliation among Victims of Violence and Participants of the Greensboro Truth and Reconciliation Commission', *Contemporary Justice Review*, 13(3): 269–285.

Arbour, L. (2006) *Economic and Social Justice for Societies in Transition*, Working Paper, New York University. https://nyujilp.org/wp-content/uploads/2013/02/40.1-Arbour.pdf (accessed 13 July 2020).

Archila Neira, M. (2003) *Idas y venidas, Vueltas y revueltas: protestas sociales en Colombia 1958–1990*. Bogotá: ICANH/CINEP.

Aulin, J. (2019) 'Civil Society Inclusion in Peacebuilding', in A. Carl (ed) *Navigating Inclusion in Peace Processes, Accord: An International Review of Peace Initiatives*, London: Conciliation Resources, pp 39–41.

Baines, E.K. (2015) '"Today, I Want to Speak out the Truth": Victim Agency, Responsibility, and Transitional Justice', *International Political Sociology*, 9(4): 316–332.

Baines, E.K. (2017) *Buried in the Hearts: Women, Complex Victimhood and the War in Northern Uganda*, Cambridge: Cambridge University Press.

Baker, C. and J. Obradovic-Wochnik (2016) 'Mapping the Nexus of Transitional Justice and Peacebuilding', *Journal of Intervention and Statebuilding*, 10(3): 281–301.

Bar-Tal, D. (2000) 'From Intractable Conflict through Conflict Resolution to Reconciliation: Psychological Analysis', *Political Psychology*, 21(2): 351–365.

Bar-Tal, D. (2013) 'Introduction', in *Intractable Conflicts: Socio-psychological Foundations and Dynamics*, Cambridge: Cambridge University Press, pp 1–30.

Bar-Tal, D. (2014) 'Collective Memory as Social Representations', *Papers on Social Representations*, 23: 70–96.

Bar-Tal, D. and G.H. Bennink (2011) 'The Nature of Reconciliation as an Outcome and as a Process', in Y. Bar-Siman-Tov (ed) *From Conflict Resolution to Reconciliation*, New York: Oxford University Press, pp 11–38.

Bar-Tal, D., L. Chernyak-Hai, N. Schori and A. Gundar (2009) 'A Sense of Self- Perceived Collective Victimhood in Intractable Conflicts', *International Review of the Red Cross*, 91(874): 229–258.

Bell, C. (2006) 'Peace Agreements: Their Nature and Legal Status', *American Journal of International Law*, 100(2): 373–412.

Bell, C. (2009) 'Transitional Justice, Interdisciplinarity and the State of the "Field" or "Non-field"', *International Journal of Transitional Justice*, 3(1): 5–27.

Bell, C. (2011) 'Post-conflict Accountability and the Reshaping of Human Rights and Humanitarian Law', in O. Ben-Naftali (ed) *International Humanitarian Law and International Human Rights Law*, Oxford: Oxford University Press, pp 328–370.

Bell, C. (2017) 'Peace Settlements and Human Rights: A Post Cold-War Circular History', *Journal of Human Rights Practice*, 9(3): 358–378.

Bell, C. (2018) 'Contending with the Past: Transitional Justice and Political Settlement Processes', in R. Duthrie and P. Seils (eds) *Justice Mosaics*, New York: ICTJ, pp 84–115.

Bell, C. (2019) 'New Inclusion Project', in A. Carl (ed) *Navigating Inclusion in Peace Processes, Accord: An International Review of Peace Initiatives*, London: Conciliation Resources, pp 11–18.

Bell, C. and K. McNicholl (2019) 'Principled Pragmatism and the 'Inclusion Project': Implementing a Gender Perspective in Peace Agreements', *Feminists at Law*, 9(1): 1–51.

Berat, L. and Y. Shain (1995) 'Retribution or Truth-Telling in South Africa? Legacies of the Transitional Phase', *Law & Social Inquiry*, 20(1): 163–189.

Björkdahl, A. and L. Warvsten (2021) 'Friction in Transitional Justice Processes: The Colombian Judicial System and the ICC', *International Journal of Transitional Justice*, 15(3): 636–657.

Bloomfield, D., T. Barnes and L. Huyse (2003) 'Introduction', in D. Bloomfield, T. Barnes and L. Huyse (eds) *Reconciliation after Violent Conflict: A Handbook*, Stockholm: International Idea, pp 10–17.

REFERENCES

Brett, R. (2008) *Social Movements, Indigenous Politics and Democratisation in Guatemala, 1985–1996*, Amsterdam/Boston: CEDLA/Brill.

Brett, R. (2017a) *La Voz de las Víctimas en la Negociación: Sistematización de una Experiencia*, Bogotá: United Nations.

Brett, R. (2017b) 'The Role of Civil Society Actors in Peacemaking: The Case of Guatemala', *Journal of Peacebuilding & Development*, 12(1): 49–64.

Brett, R. (2017c) 'Understanding Societal Fragmentation in Colombia and Guatemala: Transitions and the Building Blocks for Inclusive Social Contracts', in S. Kaplan (ed) *Inclusive Social Contracts in Fragile States in Transition: Strengthening the Building Blocks of Success*, Washington DC: IFIT, pp 50–71.

Brett, R. (2021a) 'In the Aftermath: Guatemala's Failed Reconciliation', *Peacebuilding*, 10(4): 382–402.

Brett, R. (2021b) 'Political Violence and Terrorism in Colombia', in R. English (ed) *The Cambridge History of Terrorism*, Cambridge: Cambridge University Press, pp 387–419.

Brett, R. (2022) 'Victim-Centred Peacemaking: The Colombian Experience', *Journal of Intervention and Statebuilding*, 16(4): 475–497.

Brett, R. and A. Delgado (2005) *The Role of Constitution-Building Processes in Democratization*, Stockholm: International IDEA, https://constitutionnet.org/sites/default/files/CBP-Guatemala.pdf (accessed 12 October 2023).

Brett, R. and L. Malagon (2013) 'Overcoming the Original Sin of the "Original Condition": How Reparations May Contribute to Emancipatory Peacebuilding', *Human Rights Review*, 14(3): 257–271.

Brett, R. and A. Santamaria (eds) (2010) *Jano y las caras opuestas de los derechos humanos de los pueblos indígenas*. Bogotá: Universidad del Rosario.

Brett, R., R. English, É. Féron and V. Rosoux (2022) 'Embodied Reconciliation: A New Research Agenda', *Peacebuilding*, early online version.

Bries Silva, N. (2024) 'Discovering What Is Already Known: The Afro-Colombian Ancestral Justice System before the Special Jurisdiction for Peace', *International Journal of Transitional Justice*, early online publication.

Brinton Lykes, M. and C. Murphy (2023) 'Decolonizing Transitional Justice: Soft, Radical or Beyond Reform', *International Journal of Transitional Justice*, 17(3): 361–369.

Brittain, J. (2010) *Revolutionary Social Change in Colombia: The Origin and Direction of the FARC-EP-EP*, New York: Pluto Press.

Burnyeat, G. (2018) *Chocolate, Politics and Peace-building: An Ethnography of the Peace Community of San José de Apartadó, Colombia*, Basingstoke: Palgrave Macmillan.

Bushnell, D. (1993) *The Making of Modern Colombia: A Nation in Spite of Itself*, Berkeley: University of California Press.

Castano, E., D. Muñoz-Rojas and S. Čehajić-Clancy (2020) 'Thou Shalt Not Kill: Social Psychological Processes and International Humanitarian Law among Combatants', *Peace and Conflict: Journal of Peace Psychology*, 26(1): 35–46.

Charmaz, K. and R. Thornberg (2017) 'The Pursuit of Grounded Theory', *Qualitative Research in Psychology*, 18(3): 305–327.

Cheng, C., J. Goodhand and P. Meehan (2018) *Securing and Sustaining Elite Bargains That Reduce Violent Conflict*, London: UKMG.

Chernick, M. (1999) 'Negotiating Peace amidst Multiple Forms of Violence: The Protracted Search for a Settlement to the Armed Conflicts in Colombia', in C. J. Arnson (ed) *Comparative Peace Processes in Latin America*, Stanford: Stanford University Press/Washington DC: Woodrow Wilson Center Press, pp 159–200.

Coleman Montesinos, L. (2024) *Struggles for the Human: Violent Legality and the Politics of Rights*, Durham, NC: Duke University Press.

Cooke, B. and U. Kothari (eds) (2001) *Participation: The New Tyranny*, London: Zed Books.

Cornwall, A. (2008) 'Unpacking "Participation": Models, Meanings and Practices', *Community Development Journal*, 43(3): 269–283.

Crisis Group (2012) 'Colombia: Peace at Last?', Report 45.

Crocker, D.A. (2002) 'Punishment, Reconciliation, and Democratic Deliberation', *Buffalo Criminal Law Review*, 5(2): 509–549.

David, R. and S.Y.P. Choi (2005) 'Victims on Transitional Justice: Lessons from the Reparation of Human Rights Abuses in the Czech Republic', *Human Rights Quarterly*, 27(2): 392–435.

Davidovic, M. (2021) 'The Law of "Never Again": Transitional Justice and the Transformation of the Norm of Non-recurrence', *International Journal of Transitional Justice*, 15(2): 386–406.

Davis, A., C. Nsengiyumva and D. Hyslop (2019) *Healing Trauma and Building Trust and Tolerance in Rwanda*, Interpeace Peacebuilding in Practice, Paper No. 4.

De Coning, C. (2016) 'From Peacebuilding to Sustaining Peace: Implications of Complexity for Resilience and Sustainability', *Resilience*, 4(3): 166–183.

De Greiff, P. (2006) 'Justice and Reparations', in P. de Greiff (ed) *The Handbook of Reparations*, New York: Oxford University Press, pp 451–477.

De Greiff, P. and R. Duthie (eds) (2009) *Transitional Justice and Development: Making Connections*, New York: Social Science Research Council.

De Oliveira Andreotti, V., S. Stein, C. Ahenakey and D. Hunt (2015) 'Mapping Interpretations of Decolonization in the Context of Higher Education', *Decolnization: Indigeneity, Education & Society*, 4(1): 21–40.

De Waardt, M. and S. Weber (2019) 'Beyond Victims' Mere Presence: An Empirical Analysis of Victim Participation in Transitional Justice in Colombia', *Journal of Human Rights Practice*, 11(1): 209–228.

Deas, M. (1995) *Dos ensayos especulativos sobre la violencia en Colombia*, Bogotá: FONADE.

DeMeritt, J., A. Pulido, D.T. Mason and J. Meernik (2019) 'Land, Violence, and the Colombian Peace Process', in J. Meernik, J. DeMeritt and M. Uribe-Lopez (eds) *As War Ends: What Colombia Can Tell Us about the Sustainability of Peace and Transitional Justice*, Cambridge: Cambridge University Press, pp 68–90.

Druliolle, V. and R. Brett (eds) (2018) *The Politics of Victimhood in Post-conflict Societies: Comparative and Analytical Perspectives*, Basingstoke: Palgrave Macmillan.

Durch, W.J. (ed) (1994) *The Evolution of UN Peacekeeping*, London: St Martin's Press.

English, R. (2010) *Terrorism: How to Respond*, Cambridge: Cambridge University Press.

English, R. (2013) *Modern War: A Very Short Introduction*, Oxford: Oxford University Press.

Engstrom, P. (2013) 'Transitional Justice and Ongoing Conflicts', in C. Sriram Lehka, J. García-Godos, J. Herman and O. Martin-Ortega (eds) *Transitional Justice and Peacebuilding on the Ground: Victims and Ex-combatants*, Abingdon: Routledge, pp 41–61.

Evrard, E., G. Mejía Bonifazi and T. Destrooper (2021) 'The Meaning of Participation in Transitional Justice: A Conceptual Proposal for Empirical Analysis', *International Journal of Transitional Justice*, 15(2): 428–447.

Firchow, P. (2017) 'Do Reparations Repair Relationships? Setting the Stage for Reconciliation in Colombia', *International Journal of Transitional Justice*, 11(2): 315–338.

Firchow, P. and Y. Selim (2022) 'Meaningful Engagement from the Bottom-up? Taking Stock of Participation in Transitional Justice Processes', *International Journal of Transitional Justice*, early online publication.

Fisas, V. (2004) *Procesos de paz y negociación en conflictos armados*, Barcelona: Ediciones Paidós.

Fukuyama, F. (2015) *Political Order and Political Decay: From the Industrial Revolution to the Globalisation of Democracy*, London: Profile Books.

Garcia-Godos, J. (2016) 'Victims in Focus', *International Journal of Transitional Justice*, 2(10): 350–358.

Garcia-Godos, J. and O. Knut Andreas (2010) 'Transitional Justice and Victims' Rights before the End of a Conflict: The Unusual Case of Colombia', *Journal of Latin American Studies*, 42(3): 487–516.

Gates, S., H. Mokleiv Nygård and E. Trappeniers (2016) 'Conflict Recurrence', *Conflict Trends*, 2, Oslo: PRIO.

Goldstein, D. and E. Arias (eds) (2010) *Violent Democracies in Latin America*, Durham, NC: Duke University Press.

Goman, C. and D.L. Kelley (2016) 'Conceptualizing Forgiveness in the Face of Historical Trauma', in M. Casper and E. Wertheimer (eds) *Critical Trauma Studies: Understanding Violence, Conflict and Memory in Everyday Life*, New York: New York University Press, pp 78–98.

Gomez-Suarez, A. (2007) 'Perpetrator Blocs, Genocidal Mentalities and Geographies: The Destruction of the Union Patriotica in Colombia and Its Lessons for Genocide Studies', *Journal of Genocide Research*, 9(4): 637–660.

Gomez-Suarez, A. (2017) *Genocide, Geopolitics and Transnational Networks: Contextualising the Destruction of the Unión Patriótica in Colombia*, Abingdon: Routledge.

Gomez-Suarez, A. (2017a) 'Peace Process Pedagogy: Lessons from the No-Vote Victory in the Colombian Peace Referendum', *Comparative Education*, 53(3): 462–482.

Gonzalez-Ocantos, E.A. (2020) *The Politics of Transitional Justice in Latin America*, Cambridge: Cambridge University Press.

Goodwin, J. (2006) 'A Theory of Categorical Terrorism', *Social Forces*, 84: 2027–2046.

Goulding, M. (1993) 'The Evolution of United Nations Peacekeeping', *International Affairs*, 69(3): 451–464.

Gready, P. and S. Roberts (2017) 'Rethinking Civil Society and Transitional Justice: Lessons from Social Movements and "New" Civil Society', *International Journal of Human Rights*, 21(7): 956–975.

Grewal, K. (2016) 'Can the Subaltern Speak within International Law? Women's Rights Activism, International Legal Institutions and the Power of "Strategic Misunderstanding"', in N. Dhawan, E. Fink, J. Leinius and R. Mageza-Barthel (eds) *Negotiating Normativity: Postcolonial Appropriations, Contestations and Transformations*, New York: Springer, pp 27–44.

Guelke, A. (2012) *Politics in Deeply Divided Societies*, London: Polity Press.

Gutiérrez Sanín, F. (2007) *¿Lo que el viento se llevó? Los partidos políticos y la democracia en Colombia, 1958–2002*, Bogotá: Norma.

Gutiérrez Sanín, F. and F. Barón (2006) 'Estado, control territorial paramilitar y orden político en Colombia', in F. Gutiérrez Sanín, M. Wills and G. Sánchez (eds) *Nuestra guerra sin nombre: Transformaciones del Conflicto en Colombia*, Bogotá: Norma, pp 267–311.

Hamber, B. (2009) *Transforming Societies after Political Violence: Truth, Reconciliation and Mental Health*, New York: Springer.

Hancock, L. and C. Mitchell (eds) (2007) *Zones of Peace*, Boulder: Lynne Rienner.

Haspeslagh, S. (2021) *Proscribing Peace: How Listing Armed Groups as Terrorists Hurts Negotiations*, Manchester: Manchester University Press.

Hayner, P.B. (1994) 'Fifteen Truth Commissions – 1974 to 1994: A Comparative Study', *Human Rights Quarterly*, 16(4): 597–655.

Heaney, S. (2018) *The Cure at Troy: Sophocles' Philoctetes*, London: Faber & Faber.

Herbolzheimer, K. (2019) 'Negotiating Inclusive Peace in Colombia', in A. Carl (ed) *Navigating Inclusion in Peace Processes, Accord: An International Review of Peace Initiatives*, London: Conciliation Resources.

Hickey, S. and G. Mohan (eds) (2004) *Participation: From Tyranny to Transformation? Exploring New Approaches to Participation in Development*, London: Zed Books.

Hirblinger, A.T. and D.M. Landau (2020) 'Daring to Differ? Strategies of Inclusion in Peacemaking', *Security Dialogue*, 51(4): 305–322.

Holmes, J. (2019) 'Terrorism in Latin America', in E. Chenoweth, R. English, A. Gofas and S. N. Kalyvas (eds) *The Oxford Handbook of Terrorism*, Oxford: Oxford University Press, pp 559–568.

Hristov, J. (2009) *Blood and Capital: The Paramilitarization of Colombia*, Athens, OH: Ohio University Press.

Hristov, J. (2016) *Paramilitarism and Neoliberalism: Violent Systems of Capital Accumulation in Colombia and Beyond*, New York: Pluto Press.

Hughes, J. (2018) 'Agency versus Structure in Reconciliation', *Ethnic and Racial Studies*, 41(4): 624–642.

Human Rights Watch (2001) *World Report: Colombia*, New York: HRW.

Huneeus, A.A.V. and P. Rueda-Saiz (2021) 'Territory as a Victim of Armed Conflict', *University of Wisconsin Legal Studies Research Paper* No. 1720.

Hylton, F. (2006) *Evil Hour in Colombia*, London: Verso.

Iturralde, M. (2003) 'Guerra y derecho en Colombia: El decisionismo político y los estados de excepción como respuesta a la crisis de la democracia', *Revista de Estudios Sociales*, 15: 29–46.

Jacoby, T. (2015) 'A Theory of Victimhood: Politics, Conflict and the Construction of Victim-Based Identity', *Millennium Journal of International Studies*, 43(2): 511–530.

Jamar, A. (2018) *Victims' Inclusion and Transitional Justice: Attending to the Exclusivity of Inclusion Politics*. PA-X Report Transitional Justice Series, University of Edinburgh.

Jamar, A. and C. Bell (2018) *Transitional Justice and Peace Negotiations with a Gender Lens* (Gender Briefing Series), UN Women.

Jamison, M. (2011) 'Humanitarian Intervention since 1990', in B. Simms and D.J.B. Trim (eds) *Humanitarian Intervention: A History*, Cambridge: Cambridge University Press, pp 365–379.

Jones, B., L. Ott, M. Rauschenbach and C. Sanchez (2023) 'Hiding in Plain Sight: Victim Participation in the Search for Disappeared Persons, a Contribution to (Procedural) Justice', *International Journal of Transitional Justice*, 17(2): 233–251.

Joshi, M. and P. Wallensteen (eds) (2018) *Understanding Quality Peace: Peacebuilding after Civil War*, Abingdon: Routledge.

Kalyvas, S. (2006) *The Logic of Violence in Civil War*, Cambridge: Cambridge University Press.

Kaplan, O. (2017) *Resisting War: How Communities Protect Themselves*, Cambridge: Cambridge University Press.

Kapoor, I. (2004) 'The Power of Participation', *Current Issues in Comparative Education*, 6(2): 125–129.

Karl, R. (2017) *Forgotten Peace: Reform, Violence and the Making of Contemporary Colombia*, Los Angeles: University of California Press.

Kerr, R. (2007) 'Peace through Justice? The International Criminal Tribunal for the Former Yugoslavia', *Southeast European and Black Sea Studies*, 7(3): 373–385.

Kew, D. and A. Wanis-St John (2008) 'Civil Society and Peace Negotiations: Confronting Exclusion', *International Negotiation*, 13: 11–36.

Krause, K. and O. Jütersonke (2005) 'Peace, Security and Development in Post-conflict Environments', *Security Dialogue*, 36(4): 447–462.

Klinkner, M. and H. Davis (2021) *The Right to the Truth in International Law: Victims' Rights in Human Rights and International Criminal Law*, Abingdon: Routledge.

Krystalli, R. (2021) 'Narrating Victimhood: Dilemmas and (In)Dignities', *International Feminist Journal of Politics*, 23(1): 125–146.

Lambourne, W. (2009) 'Transitional Justice and Peacebuilding after Mass Violence', *International Journal of Transitional Justice*, 3(1): 28–48.

Lambourne, W. (2013) 'Transformative Justice, Reconciliation and Peacebuilding', in S. Buckley-Zistel, T. Koloma Beck, C. Braun and F. Mieth (eds) *Transitional Justice Theories*, Abingdon: Routledge, pp 19–39.

Lambourne, W. and L.W. Gitau (2013) 'Psychosocial Interventions, Peacebuilding and Development in Rwanda', *Journal of Peacebuilding and Development*, 8(3): 23–36.

LaPlante, L. (2015) 'Just Repair', *Cornell International Law Journal*, 14: 513–578.

Leader Maynard, J. (2019) 'Ideology and Armed Conflict', *Journal of Peace Research*, 56(5): 635–649.

Lederach, J.P. (2010) *The Moral Imagination: The Art and Soul of Building Peace*, New York: Oxford University Press.

Lederach, J.P. (1997) *Building Peace: Sustainable Reconciliation in Divided Societies*, Washington DC: United States Institute of Peace Press.

Leebaw, B.A. (2008) 'The Irreconcilable Goals of Transitional Justice', *Human Rights Quarterly*, 30(1): 95–118.

Leech, G. (2011) *The FARC-EP: The Longest Insurgency*, London: Zed Books.

LeGrand, C. (2003) 'The Colombian Crisis in Historical Perspective', *Canadian Journal of Latin American and Caribbean Studies*, 28(55–56): 165–209.

Lipson, M. (2007) 'A Garbage Can Model of UN Peacekeeping', *Global Governance*, 13: 79–97.

Lundy, P. and M. McGovern (2008) 'Whose Justice? Rethinking Transitional Justice from the Bottom up', *Journal of Law and Society*, 35(2): 265–292.

Mac Ginty, R. (2011) *International Peacebuilding and Local Resistance: Hybrid Forms of Peace*, Basingstoke: Palgrave Macmillan.

Mac Ginty, R. (2012) 'Routine Peace: Technocracy and Peacebuilding', *Cooperation and Conflict*, 47(3): 287–308.

Mac Ginty, R. and O. Richmond (2007) 'Myth or Reality: Opposing Views on the Liberal Peace and Post-war Reconstruction', *Global Society*, 21(4): 491–497.

Malagón Diaz, L. (2019) 'The Role of Victims in Shaping Transitional Justice Mechanisms in Colombia', unpublished PhD, University of Ulster.

Mallinder, L. (2019) *Amnesties and Inclusive Political Settlements* (PA-X Report: Transitional Justice Series). Edinburgh: Global Justice Academy, University of Edinburgh.

Malone, D.M. and K. Wermester (2000) 'Boom and Bust? The Changing Nature of UN Peacekeeping', *International Peacekeeping*, 7(4): 37–54.

Matanock, A.M. and M. García-Sánchez (2017) 'The Colombian Paradox: Peace Processes, Elite Divisions and Popular Plebiscites', *Daedalus: The Journal of the American Academy of Arts and Sciences*, Fall: 152–166.

Mayall, J. (ed) (1996) *The New Interventionism 1991–94: United Nations Experience in Cambodia, Former Yugoslavia and Somalia*, Cambridge: Cambridge University Press.

Mazzei, J. (2009) *Death Squads or Self-Defense Forces? How Paramilitary Groups Emerge and Challenge Democracy in Latin America*, Durham, NC: University of North Carolina Press.

McEvoy, K. and K. McConnachie (2012a) 'Victimology in Transitional Justice: Victimhood, Innocence and Hierarchy', *European Journal of Criminology*, 9(5): 527–538.

McEvoy, K. and K. McConnachie (2012b) 'Victims and Transitional Justice: Voice, Agency and Blame', *Social & Legal Studies*, 22: 489–513.

McKeon, C. (2004) *Owning the Process: The Role of Civil Society in Peace Negotiations*, London: Conciliation Resources.

Mendeloff, D. (2004) 'Truth-Seeking, Truth-Telling, and Postconflict Peacebuilding: Curb the Enthusiasm?', *International Studies Review*, 6(3): 355–380.

Mendes, I. (2019) 'Inclusion and Political Representation in Peace Negotiations: The Case of the Colombian Victims' Delegations', *Journal of Politics in Latin America*, 11(3): 272–297.

Mendes, I., M. Siman and M. Fernández (2020) 'The Colombian Peace Negotiations and the Invisibility of the "No" Vote in the 2016 Referendum', *Peacebuilding*, 8(3): 321–343.

Méndez, J. (2016) 'Victims as Protagonists in Transitional Justice', *International Journal of Transitional Justice*, 10(1): 1–5.

Miller, G. (2020) 'Toward a Trans-scalar Peace System: Challenging Complex Global Conflict Systems', *Peacebuilding*, 8(3): 261–278.

Miller, Z. (2008) 'Effects of Invisibility: In Search of the "Economic" in Transitional Justice', *International Journal of Transitional Justice*, 2(3): 266–291.

Minow, M. (1998) *Between Vengeance and Forgiveness: Facing History after Genocide and Mass Violence*, Boston: Beacon Press.

Molano, A. (2007) 'The Evolution of the FARC-EP: A Guerrilla Group's Long History', *NACLA Report on the Americas*.

Monning, W. (2002) 'The Colombian Conflict: A War on Drugs? A War on Terrorism? A War on the Poor?', *Guild Practitioner*, 59: 161–164.

Moyano, M.J. (1995) *Argentina's Lost Patrol: Armed Struggle 1969–1979*, New Haven: Yale University Press.

Murphy, C. (2010) *A Moral Theory of Political Reconciliation*, Cambridge: Cambridge University Press.

Nagle, L. (2005) 'Global Terrorism in Our Own Backyard: Colombia's Legal War against Illegal Armed Groups', *Transnational Law and Contemporary Problems*, 15: 5–86.

Nagy, R. (2008) 'Transitional Justice as Global Project: Critical Reflections', *Third World Quarterly*, 29(2): 275–289.

Nasi, C. (2009) 'Colombia's Peace Processes, 1982–2002: Conditions, Strategies and Outcomes', in V. Bouvier (ed) *Building Peace in a Time of War*, Washington DC: United States Institute for Peace, pp 39–64.

National Centre for Historical Memory (2012) *Basta Ya!* Bogotá: NCHM.

Nee, A. and P. Uvin (2010) 'Silence and Dialogue: Burundians' Alternative to Transitional Justice', in R. Shaw and L. Waldorf, with P. Hazan (eds) *Localising Transitional Justice: Interventions and Priorities after Mass Violence*, Stanford: Stanford University Press.

Nilsson, D. (2012) 'Anchoring the Peace: Civil Society Actors in Peace Accords and Durable Peace', *International Interactions*, 38(2): 243–266.

Nussio, E., A. Rettberg and J. Ugarrizo (2015) 'Victims, Nonvictims and Their Opinions on Transitional Justice: Findings from the Colombian Case', *International Journal of Transitional Justice*, 2(1): 336–354.

O'Donnell, G., P. Schmitter and L. Whitehead (1986) *Transitions from Authoritarian Rule: Comparative Perspectives*, Baltimore: Johns Hopkins University Press.

Office of the United Nations High Commissioner for Human Rights in Colombia (2015) *Annual Report*.

O'Reilly, M. (2016) 'Peace and Justice through a Feminist Lens: Gender Justice and the Women's Court for the Former Yugoslavia', *Journal of Intervention and Statebuilding*, 10(3): 419–445.

Paffenholz, T. (2014) 'Civil Society and Peace Negotiations: Beyond the Inclusion–Exclusion Dichotomy', *Negotiation Journal*, 30(1): 69–91.

Paffenholz, T. (2015) *Main Results of Broader Participation in Political Negotiations and Implementation*, Geneva: Inclusive Peace and Transition Initiative, Graduate Institute of International and Development Studies.

Palacios, M. (2007) *Between Legitimacy and Violence: Colombia 1875–2002*, Durham, NC: Duke University Press.

Palma, O. (2019) 'The Changing Meaning of Terrorism: A Matter of Discourse', in M. Boyle (ed) *Non-Western Responses to Terrorism*, Manchester: Manchester University Press, pp 246–270.

Paredes Zapata, G. (2003) 'Terrorism in Colombia', *Prehospital and Disaster Medicine*, 18(2): 80–87.

Paris, R. (2000) 'Broadening the Study of Peace Operations', *International Studies Review*, 2(3): 27–44.

Paris, R. (2012) *At War's End: Building Peace after Civil Conflict*, Cambridge: Cambridge University Press.

Payne, L., T.D. Olsen and A.G. Reiter (2010) 'The Justice Balance: When Transitional Justice Improves Human Rights and Democracy', *Human Rights Quarterly*, 32(4): 980–1005.

Peace Accords Matrix (2022) *Las víctimas al centro: estado de la implementación del Acuerdo Final desde la perspectiva de sus derechos*, South Bend, IN: Kroc Institute for International Peace Studies, University of Notre Dame, https://curate.nd.edu/downloads/1544bp0284m (accessed 10 March 2023).

Peace Accords Matrix (2023) *Towards Implementation of Women's Rights in the Colombian Final Peace Accord: Progress, Opportunities And Challenges. Special Report on the Monitoring of the Gender Commitments*, South Bend, IN: Kroc Institute for International Peace Studies, University of Notre Dame.

Pearce, J. (1990) *Colombia: Inside the Labyrinth*, London: Latin America Bureau.

Pécaut, D. (2003) *Violencia y política en Colombia. Elementos de reflexión*, Medellín: Hombre Nuevo/Universidad del Valle.

Pécaut, D. (2008) *Las FARC-EP: Una guerilla sin fin o sin fines?*, Bogotá: Norma.

Posada-Carbo, E. (1997) 'Limits of Power: Elections under the Conservative Hegemony in Colombia, 1886–1930', *Hispanic American Historical Review*, 77(2): 245–279.

Prieto, J.D. (2012) 'Together after War While the War Goes on: Victims, Ex-combatants and Communities in Three Colombian Cities', *International Journal of Transitional Justice*, 6(3): 525–546.

Quinn, J.R. and M. Freeman (2003) 'Lessons Learned: Practical Lessons Gleaned from inside the Truth Commissions of Guatemala and South Africa', *Human Rights Quarterly*, 25(4): 1117–1149.

Rajca, A. (2018) *Dissensual Subjects: Memory, Human Rights, and Postdictatorship in Argentina, Brazil, and Uruguay*, Chicago: Northwestern University Press.

Ramsbotham, O. (2000) 'Reflections on UN Post-settlement Peacebuilding', *International Peacekeeping*, 7(1): 169–189.

Rettberg, A. (2015) 'Victims of the Colombian Armed Conflict: The Birth of a Political Actor', in B. Bagley and J. Rosen (eds) *Colombia's Political Economy at the Outset of the 21st Century: From Uribe to Santos and Beyond*, New York: Lexington Books, pp 111–139.

Riano Alcala, P. and M.V. Uribe (2016) 'Constructing Memory amidst War: The Historical Memory Group of Colombia', *International Journal of Transitional Justice*, 10: 6–24.

Richmond, O. (1998) 'Devious Objectives and the Disputants' View of International Mediation: A Theoretical Framework', *Journal of Peace Research*, 35(6): 707–722.

Richmond, O. (2004) 'UN Peace Operations and the Dilemmas of the Peacebuilding Consensus', *International Peacekeeping*, 11(1): 83–101.

Roberts, A. and B. Kingsbury (eds) (1996) *United Nations, Divided World: The UN's Roles in International Relations*, Oxford: Oxford University Press.

Robins, S. (2011) 'Towards Victim-Centred Transitional Justice: Understanding the Needs of Families of the Disappeared in Postconflict Nepal', *International Journal of Transitional Justice*, 5: 75–98.

Robins, S. (2012) 'Transitional Justice as an Elite Discourse: Human Rights Practice Where the Global Meets the Local in Post-conflict Nepal', *Critical Asian Studies*, 44(1): 3–30.

Robins, S. (2015) 'Mapping a Future for Transitional Justice by Learning from Its Past', *International Journal of Transitional Justice*, 9: 181–190.

Robins, S. (2017) 'Failing Victims? The Limits of Transitional Justice in Addressing the Needs of Victims of Violations', *Human Rights and International Legal Discourse*, 1: 41–58.

Roht-Arriaza, N. and J. Mariecurrenz (eds) (2012) *Transitional Justice in the Twenty-First Century: Beyond Truth versus Justice*, Cambridge: Cambridge University Press.

Rojas-Perez, I. (2017) *Mourning Remains: State Atrocity, Exhumations, and Governing the Disappeared in Peru's Postwar Andes*, Palo Alto: Stanford University Press.

Rosoux, V. and M. Anstey (eds) (2017) *Negotiating Reconciliation in Peacemaking: Quandaries of Relationship Building*, London: Springer.

Safford, F. and Palacios, M. (2002) *Colombia: Fragmented Land, Divided Society*, Oxford: Oxford University Press.

Sajjad, T. (2016) 'Heavy Hands, Helping Hands, Holding Hands: The Politics of Exclusion in Victims' Networks in Nepal', *International Journal of Transitional Justice*, 10(1): 25–45.

Sánchez, G. and P. Bakewell (1985) 'La Violencia in Colombia: New Research, New Questions', *Hispanic American Historical Review*, 65(4): 789–807.

Sánchez, G. and D. Merteens (2001) *Bandits, Peasants, and Politics: The Case of 'La Violencia' in Colombia*, Austin: University of Texas Press.

Sandoval, C., H. Martínez-Carrillo and M. Cruz-Rodríguez (2022) 'The Challenges of Implementing Special Sanctions (*Sanciones Propias*) in Colombia and Providing Retribution, Reparation, Participation and Reincorporation', *Journal of Human Rights Practice*, 14(2): 478–501.

Santamaría, A., D. Muelas, P. Caceres, W. Kuetguaje and J. Villegas (2020) 'Decolonial Sketches and Intercultural Approaches to Truth: Corporeal Experiences and Testimonies of Indigenous Women in Colombia', *International Journal of Transitional Justice*, 14(1): 56–79.

Santana, P.R. (1989) *Los Movimientos Sociales en Colombia*. Bogotá: Foro Nacional.

Santos Calderón, E. (2016) *Así Empezó Todo: el Primer Cara a Cara Secreto Entre el Gobierno y las FARC-EP en La Habana*, Bogotá: Intermedio Editores.

Santos Calderón, J.M. (2021) *The Battle for Peace: The Long Road to Ending a War with the World's Oldest Guerrilla Army*, Kansas City: University of Kansas Press.

Seils, P. (2017) *The Place of Reconciliation in Transitional Justice*. New York: ICTJ.

Sesay, M. (2022) 'Decolonization of Postcolonial Africa: A Structural Justice Project More Radical Than Transitional Justice', *International Journal of Transitional Justice*, 16(2): 254–271.

Shnabel, N., S. Halabi and M. Noor (2013) 'Overcoming Competitive Victimhood and Facilitating Forgiveness through Re-categorisation into a Common Victim or Perpetrator Identity', *Journal of Experimental Social Psychology*, 49: 867–877.

Sharp, D. (2012) 'Interrogating the Peripheries: The Preoccupations of Fourth Generation Transitional Justice', *Harvard Human Rights Journal*, 26: 149–178.

Sharp, D. (2013) 'Beyond the Post-conflict Checklist: Linking Peacebuilding and Transitional Justice through the Lens of Critique', *Chicago Journal of International Law*, 14: 165–196.

Shaw, R. and L. Waldorf (2010) 'Introduction: Localizing Transitional Justice', in R. Shaw and L. Waldorf, with P. Hazan (eds) *Localizing Transitional Justice: Interventions and Priorities after Mass Violence*, Stanford: Stanford University Press, pp 3–26.

Shaw, R. and L. Waldorf, with P. Hazan (eds) (2010) *Localising Transitional Justice: Interventions and Priorities after Mass Violence*, Stanford: Stanford University Press.

Sikkink, K. (2012) *The Justice Cascade: How Human Rights Prosecutions Are Changing World Politics*, New York: W.W. Norton & Co.

Sisson, J. (2010) 'A Conceptual Framework for Dealing with the Past', *Politorbis*, 50(3): 11–17.

Sriram Lehka, C. (2007) 'Justice as Peace? Liberal Peacebuilding and Strategies of Transitional Justice', *Global Society*, 21: 579–591.

Staub, E. (1998) 'Breaking the Cycle of Genocidal Violence: Healing and Reconciliation,' in J. Harvey (ed) *Perspectives on Loss*, New York: Routledge, pp 231–238.

Staub, E. (2006) 'Reconciliation after Genocide, Mass Killing, or Intractable Conflict: Understanding the Roots of Violence, Psychological Recovery, and Steps toward a General Theory', *Political Psychology*, 27(6): 867–894.

Staub, E. (2011) *Overcoming Evil: Genocide, Violent Conflict, and Terrorism*, Oxford: Oxford University Press.

Steele, A. (2017) *Democracy and Displacement in Colombia's Civil War*, Ithaca: Cornell University Press.

Stokes, D. (2003) 'Why the End of the Cold War Doesn't Matter: The US War of Terror in Colombia', *Review of International Studies*, 29(4): 569–585.

Tate, W. (2001) 'Paramilitaries in Colombia', *Brown Journal of World Affairs*, 8(1): 163–175.

Teitel, R. (2003) 'Transitional Justice Genealogy', *Harvard Human Rights Journal*, 16: 69–94.

Teitel, R. (2000) *Transitional Justice*, Oxford: Oxford University Press.

Theidon, K. (2010) *Intimate Enemies: Violence and Reconciliation in Peru*, Pittsburgh: Pennsylvania University Press.

United Nations (2005) *Basic Principles and Guidelines on the Right to a Remedy and Reparation for Victims of Gross Violations of International Human Rights Law and Serious Violations of International Humanitarian Law*, New York: United Nations.

United Nations, National University of Colombia, Episcopal Conference (2014) *Balance from the Organisers at the End of the Visits of the Victims to Havana*, Bogotá: UN, National University of Colombia, Episcopal Conference.

Uprimny Yepes, R. (2009) 'Between Corrective and Distributive Justice: Reparations of Gross Human Rights Violations in Times of Transition', inaugural address as Visiting Professor to the UNESCO Chair in Education for Peace, Human Rights and Democracy, 21 October, Utrecht University.

Uran Bidegain, H. (2020) *Mi vida y el Palacio: 6 y 7 de noviembre de 1985*, Bogotá: Editorial Planeta.

Valentino, B. (2004) *Final Solutions: Mass Killing and Genocide in the 20th Century*, Ithaca: Cornell University Press.

Verdeja, E. (2009) *Unchopping a Tree: Reconciliation in the Aftermath of Political Violence*, Philadelphia: Temple University Press.

Villamizar, D. (2017) *Las Guerrillas en Colombia: una historia desde los origines hasta los confines*, Bogotá: Random House/Debate.

Vogel, B. (2016) 'Civil Society Capture: Top-down Interventions from Below?', *Journal of Intervention and Statebuilding*, 10(4): 472–489.

Volkan, V. (2001) 'Transgenerational Transmissions and Chosen Traumas: An Aspect of Large-Group Identity', *Group Analysis*, 34(1): 79–97.

REFERENCES

Waisberg, T. (2008) 'Colombia's Use of Force in Ecuador against a Terrorist Organisation: International Law and the Use of Force against Non-state Actors', *ASIL Insights*, 17, https://www.asil.org/insights/volume/12/issue/17/colombias-use-force-ecuador-against-terrorist-organization-international (accessed 19 October 2022).

Waldorf, L. (2012) 'Anticipating the Past: Transitional Justice and Socio-economic Wrongs', *Social & Legal Studies*, 21(2): 171–186.

Walker, M. (2006) 'The Cycle of Violence', *Journal of Human Rights*, 5(1): 81–105.

Weinstein, J. (2011) *Inside Rebellion: The Politics of Insurgent Violence*, Cambridge: Cambridge University Press.

Wood, E. (2014) 'Conflict-Related Sexual Violence and the Policy Implications of Recent Research', *International Review of the Red Cross*, 96(894): 457–478.

Index

References to tables appear in **bold** type.

A

accountability 9, 10, 165, 235–246
  frameworks shaped by victims 251
  for HR violations 107–108
  informed by victim experience 137
  mechanisms 122
acts of terror
  see terrorism, acts of
Adler, E. 21
African palm 63
Afro-Colombian peoples 6, 99, 166, 219, 259
  and the Constitution 102
  and land 101
Agreement Regarding the Victims of the Conflict 93, 104, 237–244
  and delegates proposals 246, 247
  in negotiations 121
  public forums agreed 111
  ten core principles 109–110
  and transitional justice 7–8, 32
  truth commission 258–259
  see also Comprehensive System for Truth, Justice, Reparations and Non-recurrence
agricultural sector opposition to talks 97
Allport, G. 30
amnesty 9, 10, 28, 84, 121, 224, 241, 259
  for HR violations 107–108
  offered by National Front 48
  offered by Pinilla 46
  see also penal justice
ancestral privileges 37
Andean departments 82–84
Annan, Kofi 74
Antioquia 45
Arbour, Louise 211
Argentina 5, 9, 31, 61, 71
Arias, Armando 57
armed conflict in Colombia
  see Colombia

assassinations 39, 53, 56
  by FARC-EP 60
  of FARC-EP leaders 83
authoritarian countries 9, 106

B

Balkans 39
banana regions 59, 66
Barco, Virgilio 55, 59–60
Barrancabermeja 65, 115
  killings in 60
Barranquilla 115
Bar-Tal, D. 19, 38, 43, 271
Bartlett, M. 21
basic needs 12–13, 87, 230
  neglected by transitional justice 212
beliefs
  see social groups and their beliefs
Bell, C. 139
Bogotá 53, 56
  Bogotazo 39, 43
  bombing 77
Bojaya massacre 76
  FARC-EP apology 199
Bolivar, sword of 53
bombings 1, 46, 55, 56, 61, 76, 83
Bonilla, R.L. 56
Bosnia and Herzegovina 30
Boutros-Ghali, B. 9
Boyacá 44, 45
Brazil 31
Brett, R. 174
Brinton Lykes, M. 12
Burundi 139
Bush, President 78
Bushnell, D. 53
business sector 97
buy-in, wide 17, 24, 26, 165, 276

C

Caguán peace talks 72–75
Caldas 45

306

INDEX

Cali 115
Cano, G. 56
Carbo, Posada 37
Caro, Sergio Jaramillo 33
Casa de Mujer 158, 160
Castaño, Carlos 64
Castaño, Fabio 59
Castro, L.G. 44
cattle ranchers 45, 48, 55, 59
   opposition to peace talks 97–98
ceasefires 72, 75, 93, 96, 232, 260
Chad 212
Chavez, Hugo 95, 98
Chengue 65
Chernyak-Hai, L. 43
children
   disengagement of 233
   see also minors, recruitment of
Chiquita Banana 66
Choco 64
church role in peacemaking 140–142
Cifuentes, L.J. 55
CISMA Mujer 158
civilians and civil society 3, 54, 99–104
   affected by Uribe's policies 80
   civic projects 48
   inclusion in talks 99–104
   killed in 1990s 76
   mobilization of 72
   and peacebuilding 73, 89–90
   restoration of 83
   violence against 5, 67, 81
Civil Society Assembly (ASC) 73, 89–90, 119, 141
Clinton, President 78
clothing, red neckties 47
coexistence 19, 21, 38, 174, 242, 245, 261
coffee-producing regions 44, 45
Cold War, end of the 3, 9, 44
   effects on Colombia 69–72
Colombia, violence in
   during the 1980s 53–59
   during the 1990s 60–66
   brief history of 1–6
   complexity of violence in (brief) 66–68
   conflict since 19th Century 250
   internal conflict 1948–53 43–47
   internal conflict 1958–74 47–50
   internal conflict post 1964 50–53
   'La Violencia' 1946–1964 38–43
   post-independence 36–43
   since peace process 30
Colombian Armed Forces 51, 65, 69, 80
Colombia Viva 81
Communist Party 42, 45, 47, 48, 51, 54
   anti-communism 44, 46
   exclusion from politics 51
   guerilla groups 50

community reconciliation 242
compensation 93, 226, 233, 238, 239, 260
competitive victimhood 43–44, 47, 48
composition of victims' delegation 140–143
Comprehensive System for Truth, Justice, Reparations and Non-recurrence 209, 236, 238–239, 240
   and sustainable peace 241
   see also Special Jurisdiction for Peace (JEP); Truth, Coexistence and Non-Recurrence Commission; Unit for the Search for Persons Presumed Disappeared (UBPD)
conflict
   conflict-peace continuity nexus 36
   proximate drivers of conflict 51
Conservative Party 3
   Conservative/Liberal parties 47–50
   in power until 1930 37
   returned to power in 1946 38
contact theory 22–23, 29–30
context-specific relevance 138, 168, 212, 251, 273
convergence with victims' demands 264
'third parties' issue 262
Convivor security 63, 81
Cordoba 59, 64
counterinsurgency under Turbay 54
counter-terrorism, Uribe's policies 78
COVID-19 98
credibility for peace talks 123, 124, 132, 140, 200
crimes against humanity 241, 258
crop substitution plans 261
Cuba 51

D

databases of victims 146–147
death squads 52, 55
Death to Kidnappers (MAS) 55–56
de-escalation of conflict 27, 175, 189, 204, 207, 256
Defence of Democracy, Statute of 59–60
de Grieff, Pablo 226
dehumanization 20, 23, 29, 41, 126, 191, 234, 260
de la Calle, H. 98
democracy 10, 87
Democratic Defence and Security (DSP) 79–84, 91
denials of crimes 11, 125, 152, 194, 196–197, 207, 253
depoliticization of survivors 24, 31, 34, 128, 139, 247
de Roux, Francisco 8
disappeared 2, 4, 59, 225
   bodies of the 219–20, 222, 225
   CEV and UBPD 209, 240–241, 261
   during *La Violencia* 40
   Palace of Justice occupation 54, 57
   Relatives Association 99

Santos apology 199
in testimonies 3, 60, 178, 201, 224
disarmament, demobilization and reintegration (DDR) 6, 10, 60, 71, 84, 107, 232
displacements 2, 4, 81, 133, 163
  forced 63, 93, 144, 150
  mass 48, 77
  number of 40, 46, 65, 78
  return of refugees 229, 243, 260
  of UP supporters 58
disposal of bodies 5, 58
distrust, mutual 18, 23, 41
diverse populations 150, 166
divided communities
  see societal cleavages
drug organizations and trafficking
  and Barco 59
  Bush war on drugs 78–79
  combatted by DSP 80
  drug trade agreement 109, 245, 261
  extradition to the US 56
  finance of AUC 81
  finance of conflict 53–54, 62, 63, 67, 69, 71
  finance of ELN 51
  finance of FARC-EP 60
  and violence 3, 4, 7, 40, 55–56, 68
Duque, Ivan 31
Duzán, M.J. 56

E

Eastern Llanos 38, 44, 45, 46, 54
East Timor 212
economics
  business sector 97
  economic and social factors 21, 25, 211
  economic reforms by NF 48
  the economy 17, 48, 96, 267
  industrial sectors 97
  neoliberal economics 10, 87, 96–97
  rural/agrarian reform 227–229
  Santos economic plans 96–97
Ecuador 83, 95
education 17, 30, 240, 245, 261
elite actors 3, 15, 25, 28, 31, 55, 58
  Conservative/Liberal elites 37
  contesting peace talks 18
  convergence with victims' demands 209–210
  instrumentalization of victims 151
  interests of 244, 248
  Liberal elites 45
  and the National Front 47–50
  and peace process 267
  and Santos approach 96
  victims' subordinated to 120
  see also land and land ownership
El Nogál club 77
El Salvador 70, 71
emotional reactions 174, 178, 278
  empathy 184

pain 14, 23, 82, 184, 185, 254
recovery 242
to taking part in talks 177
employment 12, 212, 229, 260
empowerment 27, 31, 129–133, 181–182
  and peacebuilding 252–258
  and peacemaking 258–265
encounter/contact 18, 22, 28–29, 172, 251, 253, 276
  and beliefs 24
English, R. 76
Episcopal Conference of the Catholic Church (ECCC) 8, 20, 111, 140–142
  role in public forums 117
Escobar, Pablo 56
ESMAD (anti-riot police) 233, 261
ethnic groups 17, 100–101, 102, 166, 240, 270
  Afro-Colombian peoples 6, 99, 101, 102
  indigenous peoples 6, 99, 166, 224
European Union
  Terrorist Organization list 62
  victim-centred policies 13
exclusion, societal 21, 24, 30, 51, 99, 167
extortion 51, 55

F

false positives scandal 164, 187, 201, 219, 259
feminism 101
Final Agreement to End the Conflict 28, 209, 236–245, 258, 261
  and delegates proposals 247
  gender/intersectional approach 160, 257, 261
  limited nonrecurrence proposals 262–263
  referendums 268–270
forgiveness 174, 187, 197, 199
freedoms, restricting 53, 59
future, common 19, 21, 165, 174, 176, 255

G

Gacha, G.R. 56
Gaitán, Jorge Elécier 38, 39
gender 17, 136, 166, 214
  gender ideology 270
  and liberal peacebuilding 88–89
  and power relations 139
  and selection criteria 149, 155–165
  Sub-commission on 160, 164, 168, 257
Ghana 212
global liberalism 86–89
  see also Liberal Peace paradigm
Gómez, Laureano 45–46
Gorbachev regime 70
Grewal, K. 16, 17
group identity 20, 272
  ingroup/outgroup 38–89, 43–44, 173, 176
  shaped by violence 4
Guatemala 5, 9, 70, 71, 119, 141, 247
  Civil Society Assembly (ASC) 73, 89–90
Gundar, A. 43

INDEX

H

Hamber, B. 21
Havana peace talks
  see peace talks
healing 10, 126, 178, 218, 253
health, access to 230, 245, 260, 261
health, mental 278
Heaney, S. 265
historical legacy 174
  and complexity 66
  and mythical knowledge 40
  self-glorification narratives 256
  and violence 36–37
hostage taking
  see kidnapping
housing 12, 30, 212, 245, 260, 261
  access to 230
  destroyed 45, 64
Hughes, J. 30
Huila 45, 48
humanitarian disaster 33, 84
human rights 9, 10, 87
  defenders 234, 245, 260, 261
  organizations/movements 6, 54, 59, 72, 80, 99–100
  under Uribe's policies 81
  see also human rights violations
human rights violations 9, 10, 28, 41, 153, 167, 211
  accountability for 107–108, 241, 258
  by FARC-EP 77, 204
  and reparations 225, 227
  sanctions for 208, 263
  state-sponsored 34, 69, 74, 197
Hylton, F. 50

I

Ibague 46
identity 49
  conflicted identities 22
  political and ideological 40
  shared identities 30
  shared victim identity 254
  see also transformative process
ideologies 41, 51
  Cold War and new ideologies 44
  FARC-EP changes 61
  justification of violence 40, 271
  of M-19 53
  Western liberal ideas 88
illiteracy 17
income generation 260
independence and violence 4, 36–43, 66–67
indigenous peoples 6, 99, 166, 224, 259
individual reconciliation 172, 173
  transformative process 27, 176–183, 178–182
inequality 1, 12, 21, 25, 53, 211

informal breaks 165, 177, 191, 192, 276
institutions 9
  peace talks organizers 140–143
  restoration of government 87
  security sector reform (SSR) 233
  supporting human rights 100
instrumentalization 16, 26, 31, 113, 168, 247, 252–258, 258–265
  and empowerment 34, 35, 133, 172, 209, 248
  and international actors 24
intelligence files, declassification of 234
Inter-American Court of Human Rights (IACHR) 57
intergroup relations 18–19, 19, 254–255
  intergroup reconciliation 172
  intergroup transformation 188–200
internal armed conflict in Colombia
  see Colombia
International Committee of the Red Cross (ICRC) 94
International Criminal Court (ICC) 14, 108, 222
international organizations
  international companies 63
  neglect of basic needs 12
  role in peace talks 72–75, 142–143, 166
international peacekeeping operations (PKOs) 69–71
intersectionality 138, 168, 245, 257, 274
intragroup 172
  reconciliation 183–188
  victim identity 187–188, 253

J

Joinet/Orentlicher Principles 220, 231
journalists 56, 167
justice 9, 10, 107, 174
  judges 59, 73
  Justice and Peace Law 2005 7, 84, 104
  right to justice 220–225, 237
  Special Jurisdiction for Peace (JEP) 209, 240–241, 261, 262

K

kidnapping/hostage-taking 7, 51, 103, 186, 225
  false positives scandal 82, 164, 187, 201, 219, 259
  by FARC-EP 60, 61–62
  and MAS 55–56
  of police officer 154
killings 40, 47, 53
  between 1988–1990 59
  in Barrancabermeja 60
  in Chiquita by AUC 66
  civilians in 1990s 76
  executions in 1950 44
  of FARC-EP combatants 84

during *La Violencia* 39
number of 3, 41, 46, 63
in siege at POJ 57
of UP party 58
during Uribe's reign 78
Kompass, Anders 74

L

land and land ownership 37, 38, 64, 67, 245, 260
  demands for land 227–229
  landowners supporting AUC 81
  land reform proposals 39, 209, 244, 261, 262
  land restitution law 93, 104
  Liberal landowners 45
  militias of landowners 44
  and rural population 42, 48, 50, 219
  wealthy landowners 52
landmines 2–3, 4, 61, 189, 232, 256
language of international bodies 17
Latin American
  closure of conflicts 87
  effect of end of Cold War 69–71
  insurgency in 51
'La Violencia' 3, 38–43
Law for Victims and Land Restitution 93, 104
Lederach, John Paul 21, 174
left-wing activists 55, 59, 65
left-wing guerrillas 51, 52
legal political opposition 54
legislative reform for nonrecurrence 232
legitimacy of peace process 14, 122, 130, 132, 165
  confirmed by victim-centredness 15–16
  and victim inclusion 272
Lehder, Carlos 55
LGBTI + population 117, 167, 194, 240, 246, 256
  violence against 235
Liberal guerrillas 45, 48, 50
Liberal Party 3
  collapse of 38
  Liberal/Conservative parties 39, 46–50
  power 1930–1946 37
Liberal Peace paradigm 10, 87–89, 107
  and structural issues 211, 212–213
  and transitional justice 9–10, 107
Liberia 119, 212
local and subnational consideration 14
  local development 261
local turn 14, 15, 89, 90, 112, 251
logging regions 59

M

M-19 6, 53, 56–57, 60, 272, 279
  DDR process 71
Magdalena Medio Valley 55, 58
Magdalena Valley, Santander 51
magistrates assassinated 56
Mapiripan, massacre of 64
Marxist-Leninism 51
massacres 45, 198
  by AUC 65
  Mapiripan 64
  of UP party 58
McConnachie, K. 15–16, 17, 24, 113
McEvoy, K. 15–16, 17, 24, 113
McNicholl, K. 139
Medellin cartel 55, 56
Meertens 48
memorial measures 9, 31, 242
Mendeloff, D. 30
Méndez, J. 15
Mercado, Jose Raquel 53
methodology 32–33
middle class 51
migration, mass 45
military, Uribe's investment in 80
military dictatorship 46
Miller, G. 12
minors, recruitment of 4, 150, 168, 188, 241, 256, 260
  and FARC-EP 232
  Santos proposal 92
  and Victims' Law 93
Montes de Maria 83
Mora, J.E. 98
moral codes 4, 13, 41, 145
  and inclusion 122, 124, 125, 165, 236
  justification of violence 5, 20, 37, 40, 41
  Moral Imagination 22
Moyano, M.J. 61
Muralanda Velez, M. 52
Murphy, C. 12

N

Nagle, L. 65
Namibia 71
Naranjo, O. 98
National Commission for Reparations and Reconciliation 104
National Front 47–50
nationalism 53
National Liberations Army (ELN) 7, 51, 52, 55, 62
National Security Doctrine (NSD) 46, 54, 98, 262
National University of Colombia 8, 111, 140–141
  role in public forums 116, 118
National Victim's Day 267
National Women's Summit for Peace 157
negotiators
  experienced 98
  female negotiators/victims 158, 164–165
Nepal 17, 24, 113, 119, 130, 247, 251

INDEX

Nineteenth century, violence in 3
nonrecurrence 9, 10, 87, 107, 209, 260
 proposals limited 263
 right to 231–235, 237
 of violence against women 235
norms, values and behaviour 30
Norte de Santander 51, 58
Northern Ireland 24, 30, 113, 119, 130, 247, 251

O

Ochoa, M.N. 55
online portal 115, 247
Operation Marquetalia 52

P

Paffenholz, T. 216
pain and suffering 14, 23, 82, 177, 178, 184, 254
Palace of Justice occupation 56–57, 199
Palacios, M. 47
Palma 55
paramilitary groups 7, 30, 56, 62–63
 legalization of 52
 neo-paramilitary groups 84
 and political links 66
 supported by Uribe's policies 81
participation 27, 34, 114, 276–277
 effect of women's participation 161
 framing victims' 111–112
 historical demands for 120
 meaningful participatiion 209, 215, 251
 nature of 274–276
 and transitional justice 210–215
 of women in peace processes 155–158
Pastrana, Andres 72, 75
Patriotic Union (UP) 57–59, 199, 221
peace, sustainable 14, 84, 88, 266–273
 balancing expectations 108
 civil society/victims' participation 214
 transformative process 173
 and transitional justice 10, 107, 212
 victim inclusion 266–273
peace agreements 6–7
 final agreements 209, 236–245
 key principles of 87
 population unaffected by 272
peacebuilding
 commitment to 180, 181–182, 186, 187
 global processes of 34
 and groups/beliefs 21
 innovative peacebuilding 6–8, 250, 263
 priority areas for 87–88
 and reconstruction 72–75
 transformative process 212–213
 victims as peacebuilders 252–258
peacemaking
 local turn 14, 89, 90, 112, 251
 and transitional justice 8–11, 106–108

victim-centred 25, 128, 138, 207, 244, 264, 273, 278
 victim participation in 216
 victims as peacemakers 208, 258–265
peace talks 7
 and civil society 89–90, 99–104
 and elites 267
 FARC-EP at talks 150–153
 five agreements 2014 109
 and global liberalism 86–89
 Joint Declaration: Victims 109–110
 limitations on 266
 opposition to 30, 91, 209, 257, 269, 271
 rejection of individuals 258
 Santos red lines 244, 264
 see also victim inclusion; victims' delegations
peace talks, preparation for 60, 90–99
 antecedents to 108–111
 credibility of 123, 124, 132, 140, 200
 organizing institutions 140–143
 Santos support for 92
 support from neighbours 95
 victim inclusion 7–8
 Victims' Forums 113–119, 216, 247
peasants 51, 102, 167
 being dispossessed 50
 and militias 39
 mobilizing 42
 violence by 44, 45, 46, 49
 see also land and land ownership; rural areas
penal justice 121, 218, 220, 263–264
 avoidance of 224–225, 247–248, 259
 demand for 28, 109
 impeding peace 223
 JEP sanctions **242**
 see also amnesty
perestroika 70
Pérez, Mariano Ospina 37–38
perpetrators of violence 28, 31, 126, 128–130
 future rights 11
 leniency towards 270
 listening to testimonies 179
 perpetrator identity 150–155
 responsibility for crimes 197–198
 victims meeting the 14, 177
 who were also victims 136, 138, 167
 women facing the 162, 164
 see also denials of crimes; penal justice
Peru 31
Petro, Gustavo 272, 279
Pinilla, G.R. 46
Plan Colombia 78–79
Plan Lazo 51
Plazas, A. 57
Point Five
 see Agreement Regarding the Victims of the Conflict

polarized country 279
  delegates threatened 269
political actors 12, 34, 89–90, 94, 103, 121, 250
Political Participation: A Democratic Opportunity to Build Peace 245, 261
political system 51, 87
  electoral monitoring 73
  and everyday life 267
  Indigenous peoples 102
  participation agreement 109, 245, 261
  referendums 6
  reform of 10–11
  support for processes 87
  womens' participation 101
political violence 49, 53–57, 68
politicization 31, 100, 163, 171, 208, 247, 258, 278
populism 53
postconflict scenarios 106
  and DDR 10
  and liberal peace 87–89
  social repair 29
  transitional justice in 9
poverty 12, 30, 48, 211, 271, 272
power 6, 17, 203
  empowerment 27, 31, 129–133, 181–182
  empowerment and peacebuilding 252–258
  empowerment and peacemaking 258–265
  between genders 139, 168
  power relations 264
  see also instrumentalization
private sector alliances 56
  support for armed actors 209
protection of delegates 277
protests and strikes 99, 262
proxy governance 87
public apologies 198–199, 256
public forums 111, 113–119
  sectors invited 116
Puerto Tejadfa, violence in 42

Q

Quindo, violence in 42
Quintin Lame 60, 72

R

Rajca, A. 31
rape 5, 45, 76, 187
recidivism, resilient to 14, 267
reconciliation 9, 10, 87, 104, 172–176
  community reconciliation 242
  and transitional justice 18–23
reconstruction (personal) 126
referendums 269–270
refugees 46, 73, 79, 147, 229, 260
registry of victims 94
rehabilitation 119, 226, 230, 243, 260
religious groups 246

reparations 9, 10, 28, 104, 107, 209, 260
  right to 226–231, 237
representation 87, 136–140, 166
research interviews 25, 32–33
resource extraction 37, 51, 65, 96
respect and recognition 174, 190–191
responsibility for crimes 197–198, 254
restitution 7, 13, 212, 226
  land 93, 104, 229, 243
restorative justice 208, 223, 237, 240, 259, 275
  mechanisms 9, 119, 263
retraumatization 149, 171, 177, 199, 205, 258, 265
Rettberg, A. 25, 103
revictimization 31, 128, 145, 177, 200, 258, 265
Revolutionary Armed Forces of Colombia (FARC-EP) 2, 51, 69, 269
  Caguán peace talks 72–75
  delegate attacks 257–269
  denial of crimes 151, 200–202, 205
  development of 30, 46, 51–52, 54
  finance from drugs 71
  forces killed after Final Agreement 272
  informal meetings 191–192
  kidnapping by 99, 128, 166, 187, 217
  under Marulanda 52
  and Patriotic Union 57
  peace agreements 2016 6–7
  at the peace talks 151–153, 270
  against penal justice 208, 224
  public apologies 198–199, 256
  recruitment of minors 189, 190, 191, 232
  and Santos 91, 92, 93–95
  social base alienation 61–62
  Uribe military operations 33, 77–79, 82–84
  Uribe view of perpetrators 151
  violence by 60–61, 71, 129, 154, 181, 188–202, 232
rights of victims 9, 93, 208, 259
  rights framework 9–10, 107
  socioeconomic rights 12, 211, 227, 230, 267
  victims' turn 14–15, 111, 112, 137, 215
right-wing armed groups 57, 60
ritualized violence 40
Robins, S. 16, 17, 24
Rojas-Perez, I. 31
rural areas
  controlled by armed groups 52
  land reform/regeneration 227–229
  rural reform agreement 109, 245, 261
  rural violence 43, 45, 46
Ruta Pacifica 158, 160
Rwanda 30

S

safe spaces 275
Sajjad, T. 16

INDEX

Sánchez, Gonzalo 48, 140–141
sanctions by JEP 241, *242*, 263–264
San Jose Apartado 6
Santanders 44, 45, 51, 58, 149
Santos, Juan Manuel 6, 33, 83, 85, 194
   The Battle for Peace 123
   election 2014 109, 110
   negotiation red lines 244, 264
   role of 34, 86, 90–99, 104
   state apologies 199
Santos–FARC-EP negotiations
   see peace talks
Schori, N. 43
security sector 73, 87, 277
   citizen spies 79
   citizen spies/DAS 80–82
   security sector reform (SSR) 107, 233, 244, 248, 261, 262
   Security Statute 53
Segovia 58
sexual and gender-based violence (SGBV) 2, 5, 156
   and FARC-EP 60–61, 62, 201–202
   recognition of 93, 235, 256
   testimonies 162–164, 179, 187, 195, 221, 222, 230
   and Victims' Forum 117, 118
Sierra Leone 119, 212
social class 17, 51
social cleansing 59–60, 64
social groups and their beliefs 4, 24, 255, 271
   competitive victimhood 43–44, 47, 48–49
   'conflictive ethos' 19–20, 38–39
   and shared imaginary 22
   see also contact theory
socialized to violence 47
social media 257, 270, 277
societal cleavages 1, 5, 6, 18–19, 51, 271
   along party lines 37
   changed by Cold War 44
socioeconomic rights 211, 227, 230, 260, 262, 267
solidarity 184, 187–188
Solution to the Illicit Drugs Problem 245, 261
Soviet Union, finance to FARC-EP 61
Special Jurisdiction for Peace (JEP) 209, 240–241, 261
   JEP sanctions **242**
   'third parties' issue 262
spoiling actors 26, 98, 183, 225, 277
stalemate 82–84, 92
state, the
   alignment with 264
   asserting control over 4, 37
   continuing repression of 233
   denial of crimes 200–210
   national security 261
   public apologies 198–199
   statebuilding 10

state sovereignty issue 70, 71, 74
state terror 39, 41, 42, 47, 52, 57, 59
Statute for the Defence of Democracy 59
Staub, E. 23, 41, 254
stereotyping, reduction of 23, 254
stigmatization of communities 230, 234, 245, 260, 261
structural causes of conflict 12, 21, 35, 51, 227, 265
   and contact theory 30
   and liberal peace paradigm 88
   structural violence 248–249
   and transitional justice 211–213
   and Western liberal ideas 263
   see also land and land ownership; socioeconomic rights
Sub-commission on gender 160, 164, 168, 216, 235, 257, 261
sustainable peace 14, 84, 88
   balancing expectations 108
   civil society/victims' participation 214
   transformative process 173
   and transitional justice 10, 107, 212
   and victim inclusion 266–273
synderesis 145, 166

T

terror, war on 78
terrorism, acts of 40, 49, 50
   in the 1990s 60–66
   anti-terrorism statute 59
   by AUC 65
   and drug cartels 56
   by FARC-EP 76
   against HR defenders 55
   legalization of paramilitaries 52
   as a threat to national security 77
   testimonies 20, 22, 176–183, 246
   diverse 2, 117
   nature/impact of the 125–127, 190, 193–195
Texas Petroleum 55
Theidon, K. 29
'third parties' to violence 116, 210, 218, 259, 262
Tirofijo 52
Tolima 45, 48
   violence in 42, 46
Towards a New Colombian Countryside: Comprehensive Rural Reform 245, 261
trade unions 53, 54, 59, 65, 99, 167, 234, 245, 260
transformative process 113, 129, 130, 171, 254–255, 276–277
   for delegates 265
   at individual level 176–183
   intergroup level 188–200
   intragroup transformation 183–188
   limits to 200–203
   transmission chain 203–206, 236

transitional justice
  critiques of 9, 24, 136–137, 213, 236
  and human rights 107–108
  and instrumentalization 16–17
  and legitimacy 123
  and liberal peacebuilding 107
  mechanisms and representation 138
  and participation 210–215
  and peacemaking 8–11, 106–108, 251
  in Point Five 7–8
  and reconciliation 18–23
  and structural violence 211, 212, 248–249
  victim-centred 11–18
  and victims' organizations 103
  and victims' rights 111–112
  victims' turn 14, 90, 111, 215, 236, 251
  for women 155–156
  see also victim-centred peacemaking
trauma/woundedness 39
truth 28, 107, 174, 237
  international commissions 9, 212
  and sustainable peace 10
  truth commission (CEV) 209, 218–219, 258–259
Turbay Ayala, J.C. 53
Twentieth century, violence in 3

U

Uganda 119
United Nations 8, 15, 32–33, 77, 111, 140, 147
  Agenda for Peace 1992 9, 70, 86, 106
  civil society in peacebuilding 89–90
  Colombian Truth Commission 8
  nonrecurrence/reparations 226, 231
  peacebuilding policies 87–88
  peacekeeping 70–71
  and public forums 117, 118
  role in Colombia 72–75, 142–143
  victim-centred policies 13
  women and peace processes 156, 157, 158
United Self-Defence Forces of Colombia (AUC) 62, 64–66
  demobilization of 84
  and Uribe's policies 81
United States 55, 56, 92
  backing Pinilla 46
  bombing of Colombia 75
  bombing of Vietnam 51
  financial/military support 76, 78–79
  Foreign Terrorist Organizations 62, 66
  war on terror 78
Unit for the Search for Persons Presumed Disappeared (UBPD)
  see disappeared, the
universe of victims 147, 166, 252, 274
Uraba 59, 64

Uribe, Alvaro 31, 33, 63, 75–78
  democratic defence policy (DSP) 79–84
  impact of war 84
  in opposition 91, 98
  opposition to peace talks 151, 257, 269, 270
  opposition to UN 74
  and Plan Colombia 78–79
Uruguay 31

V

Valle 44
Venezuela 95
victim-centred peacemaking 25, 128, 138, 266
  in Colombia 10, 207, 244, 264, 278
  lessons from Colombia 273
victim-centred policies 111, 250–251
  claims of the 15–17
  and lasting peace 165
  peacemaking in Colombia 23
  see also transitional justice
victim inclusion 14, 18, 34
  importance of 136, 214, 236, 256, 278–279
  inclusion mechanisms 135, 137–138, 203–205, 247
  lessons from 273–278
  modalities of 216
  and peacemaking 72–75, 251
  reasons for 119–120, 121–128
  and sustainable peace 266–273
  victims as peacebuilders 252–258
  victims as peacemakers 258–265
victimization patterns 40, 77, 116, 137, 138, 166, 274
  evolution of 53–57
  represented at peace talks 144
victims
  agency of 6, 16, 31, 128, 175, 205
  competitive victimhood 43–44, 47, 48
  inclusion 34, 119–121, 121–128, 203
  Joint Declaration: Victims (2014) 109–110
  number of 3, 8, 24, 250
  organizations 103–104
  organizing institutions 2–3
  rights framework 10, 107
  and transitional justice 11–18
  universe of 166, 252
  universe of victims 147, 274
  violence as normality 47
  who were also perpetrators 136, 138, 167
  see also victims' turn
victims' delegations
  acknowledgement of 171, 180, 193
  characteristics of 149–150
  delegates' perspectives 128–133
  delegate visibility/invisibility 121, 267–268, 276
  demands and accountability 235–246
  demands for end to conflict 221

INDEX

demands for justice 220–225
demands for nonrecurrence 231–235
demands for reparations 226–231
demands for return of bodies 222
demands for socioeconomic rights 260
demands for truth 217–220
demands of the 12–13, 28, 33, 208, 209, 215–217
empowerment of 265
formal role of 7, 8, 11, 24, 31, 34, 250
intragroup identity 185
limitations on 31, 263–264, 266
meaningful participation 18, 111–213
meeting perpetrators 128–130
as peacebuilders 34, 171–172, 176, 182, 203–206, 252–258
as peacemakers 208–209, 214, 216, 246–249, 258–265
proposals/Final Agreement **238–239**, 243–246
selection and composition 140–143
selection and gender 155–165
selection and numbers 139, 274
selection and representation 136–140
selection of delegates 143–150
significance of 8, 11, 14, 18, 26–32
subordination of interests 12
treatment of delegates 257–258, 269, 277
see also victim inclusion
Victims' Forums 113–119, 216, 247
Victims' Law
  see Agreement Regarding the Victims of the Conflict
victims' turn 14, 90, 111, 215, 236, 251
Villavicencio 115
Villegas, L.C. 97
violence 1–6, 3, 33, 38, 50, 66–68
  during/after peace talks 272, 279
  atrocious 39, 40, 42, 44, 49, 53, 76, 84, 218
  by AUC 65
  circularity of violence 60
  emblematic 76–77, 154, 168
  false positives scandal 164, 187, 201, 219, 259
  historical perspective 36
  justification of 5, 20, 37, 40, 41
  as normality 5, 47, 66
  against Patriotic Union 57–59
  'third parties' to 116, 210, 218, 259, 262
  types of 4, 150, 167
  see also human rights violations; Revolutionary Armed Forces of Colombia (FARC-EP); sexual and gender-based violence (SGBV); women and girls

W

Waldorf, L. 213
war on terror 78
wealthy landowners 52, 55
welfare 87
Western liberal ideas 136, 210
  and structural violence 263
Wilsonian Triad 87
women and girls 25, 136, 214, 256–257
  effect of formal participation 161
  intragroup victim identity 187–188
  and liberal peacebuilding 88–89
  most affected by conflict 133, 144, 158, 162, 168, 218
  organizations 6, 99, 101, 160
  and peacebuilding 101, 132, 156–158, 188, 214
  power relations 139–140
  rape 5, 45, 76, 187
  selection of 114, 115, 144, 155–165
  violence against 93, 101, 117, 156, 162–164, 235, 261

www.ingramcontent.com/pod-product-compliance
Lightning Source LLC
Chambersburg PA
CBHW051527020426
42333CB00016B/1817